The American Republic

The American Republic

since 1877

John A. Schutz

Richard S. Kirkendall

FORUM PRESS

Published simultaneously in Canada.

Printed in the United States of America.

Library of Congress Catalog Card Number: 77-093846

ISBN: 0-88273-252-8

Maps designed by: Daniel Irwin

Cover and text designed by: Jerry Moore and Janet Moody

Table of Contents

Maps & Charts

Preface

THE AMERICAN REPUBLIC is an interpretation of the events, struggles, successes and failures and the lives of representative leaders which have made our country great. Historians are confronted with massive collections of stories from the past and we have to be selective in the materials which are used in developing a total picture. Our concern has been to show the growth of the nation through its system of government, its politics, its ideals and specifically, through its leaders.

History is made every day, every moment. Normally, the events transpire and the participants seldom think of that fact. Some incidents do stand out in such prominence that those involved in them realize that future generations will point back to the moment as a turning point in the life of a nation. Whatever the nature of past happenings, the historian looks back at them with a purpose. We want to profit by the experiences of past generations. History can be a tool; it can help us understand our world by showing us how it got the way it is. It inspires us with determination to build a better society by informing us of the nobility and courage of those who once lived and labored here.

To illustrate, some of the current concerns that receive wide attention are the family, health, woman's rights and the status of minority groups—Chicanos, blacks, Indians, Orientals and new immigrants. Since all groups with the exception of the American Indian are modern immigrants, the record of their relationship to one another gives us a measuring stick and some guide lines for living with one another now.

Following an account of the first British settlements at Jamestown in 1607 and Plymouth in 1620, we trace the story of the development of self-government from the first legislature in 1619 to the Declaration of Independence by the Continental Congress in 1776. We have examined the impact of the Revolution upon human rights followed by what we believe to be a simple but dramatic narrative of the early national experience of freedom.

We have emphasized the Civil War in spite of its agonies, because it is necessary to examine the meaning and effect of the momentary dissolution of the Union. Observation of the destruction of the nation should give us pause to consider how reckless persons can bring disaster to millions. We hope that the accounts of the first century of freedom will arouse sufficient interest to invite further reading and inquiry into these formative years.

THE AMERICAN REPUBLIC is available in a one-volume cloth-bound edition and in a two-volume paperbound edition. The first volume closes with the story of reconstruction following the Civil War and Volume Two opens with the same account.

In the final chapters, we have brought the story to the threshold of the 1980s. Oil and energy crises, insecurity in the cities, a crisis in the Presidency, these realities among others, are sobering thoughts to everyone. They demand creative research into our past for answers to the questions, "Where did we go wrong?" and "What can we do to heal the wounds?" This is not to say that others may not also find answers in the present moment and glimpses into what is to come. It does infer that history can help, too.

Our national history is complex and space forbids the telling of very much of it. Thus, maps, charts, graphs and pictures carry an important part of the story in THE AMERICAN REPUBLIC. The selection of these materials gives some uniqueness to the book by registering national expansion visually through the decades and by drawing upon enough illustrative material to highlight important leaders and events.

Individual persons generally highlight the events of history, even though they are sometimes only examples of the thousands or millions who have been the real determiners of national destiny. We have sprinkled our narrative with the names of men and women who have contributed to our national greatness. Presidents like Jefferson, Lincoln, Wilson and Franklin D. Roosevelt; military leaders like Washington, Lee, Pershing and Eisenhower; other leaders like Franklin, Clay, Dewey and Eleanor Roosevelt are a few of those who come in for special notice.

Our gratitude is expressed to many scholars who have helped to make this book what it is. We express appreciation to the many experts who have read chapters of the manuscript and have given advice, insight and criticism. These include:

Keith L. Bryant, Jr., Texas A & M University; Charles Bussey, Western Kentucky University; John M. Carroll, Lamar University; John A. Caylor, Boise State University; Eric H. Christianson, University of Kentucky; Ralph J. Crandall, Northeastern University; Leonard P. Curry, University of Louisville; Bailey Diffie, University of Southern California; Harold H. Dugger, Southeast Missouri State University; James Forsythe, Fort Hays State College; Bruce Glasrud, California State University - Hayward; Mike Greco, University of Houston - Clear Lake City; Nadine I. Hata, El Camino College; George Herring, University of Kentucky; James W. Hilty, Temple University; Abraham Hoffman, Los Angeles Valley College; John Howe, University of Minnesota; Franklin Hoyt, Mt. San Antonio College; Leo E. Huff, Southwest Missouri State University; Norris Hundley, University of California - Los Angeles; David E. Kyvig, University of Akron; Lester D. Langley, University of Georgia; B. B. Lightfoot, Southwest Missouri State University; Richard Lowitt, Iowa State University; Archie P. McDonald, Stephen F. Austin State University; Thomas J. McInerney, St. Thomas Seminary College; Grady McWhiney, University of Alabama; Richard H. Marcus, University of Wisconsin - Eau Claire; Franklin Mitchell, University of Southern California; Doyce Nunis, University of Southern California; Robert Oaks, University of Texas; Patrick G. O'Brien, Emporia State University; Edward B. Parsons, Miami University - Ohio; Bradley Reynolds, College of the Canyons; Glenda Riley, University of Northern Iowa; Oliver A. Rink, California State University - Bakersfield; Richard Robertson, University of Mississippi; Peter E. Robinson, Jacksonville State University; Raymond Robinson, Northeastern University; W. Stitt Robinson, University of Kansas; Philip R. Rulon, Northern Arizona University; Terry Seip, University of Southern California; Homer E. Socolofsky, Kansas State University; Arvarh Strickland, University of Missouri - Columbia; Allen Yarnell, University of California - Los Angeles; and W. Turrentine Jackson, University of California - Davis.

To Professor Dan Irwin whose maps and charts add special luster to the book we extend our special thanks. To Howard E. Short, our editor, whose help in details and manuscript preparation was always dependable, we give our sincere appreciation. Lastly, we would like to acknowledge the assistance and encouragement of Erby M. Young, Managing Director of Forum Press, who suggested our co-authorship and directed THE AMERICAN REPUBLIC in all phases of production. May this book be both an inspiration and valuable learning aid for all teachers and students.

Foreword

by Gerald R. Ford

Since history is the most active ingredient of our time, we should be aware of its power and use in our lives. From year to year, even from day to day, on a most elementary level our actions are being recorded; government bureaus, businesses, and educational institutions, in the course of their operations, take and evaluate data. Every time we use our social security number, credit cards, or badges of identification we become recorded. In this process the computer assumes an importance that is commanding and that, at times, may threaten our very privacy as citizens.

This simple form of historical research and evaluation most of us have accepted as essential to life in a modern society, even when we are apprehensive about its impact upon our lives. Another form of history, much more popular, invites us to search the origins of our families. Probably there is no more exciting pastime than the study of one's roots. Most of us belong to families that have moved a few times each generation, and many of us have lost contact with our relatives. Through family inquiry we gain, primarily, renewed admiration for the struggle to find a new life in this republic, but we gain, too, a sense of time and geography and hope. For some the roots are shallow and extend immediately to countries far older than our own; for others the roots have *Mayflower* passengers, grandfathers in the Revolution and Civil War, or followers in the expeditions of Cortez and Coronado; for some the roots extend to plantations or tribes where heoric battles for survival strengthened the ancestral ties. Admittedly, we could indulge in romantic fancy in tracing ancestors, if the rules of historical evidence are not followed and if we are only looking for aristocrats in our family's past. Most of our discoveries, we may find, will not uncover gold and purple lineage, but something more important in my opinion: ancestors, perhaps, who struggled for centuries in poverty and obscurity, and then a daring person decided to break with tradition and cross the oceans to the Western Hemisphere. His decision and experiences surely are worthy of study, for the meaning of family and the hope of our country.

While this history is a personal and family experience, there is history which associates many experiences with our own. This process brings new meaning to our lives and gives meaning to the world about us. We become part of larger movements in society which allow us to participate in them as much or as little as we may wish. Sometimes within our hands are creative forces that give us alternatives: obscurity or prominence, selfishness or responsibility, disinterestedness or involvement. Historians will evaluate whatever we do, often within the context of broader movements that seem to be directing the actions of human beings.

Individuals are constantly confronted by forces with which they must seek terms. They are born into society with no choice of time or place and must come to terms, to live happily, with these forces. The prevailing social ones like style, conventions like language, attitudes like those of race or class must be met, sometimes accepted or confronted. Customs of this kind can be productive of good or evil, or shades in between. Legal norms, for example, have a long history, extending often into the Middle Ages. Procedures in our courts developed slowly, but have become time-tested and helpful in assuring justice. Slavery has a long history too, but society has struggled to root it out, for obvious reasons. The inequality of race or sex, and that of religions derived from religious preference, has no place in modern society, yet it has taken human beings countless centuries to rise above the evil. The record of this success, nonetheless, is an extraordinary chapter in the history of human achievement. As we look about us and see poverty, ignorance, civil strife, and countless other human problems, we should study the record, measure our progress, and chart a course of action.

May I add some personal reflections. When I was President of our nation, I was impressed how my actions became part of the national record. Every time I spoke, it seemed, the record added another line. My actions whether in the office or on the golf course had some interpretative significance. I realized what it meant to be in the center of our political process, and of what responsibility I shared in setting the pattern of United States development. My actions in the presidency will be interpreted by me and others; that process is rightly called history. It is a dynamic process involving the observer, his use of evidence, and certain forces both within and beyond his control.

Our nation's past has been blessed by a strong people who possesed common sense, genius for government, tolerance, and creativity in the pursuits of life. Every generation thus far has produced leaders, ideas, and achievements, and also a few failures. Probably our greatest achievement has been the will of each generation to hand the next a heritage of responsible government and institutions.

From the days of John Winthrop in Massachusetts-Bay, the concern was repeatedly expressed that we live according to the law. The Bible and the spirit of God as revealed through nature were guide posts. People kept diaries or journals to record events, thus to know the will of God. By the Revolution history had become secular, but with a reverence for human rights as nature's law. Thomas Jefferson in the Declaration of Independence evoked these rights to justify the founding of the nation, and he recited a litany of grievances against British rule. Both George Washington and Jefferson worried about safeguarding these rights as they charted the direction of the new republic, and both were watchful that their actions set patterns of stability and republicanism for future generations. They left public papers so that others might know their intentions. Presidents through the decades have spoken of policy and direction of the nation at their inaugurations or in their reports to Congress or the people. In recent times many have deposited their papers in special libraries, with an understanding that the papers should be studied to determine the future of republican policy. Harry S Truman maintained an office in the presidential library at Independence, Missouri, and invited the public to study the nation's record during his years in office.

As a lawyer myself, I am proud of the legal profession's regard for history. From John Jay to Warren E. Burger, judges of the United States Supreme Court have consistently cited the record in seeking the best interests of the nation. John Marshall's impact is evident from his great cases, but we were also fortunate to have him serve as chief justice for nearly thirty-six years. Most justices of the Court have left records of experience, citation, and opinion that reveal struggles to find justice among conflicting evidence. In our time Earl Warren presided over the Court when it reversed judicial policy of nearly sixty years because it felt that separate but equal in the treatment of human beings did not accord with American republicanism. Its new reading of the historical record compelled it to change the law.

The Court decisions point up the fact that finding national direction is not easy. Controversies in society arise because most issues have naturally attracted supporters who are emotionally committed to their causes. Society is full of such issues, and at any time in our national life controversy may obscure our direction. Sometimes issues press hard the rationality of our institutions and leaders, and the people turn to extralegal devices. The Civil War was an obvious failure of democratic leaders to find a solution for regional differences. Over the years, however, most issues have been resolved—sometimes not easily or well, but in a reasonable fashion to satisfy the majority.

My feeling about controversy is not much different from other former Presidents. While in office I welcomed diversity of opinion, but hoped that we could confine our arguments within democratic bounds so that progress could be made. My approach to government was determined by philosophy and common sense, but I paused to read the history of our nation. Like Woodrow Wilson I valued the historical record and puzzled out the daily controversies to find what seemed to be the direction of the nation. I accepted the fact that historians often disagree on the interpretation of facts, but I read widely, called upon advisors for help, and pondered my course of action. My decisions as evaluated in time and associated with other events become history.

Introduction

As the United States approached its Bicentennial, a prominent historian wrote, "We find ourselves at this Bicentennial, for all the show-business clatter of the Fourth-of-July celebrations, an essentially historyless people. Businessmen agree with the elder Henry Ford that history is bunk. The young no longer study history. Intellectuals turn their backs on history in their enthusiasm for the ahistorical behavioral sciences." According to a 1975 report, "Confidence and interest in history are not nearly as widespread and strong among students, educational administrators, and politicians as they were only a few years ago."

Doubts about history's usefulness for the individual eager to find a job and for a society eager to solve its problems, especially doubts about its usefulness in a time of rapid change, appear to be largely responsible for the recent decline in interest in historical study and the move away from it to more "relevant" and "practical" subjects. This skepticism about the utility of history has gained renewed strength in the unusual circumstances of the past decade and has affected both curricular decisions and student choices. Increasingly free to stay away as history requirements are removed, students have chosen to do so in growing numbers for history seemed useless to them.

History does not occupy the large and high place in America's schools and colleges that it enjoyed a decade and more ago. During the first two decades following World War II, students flocked to history classes, often, to be sure, forced to do so by rules imposed by curriculum planners, school boards, and legislatures, many of whom had been alarmed by reports that many schools and colleges did not require American history. Most high school graduates had only a smattering of knowledge about it and that seemed to suggest that Americans did not understand and might lack enthusiasm for the institutions and ideals for which the war was fought. Accused by their critics of 'not learning from history and being indifferent to the past !' spokesmen of the student movement reply, "a president of the American Historical Association reported several years ago . . . there is no historical precedent for our generation." More recently, a historian was persuaded that a fundamental change was taking place, that "The people of plenty have become a people of paucity," suggested that his most useful function as a teacher of undergraduates "would be to disenthrall them from the spell of history, to help them see the irrelevance of the past."

Those who insist that history is irrelevant because we live in a time of rapid change, understand neither the nature of historical study nor the character of the historical process. History is the discipline that specializes in the study of change in human affairs, and the historical process, even when moving at its most rapid pace, does not leave all features of the past behind. "Indeed, if there is any one subject with which history is concerned," David Potter wrote some years ago, "that subject is change—how things ceased to be as they had been before, how they became what they had not been." ". . . the various branches of the social sciences and humanities often tend to produce a static view . . .," Edwin O. Reischauer points out. "History . . . is focused on change, and change is the heart of the story, especially in our day." "If there is one thing clearer than another," Dexter Perkins observed, "it is that change is the law of life, one of the deepest and most inevitable of all human phenomena;" yet, continuity, what John Jay called "the continuing tie," is also a "law of life." Human affairs are dynamic, but not all parts of the past pass away. Many remain important in the present, and features of the past and present will be with us significantly in the future. As one historian put it, "the immediate, sudden appearance of something, its creation by an individual or a group at some one moment of time, is unknown in history." Instead, as another mentioned, "each event is harnessed to the other, and the present emerges from the past." And a third agreed: "Past, present, and future are linked together in the endless chain of history."

Those who are unhappy with the present can deplore the elements of continuity—the forces of resistance and the representatives of the past, but they are inevitably present in every historical situation.

They are realities that must be recognized and that are not easily brushed aside by a champion of a vision of the future. It is a historian's duty to alert people to the elements of continuity just as it is a historian's duty to point out that all things cannot remain as they were. "The best use of history is as an innoculation against radical expectations and, hence, against embittering disappointments," George F. Will suggests. It should also innoculate against the expectations of the champions of the status quo. "No trained historian can possibly put himself in the position of the thick-and-thin exponent of the static," Perkins insisted. ". . . We have our choice . . . between the gradual reconciliation of the old and the new and the more violent processes which destroy much that is good along with much that is evil.'

As the discipline that specializes in the study of continuity and change, history promotes understanding of important realities and supplies an intellectual foundation for intelligent, effective action. "Mankind is always more or less storm-driven," Allan Nevins wrote, "and history is the sextant and compass of states which, tossed by wind and current, would be lost in confusion if they could not fix their position." If students are to understand change today and prepare to shape their own world, they must be able to appreciate their own position in time and space and understand the processes of continuity and change. If students are to make sound judgments about the direction in which they wish to go, they must know the choices open to them. The study of history is indispensable to people living in times such as ours. An understanding of the past supplies insights useful in attempts to guide the course of the present and affect the shape of the future.

THE AMERICAN REPUBLIC was influenced by convictions about the importance of these concepts—change and continuity—and the consequent value of historical study as a way of gaining understanding of human affairs. Convictions about the importance of knowing institutions, such as the American institutions of self-government, and knowing people, including American leaders from Winthrop to Carter, also affect the pages that follow. The study of American history, although it must not be merely an effort to memorize facts about the past, should supply a body of information about people, institutions, dates, and events. To function effectively, everyone needs a body of historical information—information on the experiences of people—as well as an understanding of the dynamic character of human affairs.

That information should be representative of the diversity and complexity of American life. No longer narrow, the discipline of history covers all aspects of human affairs. It now has a unique and valuable scope or range. ". . . each of the social sciences and humanities selects one major facet form a culture as a whole and then studies it in detail," Reischauer writes. ". . . Only history tries conscientiously to fit all the parts into a meaningful whole."

This book captures the experiences of a diverse and complex

people over the full sweep of their history. These pages should enlarge the range of experience available to the reader, combatting narrowness, the overwhelming preoccupation with the present narrowness, the overwhelming preoccupation with the present that is a characteristic of most people, and their tendency to learn from one set of experiences at a time, those supplied by the recent past. People need to see the present in relation to various pasts, not just one, and to draw the "lessons" of history from all significantly relevant episodes, rather than from only one set of experiences.

Although not utopian, THE AMERICAN REPUBLIC is not pessimistic or cynical. It expresses admiration for many features of American life, especially self-government, which has grown from small beginnings and gained strength from tests and trials. The book expresses admiration for the capacity demonstrated by the many different groups in American society to produce leaders who, in turn, have promoted improvements in the quality of American life. We do call attention to present difficulties, including a "leadership crisis' and the possibility that economic growth, one of the main features of the story, may be displaced by economic stagnation or decline. When that point is reached, the readers will have already studied the history of a people who have encountered more than a few difficulties without being overwhelmed by them and look toward a New America.

The
American
Republic

10

Reconstruction and Rebirth of the South

THE TASK OF 1865, IN LINCOLN'S WORDS, was "to bind up the nation's wounds" and "to do all which may achieve and cherish a just and lasting peace." From the beginning of the war Lincoln had affirmed his belief in the Union, which he felt was older than the states, and the Union was perpetual regardless of the wishes of any state. Since the Constitution said nothing about secession and nothing about disobedient states, he had used force in 1861 to compel obedience. In his eyes, Southerners were rebels and liable to penalties for disobedience and treason. He hoped in 1865, to soften the punishment by returning them quickly to "that proper practical relation" which they had enjoyed before secession. They would be required, however, to ratify the Thirteenth Amendment of the Constitution, which outlawed slavery throughout the United States.

Lincoln had thought of himself as the architect of a restored Union, in the sense that he would guide the rebel states back to full partnership in the government. As commander-in-chief he claimed the power to impose martial law, to grant pardons, and to set tests for loyalty. As his reconstruction program unfolded, he was cautious in his explanations, but firm in his actions. In 1863, he offered the "ten-percent plan" to any group of voters who equalled one-tenth of the 1860 voting population and who took an oath of allegiance, the privilege of organizing a new state government. It would then abolish slavery as a condition for recognition of readmission. He was aware, nonetheless, that Congress considered the return of the South as a proper matter for legislation and wanted to assume responsibility for setting the standards of readmission for the rebel states.

Congressmen were sensitive, and Lincoln, as a political realist and leader, was careful to keep rivalry over policies with Congress within bounds. Like Congress he was well aware of the danger of a unified southern vote, but he counted upon the South to return to Congress as many former Whigs as Democrats. His reconstruction policy, therefore, reflected the sensibilities of Republicans regarding the control of Congress. He was intent, too, to restore peace and prosperity to the old South, to repair the damage of war, and to adopt a reasonable policy toward the black as a free partner in southern life. He was careful in his instructions to southern leaders, but he would let them decide upon the degree of black involvement in the restored governments. Lincoln felt, even in 1865, that the blacks should be persuaded to migrate to Africa.

Lincoln risked much in developing these policies because some Republicans in Congress wished to impose severe punishment upon the South. They accused Lincoln of being "soft," foolish, and wrongheaded, and a few believed in April 1865 that his assassination was a "godsend to the country." Republicans were worried about the political consequences in Congress of southern votes and reflected northern bitterness over the death of 360,200 soldiers in the war. The victory won on the battlefield they did not want lost on the floors of Congress. A rejuvenated Democratic party, however, might easily overturn Republican control of Congress. Since Lincoln's policy might let southern leaders return easily to office, the threat was immediately raised, and Republicans questioned Lincoln's wisdom.

Andrew Johnson's Reconstruction

Lincoln's death brought his Vice President, Andrew Johnson, into office. A war Democrat and a self-made man, the new President rose out of poverty in the South to become a member of Congress, wartime governor of Tennessee, and Vice President of the United States in 1865. He was outspoken in his hatred for southern aristocracy and secessionists and his frequent, violent speeches had embarrassed Lincoln. Most people agreed that he lacked Lincoln's finesse, nobility of language, and sense of destiny, but in office he surprised friend and foe alike by showing a willingness to bind up the nation's wounds. Johnson was above everything else a Democrat, and he looked to Andrew Jackson and Thomas Jefferson for inspiration. He idealized the self-sufficient farmer, liked the rural environment, and favored the states over the national government. He wanted the new South to reflect his interests in agrarianism. Though he admired Lincoln, he did not appreciate the changes occurring in the North, the railroads, manufacturing, and urbanization. The new business classes that were emerging with Republican help frightened him. These people violated his preconceptions of an ideal society.

Johnson's democratic ideas, however, had not made him an emancipationist. Slavery he had defended before the war, and freedom for the black he reluctantly accepted at its end. Johnson had been less concerned with the black than with the power of the old southern aristocracy. Slave ownership widely spread among the yeomen, he had thought, would be a blessing for everyone in the South.

Johnson's reconstruction policy, therefore, had old-time Democratic ideas in it. The states would decide upon policy; the common folk would rise to power; the blacks would be guided to freedom. He formulated his ideas, unfortunately, in the face of known hostility of Congress, which insisted on federal supervision of the South. Instead of calling Congress into session during the mourning period following Lincoln's death in April, he went his own way until the next December. He allowed the southern states to elect officials and reestablish civilian governments, to plan their own reconstruction, and to handle the problems of the freed black. Wanting the South back in the Union as quickly as possible, he overlooked southern policies that were certain to irritate northern opinion, especially that of the abolitionists, who were agitating to make the ex-slave an equal member of American society. He failed to weigh public reaction to southern treatment of the black. How could he justify the fact that not one southern state granted the franchise to the black—not even to educated blacks? That most states formed special black codes to regulate black affairs, codes that appeared to reimpose servitude? Perhaps even more shocking to the sensibilities of the North was the election of many Confederate officers and leaders to public office; some tried to resume their prewar offices in Washington!

Johnson was obviously embarrassed by this southern arrogance. The black codes, in particular, tied blacks to the land, imposed heavy penalties for disobedience, and laid down rules to separate the races. The southern legislatures, furthermore, refused to accept the consequences of defeat. Some voted pensions to Confederate veterans; others refused to repudiate Confederate debts. Johnson's plans for a yeoman-controlled South were ignored. The President had failed when Congress convened in December 1865 and took matters into its own hands.

Congressional Opposition

Seven months after Johnson took office, the Thirty-Ninth Congress

assembled. It was divided into four or five uneven groups, the largest
of which was the moderate Republicans. Johnson could not count on
any warm support because he was a War Democrat, but he had usual
support, nonetheless, from those who honored the Presidency and accepted him as head of the party. Believing that once he realized how
badly he had missed the mark in his reconstruction policy, Congressmen
hoped he would join the Congress in developing another policy. Some
Congressmen were willing to wait for presidential direction, long after
Congress had organized. As the months passed, however, the moderates
became increasingly bewildered by Johnson's uncompromising attitude, and drifted toward the radical group who insisted upon stern measures for southern reconstruction.

These Radicals, often lead by Thaddeus Stevens and Charles
Sumner, were a diverse group, but many favored giving blacks economic equality. Stevens wanted to confiscate large landholdings in
the South and distribute the land to those without property, blacks
and whites alike. He would, likewise, assure suffrage to blacks and
equality to all others before the law. A bitter man, his bark and bite
often disguised his true opinions, but he was genuinely interested in
the welfare of freedmen. His Radical colleagues wanted to preserve
the war tariff, retain legislation that favored the North, such as banking
and taxes and which promoted the development of railroads. Stevens
favored high tariffs too. The Radicals wanted, like Stevens, congressional control of the South, and in various degrees they disliked Johnson for his racism and hostility to business.

By the summer of 1866 these Radicals had a working majority
in Congress. They had already prepared for this time of power by
joining moderates in an investigation of the South. A committee of
fifteen members, formed in December 1865, had formulated a series
of policies that were then put into bills. One after another Congress
passed, as it developed its own plan of reconstruction, only to have
most of them vetoed. It rewrote some bills and passed others over the
veto. It strengthened the Freedman's Bureau, then under the direction of Oliver O. Howard, and invested it with multiple duties—to
distribute food, help the black find employment, and protect him during
the transition period to full citizenship. The Bureau also provided
other enormously worthwhile services, like hospital care, educational
support (247,333 pupils in 4329 schools), and the distribution of land.
To be sure that the black enjoyed these advantages of citizenship,
Congress passed over the President's veto a civil rights act and later
incorporated many of its major provisions into the proposed Fourteenth Amendment. It defined citizenship and empowered the federal
government to guarantee it. The reaction in the South was severely
hostile, and ten of the eleven states rejected the amendment (with
Johnson's encouragement). Their action undoubtedly alienated both
the South and Johnson from moderate opinion in the North.

Reconstruction of South, 1866-1877

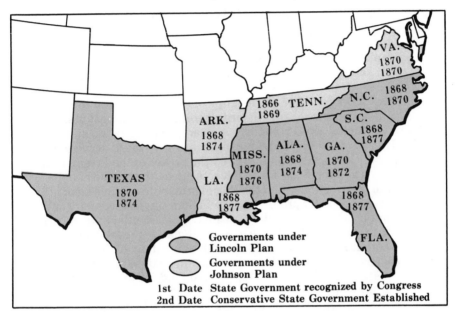

Governments under
Lincoln Plan

Governments under
Johnson Plan

1st Date   State Government recognized by Congress
2nd Date   Conservative State Government Established

In defending his vetoes, Johnson spoke courageously, but foolishly and incautiously, indulging in name-calling that only drew
further fire from Congress. On an election tour in 1866 he blistered
his opponents, frequently using inappropriate language and exposing
himself to undignified opposition. Newspapers burlesqued his remarks;
cartoonists exaggerated his foibles; congressional speakers ridiculed
his ideas. These election antics awakened—or more properly created—
hatred of the South, associated Johnson with the South, and inspired
all sorts of people to spread propaganda. Released northern prisoners
told accounts of southern brutality; people who had traveled in the
South gave impressions that the people were barbarians, undeserving
of compassion, and only the black was worth saving from the poverty
of war; publicists asserted that Democrats were in league with ex-
Confederates. In facing the assault, Johnson left the impression that
he was a madman and drunkard, favored Southerners and Democrats,
and was a dissembler and traitor. Many honest and well-meaning people
read him out of the Republican party and some even would have liked
to remove him from the Presidency.

While congressional elections are often difficult to interpret,
the results of those in 1866 were obvious. The Radicals and their friends

won a two-thirds majority in the Congress and swept the elective offices in most states. Radical leadership now was able to impose federal standards of citizenship upon the South and, in its arguments with the President, put the direction of the program in the hands of a small group of Congressmen, including such luminaries as Stevens of Pennsylvania and Sumner of Massachusetts.

To put salt into Johnson's election wounds, they urged the "Lame Duck" Thirty-ninth Congress to move the meeting time of its December session back to March 1867, in the hope of keeping Johnson from taking the reins of government. The majority agreed to this illegal maneuver, and also restricted the President's power as commander-in-chief by making Ulysses S. Grant the responsible military leader. It passed, too, the Tenure of Office Act which limited the power of the President over appointments and removals from office. In effect, the Senate had the last word on the fate of men whom the President would remove from office. Congress was especially protecting Edwin Stanton, the Secretary of War, who had opposed Johnson and whose help was essential in reconstructing the South. Finally, the House of Representatives resolved to inquire into the conduct of the President, with the intent of impeachment. The Judiciary Committee launched an investigation of Johnson's policies that lasted three months, but concluded, in June 1867, that there were no legitimate charges.

The session ended with the passage of the First Reconstruction Act. It divided the South into five military districts, imposed martial law upon the citizens, and ordered the former states to hold constitutional conventions. Most Confederate officeholders were excluded from participation in the new governments. Before the states could apply for admission to the Union, they were compelled to extend the franchise to all eligible males who now included blacks and ratify the Fourteenth Amendment. Each district was placed in charge of a military governor who had at his disposal units of the national army. Congress thus wiped away what Johnson had done since 1865 and challenged in addition any lingering ideas of states rights.

Congressional Reconstruction

When the Fortieth Congress met on March 4, 1867, in its extra-legal session called by the previous Congress, it proceeded to carry out the work of its predecessor. Supplementary reconstruction acts were passed one after another. The purpose of these acts, like the original one, was intended to impose the congressional will upon the South. In Congress discipline was maintained by unseating several Democrats. The Senate used its power to confirm presidential appointees by rejecting men whose loyalty was doubtful to the Radical cause. With these rough measures (as well as others), Congress exercised considerable power inspite of the repeated vetoes of the President, and it moved even against him with new plans for impeachment.

In the South, meantime, the military governors were frequently arbitrary, but they imposed peace on the states, took steps to hold conventions by enrolling the electorate, and ordered some changes in the economies. The new constitutions represented advances over the older ones. Suffrage was broader, the criminal laws more humane, and property laws more protective of debtors.

The new legislatures were dominated by outsiders, carpetbaggers who came South to assist the blacks and take advantage of political opportunities. Thousands of these people directed various organizations, companies, and governmental bureaus. In Republican party politics they were charged with the job of turning blacks into Republicans, separating them from their former masters, and seeing that they were registered as voters. While Republican rule was occasionally corrupt in the states, as legislators deflected funds into public display or into personal luxuries, much progress also was achieved in financing railroad construction, improving roads, rivers, and harbors, and extending public education and social services.

This corruption, wherever it existed, should be measured against the boss rule in New York, the management of western railroads, and the conduct of Indian affairs. It should be measured, too, against the experience of the people serving in the southern legislatures. Most of the men, white and black, were unfamiliar with their tasks; in South Carolina the majority for one session were freed blacks anxious to learn; elsewhere carpetbaggers who had only recently come to the South shared control with blacks and scalawags. Their record was nonetheless comparable to those of other legislatures outside the South, at least in the promotion of progressive reforms.

Congress stood behind the southern legislatures by passing protective laws. It insisted that Amendments 14 and 15 to the Constitution be ratified, guaranteeing civil rights and prohibiting race as a bar to citizenship. It passed enforcement acts beginning in 1870 protecting citizens from such organizations as the Ku Klux Klan. The Klan, a southern subversive organization, had spread widely over the South in answer to the Reconstruction. It used methods of terror and intimidation against blacks and other Republicans and forced the Radicals to employ the army and courts to beat down resistance through the use of prosecutions and fines. The Force Law of 1871 imprisoned and fined hundreds of Klan members and, by 1872, crushed the organization for the time being.

The Impeachment of Johnson and the Election of 1868

As the power of the Radicals mounted, they gained courage to assault directly the President who had been unable to stop Radical legislation with his vetoes. Though his influence with the people had declined sufficiently to encourage the Radicals to make the fight, they awaited an occasion that would give them reasonable grounds. The opportunity to impeach him occurred in February 1868 when he removed Edwin Stanton from the cabinet. Challenged thus, Congress moved to enforce the Tenure of Office Act by removing the President.

In its statement of charges to the Senate, the House listed nothing specific, as would be proper, but made a bold demand for impeachment against Johnson, accusing him of "high crimes and misdemeanors." The House then instructed its committee to press the Senate for a vote of impeachment, promising that charges would be provided as soon as possible. It also instructed the committee to ask the Senate to summon Johnson to answer the charges!

The House managers had some difficulty refining the charges against Johnson. But the charges were incidental to the purpose of the trial, as Sumner described the motivation of Congress: "this proceeding . . . is political in character—before a political body—and with a political object. . . . I have . . . called it one of the last great battles with slavery."

The trial began on March 5 and dragged on until May 26. One by one the charges were presented, and the managers of the impeachment and the defenders of the President spoke long and convincingly in supporting their positions. The President's chief defense attorney, William M. Evarts, presented powerful rebuttals of the charges, accusing the House of attempting to upset the balance of power by removing the President. Evarts regarded the President's removal of Stanton as a constitutional test of the Tenure of Office Act, a test and not a crime. Evarts' appeals surely had impact, for all the final votes, taken from May 16 to 26, were decided by votes of 35 to 16, one fewer than the required number for conviction. Many of those voting for conviction emphasized that the impeachment proceedings should not be considered a trial in the judicial sense. They believed, quite rightly, that Johnson had lost the confidence of his adopted party and should be removed from office. Others, with greater hesitation, wondered if impeachment were the best method for ridding the nation of a poor leader.

Since the President could not be ousted, members of the Republican party turned to the alternative method for getting rid of a President. As their presidential candidate for 1868, they selected the popular military leader Ulysses S. Grant, who had carefully avoided involvement in the impeachment proceedings so that he could remain acceptable to most members of the party. For Vice President they chose Schuyler Colfax, Speaker of the House, a firm supporter of national reconstruction and a widely known former newspaper editor well connected with industry. While the Democrats sympathized with Johnson, they nominated, after much argument, the distinguished Horatio Seymour of New York, a critic of the reconstruction. The campaign was a vigorous affair, and the popular choice was closer than the electoral results (214 to 80) would indicate, but the Republicans reaped the advantages of backing the blacks and having control of the South.

The Grant Administrations

The coming of Grant to office closed the painful contest between Congress and Andrew Johnson, but opened under Grant two terms of unusual corruption in the Presidency. Historians agree that he was an honest man who was abused by his friends. They feel, moreover, that he did not have the fortitude to face up to national problems and dipped at times into partisan politics that "became a national scandal." His administration, they believe, spread corruption to politics on all levels.

For a time after his election Grant's officials exercised firm control of the South. The process of reconstructing governments continued, and state after state qualified for readmission to the Union. In these states some military forces remained, but the occupation was limited to troubled areas. The Klan officers were rounded up and prosecuted, and surveillance was provided for a few ex-Confederate officers. Grant's government, however, also began its withdrawal from the South at this time. It discontinued the supervisory services of the Freedmen's Bureau and returned to the states initiative to guard the liberties of all citizens. Elections were not supervised, and more and more conservatives replaced Republicans in local government. The state courts, also filling with conservative southerners, adopted new attitudes toward the black, and the decisions were backed by the Supreme Court, which sought to reestablish the traditional pattern of federal-state relations.

The attention of Congress to the South became less intense as Sumner, Stevens, and men of their opinion died or retired, and there was a change of ideology and political goals even by those old Radicals who remained in Congress. The new leaders, facing new issues and new crises, were less concerned with the welfare of blacks than with the possibility of personal profit. The Civil War remained in the background, however, and was used for emotional purposes during a campaign or to humble Southerners or to exploit blacks.

The New Spoils System

In the 1870s the spoils of office dominated the minds of many leaders, but political corruption had been evident in a serious form since the 1850s. Political morals seem to be lower in this decade as leaders filled their pockets with bribes. The spread of corruption from the Vice President to congressmen, from state to local officials, amazes modern eyes. Almost everywhere, it seems, politicians found ways of collecting fees. The public became aroused when Congress voted salary increases and two years' back salary, but nearly everyone

A Thomas Nast's Cartoon of Grant's Troubled Presidency
(*University of Southern California*)

in the President's Cabinet, save Secretary of State Hamilton Fish, was exploiting his office for personal gain. The larger scandals surfaced after Grant was reelected in 1872.

Election results showed that the people retained admiration for the President, but he was totally unfit to meet the challenges of office. Bewildered and inexperienced in politics, he hardly knew what he was doing and was badly advised by his Cabinet and friends. He was loyal to his subordinates but blind to their weaknesses. He was willing to hear advice, but unable to select the appropriate course of action. He had little feeling for what the country needed, and events had little significance for him.

Politics reflected the rise of a new order. Since the 1850s railroad construction, textile manufacture, and steel production had made great strides. In 1869 the Union Pacific joined the Central Pacific in Utah to complete the first continental railroad linkage of the East with the Far West. Changes in the northern economy were apparent in the demand for products, the need for investment funds, the marketing of merchandise, and the enlargement of the work force. The South, too, was falling under the domination of new financial and industrial combinations. Its cotton crops went North over railroads rebuilt and controlled by Northerners, and its politicians, accepting gifts of stock and money, resembled their opposite number in the North. The need for agricultural workers rose dramatically, and the black, who was mostly unskilled, drifted into manual labor. Soon he found himself bound by a caste system and kept from schools, professions, and social institutions that would have enabled him to rise.

Such issues as the tariff, the civil service, and the scarcity of money dominated politics. The tariff had often been raised during the war, principally for revenue purposes, but it had remained nearly unchanged since 1865. The prices of commodities were held at unnatural levels, providing high margins of profit and monopoly control of the market at a time when costs of production and wages were falling. Even when tariff reduction was agitated before Congress, only minor adjustments were made. Many politicians, corrupted by bribes, seemed insensitive to the public welfare.

A code of ethics was absolutely necessary to establish standards of public responsibility. Providing a civil service was obviously not enough, when the Senate was full of corporation executives and the House was packed with clients of manufacturers. Favoritism in legislation was detrimental to the public interest, but frequently that interest was not easily understood by the citizen. So it was with the money supply which was inflexible and controlled by those who possessed gold. With the economy expanding, the demand for investment funds increased yearly. Credit resources, however, were inadequate, and the government refused to free the currency from the limitations of a gold support system. Those who had gold could charge premium

Thomas Nast's View of the Democratic Party in 1872.

interest rates and exercise monopoly controls of the market.

These issues introduced into politics new men, who usually publicized their war records yet drew their inspiration and support, as did James G. Blaine and Roscoe Conkling, from corporate and spoils connections. Their attention was absorbed by distribution of offices and contracts and the establishment of a patronage system in their states. Conkling, the son of a well-to-do judge, never accepted bribes himself, but he managed the spoils of the New York custom house with extraordinary skill. As leader of the machine, he bought and sold offices in the market for personal and party power. He regarded reformers as rivals for "office and plunder."

With Conkling as an example, many politicians tried to imitate his success; others reacted with much hostility as they joined a small group of leaders known as the Liberal Republicans who preached reform. They attacked the tariff and exposed corruption in high places and were frightened by what they saw happening to democracy. They wanted the federal government to restore full citizenship to all Southerners. Hoping to separate the government from business and industry, they backed the unusual candidacy of Horace Greeley, the editor of the New York *Tribune,* who was nominated as Democratic standard bearer in 1872. These Republicans for the most part were men of good will, devoted to separate reforms, and willing to sacrifice peace of mind to work for their objectives. But they were not united as a group except in their demand for a democratic and responsible government and were frequently incapable of assessing political realities.

The Election of 1876

Their publicity nonetheless exposed the worse excesses of the Grant administration and made honesty in government a campaign issue in the 1876 elections. The contest between Rutherford B. Hayes of Ohio, who had served three terms as Republican governor, and Samuel J. Tilden of New York, who had prosecuted the Tweed Ring and served as governor of his state, occurred in depression times of heavy unemployment and numerous busines failures which had persisted since the Panic of 1873. The Democrats had won control of the House of Representatives in 1874 and the swing of popular support seemed to be to them. Reform of government became an issue, but both candidates were careful to refrain from attacking the major issues of the day—currency reform, the tariff, and a code of government ethics.

Between the candidates the public had little to choose. Since the tide was favoring the Democrats, the election of Tilden seemed imminent, but this prediction did not allow for the machinations of the parties. Nineteen electoral votes in three southern states and one vote in Oregon created much uncertainty. The Republican party, however, exercised some control in three southern states. Its men brought in electoral votes favoring Hayes, making the total electoral vote 185 to 184. The Democrats, not to be outdone, conducted their own canvass and discovered results favorable to Tilden. The confusing votes, of course, required an arbitrator, and Congress finally set up an electoral commission of fifteen men. It was agreed that there would be equal party representation from the Congress and courts and that the fifteenth member would be David Davis of Illinois, who was not firmly connected with any party. Further complicating these proceedings were disputed ballots from Oregon where the Democratic governor ousted one of the presidential electors, because he was a federal official and chose a Democratic elector who was the next highest in the popular

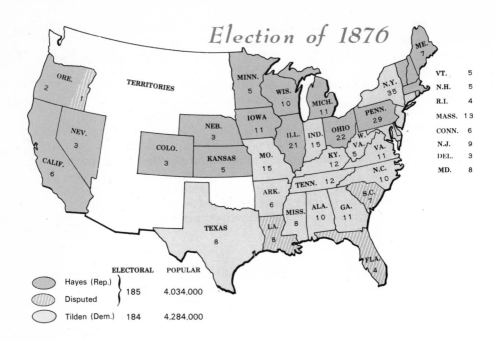

Election of 1876

VT.	5
N.H.	5
R.I.	4
MASS.	13
CONN.	6
N.J.	9
DEL.	3
MD.	8

	ELECTORAL	POPULAR
Hayes (Rep.)	185	4,034,000
Disputed		
Tilden (Dem.)	184	4,284,000

vote. The election of David Davis to the United States Senate apparently disqualified him as a commissioner.

Although the plurality of 250,000 popular votes for Tilden seemed to indicate that the Commission should select him as the next President, Davis's replacement broke the deadlock in favor of the Republicans, and in the Commission's report Hayes was given the Presidency by a margin of one electoral vote. Northern Democrats threatened a filibuster, thus a delay in acceptance of the Commission's report, and some leaders even talked of a renewal of the Civil War. To avoid this serious probability, Northern Republicans and Southern Democrats arranged a secret conference, in which their leaders bartered and compromised. Apparently the Democrats went along with Hayes's election, while the Republicans agreed to permit the South to manage its own relations with the blacks.

The Reconstruction Southern Style

Some historians have made this compromise of 1877 the equal of those in 1820 and 1850. It is difficult to prove, however, what was actually compromised, except that troops were to be withdrawn from South Carolina and Louisiana when Hayes became President. Undoubt-

edly, too, the Republicans were expected to moderate attacks on the
Democrats as the bloody plotters of civil conflict and to lessen their
support of blacks in the South. Hayes complied by naming Southerners
to posts in his government and asking help of Congress in providing
funds for internal improvements. Other understandings may have
been reached, but they are not readily apparent.

What is certain about the years after 1877 is the gradual return of
white rule to the South. Blacks were not only pushed out of office,
but were forced into an inferior position. Imposed upon them was a
peculiar system of servitude, a caste system, that was not slavery but
similar in spirit. Formed by racial bias it depended upon prejudicial
laws and bigoted social customs. The guiding principle was to establish and maintain white supremacy.

Servitude of this new kind developed fast, and laws followed
giving solid reality to what was informally happening. Segregation of
churches, schools, and public services became the rule by 1890 and
the political parties invented various kinds of devices to keep blacks
from participation. Literacy requirements determined voters; gerry-
mandering divided black power; and the appointments to office were
placed in the hands of the governor or legislature so as to by-pass
local interests. Even so, no southern state had a uniform code regulating black behavior. The only common device used among the states,
and basic to the enforcement of inferiority, was the poll tax. The financial burden it imposed was too heavy for most blacks to bear. Moreover,
literacy tests were employed, as were registration technicalities, which
limited black participation in politics.

The economic side of southern life contributed to the caste system.
Since fertile land was owned by the white population, blacks (and poor
whites) were used as day laborers and sharecroppers, or in tenancy.
With labor and land abundant, the owners of land set their rate of profit
from cotton and sugar crops, and left the blacks often very little return,
at times not even enough for subsistence. The blacks fell, as a result,
into deep poverty as debtors. Sometimes, in seeking relief, they turned
to theft, but the states reacted with harsh measures; not the least brutal
was the convict-lease system. Convict services were purchased from
the state, and the owners of service used convict labor for rail construction, mining, and field agriculture. Contractors provided the convicts
with clothing, housing, and food, and in exchange for these necessities blacks were exploited with little governmental protection. The
whip came into common use, and recalcitrant convicts were also
"softened up" by being thrown into pits and chained, given bread
and water diets, and shackled into work gangs.

The impact of black bondage upon the South was visible in the
creation of a two-class society, in the development of the Democratic
party as the voice of the dominant white, and in the persistence of an
uneasy relationship between the races. The equilibrium was main-

Black Population, 1790-1880

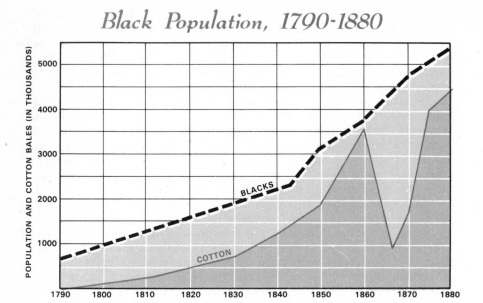

tained, unfortunately, with beatings, convict labor, and racial bias.

The New South: Industry

The decades after 1865 brought great changes in southern life. The devastation of war was quickly removed, and railroads were put into operation, then expanded and modernized. Nearly 30,000 miles of new lines were added by 1890, and rail lines in Texas and Arkansas opened new routes as transcontinental links. Southern railroads carried primarily agricultural products—cotton, tobacco, and sugar —but in the late 1870s their loads included also the raw materials from a broad range of extractive industries and finished products of textile mills that were being built in Tennessee, Georgia, and South Carolina. By 1900 the South had over four million spindles in operation, with expansion planned for millions more.

This new economic effort gradually changed the face of the land. Cities were rising, attracting immigrants as laborers, and providing urban institutions like schools and colleges, banks and insurance companies, small shops and handicraft industries. The new textile mills, often located in these cities, used indigent white laborers who had left the farm for town and city jobs. These mills were attractive to business people because of cheap labor and favorable laws—sometimes no laws at all regulated the hours of the employment of women and children. Laborers lived often in the mill towns, paying high rents for miserable housing and receiving wages barely sufficient to provide subsistence.

The New South: The Literature of Reconciliation

These harsh conditions of life, however, should not hide the beauty and charm of the South. The quiet tempo of life was reflected in the relaxed, rural atmosphere that permeated folk ways. The prevailing chivalry was captured by authors of the day in their tales of the post- and ante-bellum South. Men such as Thomas Nelson Page wove some reality into their stories, but their magnolia-scented plots lifted the commonplace into a charming, imaginative way of life. Whites were often gentle folk, while blacks were usually childlike adults, smiling and happy as they went about their daily chores. Page's use of black dialect in Marse Chan added realism to his dialogues, and his daring depiction of northern soldiers falling in love with southern belles helped foster reconciliation between sections.

The work of Henry W. Grady, moreover, hailed the coming of a new South of industry and progress. In his editorials in the Atlanta Constitution, he labeled himself the pensman of the reformed South, advocating diversity of industry and agriculture. He proclaimed the death of the old South in these words: "There is a South of union and freedom . . . thank God, [it] is living, breathing, growing every hour."

Grady was popular with Northerners who applauded his efforts to bring union and stability to the nation. They were ready to accept his solution for the black problem—a paternalism of whites over blacks —and the Democratic party leadership welcomed anything that minimized black rights as an issue. The United States Supreme Court, too, had given its support to the southern caste system and state interpretation of citizenship. In the Slaughter-House cases (1873) it had placed the protection of citizenship in the hands of the states. Years later, in 1896, it accepted the southern practice of separate but equal to the use of accommodations on trains. The rule spread to most forms of southern race relations in the coming fifty years.

Some voices were raised against southern (and northern) bias toward the blacks. Henry Cabot Lodge of Massachusetts introduced a bill in the House of Representatives setting up federal inspection of voting registration. His efforts failed, even though he won Republican endorsement of his ideas in the 1892 platform of the party. Senator Henry W. Blair of New Hampshire, in the 1880s, introduced legislation to assist schools in meeting the problems of illiteracy, but he, too, was unsuccessful. Another spokesman for justice was Booker T. Washington, the black leader who was named head of Tuskegee Institute in 1881. He spent a generation developing industrial training for blacks, and a lifetime trying to determine the future direction of blacks in American society. His fame eventually gave him platforms on which to voice the needs of blacks in the South. His gentle language and cautious program for black improvement was deceptive to racists, because he preached peace and patience. Looking into the future, however, he offered blacks the longterm objective of full integration into American society.

"Reconstruction" is a poor word to describe what happened to the South between 1865 and 1900. Lincoln planned to return the defeated South to full partnership to the union with as little punishment as possible. Johnson had a similar plan. Both Presidents would have permitted the South to devise schemes for black education and governmental participation without much federal interference. Congress, however, wanted an assurance of black involvement in the South, and it compelled the southern states to write constitutions, broaden the franchise, and accept blacks in the new governments. Much reorganization of the southern governments occurred, but Congress, in the 1870s, lost interest in following through on its program. In the breach the South developed a caste system for blacks that ground them into poverty and inferiority.

SUGGESTIONS FOR FURTHER READING

Abbott, Martin, *The Freedmen's Bureau in South Carolina, 1865-1872*. Chapel Hill, N.C., University of North Carolina Press, 1967.

Berry, Mary Frances, *Military Necessity and Civil Rights Policy: Black Citizenship and the Constitution, 1861-1868*. Port Washington, N.Y., Kennikat Press, 1977.

Belz, Herman, *Reconstructing the Union: Theory and Policy During the Civil War*. Ithaca, New York, Cornell University Press, 1969.

Brock, W. R., *An American Crisis: Congress and Reconstruction, 1865-1867*. New York, St. Martin's Press, 1963.

Cash, W. J., *The Mind of the South*. New York, Vintage Books, Random House, 1961.

Donald, David, *The Politics of Reconstruction, 1863-1867*. Baton Rouge, La., Louisiana State University Press, 1965.

Franklin, John Hope, *Reconstruction After the Civil War*. Chicago, Ill., University of Chicago Press, 1961.

McKitrick, Eric L., *Andrew Johnson and Reconstruction*. Chicago, Illinois, University of Chicago Press, 1960.

Patrick, Rembert W., *The Reconstruction of the Nation*. New York, Oxford University Press, 1967.

Perham, Michael, *Reunion Without Compromise: The South and*

Reconstruction, 1865-1868. Cambridge, England, Cambridge University Press, 1973.

Pike, James Sheperd, Republicanism and the American Negro, 1850-1882. Durham, N.C., Duke University Press, 1976.

Pressly, Thomas J., Americans Interpret Their Civil War. New York, The Macmillan Company, 1965.

Silby, Joel H., A Respectable Minority: The Democratic Party in the Civil War, 1860-1868. New York, W. W. Norton & Company, 1974.

Stampp, Kenneth M., The Era of Reconstruction: 1865-1877. New York, Random House, 1967.

Tindall, George Brown, The Persistent Tradition in New South Politics. Baton Rouge, La., Louisiana State University Press, 1975.

Trefouse, Hans L., Impeachment of a President: Andrew Jackson, the Blacks, and Reconstruction. Knoxville, Tenn., University of Tennessee Press, 1975.

_____, The Radical Republicans: Lincoln's Vanguard for Racial Justice. New York, Alfred A. Knopf, 1969.

Woodward, C. Vann, Reunion and Reaction. Garden City, New York, Anchor Books, Doubleday & Company, 1956.

_____, Origins of the New South, 1877-1913: Vol. 9, A History of the South. Baton Rouge, La., Louisiana State University Press, 1951.

11

The Continental Nation

DURING THE SIX DECADES AFTER 1848 the United States evolved into a continental nation. It owned land from sea to sea, let the people find homes on the plains and mountains, and by 1912 admitted all the western territories to statehood. It helped to put railroads into nearly every part of the West, establish farms and businesses, and weave the people into the national pattern of politics and industry. The sections of North, South, and West remained, perhaps even the frontier, but an industrial society had emerged that changed the old norms of political conduct, imposed upon leaders the responsibility to think broadly and creatively, and thrust the country into the mainstream of world politics. Over these decades the United States had increased greatly in size. By purchase in 1854 it added land about the size of Pennsylvania and now part of southern Arizona and New Mexico and, in 1867, purchased the vast territory of Alaska. In 1898 it fought a successful war with Spain, obtained Puerto Rico and the Philippines and annexed about the same time the islands of Hawaii and Samoa.

Westward Movement

The remarkable transformation of plains, mountains, and coastal

slopes into an integral part of the republic is a story of romantic exploits, heroic deeds, and down-to-earth toil. At the beginning of this
period the emotion that has been termed "manifest destiny" brought
Oregon and Texas into the Union and hastened, through war, the annexation of the Southwest and California. Following hard on the war
was the California gold rush, which attracted world-wide interest
and nearly two hundred thousand residents to California. Other gold,
silver, and land rushes drew millions to the West. The silver mines
of Washoe, now called Nevada, provided perhaps the most spectacular
discovery. The Comstock Lode, as it was named, was found in 1859.
New discoveries uncovered increasingly richer veins. A discovery in
1873 exposed a vein 57 feet wide, worth at least $300 million, and it
caused wild speculation.

While the trans-Mississippi west grew rapidly, the East also expanded. In 1850 the population of the nation was approximately 23
million; in 1917 the Atlantic states alone had nearly double that number. With the total national population five times that of 1850, the
East absorbed many people into an urban and industrial culture.
Towns one after another turned into cities and metropolitan areas,
making room for the millions of Irish, English, Germans, Italians,
and Poles who blended their Old World culture with the American.
Approximately 25 million Europeans made their way across the Atlantic; thousands of Orientals and Mexican Americans settled in the
Southwest. An observer of America, who might have met the Scots
cowboy, the Chinese or Irish railworkers, the Italian or Portuguese
grape grower, and the German factory worker, would have been hard
pressed to say whether the open frontier or the mingling of many
peoples was more important in forging the continental nation?

The Far West

The West separated into many parts, but as distance and isolation from population centers were conquered, cultural patterns similar
to the rest of the United States developed. California and Oregon became
states in the 1850s, though California's gold, wheat, and climate attracted
five times the population of Oregon. California's Spanish heritage
was quickly overshadowed by the onrush of gold seekers as people
from across the world came to work its gold fields. Anglo-Americans
came to predominate, and their language and religions influenced the
state's development in architecture and customs. The publicity that
travelers gave to California's climate and potential was ever a factor
in pulling people West. The journey was difficult overland and costly
by sea, but in 1858 the Butterfield Overland Stages began their trips
from Missouri and Arkansas to San Francisco, California, and in 1869
the transcontinental railroad was completed. The railroad stimulated
the development of a diversified agriculture in California, and in a

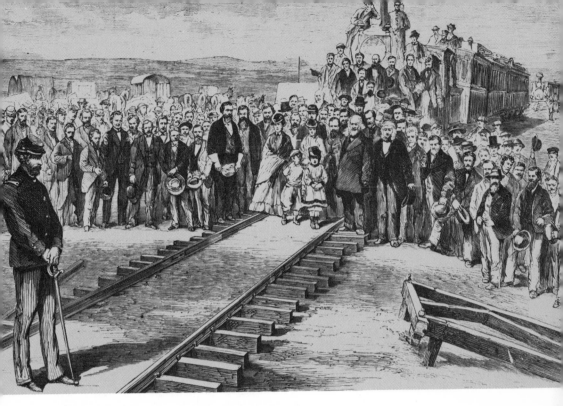

The Completion of the Union Pacific Railroad
(University of Southern California)

decade its citrus, wines, dry fruits, and walnuts were delicacies on eastern tables.

In the 1880s southern California experienced a population boom. Speculators marketed information on California's fertile lands, warm climate, and petroleum deposits; boom towns sprang up everywhere. The flooding of population quickly spread over the region, but left a strong impression, nonetheless, with the development of housing tracts, colleges, and resorts. Joining the University of California, which was founded in 1868, were such institutions of higher learning as the University of Southern California and Stanford University and a host of small, religion-supported colleges. By 1900 California had a population of one million four hundred thousand, and its orange was as popular as its gold had been a half century earlier.

Other people came West attracted by silver and copper rushes. These discoveries often took them into inhospitable country, but nearby fertile valleys, suitable for farming and cattle grazing, beckoned the disappointed miners. Permanent settlement of Colorado developed near the mining activities, giving the territory enough people for statehood in 1876. In Wyoming, however, cattle raising scattered only a few people over its plains and hills, and the territory barely qualified for statehood in 1890 when most of the Northwest was carved into states. The railroad opened the Northwest, and the pacification of the Indians and discovery of precious ores helped attract newcomers. However, vast stands of timber, abundant fishing resources, and fertile agricultural lands made Washington and Oregon prosperous, and helped Seattle and Portland to become cities. After 1900 the only remaining territories in the far west were Arizona and New Mexico, whose mining towns, Indian pueblos, and lonely villages disguised a prospering mineral industry that sustained a population of approximately three hundred thousand people. Oklahoma remained primarily an Indian territory until 1907 when it was admitted to statehood.

The Great Plains

In the Great Plains life was turbulent during the 1850s, but the population multiplied quickly. When Kansas became a state in 1861, the area had several hundred thousand people, and population expansion in that decade and the next was sustained by the opening of extraordinary fertile, agricultural lands. With the spread of cattle raising and the completion of the railroad, the population of the whole region increased dramatically. Kansas's population approached a million in 1880, Nebraska's was well over a million in 1890, and Minnesota's reached that mark in 1897. By that time the region had become great fields of wheat, corn, and barley. Where farming did not prosper, cattle grazed and were fattened for the stockyards at Kansas City, Omaha, and Chicago.

The Plains, as the name implies, were open country, and distance became a stark reality of life. Settlers were faced with scarcity of timber, shortages of water, and loneliness, and had to find expedients to solve their problems. For houses many settlers cut pieces of sod and laid the pieces together like bricks. They used wood for door- and window-casings and for rafters to support dirt roofs. Since the roofs often leaked, the settlers placed the houses near hills where they had some protection and white washed the interiors to provide modest insulation. The houses were never free of dampness, and settlers turned to other building materials when they became available. Their furnishings were crude and makeshift, but sometimes a table and rocking chair had been carried there in the covered wagons when settlers came from the East. They depended usually for necessities upon their own ingenuity, particularly for clothes, medical care, and education. The frontier, however, was less bleak after a decade of settlement, and with the building of the railroad farmers found some relief from shortages. The coming of people, too, helped diversify community services. Schools were established, but had to rely upon the availability of teachers. Education meant a one-room, ungraded school, sometimes located at a crossroads, and classes were held for only a few months each year. Churches were also distant, and services depended frequently upon an itinerant minister or priest. Life was obviously hard for most people, but pioneers found time for amusement. Church suppers, picnics, barbecues, buggy rides, and all sorts of games drew people to gatherings at a church, a river park, or a school house. Those who could travel to regional towns like Salina, Dodge City, or Sioux Falls might visit gambling halls, saloons, and brothels, as well as the few stores, traveling shows, and lectures.

Western Artists

Interest in the West, in addition to settlement, was reflected in the works of artists and writers who were fascinated by its natural beauty. In the 1860s and 70s traveling artists sketched many of the great views, and Albert Bierstadt gained fame for his paintings of Yosemite, the Merced River, and the Seal Rocks of San Francisco. In the 1890s Frederic Remington caught the poetic drama of the cowboy in sketches of the western plains, and helped make the cowboy's exploits on charging horses symbolic of western life. Others like Norton Bush and Henry Arthur Elkins tramped into the wilds and captured impressions of the Canyon of the Yellowstone and the rugged beauty of Estes Park and the Grand Canyon. Elkins's dramatic style and pallette knife technique captured magnificently the intensity of nature.

No writer left a greater impression of the natural western beauty and the urgent need to save it than John Muir. A naturalist and wanderer in the wilds, he described its grandeur in articles and books. A passage in *The Mountains of California* tells of his inspection of a glacier:

The surface-snow, though sprinkled with stones shot down from the cliffs, was in some places almost pure, gradually becoming crystalline and changing to whitish porous ice of different shades of color, and this again changing at a depth of 20 or 30 feet to blue ice, some of the ribbon-like bands of which were nearly pure, and blended with the paler bands in the most gradual and delicate manner imaginable. A series of rugged zigzags enabled me to make my way down into the weird under-world of the crevasse. Its chambered hollows were hung with a multitude of clustered icicles, amid which pale, subdued light pulsed and shimmered with indescribable loveliness.

Other writers also made contributions toward interpreting western life. Helen Hunt Jackson helped dramatize the sufferings and joys of the American Indian. Charles F. Lummis, the city editor of the Los Angeles *Times*, was a man of enthusiasm who genuinely loved the West and described its animals, trees, beaches, and open spaces in romantic terms. More serious were the writings of Henry George who saw the speculative ownership of land as a threat to western life.

Black Hawk: Kiowa Apache (Los Angeles County Museum of Natural History)

The Farmers and the Railroads

Western farmers, especially on the Great Plains, cultivated large acreage, often concentrating on a single crop and always using machinery to reduce labor costs. In selling their crops they depended on rail and/or ship transportation to distant markets, sometimes as far as western Europe. The experience for farmers was not new, but it was aggravated because they were living in a frontier area. They did not know each other; they had few societal ties; and they did not control their legislatures. Probably of equal seriousness were the technical problems of the new type of farming. Farmers were caught up in a fast-changing set of circumstances which included new machinery, increasing acreage, credit purchasing, and distant markets. Crop prices—often set in New York and London—were beyond their control, and the prices in the market centers depended upon reasonable prices of transportation and storage. The abundant production, moreover, brought falling prices so that farmers regularly bought machinery on credit in one market and paid for it in another. Their relations with the railroads and banks as mortage companies added complexity; somehow, although the farming community was surrounded by abundance, it was sinking into debt and had little return for its effort. For these problems, the desperate farmers blamed the nearest target, the railroads, which were their lifeline to the markets. The farmers did not realize that railroad corporate management was having its problems, too.

The railroads had penetrated isolated areas, especially in the West where population was sparse, and had built their lines on the expectation of business that was not to be realized for years. To help some railroads defray initial costs, Congress had provided land, credit, and subsidies. Private individuals had supplied vision and skill. Promoters like Collis Huntington and Leland Stanford had mobilized capital on the East Coast and in Europe, found settlers to emigrate, and encouraged investors to develop mines, grain elevators, and businesses near the railroads. In a decade, corporate organization, engineering know-how, and manpower development had put rails over the plains and mountains. Following the completion of the Central Pacific to San Francisco in 1869, other lines pushed West from points in the Middle West. The Santa Fe entered southern California in the 1880s and the Northern Pacific reached Washington in the 1890s.

From their vast grants some railroads sold attractive farms and sites for businesses. Using advertising, special transportation services, and credit to entice thousands of settlers, their agents were responsible for opening western Kansas and Colorado, and the Southern Pacific sold to French, Italian, and Portuguese immigrants enormous acreages in the Central Valley of California, where crops of grain and fruit were soon ready for shipment. The towns of Bakersfield and Fresno flourished, but it was Los Angeles that drew the greatest numbers of people,

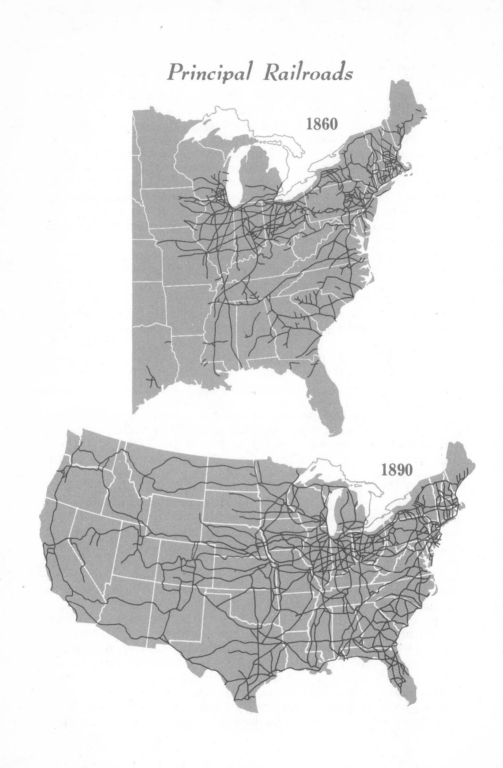

Principal Railroads

1860

1890

many of whom sought the mild climate for health and recreational purposes.

Few railroads, however, could long continue their beneficent policies toward settlers. The heavy costs of running lines through frontier country cut profits from settled areas, and freight agents were pressed to fix rates at levels that would bring back the profits. Original construction had been inordinately expensive, often because of hasty work and corrupt management, and the roads were thus overcapitalized and burdened with heavy charges. Interest rates were high, stockholders demanded good returns, and management wanted its rewards. Freight rates were set as high as possible, but they were used, too, to favor shippers and markets where the railroad might have advantages. Even so, between 1870 and 1890 many lines went bankrupt.

Farmers protested these costly services because prices were usually uncertain or inconsistent with market conditions. Rates often were not posted, and frequently were set at their dearest levels during times of peak railroad use. Other aggravations like rate discrimination for long and short hauls, insufficient service, and partnerships between railroads and some grain elevator companies often seemed to deny the farmer a fair return on his crops. He was forced eventually to seek justice in the state legislatures and courts.

Railroads nonetheless enjoyed an unusual position of power in transportation. They provided fast, dependable, safe service and enabled the East to coordinate its enormous industrial activity, raising national production yearly and inspiring inventive and creative efforts in many areas. Likewise, they enabled the West to take its abundant crops to markets.

The railroads themselves had to be responsive to new inventions and industrial improvements. For safer rails, stronger and heavier coaches, and stable bridges, railroad management relied on durable steel, a new product which helped the roads in each decade to increase the loads and speed of trains and to improve service. Many railroads also needed to be unified and to have their services standardized. Their services needed to be made attractive to investors with risk capital. Cornelius Vanderbilt, James J. Hill, and George Pullman, were a few of the persons upon whom railroads depended for management skill to keep the roads responsive to industrial and customer demands.

Few men gave the railroads better management than did Cornelius Vanderbilt (1794-1877), who late in life became interested in their problems. His great wealth had been made in shipping before the Civil War. In 1862 he began to buy shares in New York rail lines, which he rescued from bankruptcy and supplied with capital. Consolidating lines, buying new equipment, and improving service, he put them on a paying basis. He secured control of the New York Central in 1867, extending its service eventually to Chicago in the 1870s. His grandson

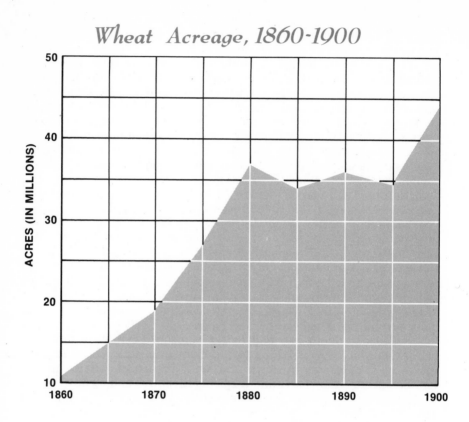

Wheat Acreage, 1860-1900

The Industrial Empires

and namesake (1843-99) expanded the railroad empire and became director of many companies supplying the roads with business.

The Industrial Empires

The Vanderbilt lines and their competitors required large quantities of steel for rails and equipment to handle the heavy loads of new products. The development of great iron ore fields in western Michigan and in the Mesabi region in Minnesota assured the industry of an enormous quantity of easy-to-mine ore. By rail and by ship through the Great Lakes, the ore was conveyed to furnaces where ample supplies of coal were at hand. The perfection of smelting with the Bessemer and Siemens-Martin processes guaranteed manufacture of an unusually fine quality steel at astonishingly low costs. Abram Hewitt and Andrew Carnegie, with daring and skill, introduced inventions and management techniques that made American steel competitive on the world market.

The pioneer producer Andrew Carnegie (1835-1919) began his

career as private secretary for the Pennsylvania Railroad executive Thomas A. Scott and continued in the firm until 1865 as a talented salesman and judge of men. In the decade after the Civil War he sold securities, dealt in oil, built bridges, and speculated in steel stocks, all with unusual success. After 1873 he interested himself in steel, attracted good talent to him, and using shrewd business methods took his partnership from its modest origins to the pinnacle of corporate greatness. His career was interwoven with the rise of the steel industry. Using up-to-date methods and inviting experimentation, he controlled the process of steel making from the ore fields to the finished product. He struggled also to provide competitive quality and prices behind a tariff wall.

Better and cheaper steel helped the machinery industry make new, stronger equipment for textile manufacturers and railroads as well as farm implements, building materials, and household items. These consumer industries, in turn, produced merchandise that raised the standard of living. The petroleum industry, developing in Pennsylvania and California, gave the home user inexpensive heating and lighting and supplied eventually western railroads with fuel for steam power when proper burning methods were perfected.

The new products were marketed increasingly on a continental scale. To win customers, manufacturers were forced to standardize the quality of merchandise, and some businesses employed scientists to assure quality control. Mass production through assembly-line operations standardized clothing sizes, styling of products, and trade names. By the first decade of the twentieth century such merchandise companies as J. C. Penney, Montgomery Ward, Sears Roebuck, and the Great Atlantic and Pacific Tea Company had developed marketing practices that served customers in distant areas. Improved refrigeration on ships and railroads made shipping of processed meat possible, and Gustavus F. Swift and Philip Armour unified the meat packing industry into a monopoly.

American ingenuity in industry was backed financially by investment bankers in New York and Philadelphia. Men like J. Pierpont Morgan mobilized capital in the East and Europe and invested it in American industry. They were careful to guard the safety of their clients' money in the securities' market and demanded a voice in management in exchange for securing these funds. Setting standards of competition and giving advice on corporate affairs, they salvaged the assets of weak enterprises for stockholders and sometimes strengthened the market. They also exploited opportunities to combine companies and accelerated the formation of trusts, interlocking directorates, holding companies, and various agreements to reduce competition, often concentrating in their own hands power that involved the welfare of millions. While consolidation was frequently beneficial to all—settling market conditions, raising quality of merchandise, and insuring stockholders good dividends—corporation size, power, and monopolies threatened the independent action of government itself. The discretion of a few persons could determine the course of industry: manage prices, set patterns of development, allocate benefits. Some company executives drew annual salaries of more than $100,000; chief stockholders often accumulated millions in dividends and services. The control of wealth by this minority created a class of "superdemocrats" who firmly believed in the nation's principles, distributed alms to the poor, and founded hospitals and universities, and contributed heavily to both political parties. They were society's chosen people, "the fittest," who had heard Andrew Carnegie describe them as the bees who "make the most honey, and contribute most to the hive even after they have gorged themselves full. Here is the remarkable fact, that the masses of the people in any country are prosperous and comfortable just in proportion as there are millionaires."

While the sheer size of industry troubled most observers of corporate activity, it was not the primary problem of the day. Reformers repeatedly attacked corporate size, nonetheless, and sponsored measures to control trusts, holding companies, and interlocking directorates. Perhaps management responsibility toward stockholders and the public was more improtant than size in terms of safeguarding investments, providing dividends, and manufacturing quality products. Directors of some railroads, for example, undermined their company's solvency by awarding contracts to firms in which they had private interests. Without competitive bidding, directors of the Union Pacific Railway used the Credit Mobilier to drain profits into their own pockets, even assuring themselves of congressional protection by giving shares in the Credit Mobilier to leaders of the Grant administration. Corporate evils also arose from the sale of substandard merchandise. In the meat industry, packers slaughtered diseased cattle or employed artificial preservatives to disguise quality. Drug manufacturers released preparations to the public without proper scientific testing and with improper labeling. Corporate evil, however, was worst in its use of power, through monopoly prices, graft, and corruption. It denied the people what was rightly theirs: democratic government.

The industrial system thus had serious imperfections, but in a democratic society inequities of wealth and the amoral conduct of some industrialists were problems for the political order to solve. To find the public interest amid the complexities of industrialism was an intricate problem that was not well understood by the people, most of whom were proud of what was happening and applauded enterprise. Laborers found many new jobs in the factories, mills, and mines. Immigrants by the hundreds of thousands accepted positions in the industrial system and saved their money to send for relatives. While hours were long, wages low, and housing poor, the mobility, city living, and relief from old-country customs were counted as benefits.

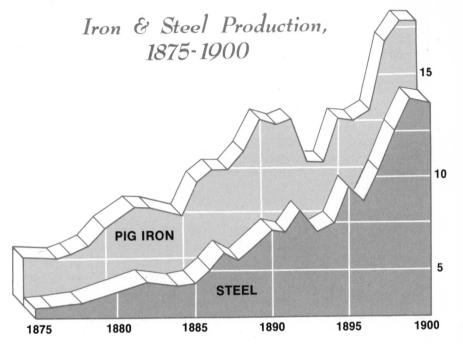

Iron & Steel Production, 1875-1900

PIG IRON

STEEL

SHORT TONS (IN MILLIONS)

15

10

5

1875   1880   1885   1890   1895   1900

For many the standard of living was an improvement over European conditions. Thousands, however, found life in America lonely and disappointing, and they returned to Europe penniless and bitter.

Labor Problems and Organization

During these decades laborers needed bargaining power to cope with the nationwide spread of industry and the development of assembly-line production. They joined a large work force in expanding factories where management was distant and impersonal, and fellow workers were separated by tasks, noise, and numbers. Their jobs were becoming more and more routine, and skill was a lesser asset than youth and agility. Their health was threatened by fumes, poisonous chemicals and dust, unprotected sawblades and other cutting instuments, and improper ventilation.

As their work became dehumanized or depersonalized by machines and assembly lines, laborers tried to remedy the situation through organization. Craft unions helped typesetters, cigarmakers, shoemakers, and other craftsmen, but the need for common action among the less skilled was desperate. At first they formed general labor associations like the National Labor Union and the Knights of Labor, and enrolled members in great numbers. Under the leadership of Terence V. Powderly the Knights rallied working people into a party devoted to social action, cooperation, and democracy. They sponsored educational programs and legislation to improve living conditions, and backed strikes against railways, factories, and mining operations. However, they lacked a powerful, committed membership that could demand political support, and they faced the prejudice of people who saw labor resistance as conspiratorial and as a violation of the rights of private property. Courts were willing to grant injunctions and governors ready to send troops into troubled areas. Both Presidents Hayes and Cleveland employed federal troops to break up strikes. Employers used strikebreaking devices such as lockouts, Pinkerton detectives, spies, and black lists in order to beat down opposition.

The Chicago Haymarket Square riot of 1886 irreparably damaged the reputation of the Knights of Labor. When a general strike for the eight-hour day became disorderly, police trying to contain the violence shot and killed some of the demonstrators. The following day, during a gathering of labor agitators in Haymarket Square to protest the shootings, a bomb exploded in the crowd. Rioting began; eleven persons were killed and more than one hundred wounded. Eight anarchists finally stood trial for murder and disorder, and, although no personal involvement other than their presence in the mob was proved, seven of them were convicted of murder, and four were hanged. The harsh penalties were generally applauded by the public; when Illinois Governor John P. Altgeld in 1893 pardoned two of the convicted leaders who were serving life sentences, he was assailed in the press and legislature and defeated later for reelection.

Governor Altgeld's sympathy for railroad workers during the Pullman strike in 1894 was also well known, but he was powerless when President Cleveland used federal troops to crush the strike. In the face of such hostility, labor leaders gave up massive strikes and turned to methods of persuasion.

The American Federation of Labor was formed by Samuel P. Gompers in the 1880s. An organization of trade unions and industry-wide workers, the A. F. of L. sought shorter hours and the abolition of child labor but refrained from most political activity. It never seriously espoused the cause of a union for all laborers. In his forty years as its leader, Gompers guided the organization along moderate paths, advocating legislation to solve labor's ills and using collective bargaining and moral pressure with employers.

In the 1890s and the first decade of this century, labor had the unwanted help of socialist leaders who painted for the workers a picture of a society without the burdens of private capital and property. Laurence Gronlund and Eugene V. Debs, widely known by laborers, were not revolutionists, but sober persons who felt deeply the evils of society and wanted to find solutions to them. In The Cooperative Common-

wealth, Gronlund urged that citizens possess enough property for their private use, but that the state own the industrial production. The state itself was to be run by administrators chosen by the people, whose duty would be to plan the economy and distribute the product. The state, according to Gronlund, "is the organic union of us all to wage that war, to subdue Nature, to redress natural defects and inequalities. The State therefore, so far from being a burden to the 'good,' a 'necessary evil,' is man's greatest good." Gronlund emphasized cooperation, the coordination of production for social good, and rewards shared according to one's deeds.

Americans did not become socialists, but their ideas were influenced by these attacks on capitalism. Writers and scholars in larger and larger numbers questioned the application of Herbert Spencer's principles to the industrial society: Did the unusual suffering of laborers and farmers, the amassing of fortunes by industrialists, and the growing dominance of economic life by impersonal corporations permit the kind of struggle that the Social Darwinians advocated? The socialist emphasis upon the welfare of men and the social use of property convinced sociologist Lester F. Ward that society should have a positive role in the human struggle for survival and that state resources should be used to battle suffering and greed. Richard T. Ely and Thorstein Veblen, both professional economists, analyzed the economic system and concluded that there was nothing natural about its operation, that the economy required study and direction if society were to receive its full benefits. In *The Theory of the Leisure Class,* Veblen attacked the business community, separating it from the workmen, engineers, inventors, and technicians who were making contributions to human welfare and deserved rewards for their services.

The Cities

Most industrial laborers lived in the expanding cities, where housing and the general environment were indescribably poor. In New York, Philadelphia, Chicago, St. Louis, and Pittsburgh industry brought a rapid concentration of population. City size increased with each decade and leaders were puzzled by the problems confronting them. Coal smoke, factory ugliness, noise, tenements, disease, and congestion added a measure of suffering to anything the employer provided at the plant. The cities too often were in the hands of political machines that used public services for patronage, and the people paid the price in adequate schools, police protection, sanitation, and zoning.

Trying to expose social problems in the cities, Jacob A. Riis studied tenements in New York City and made this shocking report in 1890:

It is said that nowhere in the world are so many people crowded together on a square mile as here. The average five-story tenement adds a story or two to its stature in Ludlow Street and an extra building on the rear lot. . . . Here is one seven stories high. The sanitary policeman whose beat this is will tell you that it contains thirty-six families, but the term has a widely different meaning here and on the avenues. In this house . . . there were fifty-eight babies and thirty-eight children that were over five years of age. In Essex Street two small rooms in a six-story tenement were made to hold a "family" of father and mother, twelve children and six boarders. . . . These are samples of the packing of the population that has run up the record here to the rate of three hundred and thirty thousand per square mile. The densest crowding of Old London . . . never got beyond a hundred and seventy-five thousand.

The city, however, brought new institutions into American life. Aggressive metropolitan newspapers developed during these years, with such energetic editors as Joseph Pulitzer and William Randolph Hearst and news services like the Associated Press giving wide coverage to world and national events. Research libraries were founded, scientific laboratories endowed, and universities created. The University of Chicago, generously endowed by John D. Rockefeller in 1892, soon rivaled eastern institutions that had been established for centuries. Cities became centers for professional sports—especially baseball; fraternal societies; fairs; and social institutions. The foreign populations, sometimes living in ghettos, gave a rich variety to life in song, dance, and cuisine. Their religious institutions, particularly those of Roman Catholicism and Judaism, brought social services (like hospitals) that challenged the Protestant ones. With the support of industrialists like Cornelius Vanderbilt, newly-arrived Americans erected schools, orphanages, hospitals, and relief centers. Private initiative made up for the lack of public support; fraternal societies provided group life insurance, leisure activities, fellowship, and social work. The German societies in St. Louis, for example, held picnics almost every weekend throughout the summer with singing groups, dancing, gymnastic contests, and card playing. The German Catholic and Lutheran churches provided language instruction to the young, and merchants opened beer gardens and outdoor amusement centers.

As more Americans became city dwellers than at any time in the past, the city itself was also becoming diversified, with opportunities for employment, amusement, and education. Citizens in large numbers were finding careers as artists, architects, writers, musicians, and scholars. Architects Frank Lloyd Wright and Louis Sullivan designed the famous transportation building for the Chicago's World Fair in 1892, and both gave inspiration to the design of residences, churches, and public buildings. John Singer Sargent, the painter, was influenced by the sophistication of society. Born in Florence, he studied in Europe, but adopted Boston as his American home (but was rarely there). He painted the wealthy, the politicians, and so-

Immigration, 1820-1910

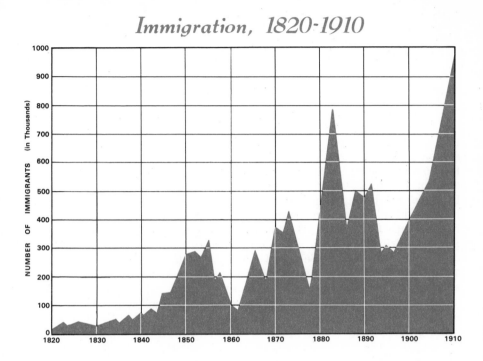

ciety's leaders, and his work is acclaimed as brilliant. His murals in the Boston Public Library, moreover, are expresive and magnificient, even spectacular. In music the cities of New York, Boston, and Chicago developed orchestra, and Theodore Thomas, the German immigrant, finally won national esteem for his efforts in Chicago. Popular music, however, immediately gained great audiences, with the works of Victor Herbert and John Philip Sousa. Sheet music publishers produced such favorites as the "Sidewalks of New York," "After the Ball," and "On the Banks of the Wabash."

The city also had its journals of opinion and amusement. In the 1870s *Scribner's Magazine* gained wide attention for short stories, but it was the *Ladies' Home Journal* that had the wide reading audience and the challenging articles, which entertained, informed, and aroused. *McClure's*, however, achieved a reputation for its exposés of graft and corruption, of life in high government places. The journals attracted many writers who experimented with ideas and style, and an informed literature was available to the English-speaking public. More serious readers, moreover, had a wide selection of first-rate American novels.

Stephen Crane's *Maggie: A Girl of the Streets* and Theodore Dreiser's *Sister Carrie,* filled with realism, social criticism, and daring, proved to be shocking and lucrative for their publishers.

Politics

This brilliance in arts and letters did not find a counterpart in politics. From Ulysses Grant to Theodore Roosevelt, with the possible exception of Grover Cleveland, the Presidents were usually devoted public servants, honest and capable, but their vision hardly reached across the Potomac River. Rutherford Hayes concentrated on giving the nation an honest administration, naming men of intelligence and integrity to office, but he did not wish to involve government as a partisan in labor's struggle for justice or in the blacks' struggle for electoral rights in the South. Chester A. Arthur, who succeeded the assassinated James A. Garfield in 1881, was interested in attracting better men to federal office. With the help of Senator George Pendleton of Ohio, he secured a bill that allowed the President to add classes of positions to the civil service. His successors continued the work with remarkable faithfulness so that by 1917 nearly sixty percent of federal jobs were under the merit system. Otherwise, his administration achieved little that was noteworthy.

In 1885 Cleveland began the first of two terms, divided by the four-year administration (1889-93) of Benjamin Harrison, and established a reputation among his fellow Democrats as a courageous President. Vetoing more bills than all past Presidents together, he struck out against vice and attacked military pension bills, special privilege, and corruption in public office. He favored tariff reform, regulation of railroads, and citizenship for Indians, finally winning legislation that partially solved these problems. For example, the Interstate Commerce Commission in 1887 was created as a regulatory body but lacked the power to set railroad rates. Cleveland failed to sympathize with labor's plight in the Pullman strike of 1894 and let his pro-business Attorney General use federal troops to break the strike.

His close electoral college defeat in 1888 (when he won a popular victory of more than 100,000 votes) brought Harrison to the Presidency. The Republicans, determined to strengthen their hold on national politics, admitted a group of territories in the Pacific Northwest to statehood. They backed higher duties on manufactured goods (the McKinley tariff), generous pensions for Civil War veterans, and purchased quantities of silver as a subsidy for the mining interests of the newly admitted states. A less partisan measure was the Sherman Anti-Trust Act of 1890, which became the foundation for future legislation to regulate business; the Act outlawed "every contract, combination in the form of trust or otherwise, or conspiracy in restraint of trade or commerce among the several states, or with foreign nations," set modest penalties, and gave triple damages to any person injured by the unlawful actions defined under it.

In 1892 the harmful results of the McKinley tariff, together with a spreading depression, helped return to office the uninspiring Cleveland. The dullness of national politics reflected the personalities of the leaders, and the issues were artificial. The elections of 1884 and 1888 were full of exposés and emotion, but the excitement was caused by charges external to the basic national issue of industrialism. Cleveland was accused of immorality—at least of loose morals—because he had fathered a child out of wedlock, and pious Republicans chanted "Ma, Ma, where's my pa; Gone to the White House, ha ha ha." The Democrats manufactured a saying to reveal the flexible morals of James G. Blaine. Slander of the candidates should have been incidental to national issues, but neither man had much imagination about the responsibility of government toward the farmer or the laboring man, even less toward the black or the immigrant.

The Courts

The Supreme Court under Morrison R. Waite responded more to popular developments than the Presidents or Congress, but it frequently limited government power to regulate corrupt business or legislative practices, and made reforms difficult to formulate. In the Slaughterhouse Cases of 1873, announced a year before Waite became Chief, Justice, the Court had decided that a Louisiana law creating a monopoly under corrupt circumstances did not violate national rights. The Court had refused to vest the federal government with power to set standards of citizenship, and instead had followed the traditional policy of letting the people of the states handle issues of civil liberties. The cases had profound significance upon the decision of other issues during Waite's tenure (1874-88). The court permitted most state statutes in the exercise of police power to be judged constitutional, without considering the problem of discrimination. It approved thus harsh municipal ordinances regulating the laundry business in San Francisco where the Chinese alone were concerned, because it refused to determine impact or consequences of legislation. So also did it refuse to accept suffrage as a base right of citizenship, permitting Missouri to refuse the franchise to women (Minor v. Happerset).

This narrow view of the Fourteenth Amendment also applied to the regulation of railroads. In Munn v. Illinois and other Granger Cases in 1877 the Court through Chief Justice Waite decided to protect property rights by giving the public interest a narrow definition (allowing for regulation according to the degree of public service). The definition was not narrow enough for some states, which limited governmental action severely, making regulation of labor conditions, simple matters of zoning, and corporate practices nearly impossible. In the hierarchy of rights, property had a supreme position, and unscrupulous employers acting under the cover of property rights maintained sweatshop conditions, child labor, and other dubious practices without fear of governmental penalties.

These *Granger Cases*, nonetheless, gave government wide powers to regulate those businesses "clothed with a public interest." Legislatures in the farming states thus passed bills to regulate the business practices of railroads and grain elevators, and much progress in the 1870s was made to establish standards of business conduct. However, the economic resources of the railroads was such that their pressure upon state legislatures in the 1880s was irresistible, and the laws were generally weakened.

The Supreme Court, also, modified its ideas of this kind of business regulation. It intervened now directly into the regulatory process by applying the rule of "due process." In *Stone v. Farmers' Loan and Trust Company* (1886) it asked commissions to justify the fairness of regulation, giving itself a voice in deciding whether the regulation was reasonable. In short, it assumed the final determination of rates instead of the task of assuring the railroads of a lawful hearing. By making decisions on "substance," the Court not only assumed the work of the commissions, but was soon investigating the purposes of legislation and examining the mind of Congress. In the famous Wabash Case (1886) the Court removed most railroad rates from state regulation because of the interstate effect of most rates. The case forced the federal government to enact regulatory legislation.

At this point in 1888 Waite died and Melville Weston Fuller of Illinois became Chief Justice. His office, to 1910, gave continuity to the court's policy of protecting business from long service in government regulations. Fuller was also hostile to the increase of national power, decrying at times the centralizing tendencies of the federal government. The court, however, left a "no man's land" where neither states nor federal government could enter to regulate business or income. In *United States v. E. C. Knight Company* (1895) the Court rejected the federal tenet that manufacturing was interstate commerce. Though the Knight Company had a monopoly on sugar refining, the Court refused to permit a federal antitrust action under the authority of the Sherman Act. In *Pollock v. The Farmers' Loan and Trust Company* (1895) the Court denied the federal government power to levy an income tax. With a profound display of logic, it declared income to be protected by the same constitutional guarantees that restricted taxation on land, reversing precedents of nearly a century's standing. Justice Stephen J. Field, long a spokesman for industry, explained the position of the majority when he labeled the income tax an assault on capital, a war of the poor upon the rich, and a sign of revolution. The decision, however, denied government power to tax income, in a period when securities such as stocks and bonds were becoming an important source of wealth.

Additional support was given to the creation of a caste society when the Court in *Plessy v. Ferguson* (1896) approved "separate but equal" facilities on railroad coaches for blacks and whites. In *Cumming v. County Board of Education* (1899) it permitted the rule to be extended to education.

The nation between 1850 and 1900 had experienced great changes. Spreading across the continent and overseas, it created a vast railroad network, an industrial order, and a consumer's market. The wealth of production from farm and factory was unbelievably great, and impressively collected and marketed over vast distances. The distribution centers grew into cities, and millions of people were soon living in urban centers. The urbanization of the nation, like its expansion across the continent, had great impact upon national development, creating new institutions and diversity. Society benefited some from these changes, but there was a political imbalance. Democratic society was challenged by accummulated wealth and power, and political leaders struggled to find solutions for the regulation of industry and the improvement of society.

SUGGESTIONS FOR FURTHER READING

Athearn, Robert G., *Union Pacific Country*. Chicago, Ill., Rand McNally and Company, 1971.

Clark, John G., ed., *The Frontier Challenge: Response to the Trans-Mississippi West*. Lawrence, Kansas, University Press of Kansas, 1971.

Daniels, Roger, *Politics of Prejudice: The Anti-Japanese Movement in California and the Struggle for Japanese Exclusion*. New York, Atheneum Publishers, 1968.

Davison, Kenneth E., *The Presidency of Rutherford B. Hayes*. Westport, Conn., Greenwood Publishing Company, 1972.

Dick, Everett, *The Sod-House Frontier, 1854-1890*. New York, D. Appleton-Century Company, 1937.

Dubofsky, Melvyn, *Industrialism and the American Worker, 1865-1920*. New York, Crowell, 1975.

Elliot, Russell R., *History of Nevada*. Lincoln, Nebr., University of Nebraska Press, 1973.

Franklin, John Hope, ed., *Three Negro Classics*. New York, Avon Books, The Hearst Corporation, 1965.

Galambos, Louis. *The Public Image of Big Business in America, 1880-1940*. Baltimore, Md., Johns Hopkins University Press, 1975.

Hicks, John D., *Populist Revolt: A History of the Farmers' Alliance and the People's Party*. Lincoln, Nebr., University of Nebraska Press, 1961.

Higham, John, *Strangers in the Land*. New York, Atheneum Publishers, 1965.

Hine, Robert V., *The American West: An Interpretive History*. Boston, Little, Brown and Company, 1973.

Jacobs, Clyde E., *Law Writers and the Courts*. Berkeley and Los Angeles, University of California Press, 1954.

Josephson, Matthew, *The Robber Barons: The Great American Capitalists, 1861-1901*. New York, Harcourt, Brace and Company, 1934.

Osgood, Ernest Staples, *The Day of the Cattlemen*. Chicago, Phoenix Books, University of Chicago Press, 1957.

Persons, Stow, ed., *Selected Essays of William Graham Sumner: Social Darwinism*. Englewood Cliffs, N.J., Spectrum Books, Prentice-Hall, Inc., 1963.

Porter, Glenn, *The Rise of Big Business, 1860-1910*. New York, Thomas Y. Crowell, 1973.

Pratt, Julius W., *Expansionists of 1898*. Chicago, Quadrangle Books, 1963.

Starr, Kevin. *Americans and the California Dream, 1850-1915*. New York, Oxford University Press, 1973.

Thernstrom, Stephen, *The Other Bostonians: Poverty and Progress in the American Metropolis, 1880-1970*. Cambridge, Mass., Harvard University Press, 1973.

Unger, Irwin, *Greenback Era: A Social and Political History of American Finance, 1865-1879*. Princeton, N.J., Princeton University Press, 1964.

Ware, Norman J., *Labor Movement in the United States, 1860-1895: A Study in Democracy*. New York, Vintage Books, Random House, 1964.

Warner, Sam Bass, Jr., *The Urban Wilderness: A History of the American City*. New York, Harper and Row, 1972.

Westermeir, Clifford P., *Colorado's First Portrait: Scenes by Early Artists*. Albuquerque, N.M., University of New Mexico Press, 1970.

Woodward, C. Vann, *Origins of the New South, 1877-1913,* Vol. IX, *A History of the South*. Baton Rouge, La., Louisiana State University Press, 1975.

Political Unrest and Expansion into Foreign Lands

FROM THE 1860s ON, AGITATION for reform was ever pressing itself into the public consciousness. Reform, however, was centered on individual issues, on regional problems, and on worker-employer relations until late in the century. Few voices were heard nationally, but men and women of goodwill were energetically working everywhere for the improvement of society. Spokesmen for causes gathered their followers, published pamphlets and books, and held rallies, but there resulted no national surge for reform.

The Stirrings of Reform

With the political parties dominated by business interests, experiment by state legislatures was held suspect and reformers were often turned out of office when they challenged vested groups. People of reform disposition thus acted to change institutions by private effort. In education, particularly, major changes occurred. New colleges were established everywhere, often with limited funds but with great community enthusiasm; older ones examined their traditions by approving new programs and making changes in their educational requirements. Many institutions endowed graduate and professional schools, encouraged investigations of public health and disease, and vied with each other for knowledgeable scholars of history, political economy, and science.

At Harvard University, President Charles W. Eliot pressed his colleagues in the medical school to make significant changes in policy. Entrance requirements were raised, laboratory courses provided, and the faculty enlarged. In Harvard College Eliot's famous elective system gave students a wide selection of courses. At Cornell University, Andrew D. White defied predictions of failure and enticed scholars from other universities to join the faculty and participate in his great experiment in democratic education. The curricula were broadened, with courses in electrical engineering, forestry, animal husbandry, and horticulture as well as the more traditional pursuits. At both Harvard and Yale graduate divisions were established, but at Johns Hopkins University, effort was concentrated on advanced study. Its president Daniel Coit Gilman secured money for laboratories where research was emphasized for graduate instruction. Leaders of the University of Wisconsin had great difficulty in finding money to experiment, but they succeeded, nevertheless, in creating an atmosphere of scholarship that drew to Madison some of the nation's brightest educators and students. These developments, in lesser degrees, took place in many other institutions because education always has been decentralized in the United States. Local colleges and universities, acting according to their resources, adopted the practices of the leading institutions. Many men and women with professional qualifications soon found places in business and government.

This new knowledge, with well-educated graduates and resourceful universities ready to apply it, had an impact on government in the 1890s—especially knowledge of taxation, agriculture, habits of society, and the structure of government. Federal agencies employed graduates in the Bureau of Ethnology and the Geological Survey, recruiting J. Wesley Powell as head of these organizations. The Department of Agriculture drew heavily upon the research activities of men like Eugene W. Hilgard of the University of California in maintaining its bureaus of chemistry, entomology, statistics, and animal husbandry. The states utilized the knowledge of professors and students in establishing experiment stations, and thousands of industrial firms hired chemists and engineers. These experts, in turn, founded professional associations which exchanged ideas, set standards of conduct, and certified members' competence.

A differently educated society was obviously emerging. With less knowledge of the classics, languages, and traditional disciplines, it was concerned with the problems of the industrial society. In general, it accepted the evolutionary philosophy of Herbert Spencer, who thought of change as a natural phenomenon that must not be disturbed by government; for most people evolution meant survival of the fittest and a laissez-faire society. Yet many intellectuals speculated on the possibility of controlling the environment. Could progress be accelerated by regulating society? Need men stand off from society and permit unseen forces to operate? Was turmoil necessary for beneficial change? For scholars like John R. Commons, an economist from the University of Wisconsin, the industrial system without some regulation was a jungle. For jurists like Oliver Wendell Holmes of Massachusetts, present society was the result of layer upon layer of human experience, evolutionary but of human design. For others, society was a struggle of classes, poor against rich, the common people against vested interests, and society at any time was merely a reflection of these economic forces. Louis D. Brandeis, a distinguished Boston lawyer, envisioned a balance between voluntary action and societal control, and hoped to find a creative role for law that would restore traditional values like individual initiative, competition, morality, and democracy to the industrial society.

The reflections of these men were examples of the growing interest in reform. Many novelists, publicists, ministers, and journalists joined the cause. They described the realities of the industrial system, and like Harriet Beecher Stowe they tried to arouse the public. Frank Norris's The Octopus described the impact of railroad and environment on the farmers and workers of the San Joaquin Valley of California; in this world the impersonal forces of industrialism had greater power to do evil than did the corporation executives who supposedly controlled them, making all victims of an economic determinism that would eventually destroy them and the traditional values of society. Publicists offered biographies of industrialists—the Robber Barons— and described greed, trickery, and foul play as the forces that motivated them. Ida Tarbell, in her life of John D. Rockefeller, so tarnished his reputation that later generations had great difficulty appreciating his genius as a pioneer industrialist. Accounts similar to hers became the basis for a literature of exposé, filling magazines like McClure's in the 1890s and early 1900s.

Long before these articles appeared, some ministers had begun to question the ethical bases of industrialism. They realized that the traditional religious approach to Christianity was hardly appropriate to the prevailing suffering of society. While prayer meetings were useful, revivals salutary, and evangelical services elevating, they did not solve the problems of daily life. Ministers were generally impressed with the philosophy of Horace Bushnell, who emphasized that Christian brotherhood was developed through a lifelong contact with Christian doctrine, that conversion was not a sudden revelation but a continuous experience, and that therefore environment was important and society must be committed to Christian principles. Taking up these ideas was Washington Gladden, pastor of a Congregational Church in Columbus, Ohio, who denounced Social Darwinism and unregulated capitalism. He supported labor's right to strike and society's obligation to legislate. His ideas were shared by Walter Rauschenbusch, the influential Baptist writer at Rochester Theological Seminary, who elaborated these ideas in such widely read books as *Christianity and the Social Order*, which insisted that Christianity was meant to be lived and practiced. In the Roman Catholic Church such powerful spokesmen as James Cardinal Gibbons, the archbishop of Baltimore, defended the program of the Knights of Labor and the radical tax measures of Henry George.

Equally powerful in these years were the activities of many women leaders. Interested in a variety of social problems, from suffrage to temperance, they organized associations and put their demands before legislatures at all levels. Wyoming gave them the right to vote in 1869, then Utah and Colorado, as they agitated from state to state. The Women's Christian Temperance Union was founded in 1873, under the leadership of Francis E. Willard, who secured pledges from school children by the thousands. Women became nurses, and Clara Barton helped found the American Red Cross; and others sponsored (and staffed) various kinds of charitable institutions, foundling homes, and humane societies.

Into these charitable institutions were drawn many influential people, who served as trustees and directors and who gave their financial support. Men like Abram Hewitt, the industrialist, and James Roosevelt, director of and investor in corporations, were most interested in the improvement of society. Hewitt ran for mayor of New York City, while Roosevelt served many terms in the New York state legislature. Others, like Henry Cabot Lodge of Massachusetts and Theodore Roosevelt, sons of wealthy parents, chose politics as a matter of obligation, working within political organizations to improve leadership. Still others, like Robert La Follette, Herbert Croly, and William Howard Taft, entered politics because of university and professional connections. They read current political literature, studied the nation's development, and written its history. They were well informed, sensitive individuals—ambitious to serve and receptive to opportunities.

Agrarian Unrest

Between 1867 and 1875 many farmers of the Middle West joined the Grange, an eastern-inspired society modeled on the Masonic Lodge and other fraternal orders. It brought farmers into social and political associations that they had lost in moving West. They were invited to picnics, roundups, and church socials, where Grangemen clarified the problems they were experiencing and showed them how they could stage effective protests. At first suspicious, farmers read the Grange papers, talked together, and learned of common grievances. Finally they responded favorably to political activity and backed the new leaders who pledged relief from high railway rates, grain elevator fees, and bank interest rates. In five years the farmers were able to challenge the older parties in Illinois, Wisconsin, Minnesota, and Iowa and to obtain some remedial legislation. The Granger Laws were challenged in the United States Supreme Court because the legislation was inexpertly drawn and encroached upon private property, but the court gave state legislatures power in 1877 to regulate property "clothed with a public interest when used in a manner to make it of public consequence, and affect the community at large."

The Grange success came at a time of acute economic distress which followed the Panic of 1873. Railroads fell into the hands of receivers; the market generally was prostrate; and the farmers were seriously affected. Crop prices were falling yearly as farmers tried to meet interest payments with greater production. Debts mounted; interest rates for new equipment rose, sometimes to eighteen per cent; and the farmers looked desperately for a solution. Many joined the Greenback Movement (and left the Grangers), which promised cheaper money for mortgages, then backed the crusade for unlimited coinage of silver. To pacify them, President Hayes signed the Bland-Allison Act of 1878 which ordered the Secretary of the Treasury to purchase monthly from $2 to $4 million in silver. This limited concession to currency expansion was acceptable to the Treasury Department only when silver was redeemable by gold. The pressure upon credit was not eased enough to satisfy the farmers.

The agitation over inflationary credit brought to regional prominence James B. Weaver and Ignatius Donnelly and advertised the injustices to farmers and debtors, but failed, except in a minor way, to unite farmers, laborers, and eastern reformers into a national protest movement. The farmers, however, were now invited to join the Knights of Labor which was ready to wage a massive battle for reform. It urged all workers to join the movement, promising general societal reform, but specifically an end to child labor, labor violence, and cutthroat competition between capital and labor. Its leaders put their program before millions of people, but were unable to forge a third political force, even though membership in the Knights reached 700,000 by 1885.

The Alliances

The farmers, with their problems unsolved, reorganized in the Middle West and South in the 1880s. Under the leadership of Milton George, editor of the Western Rural, they united behind their hatred of railroads, bankers, and industrialists, and formed local societies through which they applied political pressure and ran various businesses. Blends of politics and cooperation, the societies drew in existing Grange chapters and formed Alliances. These loose federations gained control

of legislatures, promoted regulatory measures, and harassed the railroads and grain elevators. The Northern Alliance grew rapidly, engaged
in politics, established cooperatives for buying and selling products,
and passed on information on marketing and agriculture to members.
The alliances, however, were unable to better the farmer's position substantially, and possibly their failure left him embittered. Then hard
times, a severe drought in 1887, and tight credit exacerbated farm
grievances.

In the South alliances were also formed. Their problems were
much different from those in the Middle West. Southern farmers,
usually tenants, mostly impoverished blacks, over the years secured
necessary credit for crop management from their landlord or the country
store and used their share of the cotton crop to guarantee their debt. In
his relations with the storekeeper the farmer was a victim of the southern system. The South had not developed an independent credit system,
banks were scarce, interest rates were dear, and the tenant farmer,
having no recourse, borrowed money from his supplier of merchandise,
the country store, where prices were high. He grew a single crop, usually cotton, which did not permit any related occupation such as raising
and fattening cattle or cultivating a truck garden. Most of what he
needed he had to buy, and he was totally dependent on his cash crop to
pay his yearly expenses. Even worse, he had no choice of political party.
In most areas the landowners and merchants, in cooperation with
townsmen and industrialists, held political power and consolidated
it by making the Democratic party a symbol of the old South, feeding
on white racism and exercising community pressure to compel loyalty.

The Alliance was attractive to the white farmers of Texas in the
1880s, but experimentation with various kinds of cooperation turned
leaders there, and later in the Deep South, toward political action. Men
like Leonidas L. Polk, Tom Watson, and Ben Tillman fought political
apathy and pledged themselves to work for reform within the Democratic party. Their preliminary efforts in 1890 were generally successful; they won important victories in Tennessee, Alabama, and
Florida. The Democratic party, showing unusual flexibility, adopted
many Alliance ideas as part of its political creed.

The Populists

In the Middle West the farmer's protest was less successful than
in the South, but victories were won in Kansas and South Dakota, and
an enthusiastic leadership pressed for the formation of a people's
party. Their demand for a third party was accepted only reluctantly
by southerners, but Northern Alliance delegates met at Cincinnati in
May 1891 to form their party, and nearly a year later at Omaha to nominate candidates for the 1892 elections. Their platform, the first syste-
matic statement of reform by a political party since the Civil War,

pledged the Populists to work for more currency, either paper or silver, government ownership of railroads and communication services, and popular government in the form of direct election of United States senators, the secret ballot, the initiative and referendum, a graduated income tax, and a single term for President and Vice President. The platform also asked for a subtreasury system, the establishment of federal grain depositories, and a system of government credit on the stored grain. Finally, it backed a shorter working day for laborers.

On the eve of the Omaha convention. Leonidas Polk, the party's most popular candidate for the Presidency, died suddenly. His candidacy had been awaited with enthusiasm in the South and might have drawn people from the Democratic party. As it was, the Populists had to turn to James B. Weaver of Iowa, a veteran of the Union Army, and James Field of Virginia. Neither man had the magnetism of a great candidate, but they were well supported by an exciting press and talented speakers. Folk characters like "Sockless" Jerry Simpson and Mary Elizabeth Lease exhorted their audiences to raise less corn and more hell.

The older parties followed the expected pattern by nominating Harrison and Cleveland, but signs of rebellion were in the air. In the South, Democrats protested against the conservative-dominated party leadership, and nearly every legislature endorsed principles that were closer to populism than to the democracy of Grover Cleveland. In both Republican and Democratic conventions strong opposition to national leadership arose. The November elections gave Cleveland an overwhelming electoral victory of 277 to Harrison's 145, and control of the houses of Congress, but the long-term significance of the substantial Populist vote should have made party leaders pause: the Populists collected more than one million popular votes and twenty-two electoral votes.

Cleveland nevertheless interpreted the election victory in conservative terms. Using his vast powers over patronage, his veto, and his presidential position to control Congress, he backed Democratic leadership in applying pressure upon party workers at home. The reaction was sharp. Anger among rank and file Democrats mounted to revolutionary levels in the party. Though opposition was driven underground in the South, many Democrats joined Populists in violent attacks on Cleveland. More and more through the South the issue of free and unlimited coinage of silver came to represent a cure for all national ills—tight money, high interest rates, and eastern dominance of the economy.

In the Middle West, Cleveland's second term disappointed Democrats and temporarily revived populism. As depression conditions worsened in 1894 and tariff and taxation reform faltered in 1895, agitation for new leadership increased. Many Democrats were quickly attracted to a youthful critic of the administration, William Jennings

A Poster from the Election of 1896 *(Library of Congress)*

Bryan, of Nebraska, who attacked the tariff. His deep feeling for the suffering farmer, his imposing presence as an orator, and his biblically colored words were expressions of a secular revivalist, and he touched the emotions of his audiences. He had the experience of four years in the House of Representatives and the backing of powerful farm and mining interests.

As their leader in 1896 the Democrats chose on the fifth ballot the thirty-six-year-old Bryan. They now had a presidential candidate who was attractive to westerners and who could draw Populist votes and stem the revolt of southern farmers. His appeal to the lower classes, some laborers, and the Populists proved to be exceptionally strong. His great energy as a campaigner took the message of the campaign into the countryside. Counterbalancing these strengths as a candidate, he had some serious weaknesses. He leveled his attack primarily at currency problems, demanding free and unlimited coinage of silver. The simplicity of his solution may have won some lower class votes, but it permitted an emotional assault upon him that unsettled eastern Democrats and intellectuals. His integrity and his knowledge of government were questioned, and men of wealth and substance were frightened for the safety of the nation should Bryan and silver win the election.

The Republicans nominated the former governor of Ohio, William McKinley, a member of Congress for sixteen years and a party regular well known for his safe positions on the tariff and currency. McKinley was fortunate in having the industrialist Mark Hanna as his campaign manager. With nearly unlimited funds at his disposal, Hanna spread heavy layers of propaganda across the East and Middle West and rallied the forces of industry and tradition. Even then McKinley's popular victory was less than Cleveland's had been in 1892.

Shortly after his inauguration McKinley called Congress into special session, and the Republican-dominated legislature passed the highest protective tariff (the Dingley tariff) in the nation's history. Its duties on steel rails, wool and cotton products, and a variety of other items like hides and sugar were designed to discourage foreign imports. The party waited three years before it passed a gold standard act. By that time gold rushes in the Klondike, South Africa, and Australia had expanded the international gold supply so that the law was not so harmful as it would have been a decade or two earlier. Soon after McKinley entered office prosperity returned, and Republicans, emphasizing the turn of events, associated good times with the party's policies. For the next three or four decades a vote for Republican candidates was popularly believed to be a vote for prosperity.

Defeat in the 1896 election brought gloom to many Democrats and reformers; it reflected their inability to formulate a program that had majority appeal. The silver issue had been too simple and had frightened voters in New England and the old Northwest. Bryan himself was a man of his section, without the popular characteristics

Election of 1896

	ELECTORAL	POPULAR
McKinley (Rep.)	271	7,035,000
Bryan (Dem.)	176	6,468,000

of Jackson and Lincoln, the imagery of Indian fighting and rail splitting, to make him nationally attractive. His was a voice undoubtedly crying for justice, but neither he nor his party was ready to reform the old order.

America's Entry into World Affairs

While the agitation of the 1890s had caused some Americans to be critical of society, most were exceedingly proud of what their industrial society had accomplished. The nation's wealth equaled that of any country in Europe; in steel production the United States was surpassing the combined output of all world competitors; in the manufacture of consumer goods it had few rivals. In 1889, the centennial of Washington's inauguration, the people of the United States examined the strength, territorial size, and population growth of their nation, and they were proud of its achievements.

With approximately 62 million people scattered from coast to coast, the United States was experiencing the power of being an industrial nation. Its interests in neighboring lands were expressed boldly for the first time; Americans revealed their aspirations in books, newspapers, and speeches. The excitement of international affairs had touched some of the nation's younger politicians and was distracting

President Grover Cleveland Protests Treatment by
the Press *(University of Southern California)*

attention from domestic events, certainly minimizing the impact of
reform speeches by the Bryan Democrats. Tariff protection, industrial
growth, and monetary stability rose as issues of great importance because they contributed to the nation's power in world affairs. It is
possible that the winning issue of the 1896 election for the Democrats
might have been American participation in world affairs, with only
incidental emphasis on domestic reform.

In the 1890s manifest destiny influenced another outbreak of national discussions of power. For a century the emphasis had been on
western expansion, population growth, and democratic institutions, but
comparisons of British and American power were always present in
American minds. The importance of Britain's navy to her power influenced many American leaders, and Cleveland in his first administration initiated policies to modernize the larger American vessels. Alfred
T. Mahan, an American naval officer, popularized the greatness of the
British navy in a persuasive book, *The Influence of Sea-Power on History, 1660-1783.* Other Americans were equally impressed by Britain's
imperialist ventures in which she brought the "blessings" of a high
civilization to backward areas; they viewed acceptance of the "white
man's burden" as a mark of a great nation, and felt that the United
States, like Britain, should accept a sphere of influence and share American institutions with the less fortunate.

Latin America as a Sphere of Influence

To most North Americans, Latin America seemed the proper area to influence. They reflected Anglo-Protestant prejudice in their views on Hispanic culture, and were eager to extend a civilizing hand. From 1789 the United States had hoped that republics would one day be established in Latin America. Both Thomas Jefferson and John Quincy Adams had held the philosophy that the Latin American people were to be encouraged in republicanism and to be aided in their struggle against European imperialism. The Monroe Doctrine, conferences with Latin Americans, and assurances of sympathy in revolutions against colonial powers became traditional policy. A significant step was made in 1881 and another in 1889, when Secretary of State James G. Blaine presented proposals for a hemispheric association.

The first of the Pan-American conferences convened in Washington on October 2, 1889, and gave Blaine and President Harrison a chance to display the grandeur of the United States. While the conferees discussed many questions of minor importance, they took some steps toward establishing an international bureau in Washington and a postal union. A few of the issues raised were too complex for the brief meeting and were to require years of negotiation. The conference ended with mixed impressions, especially in Washington. Blaine had tried to promote peace, friendship, and conciliatory methods for solving hemispheric disputes as the principal business of the conference, yet he soon revealed his inability to accept the Latin Americans as equals.

In 1891 a civil war in Chile temporarily split the nation into warring factions. the United States got triply involved in interrupting the flow of arms and using its diplomatic facilities to provide asylum for refugees. Some Chileans also were angry over this interference, and when a few sailors from the U.S.S. *Baltimore* came ashore at Valparaiso, feelings were intense and a brawl resulted in which two sailors were killed, others injured, and some imprisoned.

Chile did not express regret, and the United States insisted upon an apology or, in the words of President Harrison to Congress, "I will . . . bring this matter again to the attention of Congress for such action as may be necessary." Chile also rattled her sabers; the United States repeated through Blaine a request for an apology and an indemnity; and Harrison offered war to Congress as a solution for the disagreement with Chile. Finally, Chile paid $75,000 to the families of the injured and deceased. Blaine was severely accused in the press and by some Democrats as a warmonger, but he was probably less angry than the President was.

The Democrats exhibited a similar aggressive spirit under Cleveland. During a boundary controversy between Venezuela and British Guiana, the United States sympathized with Venezuela because of propaganda and a fear of British meddling in the Caribbean. Newspapers

American Imperialism in the Caribbean

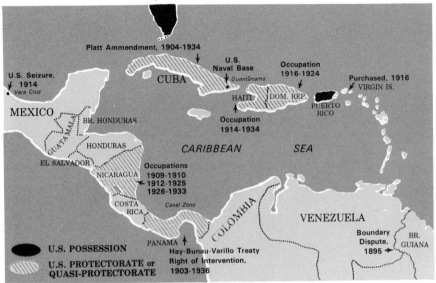

gave much space to the controversy; two state legislatures condemned Cleveland's lack of decision; and leaders such as Theodore Roosevelt and Henry Cabot Lodge whipped up popular feeling in public addresses. Responding to this pressure, Cleveland, through Secretary of State Richard Olney, declared that the United States had sovereignty over the whole Western Hemisphere and demanded that Britain arbitrate her disagreement with Venezuela. The saber rattling naturally irritated the British prime minister who took four months to answer the American demand. Then the response made Cleveland "mad clear through," and he told Congress he would draw the boundary and defend the line with United States forces. Though American bluster excited the British, their affairs in South Africa were equally critical. A telegram of support from the German Kaiser to the Boer leaders was enough to make the British whistle "Yankee Doodle." They finally agreed to aribtrate the boundary dispute and seek other ways of getting along with the sensitive Americans.

Pulling the tail of the British lion was dangerous fun and won Cleveland popularity in the country, even some half-hearted respect in Britain. But U.S. imperialists were hardly Anglophobes; they had a healthy regard for Britain and sought to imitate rather than fight her. They were uncertain about what they really wanted and were divided

Anti-Imperialism (University of Southern California)

among themselves on tactics. Under Blaine they challenged Germany over the control of Samoa, then exchanged a possible war with Germany for a joint protectorate of the islands. Under Cleveland they postponed the annexation of Hawaii even when interests in the U.S. and in the islands had arranged the union.

The Spanish-American War

In Cuba the United States had more sustained interest. About $50 million had been invested in the island's industries by U.S. business, and the investment was threatened by disputes between insurgent Cubans and Spain. The insurgents, trying to involve the United States in the dispute, destroyed North Americans' property, compromised the neutrality laws by running arms, and spread propaganda. Cleveland was aware of these tactics, but he had great difficulty in holding a steady course. When the dispute in Cuba heated in 1896, Spain attempted to break the resistance by using concentration camps to hold rebel prisoners; however, her officials failed to maintain humane standards of care and thousands of prisoners died. Reports of atrocities multiplied, partly through the Hearst and Pulitzer presses, and stimulated demands from the American people and Congress itself for an end to the barbarity. Even college students demonstrated; citizens boycotted Spanish products; the Cleveland administration finally offered to mediate the dispute. Though the President formally told Congress that intervention in Cuba seemed inevitable, he privately resisted belligerency. He hoped, as many people did, that Spain would reform the Cuban government and awaited only an appropraite opportunity to do so. His successor, William McKinley, also tried to avoid war while guarding U.S. investments and neutrality, but he let the battleship *Maine* schedule a friendly visit to Havana in spite of warnings from advisors that he was courting disaster.

During these months the United States applied steady pressure upon Spain, demanded assurances of reform in the Cuban government, and received favorable replies. Negotiations were set back, however, when a private letter written by the Spanish minister to Washington, Dupuy de Lôme, fell into the hands of a Cuban sympathizer and then into the hands of Hearst. In it Dupuy de Lôme criticized McKinley as "a bidder for the admiration of the crowd" and revealed bad faith on Spain's part in her negotiations with the United States. An exposé in the Hearst press set off a wave of hysteria, followed by angry oratory in congress. Then, on February 15, 1898, the *Maine* was sunk in Havana harbor with a loss of 260 men. Whoever had planted the deadly bomb aboard her had calculated well the emotional effect of the disaster. Reason was swept aside in America; the people demanded war, and Congressmen, launching a holy crusade, voted to make Cuba an independent republic. War was declared by an act of Congress on

April 25, and the Army was quickly raised from 28,000 to 153,000 men.

With the halls of Congress echoing "Dixie" and celebrations taking place across the land, the United States plunged into a popular war. Men enlisted quickly; the young Assistant Secretary of the Navy, Theodore Roosevelt of New York, began recruiting a regiment of cavalrymen, whom he pledged to join as an officer. Popular emotion intensified and crowds gathered to cheer "the boys" as they marched to the railroad stations, and people brought picnic lunches to the training camps. The haste, inexperience of leaders, and inadequacy of supplies created chaos. While soldiers awaited transports at Tampa, the U.S. fleet in the Far East under Admiral George Dewey was ordered to attack the Spanish fleet in Manila Bay. In a swift battle in which eight Americans were wounded, Dewey destroyed the Spanish squadron. He then besieged Manila until ground forces were dispatched for the land operations, a two-month delay that gave the insurgents under Emilio Aguinaldo time to raise their own troops for an attack upon Spain and gave German and British warships time to arrive and drop anchor in Manila Bay. Bickering with the Germans threatened Dewey's operations and irritated Americans at home, but did not prevent the final conquest of Manila.

Dewey's problems had the immediate result of bringing the annexation of Hawaii, to allow the United States to "bridge the Pacific." President McKinley set the tone when he called the annexation not change, but consummation. In 1899, Samoa was also divided with Germany.

In the meantime, U.S. military operations in Cuba awaited information on Spanish naval maneuvers. The Spanish fleet arrived in the Caribbean in late May and slipped successfully into the harbor of Santiago, Cuba. Its relative safety from attack and its potential firepower forced U.S. officials to blockade the port and plan its destruction. The only feasible way, however, was by land, and the U.S. Army was not ready to make the challenge, perhaps because of the imagined strength of Spanish island forces. Newspapers put the enemy army at 200,000 men.

In Tampa army leaders were confused. The commanding general, William R. Shafter, was unable to make order out of the mobilization and reacted irrationally to instructions from his Washington superiors. When campaign plans were finally completed calling for an invasion of Puerto Rico and ground support for the navy at Santiago, troops were put on the transports but delays prevented immediate departure. On June 14, more than seventeen thousand troops embarked for Santiago; on June 25, the entire force was ashore in Cuba.

Though the object of the invasion was an attack upon the Spanish fleet and the city, volunteers—including Roosevelt's Rough Riders—under Fighting Joe Wheeler of Confederate Army fame set out for themselves and engaged the Spanish first. Most of the action involved taking strategic hills guarding Santiago harbor, particularly Kettle

Hill. The Rough Riders were tested more than they had ever expected to be; they exerted themselves well under fire, counting their fatalities and sufferings as heroic deeds.

The Spanish, short of food and ammunition, were discouraged by the U.S. advance and finally decided to abandon Santiago. When their fleet tried to run the blockade, American cannon fire set the wooden vessels aflame. The end of the fighting came, significantly, on the Fourth of July. Before the smoke cleared at Santiago and Cuba was fully pacified, an expedition was hastening to Puerto Rico in anticipation of peace negotiations; by August 1 the island was taken with little resistance.

Negotiations with Spain proceeded swiftly at Paris. Spain agreed to cede Cuba and Puerto Rico to the United States and sell the Philippines for $20 million. President McKinley insisted on the purchase of the Philippines, even though only part of Manila was in American hands at the time of the armistice on August 12. He was intent on the mission of giving these far-off islands the benefit of advanced civilization, on uplifting and Christianizing them.

Imperalism After the War

McKinley's insistence on annexing the Philippines upset many members of his party and gave some Democrats a chance to denounce him. Also many leaders in education and public affairs opposed him and the Republican party faced a severe split in its ranks. But McKinley was firm and used his political patronage. He had invaluable support from Senator Beveridge who saw the acquisition as part of "God's great purpose" and of Senator Lodge who led the fight for treaty ratification. They welcomed too the unexpected help of William Jennings Bryan, an avowed anti-imperialist who wanted peace with Spain and independence for the Philippines. The hard fight in the Senate probably forced McKinley later to think of Theodore Roosevelt as a runningmate in the 1900 elections, while it encouraged the Democrats to turn to the moderate Bryan who denounced imperialism. Though, McKinley suffered the revolt of many intellectuals from his party, he benefited from an upturn in business and farm prices, the popularity of the war, and the glamour of his young runningmate. His electoral victory of 292 to 155 and popular victory of 7,219,525 to 6,358,737 was substantial.

Six months after his second inauguration McKinley was shot by an anarchist while attending the Pan-American Exposition at Buffalo. He died a few days later. His successor, Theodore Roosevelt, was more than most politicians of the day a symbol of the imperialist thrust. His was the responsibility of carrying McKinley's work to a conclusion.

When Theodore Roosevelt became President, neither Cuba nor the Philippines was yet fully occupied. Serious public health problems in Cuba delayed progress as doctors fought to check yellow fever and

other diseases. Under General Leonard Wood methods of sanitation
and public health were applied to local problems: swamps were cleared
and sprayed, drinking water supplies protected, streets swept, and
hospital services improved. For the island as a whole Wood had elections held and ordered a constitution written. Congress defined relations with the new nation by laying down some apparently sensible
restrictions on Cuban independence that permitted North Americans
to supervise island affairs and intervene in times of crisis. The United
States itself expected Cuba to develop into a vigorous democracy like
the United States—a vain hope when Cuba's economy was dominated
by foreign-owned sugar producers and poverty pervaded the island. The
instability of the island was evidenced in revolts that from time to time
turned out the established governments.

The problems of ruling the Philippines were more complicated.
For nearly three years an insurrection of Philippine natives defied
U.S. authority, even when an olive branch of eventual independence
and modern government was extended. Gradually, as the insurrec-
tionists were suppressed the military officers gave way to civilians who
reformed local institutions and developed plans for a semi-independent
government. The responsibility for these matters was entrusted to
William Howard Taft, an Ohio jurist of excellent education and experience. By cautious and deliberate methods he reorganized communica-
tions, set up an educational system, and encouraged economic reforms
that increased the output of farms. When the rebels made peace in
1902, he ordered additional steps toward self-government and let
island businesses trade in the U.S. market. These economic advantages
through the next three decades brought unusual prosperity, development of resources, and a modernization of life, but the people longed
for the day when they could be independent.

The Spanish war quickened the United States' interest in world
affairs. Both Cuba and the Philippines represented areas where the
United States expanded its trade and diplomatic activity. In the early
1900s it found, however, less commerce than political turmoil in the
Caribbean. Many of the independent nations, including Cuba, erupted
periodically into violent revolutions, and the United States for various
reasons assumed the responsibility of protector. As an occupying
power it became embroiled with European nations who wanted their
loans to the Caribbean republics paid, and had to assume the obligation of paying these debts. It managed the customs, reformed the economies, and held down political revolutions. Whether it actually provided
any permanent service to these nations was debated then, as now, but
Presidents Roosevelt, Taft, and Wilson (1901-17) interfered in the
internal politics of the republics with varying degrees of success.

Theodore Roosevelt dignified these interventions in the Caribbean
by enunciating some principles which he regarded as a "Corollary" to
the Monroe Doctrine. "Brutal wrong-doing," he told Elihu Root, "or

an impotence which results in a general loosing of the ties of civilizing society may finally require intervention by some civilized nation;
and in the Western Hemisphere the United States cannot ignore this
duty." At other times, and with less dignity, he called his relations
with these republics "big-stick" diplomacy, in which the United
States assumed the role of a policeman or parent. His successor's diplomacy in this area received the less gracious title of "dollar diplomacy," a reference to Taft's unconcealed support of business interests.
In 1912 Senator Henry Cabot Lodge, an influential Republican from
Massachusetts, created his own corollary. He became aroused by
Japanese business activities in the Magdalene Bay of Mexico. Feeling
that they were a threat to California and the Panama Canal, he asked the
Senate to declare that the transfer of strategic areas in America was
contrary to United States policy and a threat to security. The resolution passed by a vote of 51 to 4, but embarrassed Taft who considered
it provocative.

The difficulties in finding a satisfactory basis for peace in Mexico

A serious problem arose in Mexico in 1911 when the aged dic-
tator, Porforio Díaz, was overthrown. The event disturbed United
States citizens because their large land, industrial, and mining properties, probably worth two billion dollars, were developed during
Díaz's rule. When the first revolution was followed by a second, then
a third, and by civil war, murder, and extortion, the United States
government lost patience. It was the attacks, however, upon United
States villages and ships that brought U.S. reprisals and an expedition
by General John Pershing deep into Mexico. Although some Americans
demanded occupation of Mexico, or its dismemberment, Wilson resisted the pressure, and held off, too, European reprisals against Mexico.
Upon the rise of Venustiano Carranza to the presidency, conditions
gradually improved in Mexico. Wilson then moved to normalize relations, even though he was not pleased with Carranza's policies.

The difficulties in finding a satisfactory basis for peace in Mexico
and security for U.S. investments perplexed Wilson and brought forth
many bungling policies. Perhaps, no clear-cut solution was possible,
for he had the U.S. border to protect, U.S. citizens to satisfy, and Europe
to ward off. He was wise, it seems, in avoiding a war with Mexico.

Except for Mexico and Cuba, U.S. investments were insignificant
in the formulation of policy. The "banana republics," however, were
within the sphere of United States influence, and North Americans
felt that their great nation had the responsibility for maintaining law
and order. If additional economic rewards developed, those were accepted as the fruits of occupation. Taft was accused of dollar diplomacy,
and Wilson, too, furthered national aspirations within the region.

The Panama Canal

President Roosevelt decided that a canal across the Central Amer-

The President in Panama *(Library of Congress)*

ican isthmus was essential to national defense, for it would permit the
fleet to shift speedily from ocean to ocean during crises. Congress
backed the President, and was ready to build in spite of obligations
under the Clayton-Bulwer Treaty of 1850, which provided for joint
British-American control of a canal. Roosevelt decided to negotiate
another treaty, rather than violate the Clayton-Bulwer Treaty and in-
flame the British government. His tactful course was eventually successful; Britain, eager to keep American friendship, conceded to the
United States every point the President asked for—the right to build,
control, and fortify it. Newspapers gave the negotiations extensive
coverage, and irresponsible Congressmen repeatedly demanded full
authority to build and defend the canal.

When the treaty was finally signed, the President turned to the problem of negotiating a route for the canal. The route across the isthmus of Panama soon became the favorite. It required an agreement with Colombia and the purchase of certain rights from a French company that had unsuccessfully attempted to build a canal. A treaty was quickly negotiated by Secretary of State John Hay with Tomás Herrán of Colombia, providing for a ninety-nine year renewal and annual payments of rent. To the surprise of the United States, the Colombian Senate unanimously rejected the treaty because it did not give Colombia enough money. The price was $25 million, an insignificant sum considering the value of the property. President Roosevelt and Congress, however, not only would not raise the price but denounced the Colombians as bandits and cutthroats. Roosevelt resented Colombia's opposition and planned to secure the territory by other means.

Like other Latin countries, Colombia was unstable, and its district of Panama was often in rebellion. If the Panamanians were to revolt again, reasoned Roosevelt, the United States could agree to protect their rights and could obtain land for the canal as a price for cooperation. Conspirators soon formed the plot and, with the help of the United States Navy, created in a few months the Republic of Panama. The new nation negotiated a treaty with terms very favorable to the United States, and the Senate approved it by a vote of 66 to 14. While some Congressmen and a few newspapers criticized the President's methods, the overwhelming response across the United States was enthusiastic. From 1904 to 1914 the great earth-moving enterprise kept alive national interest in Caribbean politics and symbolized U.S. ingenuity and greatness as an industrial nation. Roosevelt described his diplomacy in these words during an address at Berkeley, California, in 1911:

> I am interested in the Panama Canal because I started it. If I had followed traditional, conservative methods I would have submitted a dignified State paper of probably 200 pages to Congress and the debates on it would have been going on yet; but I took the Canal Zone and let Congress debate; and while the debate goes on the Canal does also.

The Open Door for China

As with the Panama Canal and the Caribbean, occupation and government of the Philippines focused American attention on the Orient. While trade never was extensive in this area, Americans had some trade with China and Japan and were prepared to expand it. During the Spanish-American War the United States annexed Guam and Wake Island, and developed Pearl Harbor in Hawaii as an advanced base for the Navy. Occupation of the Philippines gave the United States home ports within the Orient as well as trade possibilities.

To exploit Oriental trade the United States needed to convince world powers that Chinese territorial integrity should be respected and that those ports already controlled by outsiders should be opened to the commerce of all nations. Hardly had Secretary Hay proposed the Open Door policy when Chinese agitation against foreigners broke into the Boxer Rebellion. While the United States joined the expedition to rescue missionaries and diplomats imperiled by the rebellion, it acted also as a moderating force to reduce to reasonable levels the reparations assessed against China, and urged again the need for an Open Door policy. Most American traders dreamed of great commerce in the area if China were modernized and foreigners shared trade in the territories they occupied along China's coasts.

From 1898 the safety of the China trade and of the Philippines became a concern of the United States. Leaders worried about the power of Japan, its desire to expand, and its relations with Britain. Under the leadership of Elihu Root, the Secretary of War, the army was reorganized and the military practices that had proven inefficient in the Spanish-American War were eliminated. A general staff was established, the War College founded, and the training of the state militia updated. The navy was enlarged, strengthened, and modernized, often under the direct supervision of President Roosevelt, who had a particular fondness for it. In 1907 he advertised the navy's presence as a fighting force by sending it around the world.

The Imperialist Thrust Versus Traditional Policy

America's interest in the Orient was in sharp conflict with its traditional policy of isolation. For more than a century the United States had based its security on its distance from Europe, its continental position, and its concentration of power in the Western Hemisphere. From time to time its naval vessels had been in European and Oriental waters in order to defend commerce, but America had depended primarily upon the good will of Europe, particularly that of Great Britain, to keep the trade lanes open. The relationship had worked very well, for Britain had poured money into the development of United States industry and agriculture and had absorbed vast quantities of cotton and foodstuffs. America's new interests in the Orient, however, put its traders in competition with Britain and her ally Japan, and into a military area where Japan was fast becoming the predominating power.

The United States was thus confronted with the problems of changing its attitude toward world affairs. Roosevelt offered American help in ending the war between Japan and Russia in 1905 and later hosted the peace conference at Portsmouth, New Hampshire. He negotiated an agreement with Japan in 1908 that guaranteed each other's territories and the Open Door for China, and attempted to conciliate Japan by recognizing her territorial ambitions in Manchuria. Roosevelt also used the occasion to deal with an emotional issue with Japan. Relations were severely strained over anti-Japanese feeling in California where Japanese laborers had immigrated in modest numbers. The twenty-two thousand in 1907 brought cries of "yellow peril," and some newspapers aggravated the issue. San Francisco segregated white and oriental students in the local schools. In Japan the leaders talked of retaliation, even of waging war. Roosevelt persuaded Japan to stop the labor immigration in exchange for San Francisco's withdrawal of its segregation ordinance and an agreement not to bar Japanese formally from the United States.

Though Roosevelt was applauded for what he accomplished, his deals with Europeans raised questions from isolationists. With Britain he negotiated settlement of the Alaskan boundary and convinced her to accept arbitration of a dispute with Venezuela. British relations generally became cordial as the cultural heritage of America and Britain was emphasized. With France and Germany relations were also friendly, and Roosevelt was able to set up an arbitration conference for them that settled a dispute over Morocco. Some Americans, however, resisted committing the nation to intervention in Morocco, and a bloc of Senate Democrats fought the President's plans for a conference. They attached to the bill giving approval of representatives a statement that their permission should not be interpreted as a departure from "traditional American foreign policy."

Traditional policy included even opposition to the negotiation of arbitration treaties among nations. Under Secretary Root the United States signed twenty-five such treaties in 1908 and 1909. In 1911, Taft tried to strengthen their provisions but encountered strong resistance from the Senate. Most isolationists, however, appreciated the prominence of the United States as a world power. They supported expanded trade, naval bases, colonies, and a strong navy as necessary additions to national power. They accepted, sometimes with reservations, the movement of Americans from their borders to trade and travel, to put the politics of other nations in order, and to spread American culture. They admired the growth and potential of the nation and wanted to safeguard independence by keeping the country free of alliances.

The rise of the United States as an industrial power was rapid and dramatic. The nation was the world's largest producer of steel and foodstuffs and was contesting Britain's supremacy in textiles and pottery. Its material growth in manufacturing products and in standard of living was astonishing. But in this land of abundance, the life was not measuring up to the dream. The political order was dominated by industrialists, and the distribution of national wealth was uneven. While many people were aware of this strange situation, they were not ready to force changes in the society that had accomplished such wonders.

SUGGESTIONS FOR FURTHER READING

Barker, Charles A., *Henry George*. New York, Oxford University Press, 1955.

Buck, Paul, *The Road to Reunion, 1865-1900*. New York, Vintage Books, Random House, 1937.

Buck, Solon J., *Granger Movement: A Study of Agricultural Organization and its Political, Economic, and Social Manifestations, 1870-1880*. Lincoln, Nebr., Bison Books, University of Nebraska Press, 1963.

Daniels, Roger, *Politics of Prejudice: The Anti-Japanese Movement in California and the Struggle for Japanese Exclusion*. New York, Atheneum Publishers, 1968.

Franklin, John Hope, ed., *Three Negro Classics*. New York, Avon Books, The Hearst Corporation, 1965.

Hicks, John D., *Populist Revolt: A History of the Farmers' Alliance and the People's Party*. Lincoln, Nebr., University of Nebraska Press, 1961.

Higham, John, *Strangers in the Land*. New York, Athenaeum Publishers, 1965.

Hunt, Michael H., *Frontier Defense and the Open Door: Manchuria in Chinese-American Relations, 1895-1911*. New Haven, Yale University Press, 1973.

Iriye, Akira, *Pacific Estrangement: Japanese and American Expansion, 1897-1911*. Cambridge, Mass., Harvard University Press, 1972.

Jacobs, Clyde E., *Law Writers and the Courts*. Berkeley and Los Angeles, University of California Press, 1954.

Miller, George H., *Railroads and the Granger Laws*. Madison, Wisconsin, University of Wisconsin Press, 1971.

Nesbit, Robert C., *Wisconsin: A History*. Madison, Wisconsin, University of Wisconsin Press, 1973.

Nordin, D. Sven, *Rich Harvest: A History of the Grange, 1867-1900*. Jackson, Miss., University Press of Mississippi, 1974.

Osgood, Ernest Staples, *The Day of the Cattlemen*. Chicago, Ill., Phoenix Books, University of Chicago Press, 1957.

Persons, Stow, ed., *Selected Essays of William Graham Sumner: Social Darwinism*. Englewood Cliffs, N.J., Spectrum Books, Prentice-Hall, Inc., 1963.

Pratt, Julius W., *Expansionists of 1898*. Chicago, Ill., Quadrangle Books, 1963.

Unger, Irwin, *Greenback Era: A Social and Political History of American Finance, 1865-1879*. Princeton, N.J., Princeton University Press, 1964.

Wall, Joseph Frazier, *Andrew Carnegie*. New York, Oxford University Press, 1970.

Ware, Norman J., *Labor Movements in the United States, 1860-*

1895: A Study in Democracy. New York, Vintage Books, Random House, 1964.

Weinstein, Allen, *Prelude to Populism: Origins of the Silver Issue, 1867-1878.* New Haven, Conn., Yale University Press, 1970.

Woodward, C. Vann, *Origins of the New South, 1877-1913,* Vol. IX, *A History of the South.* Baton Rouge, La., Louisiana State University Press, 1951.

Reforms, War and Peace

AMERICANS ENTERED THE TWENTIETH CENTURY convinced that their democracy was a remarkable success. Optimistic and proud of the nation's achievements, they had boundless faith in the future and expectations of new national glory. This optimism, however, did not blind them to the imperfections of society. Since the Civil War political power had been shifting from a wide agricultural base to a narrow, industrial one. The shift was obviously threatening political values and raising the need for rethinking the basic premises of democracy. In the vanguard of the reform movement were practical leaders, coming from a new middle class, who wanted to eliminate cut-throat competition, the destruction of raw natural resources, and economic instability. They hoped to bring order to urban life thorugh the employment of experts, and some regarded business and industry as their chief allies. Leaders like Robert La Follette and Herbert Croly, who called themselves Progressives, wished somehow to blend the virtues of the old America with the advantages of the new. They asked how the energy of industrialization could be harnessed to provide living conditions comparable with the agrarian society of Jefferson's day; how industry could expand without the existence of urban slums and rural poverty; how democracy was possible in the midst of political and social inequality. Most reformers, in seeking solutions for the nation's problems, viewed the issues in moral terms and wanted to restore to the country old virtues and principles.

A Tradition of Opposition

When Populists had asked these questions, city dwellers had not been ready to join them. When William Jennings Bryan had appealed to them, his free silver crusade had seemed undignified, narrow, and simple. The white collar workers, associating with professional groups in the cities, had been pressed by falling prices, fixed incomes, and poor city governments, and had feared that Bryan's inflationary policies might extend the depression.

When the Populists discarded the silver issue, and the farmers themselves were again prosperous, city workers and farmers allied as Progressives. They retained their traditional values—an agrarian society, private ownership of wealth, and simple government—but accepted as their leaders urban professional people: lawyers, newspaper editors, college professors, and social workers. The Progressives belonged to a tradition of opposition. As the Liberal Republicans of the 1870s, the Mugwumps of the 1880s, the National Municipal League of the 1890s, and the muckrakers of the 1900s, they attacked the evils of the new industrialism in terms of the old values. Although not united as a party, they shared a common anger over "corporate arrogance" and social evil, and labored for a free economy without industrial barons, union leaders, and political spoilsmen. They drew their inspiration from experiences as workers in the hospitals, orphanages, and relief agencies or, like Eleanor and Franklin Roosevelt who toured Europe in 1905, they met English reformers and were introduced to socialist ideas. Others compared the exposé literature of *Harper's Weekly* and *McClure's* magazine with their own observations. The startling articles by Lincoln Steffens revealed corruption in contracting and franchising in key American cities that seemed inconceivable in a modern nation. Others read commentaries on Pope Leo XIII's encyclical *Rerum Novarum* in which the Pope assailed the rich for imposing a yoke on the poor "little better than slavery itself." Or they read the writings of Walter Rauschenbusch, the noted Baptist minister, who believed that the misery of the slums challenged Christian worship. "For fifteen hundred years," he wrote, "those who desired to live a truly Christian life withdrew from the evil world to live a life apart. But the principle of such an ascetic departure from the world is dead in modern life. The Church must either condemn the world and seek to change it, or tolerate the world and conform to it."

Many of these reformers in the Church and elsewhere in the social order would not have called themselves "Progressives." While they had little opposition to the designation, they were primarily concerned with pushing their own program of reform. Women were interested in achieving equality; Prohibitionists wanted to remove liquor from the diet; labor organizers were bent upon controlling foreign immigration. Reform was in the air, however, and many people had their own personal projects.

Theodore Roosevelt in the Presidency

At a time when many people were feeling the need for reform, the accession of Theodore Roosevelt to the Presidency came as a decisive event. Though he obtained the office through the assassination of President William McKinley, he represented even more than his predecessor the national temper. Like many reform-minded leaders, he was at first conservative and cautious, disturbed by labor violence and Bryanism, but anxious to find a solution to the nation's problems without the turmoil of a social revolution. Later in his Presidency he advocated reforms and often assailed Congress and the courts when they fell short of following his leadership. Unlike other men of wealth, he had entered politics at the lowest levels, rising successively from New York assemblyman, Civil Service Commissioner, New York City Police Commissioner, Assistant Secretary of the Navy, and Governor of New York to be Vice President. His unique and varied experiences along the way gave him a public character. As rancher he had chased and captured outlaws in the West; as Police Commissioner he had assailed grafters; as Rough Rider he had charged San Juan Hill, (actually Kettle Hill) as an officer of a volunteer regiment in Cuba; as writer and historian he had described with skill and beauty the pageantry of winning the West. His wide smile and curious facial expressions, aided always by appropriate youthful remarks, made him attractive to audiences, who also appreciated the moral tone of his speeches and statements.

For the first time in four decades America had an exciting chief executive whose personality drew a host of loyal, devoted followers. Neither he nor they in 1901 realized how truly different he would be from his elderly predecessors. While he had no preconceived legislative program, he wanted to lead the Republican party and give the Presidency importance and vitality in national affairs. But he could not do this immediately, while the party was controlled by Mark Hanna, Nelson Aldrich, and "Uncle Joe" Cannon, nor could he move as freely as could an elected President. He acted deliberately and chose associates with care, balancing the Old Guard with new men, inviting to the White House for consultation labor leaders as well as corporate executives and seeking advice from party elders. With unusual skill he replaced or neutralized party regulars and selected colleagues who would wage an attack on corruption and privilege. Men like Henry L.

President Roosevelt's Dream of a Successful Hunt *(Library of Congress)*

Stimson and Oliver Wendell Holmes were drawn into federal service and several qualified blacks were offered posts in the South. While his appointments generally improved the intellectual quality of office-holders, he was careful to cement alliances with northern business people. His success was easily measured in 1904 when the Democrats pitted the New York conservative lawyer, Alton B. Parker, against him, and Roosevelt won by a popular majority of two and a half million, and an electoral vote of 336 to 140. Business people were more content to back his policies than to trust the Democrats who had twice nomin-ated Bryan.

The continuing prosperity pleased them as well as the people, who were celebrating the centennial of the Louisiana Purchase with the St. Louis World Fair and American progress in popular song. Roosevelt was part of the expansive spirit, and his foreign policy in Panama, Cuba, and the Philippines gave glamour to his presence in the Presidency.

Though Roosevelt changed dramatically the personnel of the executive branch, his assault upon business and industry trusts was more spectacular and better known. He urged Congress to regulate the concentration of corporate power—to supervise, not prohibit, the formation of large businesses; to set standards of conduct that would permit economic activity without undue governmental control. Specifically, he requested the establishment of a Department of Commerce and Labor, with a Bureau of Corporations to investigate the trusts. His recommendations followed earlier studies, but they met resistance in Congress and had to be taken to the people before Congress would accept them. The Bureau of Corporations during its decade of service reported in about thirty volumes the behavior of corporations; much of the information on the oil and tobacco trusts was later used in prosecuting them.

Congress was also persuaded in 1903 to prohibit railroad rebates (discounts to favorite shippers) and in 1906, in the Hepburn Act, to give the Interstate Commerce Commission power to determine rates and inspect corporate books. It allowed railroads to appeal decisions, but the burden of proof was placed upon the carrier. By 1911, over 190,000 rates were reduced by one half. The stench of Chicago's stockyards, their rats and debris claimed Roosevelt's attention and he was aroused to action by the popular impact of Upton Sinclair's The Jungle. With the president's firm support Congress passed the Pure Food and Drug Bill in 1906, which set standards for the preparation of certain kinds of foods, drugs, medicines, and liquors. Under the direction of Dr. Harvey Wiley, the administration established research centers and sent its inspectors into meat packing houses and drug laboratories.

During his two terms in office Roosevelt worried about the ethics of business management. Through Attorney General W. H. Moody and his successor, C. J. Bonaparte, the President prosecuted about twenty-five antitrust suits, mainly against the oil, beef, and tobacco industries. He moved cautiously because he doubted whether bigness of corporations was the real evil that government should be attacking. Though these prosecutions did not halt the concentration of capital, they left the impression that the government was every ready to combat evil deeds and that it was "supreme over the great corporations." He was concerned likewise about labor, though not always sure how to act, and he moved a time or two to insure improved working conditions. His attitude was generally protective, perhaps paternalistic, toward labor, without an appreciation of labor's needs to organize and strike. When he recommended legislation to regulate hours and working conditions, establish workmen's compensation, and set rail-road safety standards, he had to fight opposition from Congress and the courts and received much criticism. His retort, however, was equal-ly strong:

> While I agree heartily that the Constitution of the United States represents a fixed series of principles, yet I hold that it must be interpreted not as a strait-jacket, not as laying the hand of death upon our development, but as an instrument designed for the life and healthy growth of the nation.

The Supreme Court declared the Employer's Liability Act of 1906 un-constitutional and reversed fines against corporations for evil prac-tices. For these defeats, and others, Roosevelt had much to say, but this sentence summarizes his thought: "There is altogether too much power in the bench."

Despite these defeats, Roosevelt secured some important laws encouraging conservation of natural resources. He set aside approxi-mately 125 million acres of forest lands and additional millions of acres of mineral lands. He acted against the forces of exploitation, using the symbolism of the fight against evil that had won him suc-cesses elsewhere, and stretched laws to accomplish his purpose. But he was not interested simply in perpetuating the national wilderness for sportsmen like himself. The West also was to be developed; its water resources preserved and exploited in the public interest; its lands irrigated and planted in crops.

With the help of Francis G. Newlands he backed a reclamation program, creation of irrigation districts, and building of dams for water storage. Among the areas he secured for power and storage products were the Muscle Shoals in Tennessee and the Salt River area of Arizona. He was fortunate to obtain the services of a host of energetic young men who gave the program imaginative leadership. Gifford Pinchot, a bit older than the others, became the most famous of all. His work as a conservationist, in the forest service and as professor of forestry at Yale University, first attracted Roosevelt, but he admired, too, Pinchot's enthusiasm and his devotion to conservatism.

Local Reformers

While news of the President filled the papers and his personal idio-syncrasies made good cartoons and quotations, he had to share prom-inence with hundreds of local leaders who were doing in a smaller way what he was advocating for the nation. In Wisconsin Robert M. La Follette, "Fighting Bob," the most influential Progressive governor, carried out an exciting program of reform. Believing firmly in represen-tative government, he secured a direct primary law, secret ballot, a cor-rupt-practices law, civil service reform, and registration of lobbyists.

He won legislation for an income and inheritance tax, revision of the land taxes, a railroad commission, money for state education, and laws to protect labor unions. La Follette's Wisconsin Idea was well publicized in the press and given favorable reports by Lincoln Steffens. On the grass roots level the idea inspired renewed interest in government planning and encouraged reformers throughout the nation to examine his program. His election to the Senate in 1905 put a powerful voice for railroad control in the federal government and one willing to push the President to take advanced positions on reforms. Roosevelt was sympathetic, but risked open rebellion from conservatives in his party.

In Oregon, William S. U'Ren, a private citizen of unusual ability, originated the "Oregon system." Advocating the secret ballot, initiative, referendum, and recall, he guided a movement for popular government for nearly twenty years. At Princeton University, its new president, Woodrow Wilson, raised brilliant and daring questions. He asked the faculty whether the university was meeting its responsibilities to the nation in the quality of its education and whether the campus was truly democratic. His experiments in individualized education became the talk of the institution, and his fight against the vested interests of faculty and alumni attracted the attention of Democratic politicians in New Jersey and the nation.

During Wilson's presidency of Princeton, an astute newspaper writer, Herbert Croly, synthesized Progressive thought and sketched ingenuously the problems facing the country. *The Promise of American Life* (1909) stressed that the days of the frontiersman and individualist had passed, that it was time for Americans to reinterpret their ideals in the light of present-day circumstances. Croly asked for laws favoring federal planning and regulation and the use of taxes to equalize bargaining power among the classes. He urged also the study of ways to make business responsible in serving the needs of the nation and in helping to create human excellence. His was a faith in a nationalism that would draw people together, turn them from selfishness, and awaken in them a concern for the public interest. His was faith, too, in the federal government as a creative force which could use its legislative powers to select policies that would make the nation a better place to live in; in short, government must be a positive force and must treat citizens as individuals; it must adjust, balance, create, and inspire.

Two local reform movements that were achieving national recognition were women's rights and prohibition. For many years Susan B. Anthony led the cause of women's rights and paid for her militancy by suffering showers of fruit and eggs. But her efforts were rewarded by the extension of the franchise in local matters, the liberalization of land ownership and the relaxation of laws regulating divorce. Most women, and a few men, were not satisfied by these "concessions."

Agitation against hard liquor also was aided by women. Their Women's Christian Temperance Union (WCTU) was equally militant with the women's rights movement. Carry A. Nation, with axe in hand, led corps of followers into saloons where they broke up barrels and bottles. The movement attracted much attention and considerable support.

Taft and the Progressives

Croly's thoughts reflected as well as influenced the actions of politicians. But Republicans were severely divided by the time Roosevelt left office. His relations with Congress had deteriorated badly during 1908, and bitterness had reached a critical point a few days before he handed the Presidency to William Howard Taft. The new President had served well as federal judge, governor general of the Philippines, and Secretary of War, and held a college degree from Yale University which had considedred him for its presidency. In personality, he and Roosevelt were as unlike as two men could be. Taft lacked the dynamic qualities of a leader, the daring of a fighter, and the insight of a politician. He was content to follow the lines of policy set down by the "President." While Roosevelt had sought ways to lead and inspire, Taft was determined to administer and explain. Many conservatives welcomed him, but the young, spirited men of the party were astonished by his inability to understand the implications of Roosevelt's policies. The former President, however, had side-stepped many politically sensitive issues that Taft had to face—particularly a revision of the tariff and a reorganization of party leadership in Congress.

In making the tariff an issue, Taft knew the risks he assumed and the expectations of the reformers, who wanted a sharp cut in duties. He called a special session of Congress and then disappointed many people by leaving the specific reforms to Congress. The reformers expected him to support downward revision and interpreted interviews with him in that light. The move for tariff reform got off to a good start in the House when Serenó Payne offered a bill which extended the list of duty-free items. However, in the Senate, tariff revision fell into the hands of Nelson Aldrich, whose committee made more than six hundred changes in the House bill and who was allowed to report the bill out of committee without an explanation of committee action. Aldrich and Republican leadership challenged the liberal wing of the party.

The tariff had become by 1909 a device for keeping business profits at artificially high levels because tariff schedules in most instances had excluded lower-priced foreign goods which could offer competition. It gave industrialists monopoly profits instead of protection. These profits were not extended to workers in the form of higher wages or to consumers in quality merchandise; they went to a small segment of the population—the corporation shareholders and executives.

The battle against the tariff was waged principally in the Senate,

where La Follette was a leader. With Senators A. B. Cummins, Albert
J. Beveridge, and Jonathan Dolliver, they cited business statistics to
prove the need for lower duties and assailed the tariff, often with in-
temperance, as a payment of tribute to eastern capitalists. The undignified clashes unnerved Taft, who refused to provide presidential
support. In icy seclusion he sided with party regulars, but nevertheless
won a slight overall modification of rates and the submission of a constitutional amendment providing for an income tax. Taft was unde-
niably in a difficult position. In signing the Payne-Aldrich tariff into
law, he raised another storm by praising it.

The tariff battle alienated many of the Progressives and left the
Republican party seriously split. Middle West Progressives, already
discontented by national policies, were angered still further, and rising
prices for merchandise confirmed their opinions. Though Taft hoped
to win back this support by conducting a vigorous prosecution of the
trusts, the cases were in court for years and most dissolutions of corporations did not materially affect prices. In the end he was undoubtedly
more successful than Roosevelt in breaking up monopolies, but the
results were disappointing. Taft appeared more and more reactionary,
and the rift between him and the Progressives became permanent. One
incident will illustrate Taft's problems.

In carrying forth Roosevelt's conservation policies, he backed
legislation for irrigation projects, extended the forestry service, and
preserved much forest and mineral land. He accomplished much, but
through officials like Richard Ballinger, the Secretary of the Interior,
who were not members of Roosevelt's conservationists. Ballinger, in
fact, was a businessman who wanted to open the West to private enterprise and had little sympathy for proposals to retain large forested
areas in the federal reserve. His trouble began when he planned to re-
lease some coal land in Alaska to private exploitation. Enthusiasts for
conservation protested his decisions to Taft, to Congress, and to Roosevelt and then exposed them in national magazines. In standing with
Ballinger, Taft had to dismiss prominent conservationists and was himself caught up in the emotion that separated him from the Roosevelt
Progressives.

When Roosevelt returned home from Africa and Europe in 1910,
he took part in this controversy and joined also in the election campaigns. The party was plainly divided, and Roosevelt was uncertain
of his own position as an elder statesman. Though he pledged support
to all Republicans, he was angry with Taft and party regulars because
they had not kept pace with progressive thought. At Osawatomie,
Kansas, he acclaimed what he called a New Nationalism for the United
States and outlined principles that were inspired by men like Herbert
Croly. Backing an income tax, workmen's compensation, child labor
laws, corporation regulation, and reform of the courts, he sided with
the Progressive wing of the party and frightened the Old Guard, who

branded him a "revolutionist." Roosevelt raised more opposition than he had expected, and between October and the November elections of 1910 he tried to modify and explain some of his statements.

But he and his Progressive followers left the party divided, and the Democrats made the most of the dissension by taking a majority of seats in the House of Representatives (229-161). In the country reform-minded politicians also challenged the establishment. City governments in Los Angeles, San Francisco, St. Louis, and Cleveland, to name a few, investigated franchises, the tax structure, and contracting. Tom Johnson of Cleveland introduced civic planning which led to zoning ordinances and standards for housing. In New Jersey Woodrow Wilson stepped into the governor's office with a major victory, which challenged the Democratic organization and set the stage for a party struggle for leadership. In California Hiram Johnson won the governorship from old guard Republicans by promising a thorough reform of the state. His introduction of La Follette's Wisconsin Idea into the state gave him great prominence in national politics.

By 1910 reformers had improved upon the La Follette program. Many western states, including California, had granted the franchise to women and had appointed women to public office. Others were writing factory legislation that set safety standards and maximum hours of labor. Congress had prohibited interstate shipments of liquor, and the Mann Act had helped to break up interstate prostitution. The Sixteenth Amendment to the Constitution, providing for an income tax, had been submitted in 1909 and was near approval. (The Seventeenth, to be submitted in 1912, was to make popular election of United States senators a constitutional requirement.)

These reform movements were often supported by President Taft, but he got little credit for his efforts. Instead, reformers separated themselves from the administration and their leaders founded the National Progressive Republican League to organize their opposition to Taft's policies and to back La Follette for the Presidency. When Roosevelt committed himself to run as a Progressive candidate, the League abandoned La Follette in his favor. However, neither he nor La Follette was able to round up enough convention delegates, and Taft, supported by men like Warren G. Harding of Ohio and other party regulars, easily won renomination. The Progressives challenged the realities of politics, bolted the Republican party, and formed a third party, the Progressive party, with Roosevelt and Hiram Johnson of California as their candidates.

Candidate Wilson

The Republican division meant almost certain victory for the Democrats if the party could agree on a candidate. They had no candidates with a national reputation except Bryan, who had been thrice defeated and now stood aside while four favorite sons battled for the nomination. Woodrow Wilson was easily the choice of the urban East, while Champ Clark of Missouri had the support of party regulars, the Hearst press, and the Middle West. Oscar W. Underwood of Alabama had the solid support of Ohio Democrats. Finally, the friends of Underwood and Bryan, seeing the dangers an impasse posed to party unity, mobilized the additional votes on the forty-sixth ballot to give Wilson the victory. It was a tribute to Bryan's convention organization and his ability as a speaker and crusader—and a tribute to his party—that it accepted this unique candidate as its standard-bearer.

As the son of a Presbyterian minister and a Virginian, Wilson had grown up in an atmosphere of religion and in a tradition of southern leadership. His youth had been spent in Confederate Georgia and reconstructed South Carolina, and he had been educated at Princeton and the University of Virginia for a career in law. He had practiced law for a time in Atlanta, Georgia, but when he had found life as a lawyer unrewarding, he had enrolled at Johns Hopkins University and taken a doctorate in political economy. He had served on the faculty of several institutions before going to Princeton, where he became president in 1902. Both as its president and later as governor of New Jersey, he had been a resourceful leader, always a crusader, and frequently dogmatic in his opinions. His inspiration was drawn from the Bible and his political theory from England. His heroes were Jefferson and Lincoln, but with Lincoln there was "a little unconscious self-portraiture."

Wilson's admiration for the past should not conceal his readiness to reform society. In 1912 he conceived of his task in conservative terms; he announced his desire to restore and purify the nation's institutions. For a return to the good old days of a simpler life, he promised to help fight waste and corruption and to destroy vested interests. So that a free economy could exist, he planned to side with the small-businessman, the laborer, and the farmer against big business. Somehow, he believed, these true Americans could be helped to live fruitful lives in a democratic economy without restraint and without monopolies. He had a romantic view of the past in which society had had a balance of liberty and prosperity, freedom had been triumphant, and opportunity had been unlimited. With a touch of religious imagery and emotion, his messages had a ring of sincerity and left an intellectual impression that was attractive to many people. They greeted his program as the "New Freedom."

Great leaders like Wilson are difficult to characterize. Though he liked to speak in ideological terms, he frequently acted in practical ways. In New Jersey, he revealed a masterly understanding of political realities in the governorship. He debated issues of legislation with lawmakers; he supervised the drawings of bills; he used the press to rally popular support; he made public appearances for political purposes;

he frequently permitted his opinions to be shaped by others.

His victory in November 1912 was predictable. Roosevelt and Taft divided the Republican vote and drew some support from Wilson; although he won the electoral vote of forty of the forty-eight states— 435 votes to 88 for Roosevelt and 8 for Taft—he received only 42 percent of the popular vote. A unified Republican party might easily have defeated him. The split in its vote also helped the Democrats to win both houses of Congress with workable majorities. The combined vote of Democrats and Progressives was most impressive—it was a mandate for reform.

Progressive Gains

By 1916 Wilson had modified his attitudes on the use of federal power. He moved from a policy of mediation and restrictions to an aggressive policy of intervention. By a series of measures he accepted a policy of federal subsidies to the states, which promoted agricultural education, a system of county agents, and farm-to-market highways. He had finally realized that progressivism meant something more than creating an atmosphere of equal opportunity. It meant that government must exploit its resources of prestige, money, and power to give a better life to the people than they could receive under private initiative. The President's change of attitude reflected developments that were occurring across the nation. In education, law, medicine, science, and letters, as well as in industry, leaders were spreaidng new ideas that were having a profound impact upon the country.

After much consultation, Wilson worked closely with Senator Carter Glass of Virginia and pushed a compromise bill through Congress. It created regional banks in twelve areas; each was owned by the banks of the area and given the power to rediscount notes, issue a bank currency, and do certain things for the government in exchange for some general supervision of banking practices. While the Federal Reserve System decentralized banking and made the currency flexible, it did not destroy the money trust. It left too much power in the hands of the banks and excluded from the scope of its authority nearly a fifth of the banking system. It did not permit the United States Treasury to act in the public interest when the Federal Reserve Board was deadlocked or hesitant over policy.

Since the money monopoly continued to exist, Wilson turned to the task of revising the antitrust laws, especially those regulating interlocking directorates. Agrarian interests in the Democratic party also wanted stiff legislation controlling stock transactions, contracting, and credit practices. Labor agitated for many of these ideas, but desired most of all exemption from antitrust laws so that it could organize and strike. But Wilson was opposed to such forceful measures and turned to a favorite idea, the establishment of the Federal Trade

Commission to guide business in setting patterns of competition. By developing ethical practices, he hoped to avoid evils that would necessitate court prosecution. Size seemed less an object of concern to him than corporate ethics, and prosecutions were to give way, whenever possible, to persuasion.

When he recommended legislation to abolish interlocking directorates and other kinds of corporate devices that reduced competition, conservative Democrats opposed his plans, which they regarded as an attack upon the Sherman Anti-Trust Act. Other pressure groups within the party, however, advocated much more advanced control over corporate activities than he had in mind, and he, seeing the rise of this radicalism, decided to put his immediate faith in the corrective tactics of the Federal Trade Commission.

The FTC supervised business practices and issued warnings whenever competition was seriously violated. It could follow up its orders by recommending prosecutions, but public exposure of corporate practices was believed to be a powerful way of bringing pressure upon business for corrective change. Party leadership, nonetheless, wished to attack corporate abuses through legislation and passed the Clayton Anti-Trust Act. It declared that unions were not to be considered conspiracies in restraint of trade, a concession that Samuel Gompers of the American Federation of Labor (AF of L) hailed as "Labor's Magna Charta," but the courts continued for two decades to issue injunctions to break strikes. The Clayton Act was also exceedingly weak in correcting corporate abuses.

Actually Wilson remained cautious in his relations with business and labor, and some of the celebrated reforms of his administration were the initiative of others. At the insistence of Robert La Follette he finally approved legislation that guaranteed for seamen better working conditions on board ships and ended the tyranny of ship captains in contracting and discipline. Under Secretary W. B. Wilson, the Department of Labor formulated an extensive program of social legislation. A children's bureau was particularly helpful in offering advice to families on the care of youth. Employment studies were made that led to the Keating-Owen Act prohibiting the shipment in interstate commerce of products made by children. Other reformers found Wilson easier to approach in 1916 when he nominated the famous labor lawyer Louis D. Brandeis to the Supreme Court, favored an eight hour day for railroad workers, and approved of a workmen's compensation law. Even so, Wilson remained generally cautious in backing women's suffrage, aid for blacks, and immigration control, finding justification for inaction in traditional liberalism and his states' rights philosophy.

Wilson in Office

During the next four years Wilson exercised strong control over

Congress and devoted himself to the stated objectives of the New Freedom. Breaking a tradition of a century, he delivered in person his important addresses, and he presented bills to Congress that contained
many of his proposals already well-formulated. He kept Congress in
special session in 1913 and forced through tariff reform and banking
legislation before lobbyists could mobilize. While the Underwood
tariff reduced rates by about ten percent and enlarged the free list, the
Federal Reserve Act was undoubtedly the greatest piece of legislation
of his administration. The money monopoly had become notorious,
allowing concentration of banking in relatively few hands and making
the development of West and South secondary to the capital needs
of the North and Northwest. New bonding by states and industry was
dependent upon a few banks and bankers who collected tribute. Obviously more independence was needed in the money market, also
more flexibility of credit and more regional control, than were available
in the National Banking System.

In education, for example, the philosophy of John Dewey, then
of Columbia University, was having a revolutionary influence. He
emphasized the value of experimentation and flexibility in the educational process, insisting that "learning by doing" would help children
adjust to life's problems. The debate he started by his book, *The Child
and the Curriculum*, in which he attacked the values of memorization,
classical instruction, and age-old theories of discipline still continues.
Education for a democratic society nonetheless was widely accepted,
and states provided more and more elementary and high schools, required longer school years, and raised teacher qualifications and
salaries.

Colleges moved from classical curricula to elective programs and
widened their course offerings to include vocational subjects. Normal
schools for teachers were transformed into colleges, training lengthened
to four or five years, and the course of study made to lead to the bac-
calaureate. Colleges were even more influenced by the growth of profes-
sionalism. The emphasis on graduate work and concentration on
effort turned them into research centers and their faculty members
into specialists. The collection of data provided an enormous amount
of specific material on every aspect of life.

Progressivism benefited very much from this rise of professional
activity. La Follette enlisted economists to aid him develop attacks
on railroad rates and taxation while he was governor of Wisconsin.
His administration was full of university people, professors and their
students, who brought to government insights from their special fields
of study. In the United States Army, medical doctors did impressive
work combating yellow fever in Cuba and the Canal Zone. When the
Public Health Service was established in 1912 in order to coordinate
the work of many government bureaus, it supplied information at
an increased tempo to the states and cities concerning chlorination

of drinking water, inspection of milk, and the use of vaccines. As this and other information became available, cities and states set up services in their jurisdictions. Katherine Edson, as a member of California's first Industrial Welfare Commission, won the support of Governor Johnson for a minimum-wage law for women by using statistics and case studies to illustrate how low wages affected the lives of women and children. Louis D. Brandeis used all sorts of scientific evidence when he presented his brief in *Muller v. Oregon* to the Supreme Court, evidence that was only recently available because of the research of sociologists, economists, and social workers. His brief was not only a departure from traditional practice, but it reflected the accumulated learning already in the possession of experts. Progressives reacted differently to these social programs, because many of them could not agree on the ultimate function of government. Other reform programs might have developed had not European war between 1914 and 1918 at first distracted popular attention and then drew the nation into the conflict.

The War in Europe

Like most Americans, Wilson firmly believed that the United States should concentrate its political activities in the Western Hemisphere. Like many he favored the use of military forces to insure peace in Mexico and the Caribbean, but questioned the practicality of sending troops to Europe. Since 1900 relations between the United States and Great Britain had become very cordial. British deference to American ambitions in the Caribbean had lessened friction, and the Liberal party reform program of H. H. Asquith and David Lloyd George aroused the interest of Progressives. Wilson's own philosophical roots as a professor and scholar were in English history, and he had much sympathy for the British struggle against Germany. This sympathy was shared by the literary and scholarly community who were well acquainted with their British colleagues. Germany, on the other hand, had alienated many Americans by aggressive military policies that threatened the peace. While German-Americans had nostalgic memories of the fatherland, many had immigrated to avoid military service. They preferred Germany to Britain if faced with a choice between the two, but they valued even more the distance of the United States from Europe.

When war broke out in Europe in 1914, Wilson declared American neutrality, recalling the traditional principles of Washington and Jefferson in separating the nation from Europe. He cautioned the nation to be wary of emotional ties with the belligerents and keep peace ever as the objective:

> we must be impartial in thought as well as in action, must put a curb upon our sentiments. . . . This country of ours . . . should

show herself . . . a nation that neither sits in judgment upon others
nor is disturbed in her own counsels.

At first his warning was heeded, but in 1915 and 1916 military purchases by Britain and France turned the sluggish economy into the
greatest boom in the nation's history. Exports to these countries jumped
from $824 million in 1914 to $3 billion in 1916. To finance these purchases, Britain and France liquidated their investments and in 1915
borrowed heavily from the American people.

Trade with Germany fell off drastically because of British superiority on the high seas. British blockades of enemy ports made almost
all direct trade impossible, and her use of contraband controls limited
indirect commerce through neutral ports. The United States protested
these obstructions to regular trade, but being pro-British in sympathy
it permitted the blockade to be tightened. Its sympathy for Britain and
her allies increased when Germany invaded Belgium, and starving conditions in that battered nation brought appeals for food. News of atroci-
ties in Belgium and elsewhere by Germans also upset Americans, but
nothing irritated them as much as the sinkings by German submarines.

The Germans used in 1915 the full power of their submarine fleet
to break the British blockade. They had to surprise their victims,
strike, and disappear before the submarine was itself destroyed. They
thus often violated the spirit of international law, which provided
for determination of the ship's ownership, search and seizure, and
safety of passengers and crew: if the Germans had promised to adhere
to the traditional rules of warfare, they would have been unable to
use their submarines effectively. Their sinking of the *Lusitania* in
July 1915 aroused the American public; the sinking of the *Arabic* in
August 1915 brought a crisis and a German retreat; the sinking of the
Sussex in March 1916 inflamed the United States. Germany finally
gave a pledge to follow the traditional rules of warfare.

While tension was reduced, so much had occurred to anger Americans that they reluctantly agreed to a program of national defense.
Plans were approved to expand the Army from 80,000 to 175,000 and
to construct eight first-class battleships. Congress coordinated defense efforts by establishing a Council of National Defense, and Wilson
chose a new Secretary of State, Robert Lansing of New York, to replace
William Jennings Bryan whose pacificism irritated the President.
Wilson encountered severe opposition in Congress and throughout the
country because of his defense program. Peace Democrats rebelled
and forced restrictions on the mobilization. Leaders of the Middle
West, with Bryan often at their head, organized farmers and laborers
to block the presidential program.

Opposition remained strong within the party and threatened to
defeat the party in the presidential elections of 1916. Wilson was
renominated because of his progressive record and his apparent de-

The Rape of Belgium (*Library of Congress*)

termination to be neutral. The convention gave him a strong slogan for the campaign: "He kept us out of war." It was particularly telling when Republicans like Theodore Roosevelt and Henry Cabot Lodge seemed to be driving the nation into the war. The Republicans united behind Charles Evans Hughes of New York, then an associate justice of the Supreme Court and known for his progressive views. He had avoided taking sides on the war, and his nomination drew back into the party many Progressives. Hughes proved to be a poor campaigner, unable to control Roosevelt's outbursts, and, at a critical moment in California, failed to meet the haughty Governor Johnson who was staying in the same hotel. Even so, the election was exceedingly close. Wilson had a victory of 23 votes in the electoral college (277 to 254) and an uncertain control of Congress. His combined opposition had more popular votes than he had.

If the election had any meaning, it was an approval of progressivism. The uncertainties of peace, however, were great, and war became a possibility in January 1917 when Germany announced her intention of renewing immediately submarine warfare. Wilson reacted firmly against the declaration by breaking diplomatic relations with Germany and noting that "a madman . . . should be curbed." Nonetheless, he then assured Congress that the nation under his leadership still stood for "peace, not war." But he had taken such a firm position against the submarine that torpedoing of American vessels in March brought a recommendation for war from the Cabinet and his call for a special session of Congress. In this crisis Wilson pondered, balanced, and weighed the effect of war upon the United States. He hoped for a lasting peace, a league of nations to maintain it, and a recognition of international principles like freedom of the seas, the free determination of peoples, and the equality of nations. After much agonizing, he asked Congress to declare war. His words in the war address of April 2, 1917, expounded American ideals:

> It is a fearful thing to lead this great peaceful people into war, into the most terrible . . . of all wars. . . . But the right is more precious than peace, and we shall fight for the things which we have always carried nearest our hearts—for democracy, . . . for the rights and liberties of small nations, for a universal dominion of right by such a concert of free peoples as shall bring peace and safety to all nations and make the world itself at least free.

Within four days both houses of Congress passed easily the war resolution. Many who had been critical of Wilson's hesitancy to enter the war observed now the decisiveness of a leader who had the job in hand.

America Enters the War

During the next twelve months the nation reluctantly mobilized its total resources, and the spirit of war gradually fired emotions. The administration learned that the Allied cause was critical and that only massive war materiel and reinforcements by American soldiers would save it. From nearly peacetime conditions the nation erected war agencies, mobilized manpower through a draft, and coordinate industrial production. The War Industries Board, under the chairmanship of Bernard Baruch, was empowered to gather supplies for the Allies, and through controlled purchasing, the Board standardized products and determined production.

Under the direction of a mining engineer, Herbert Hoover, who had won the reputation of providing relief for Belgium, food production was increased, waste reduced, substitutes encouraged, and supplies conserved. Enlisting the patriotic support of the people, he set meatless and wheatless days and encouraged experiment with grains other than wheat. Farmers reacted well to government measures to increase production. Enormous new acreage was added in the Middle

West, with wheat acreage nearly doubling in two years. While the production of meat, butterfat, and other foodstuffs was equally impressive, the most important point was the success of shipments of food abroad, which rose from near 7 million tons before the war to 18 million tons in 1918-19. Wartime demand for food in the United States seemed insatiable and drove prices upward, but the rising prices were offset by adjustments in wages and profits. Hooverizing the American diet was accepted in good spirit, even the substitutes for sugar and pork, and many people found humor in experimentation with other foods.

The war mobilization put a heavy burden on transportation facilities. When railroads could not provide sufficient freight cars or move products fast enough, Congress gave Wilson power to take over and unify them. Government administrators, acting with emergency funds; invested heavily in rolling stock and forced a modernization of railroad practices. Even greater was the task of moving goods by water, since new shipyards had to be built or old ones enlarged to handle the demand. Though vast numbers of ships were constructed in record time, some of the emergency capacity was unnecessary because in a few new yards the first ships were completed just as the war ended. This was undoubtedly a worthwhile expenditure of war funds, for the expanding merchant marine, together with improved convoys, enabled the United States to deliver over 5 million tons of supplies to Europe.

Conservation of United States manpower was paramount in waging war. Congress passed a Selective Service Law in 1917, mobilized the national guard, and accepted volunteers. Eventually the nation had an army of 3.4 million men. While awaiting induction, men and boys everywhere practiced marching and a holiday atmosphere often prevailed. Some young men, however, resisted enlistment and challenged the constitutionality of Selective Service. A few went to prison. Two million men in the new army were eventually assigned to the command of General John J. Pershing.

American approached the war with great emotion, learning to hate Germans and their sympathizers, and responded excessively to the barrage of propaganda that was issued by George Creel's Committee on Public Information. His orators spread hatred across the land, inspiring thousands of neighborhood patriots to report pro-German sympathy, burn German books, and rename songs and customs. Some prominent German immigrants were put in prison, and many critics of the war were also jailed. Witch-hunting became a pastime of patriotic folk, who used suspicion, rumor, and prejudice to guide their actions. Wilson plainly used the emotion for governmental ends, permitting federal officials to prosecute on flimsy evidence and refusing to use his powers of clemency to rectify mistakes. He signed sedition and espionage acts and, much worse, let A. Mitchell Palmer, who was bent on

Suffragettes (Library of Congress)

repressive measures, become Attorney General. In this emergency
Wilson supported women's suffrage and prohibition. He regarded proposed amendments as war measures. Some male opponents angrily
denounced the proposals and they were not passed.

The Fourteen Points

The United States joined the allied side—not because it accepted
all the allied war aims as such—but because it hoped to influence the
Allies to bring about a lasting peace. Wilson considered the United
States as bearer of a mission, and he prepared to carry it out with a
world plan of reform.

From the entrance of the United States into the war, he issued
statements of principles, to patriotic groups, Congress, labor groups,

The Foes of Suffrage *(Library of Congress)*

and foreign diplomats. His freedom of action was maintained, moreover, by refusing to seek a conference with the allied powers. His decision had great risks, but he depended upon the people everywhere to support his policies. His Flag Day address in 1917 particularly expressed this idea:

> This is a People's War . . . for freedom and justice and self government amongst all the nations of the world. . . . For us there is but one choice. We have made it. Woe be the man or group of men that seeks to stand in our way.

Before January 8, 1918, he had issued in piecemeal fashion what was now presented to Congress as the Fourteen Points, upon which peace could be negotiated. Their purpose was a direct appeal to the peoples of Germany and Austria-Hungary, over the heads of their pres-

THE BIG FOUR (National Archives)

ent governments. It offered peace without victory, a peace of principles, humanity, and justice. Five points in his peace program were
general, stating principles of international diplomacy, public negotiation of treaties, freedom to trade on the high seas, equality of economic
opportunity, disarmament, and adjustment to colonial claims. The
remaining points referred to the problems of specific countries, to
their boundaries, the self-determination of minorities, the evacuation
of military forces, and the creation of an independent Poland. His
fourteenth point proposed a "general association of nations," a league
of nations, in order to guard the peace.

Without bothering to assure himself of either Congressional support or the backing of the Allies, Wilson made these proposals the
battle cry of the United States. While he received favorable comments
from British Prime Minister David Lloyd George, French Premier
Georges Clemenceau clearly stated a position that more accurately
represented the Allies: "My war aim is to conquer." There was no
assurance that the Allies would accept the Fourteen Points and, more

important still, no assurance that when emotion had decreased in the
United States the nation would be ready to abandon its traditional
isolation toward Europe.

The Battlefield

American recruits expected to win the war in less than a year.
Their armies, directed by Secretary of War Newton D. Baker, depended
for manpower upon conscription. Baker had raised within the year
almost three million men and had two million of them on their way
to France and some expeditionary forces were soon on the line of fire.
The first contingent of regular troops arrived in France in June 1917.
At the end of the first year, the land war was still bitter, but the control
of the sea was nearly complete. The length of the war surprised many
people; the losses of men were sobering.

Secretary of the Navy, Josephus Daniels, and his staff were only
partially prepared for war in 1917. Many additions to the fleet were
still in the blueprint stage, and firm plans to assist the allied cause
were not yet conceived. With the advice of Rear Admiral William
Sims, the navy decided to develop a convoy system and seek out
German submarines. Losses of shipping were gradually reduced from
881,000 tons in April to 289,000 tons in November 1917. This compara-
tivé safety made possible the transport of matériel to France in ever
greater quantities, and, of course, reinforcements of American troops.

Success on the sea equalized to some degree the impact of Italian
weakness and the Russian revolution; both permitted Germany to
remove troops from those fronts for fighting in the west. By March
1918 the Germans had achieved superiority on the western front, and
the Allies begged for the American recruits.

The first German offensive in March and April 1918 hurled the
British back from their positions, and severely weakened allied defenses. In May and June the Germans repeated these attacks upon
French lines, with nearly the same results. The reaction in America
was determined, and leaders asked that part of the front be assigned
to American troops under the leadership of General Pershing. However, Pershing regarded support of allied lines most important, and
chose instead to keep the American troops as a mobile force. His advice
seemed effective, because in late May the German drive on Chauteau-
Thierry was stopped. A month later, in another German drive, 275,000
Americans again supported allied forces at Chauteau-Thierry, and
success of allied armies then saved not only Paris but turned the tide
of the war.

Fighting continued in August and September, but the loss of
momentum had its effect upon German morale. The forces of her Allies
had suffered severe losses, and all but left the war. A great battle in
the Meuse-Argonne region then convinced German military leader-

German War Zone & Western Front, 1918

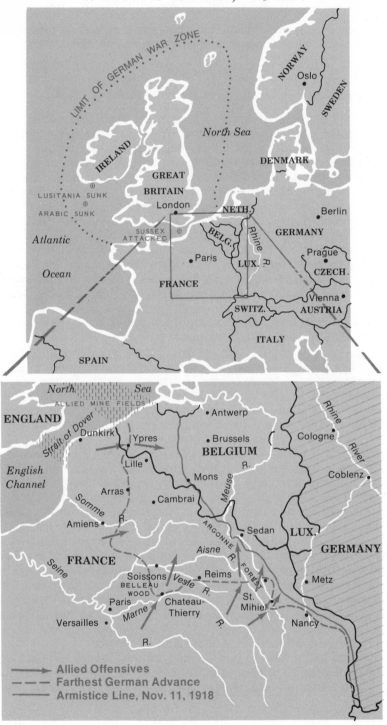

LIMIT OF GERMAN WAR ZONE

NORWAY
Oslo
SWEDEN

North Sea

IRELAND

DENMARK

GREAT
BRITAIN
London

Berlin

LUSITANIA SUNK
ARABIC SUNK

NETH.

GERMANY

Atlantic

SUSSEX
ATTACKED

BELG.

Rhine R.

Prague

Paris

LUX.

CZECH.

Ocean

FRANCE

Vienna

SWITZ.

AUSTRIA

ITALY

SPAIN

North Sea
ALLIED MINE FIELDS

ENGLAND

Strait of Dover

Antwerp

Rhine River

Dunkirk

Ypres

Brussels

Cologne

English
Channel

Lille

BELGIUM

Coblenz

Mons

Meuse R.

Arras

Cambrai

Somme R.

ARGONNE

Sedan

LUX.

Amiens

FOREST

GERMANY

FRANCE

Aisne

Seine

Soissons
BELLEAU
WOOD

Vesle R.

Reims

Metz

St.
Mihiel

Paris

Marne R.

Chateau-
Thierry

Versailles

Nancy

R.

```
⟶   Allied Offensives
– – –   Farthest German Advance
────   Armistice Line, Nov. 11, 1918
```

ship that the war could not be continued. Changes in government followed, and the Germans asked for an armistice, with the hope that a peace would be negotiated according to the principles of Wilson's Fourteen Points.

Germany was not crushed by defeat, but the reverses had made effective fighting in the future very doubtful. The Allies, too, were tired of war, and the United States was disillusioned by the potential hardships and controls of a long conflict. Americans had not given much thought to demobilation, and the suddenness of the Armistice left them unprepared. Wilson looked forward to a peace conference at Paris, but the American public wanted a return to normalcy as quickly as possible.

Wilson's Loss of Control

Even before the war had ended in November 1918, critics in the United States had begun to attack Wilson's handling of the mobilization. Opposition leaders like Theodore Roosevelt made irresponsible public statements and did great harm to the President. Disillusionment and suffering kept the people restless. Vast numbers of people had crowded into the cities, especially blacks from the South, and the appearance of so many strangers had unsettled people worried about radicalism. Businessmen and their employees had been caught up in the shift to war production, and some had suffered from the harsh realities of shortages, wartime controls, and heavy taxes. Taxes themselves had fallen unevenly on white collar workers and professional people, who had early become disenchanted with the war. Crop controls on farm commodities also had angered many.

In the November 1918 elections, just a few days before the German armistice that would end the war, the Wilson administration lost both houses of Congress by narrow margins. Wilson had foolishly chosen to make the election a vote of confidence in his policies and asked that Democrats be entrusted with the responsibility of writing the peace treaty. He exposed himself to partisan criticism, and the ever-belligerent Roosevelt made the most of the opportunity: "Mr. Wilson and his fourteen points and his four supplementary points and his five complementary points and all his utterances every which way have ceased to have any shadow of right to be accepted as expressive of the will of the American people."

These signs of opposition should have been a warning of political danger to Wilson and an inducement for consultation with the Republican leadership about the peace and the conference at Paris. To a degree Wilson did anticipate the hazards of opposition before he left for Paris. He selected a number of unusually capable experts like Bernard Baruch and Herbert Hoover, but he failed to select any of the powerful senators. His neglect of proper political tactics deprived him of a buffer when he had to explain the political conditions of the peace conference and the compromises he was forced to make. While he succeeded very well in winning better peace terms for Germany than she could have obtained herself, the peace treaty was harsh and violated the spirit of his earlier pronouncements. Its imposition of war guilt and reparations upon Germany was plainly ridiculous and, indeed, shocking to American liberals. He was criticized for concessions to Japan that put her in control of former German territories on the Shantung Peninsula of China and in the Pacific.

While the treaty reflected European war aims, it provided for a League of Nations to adjust inequities as they were discovered. To Wilson the League alone was the organization that could help mankind avoid wars, and he believed it would develop into a body that would have moral influence to stop aggression. He was sorry to make concessions in Paris, but refused to let the Senate force further changes; nor, even in the face of warnings from former President Taft, would he bend to mollify his critics. He was determined to force ratification in spite of the opposition of Senator Henry Cabot Lodge of Massachusetts and stated flatly, "The Senate is going to ratify the treaty." To rally popular support he undertook a nationwide tour in the fall of 1919. He was tired even before he began. He traveled from city to city until he nearly collapsed from exhaustion at Pueblo, Colorado, on September 25. Rushed back to Washington, he suffered a physical breakdown. For eight weeks the nation was without effective leadership in the Presidency and during these weeks the treaty came up for a vote in the Senate. Senator Lodge had succeeded in attaching fourteen reservations to the treaty. Democrats joined a group of Republican opponents of the League to reject the treaty with its reservations, and then a vote for the treaty without reservations failed overwhelmingly (38 to 53).

These votes surprised many Americans. Some prominent leaders tried to arrange a compromise between Wilson and Lodge, but stubbornness on the part of both men prevented a compromise treaty. Wilson looked to the election of 1920 for popular support, while Republicans expected the people to be tired of the Democrats and vote the Republicans into office, when they would be able to present their own treaty to the Senate.

The Return of Peace

In his preoccupation with world affairs, Wilson let domestic affairs lose their reformist direction. Many people were too interested in a return to peace and normal conditions to give thought to national reforms. While businessmen took much credit for the success of the American war effort, they urged the relaxation of controls on prices during the reconversion. They had sufficient influence to force the government to get out of business and liquidate its war enterprises.

The sudden suspension of controls allowed prices to shoot upward and unsettle the wage and price structure; food prices advanced sharply and put pressure on wages. In 1919 and 1920 the cost of living climbed nearly 105 percent over prewar levels. Workers responded with demands for wage increases, then strikes that took millions off their jobs in every part of the nation.

Negotiations in the coal and steel industries exposed serious questions concerning hours of labor, pay increases, and working conditions. When negotiations broke down, violence followed. United States Steel used thousands of strike breakers, and spread propaganda to justify its activities. The bituminous-coal miners also pressed for concessions—a wage increase of 60 percent, six-hour day, and a five day week. Wilson insisted that wartime wage controls for the coal industry be continued, and both the Attorney General Palmer and the courts enforced government policy. The miners eventually got a 27 percent increase in wages, and a court injunction enforced federal law.

In Boston a police strike challenged public authorities. The police, suffering from long hours and poor wages, organized the Boston Social Club and secured a charter from the A.F. of L. A citizen's committee readily accepted the justice of the demands, but the police commissioner, responsible only to the governor, stoutly resisted pressure and dismissed nineteen of the agitators. The police then left the city to its own resources and in the hands of rowdies who frightened the citizens by acts of violence. In desperation the mayor mobilized local militia and enlisted citizens to take over police duty. The situation was well in hand when Governor Calvin Coolidge, aroused by the principle involved in a police strike, abruptly ordered in the militia and supported the commissioner's decision not to rehire striking police. When the head of the A.F. of L. appealed to Coolidge for compassion, the Governor replied: "There is no right to strike against the public safety, anywhere, anytime." Most surprising of all, President Wilson congratulated Coolidge on his position, as did millions of Americans.

This police strike was one of numerous incidents that aroused the nation. Bombings, attempted bombings, the deaths of innocent people during strikes and labor disputes frightened many people who advocated arbitration. Others sought solutions in repression. Attorney General Palmer feared a Communist revolution like the one that had recently occurred in Russia and ruthlessly rounded up thousands of suspected aliens for deportation. American patriots to the "one hundred percent variety" consorted to deprive Catholics, Jews, and blacks of their jobs, and the Ku Klux Klan terrorized the South to hold the blacks in subjugation.

Probably no group was discriminated against more persistently than the blacks. Thousands of them had moved into the cities during the war to work in the expanding industries, and low pay and poor housing kept their living conditions little better than on the farm. When they sought collective remedial action through the National Association for the Advancement of Colored People, their civil liberties were not recognized. The Ku Klux Klan terrorized them, particularly in the South but also in the North and Southwest. Lynching of blacks increased in the South in 1918 and 1919 until more than seventy persons had died from mob violence. But the Klan was not alone in its harassment. Race riots in the northern cities accounted for many deaths and the destruction of valuable property.

While the nation was trembling over violence in its cities, Congress passed the famous Volstead Act, implementing the Eighteenth Amendment and thereby restricting the sale of all beverages containing even a trace of alcohol. This unnecessarily strict measure, a vain attempt to end all consumption of alcohol, deprived the urban masses of their beer. Prohibition became most unpopular, and its opponents accused the government of infringing on their liberty.

Return to "Normalcy"

In the midst of the postwar adjustment the 1920 elections were held. Though the political tide had turned Republican, strong factions still divided the party. The liberals and Progressives, now less ardent, put forth Herbert Hoover as their favorite candidate. This self-made man, engineer, and administrator who had distinguished himself as head of the nation's food program during the war merited his party's support. He had some opposition from Hiram Johnson of California, whose record as a Progressive governor was exceptional, but whose isolationist tactics in the United States against ratification of the League of Nations were shameful. The conservatives backed General Leonard Wood, friend of Theodore Roosevelt (who had died in 1919), and Frank O. Lowden, who offered a campaign chest full of business dollars. On the tenth ballot, however, convention delegates agreed to a deal of the party managers and nominated Warren G. Harding of Ohio, a pliable party regular, and to a platform denouncing government interference in the economy. Harding promised a "return to Normalcy," whatever that meant, and offered confusing statements on America's future role in Europe. Calvin Coolidge of Massachusetts, known for his strikebreaking activity in Boston, took the vice presidential nomination. The Democrats were unable to find a candidate or issue that could clearly take advantage of their eight-year record. Wilson's health had reduced his chances of reelection, but the swing to the Republican party in 1918 served a warning on political leaders that someone else should represent them in the Presidency. Wilson's son-in-law, William Gibbs McAdoo, was a major candidate, and A. Mitchell Palmer had much support. On the thirty-eighth ballot, however, the Democrats chose James M. Cox of Ohio, a man of moderate principles in the Wilson tradition, and Franklin D. Roosevelt of New York, Wilson's Assistant Secretary of the Navy, as their standard-bearers. Though the Democrats waged a vigorous campaign, the Republicans won an overwhelming victory, taking every state outside the Deep South and even taking Tennessee. The voters gave Harding 16,152,200 votes (and Cox 9,147,573) and control of both houses of Congress.

Life in Progressive America was exciting for most citizens. Their nation had won great prominence in world affairs since 1898, and took a commanding part in the plans for victory in 1917 and 1918. Wilson's Fourteen Points were a significant attack upon imperalism in favor of national self-determination and world cooperation to end international conflict. His failure in 1919 to secure participation of the United States in the League of Nations was serious, but the American public was divided and unwilling to make further sacrifices of its wealth and freedom for international peace.

Progressivism also had accomplished much. A new spirit entered politics, with responsible significant changes to local and state governments. On the national level the people elected their senators, women voted and income was taxed. The federal government had assumed new responsibilities to aid farmers, to assist education, and to build highways. Much needed to be done and, in 1920, the people welcomed the return of peace by electing new national leaders and accepting their pledge to give the nation "normalcy."

SUGGESTIONS FOR FURTHER READING

Anderson, Donald F., *William Howard Taft: A Conservative's Conception of the Presidency.* Ithaca, New York, Cornell University Press, 1973.

Chamberlain, John, *Farewell to Reform: The Rise, Life and Decay of the Progressive Mind in America.* Chicago, Quadrangle Books, 1965.

Chessman, G. Wallace, *Theodore Roosevelt and the Politics of Power.* Boston, Little, Brown and Company, 1969.

Croly, Herbert, *The Promise of American Life.* New York, Capricorn Books, E. P. Dutton and Company, 1964.

La Follette, Robert M., *La Follette's Autobiography,* ed. Allan Nevins. Madison, Wisconsin, University of Wisconsin Press, 1960.

Link, Arthur S., *Woodrow Wilson: The New Freedom.* Princeton, N.J., Princeton University Press, 1965.

_____, *Woodrow Wilson and the Progressive Era, 1910-1917.* New York, Harper Torchbooks, Harper & Row, 1963.

Marcell, David W., *Progress and Pragmatism: James, Dewey, Beard, and the American Idea of Progress.* Westport, Conn., Greenwood, 1974.

May, Ernest R., *The World War and American Isolation, 1914-1917.* Chicago, Quadrangle Books, 1966.

Mowry, George, *Era of Theodore Roosevelt and the Birth of Modern America, 1900-1912.* New York, Harper Torchbooks, Harper & Row, 1963.

Nash, Gerald D., *The American West in the Twentieth Century: A Short History of An Urban Oasis.* Englewood Cliffs, New Jersey, Prentice-Hall, 1973.

Parsons, Edward B., *Wilsonian Diplomacy.* St. Louis, Forum Press, 1978.

Peterson, H. C. and Gilbert C. Fite, *Opponents of War, 1917-1918.* Seattle, University of Washington Press, 1968.

Pollack, Norman, *The Populist Response to Industrial America.* New York, W. W. Norton and Company, 1966.

Porter, Glenn, *The Rise of Big Business, 1860-1910.* New York, Thomas Y. Crowell, 1973.

Pringle, Henry F., *Theodore Roosevelt: A Biography.* New York, Harvest Books, Harcourt, Brace and Company, 1956.

Stanley, Peter W., *A Nation in the Making: The Philippines and the United States, 1899-1921.* Cambridge, Mass., Harvard University Press, 1974.

Vandiver, Frank E., *Black Jack: The Life and Times of John J. Pershing.* College Station, Texas, Texas A&M University Press, 1977.

The New Era

T HE 1920s WAS A NEW ERA—or so it seemed at the time. Material abundance—or a consumer-oriented economy—was its most obvious feature; enlightened business leadership seemed largely responsible, and changes in manners and morals were also involved. We can now see that American life was very dynamic during the decade, not stagnant and reactionary as it appeared to some critics at the time and later. We can also see that the output of the economic system, although quite spectacular, was not distributed nearly as widely as it seemed to the admirers of the economic system, and that the era, although previewing some features of an economy and a society that would emerge after world War II, did not last very long. And we can see that American culture in the 1920s was plagued by tensions and conflicts. They as well as the performance of the economic system helped a champion of the new era, Herbert Hoover, rise to the top of the political system late in the decade.

The Performance and Structure of the Business System

The American business system, at least after 1922, was tremendously productive in the 1920s, more productive than any other system at the time and more productive than the American system had been in the past. One part, manufacturing, increased its output by 50 percent from 1922 to 1929. As a result, many Americans had many more material things than ever before, and the products of American industry entered into their daily lives to a much greater extent than had been possible earlier.

An increase in the efficiency of American industry contributed significantly to the change. The leading manufacturing firms applied the principles of scientific management, stepped up industrial research and enlarged their employee relations programs, even using social scientists to find out what innovations would make workers become more efficient. The results were impressive. Output per worker in manufacturing increased by 40 percent during the decade. From 1899 to 1909, also a dynamic decade, output had jumped only 7 percent.

The automobile industry had much responsibility for economic growth. In part, the industry was important because it expanded so rapidly (by 225 percent) in its production to become the largest manufacturing industry in the country and to turn out about 13 percent of the total value of the nation's manufactured products. It provided half a million jobs in the manufacture of cars, buses and trucks.

As the industry expanded it promoted other changes. Detroit, the center of the industry, jumped from a quarter of a million people in 1900 to a million and a half in 1930. There and in other places, the auto industry produced several million jobs by stimulating the expansion of established industries, such as oil, rubber, steel, and travel, and creating many new enterprises, including garages, service stations, hot dog stands, billboards and the like. The advance of the automobile stimulated the construction industry, especially in suburbia as it now became easier to live some miles away from one's job. The progress of the automobile industry created the trucking and busing industries, and these developments produced problems for the railroads and for public transportation.

The automobile industry had a broad impact for it produced for a mass market. Henry Ford was the leading figure in this development. Well before the 1920s, he had changed the auto business from a manufacturer of a luxury article into an essential industry by producing successfully the Model T Ford. His aim was a cheap, durable, easily repaired vehicle, and he began to produce one in 1908 that could be sold for $950. By employing the moving assembly line, he had cut the price below $500 by 1914. During the 1920s, he sold over thirteen million Model Ts, selling them for $290 each in 1926. Following Ford's lead, auto production in the United States jumped from 4000 vehicles in 1900 to 1.7 million in 1920 and to 4.5 million in 1929. Automobile registrations moved from nine million in 1920 to twenty-three million ten years later. This was more than 1 car for every 5 people as com-

Henry Ford and His Model T *(Ford Archives)*

pared with 1 for every 43 in Great Britain and 1 for every 7,000 in Russia. By the end of the 1920s, many Americans regarded the automobile as a necessity, and ownership was facilitated by easy-credit policies.

Production for a mass market was a characteristic of all the so-called "new industries." They included the radio, movie, electrical, chemical and food canning industries. More than ten million families had radios by 1929. A multitude of things that people had not been able to get only a short time before became parts of every day life in the 1920s. These things affected the lives and values of the American people significantly.

The highly productive business system featured large and powerful organizations. It was not a highly individualistic system. Parts of it were, but a form of private collectivism which had been developed in

most industries before the 1920s and continued to develop during that
decade. Long before, business leaders organized their sector of the
economy, developing large institutions like Standard Oil and United
States Steel, and now the organization process moved forward, and
as it did, new programs were developed to enlarge the power of the
organizations and the business system and shape the behavior of the
American people.

Economic historians have called the 1920s the "second great consolidation period," comparing it with the decade after the depression
of the 1890s. Consolidation in the business world moved forward in
several areas, including banking, electrical power and automobiles.
By the end of the decade, Ford, General Motors and Chrysler produced better than 80 percent of the automobiles in the United States
although, by then, nearly two hundred firms had tried to establish
themselves in the industry. The two hundred largest non-banking
corporations controlled nearly half of the wealth and income of all
non-banking corporations, and one giant, the American Telephone
and Telegraph Company, had assets of $4.25 billion.

The consolidation process had not created monopolies, but had
produced "oligopolies." In nearly all of the major industries, a
small number of firms, not one or many, turned out most of the products of the industry. Nine steel companies produced 82 percent of
the steel; four firms were responsible for 70 percent of the meat
packing; four turned out 66 percent of the rubber, and four produced 94 percent of the tobacco.

The large firms with large competitors tried to avoid price competition and to rely instead on advertising, salesmanship and style
changes. In automobiles, price competition was confined to the dealers
where firms were small, while the producers tended to follow the
lead of one firm, keeping prices in line with it, seeking to avoid sharp
cuts, and relying upon other devices, such as frequent style changes,
to expand sales. This represented a basic departure from the philosophy
of Henry Ford who saw style changes as a threat to his goals of efficiency and a low price. "The customer can have a Ford any color he
wants," this innovator liked to say, "so long as it's black." A change in
public taste forced Ford to change. By the mid-twenties, his competitors
were succeeding at his expense by emphasizing style. The people to
whom he was catering had more purchasing power, wanted their cars
to testify to their progress and thus were more interested in style than
price. As a result, Ford turned to the Model A in 1928, producing a
car of modern design available in a variety of colors.

The automobile industry also became one of the leading users of
advertising. The firms recognized that advertising added to costs,
but they preferred it to price warfare.

Advertising was one of the techniques of influence and control
that business developed significantly in the 1920s, seeking to change

behavior. Expenditures on advertising tripled during the decade, and advertisers employed new methods heavily influenced by modern psychology with its emphasis on the irrationality of men. They moved away from the old emphasis on simple, illustrated description of the product and employed non-rational appeals and projected a conception of the good life. "In the old days men were rated by the homes in which they lived and few but their friends saw them," an ad suggested. "Today, men are rated by the cars they drive and everybody sees them—for the car is mobile and the home is not. To own a Packard is an evidence of discriminating taste." Advertising portrayed the American home as a place of great beauty as a consequence of the workings of the economic system and exalted romantic love as an activity of great importance facilitated by the economy.

The advertising men portrayed themselves as essential in an economy capable of producing abundantly. They could, they insisted, promote the mass consumption needed in a mass production economy by undermining old habits of hard work and thrift and developing new habits of leisure and spending. Seeing themselves as crusaders for the liberation of the American middle class from the tyranny of "Puritanism," advertising men rebelled against the Protestant economic ethic, the ethic of an earlier capitalism, and their industry became a major institution, comparable to the church and the school, seeking to shape the values and hence the behavior of people, seeking to get them to function as vigorous consumers.

Advertising men and other spokesmen for American business spoke frequently of the "New Era." To them, the 1920s seemed to be a revolutionary period in which a new civilization was emerging, a civilization that would be free of poverty. According to the theory of the new era, the revolution was based upon technological developments, helped by high wages, the diffusion of ownership and advertising and led by enlightened business leaders. They constituted the American elite, superior to labor leaders, politicians, intellectuals and others because, due to the strength of the drive for material self-interest, the best men entered business and the superior men succeeded.

The American business system during the 1920s continued to move in a collectivist direction. It was dominated by large, private organizations, and most of them were developing and using sophisticated techniques designed to shape the behavior of the American people. The business system promised them happiness if they would accept the leadership offered by the great businessmen and consume the products of American industry.

The Bias of the Political System

The American political system in the 1920s, especially on the presidential level, was biased in favor of business leadership. This was, in part, a consequence of the performance and structure of the business system. The bias resulted also from the weaknesses of its critics.

The popular presidents rejected the Roosevelt-Wilson conceptions of presidential leadership and reform. Both Warren G. Harding in 1920 and Calvin Coolidge in 1924 were elected by wide margins, with Harding receiving 60 percent of the popular vote; Coolidge, 54 percent. Neither one believed that the nation faced large problems or that the Constitution empowered the president and the national government to solve problems. And both men had great confidence in business leadership. Harding's slogan was "Less Government in Business and More Business in Government," while Coolidge insisted that "This is a business country and wants a business government" and that the federal government "justified itself only as it served business."

In line with this attitude, the Presidents appointed prominent businessmen to many of the key spots in Washington. One of them was Andrew Mellon. A Pittsburgh industrialist and banker, he had become one of the wealthiest men in the country as the top man in the Aluminum Company of America, Gulf Oil, and other giants. Harding appointed him Secretary of the Treasury and Coolidge kept him in that position. As Treasury Secretary he devoted his attention to the destruction of the tax program that the progressives had developed, which hit the upper income groups hardest, taking more than 70 percent of income at the highest level. Mellon and other business leaders regarded such taxation as harmful to business and thus to the country. He said that everyone knew of "businesses which have not been started, and new projects which have been abandoned, all for one reason," high income taxes. He believed that taxes taking more than 25 percent of income destroyed initiative and insisted that capital needed to be released by the government for productive industry.

Mellon achieved great success. Resisted by Midwestern progressive Republicans and many Democrats in Congress, he was backed by a strong propaganda campaign by business groups and given strong support by Coolidge, who admired him enormously. His influence is well illustrated in the Revenue Acts of 1926 and 1928 which cut the maximum tax to 20 percent of income.

Harding appointed to this cabinet another success from the business world, Herbert Hoover, who also served throughout the Harding-Coolidge administrations. Hoover had been a very successful engineer, promoter and organizer, operating in enterprises outside the United States, and he had gained fame as an administrator during World War I. Now, he became Secretary of Commerce on the condition that he would have a voice in all important economic matters.

Hoover saw himself as a champion of a new order. He believed in an active role for government in economic affairs but feared over-reliance on its power. It should, he insisted, function as adviser and

President Harding and His Cabinet *(Library of Congress)*

coordinator in a transition period, supplying information and bringing people and groups together. Washington needed to manage, speed
up, and guide a natural tendency toward organization and association,
enabling the process to realize its full potential and preventing impatient people from turning to undesirable "statist" solutions. Then,
after the new order had come into existence, the federal government
would play a minimal role.

To accomplish his objectives, Hoover enlarged the Department of
Commerce substantially, seeking to make it responsible for the coordination of all economic activity. The department promoted the formation of and worked with a variety of associations, including trade
associations. Composed of public and private officials with businessmen especially important, they promoted cooperation and reform in
a number of areas, including foreign trade, electrical power, transportation, construction, labor relations, child welfare, relief, and techniques of production; they developed codes of fair competition de-

signed to root out inefficiencies and increase productivity and social welfare, and they gained the cooperation of the Justice Department and the Federal Trade Commission and won favorable Supreme Court rulings. Hoover assumed that everyone would benefit from government action of this sort. It would result in more and better jobs and products.

The same tendency to use government to promote the general welfare through cooperation with business appeared in the foreign policy of the Harding-Coolidge administrations. Isolationism continued to exert a large influence, blocking efforts by the Wilsonians to bring the United States into the League of Nations and the World Court, and the anti-military attitudes that were closely associated with isolationism defeated the efforts of advocates of military preparedness. The Army was cut below 200,000 men, and at the Washington Naval Conference of 1921-1922, American officials worked out agreements to reduce the size of navies and maintain a ratio among the major naval forces. Champions of a naval buildup were able to get legislation late in the decade authorizing the addition of fifteen cruisers to the United States Navy.

The peace movement, strengthened by revulsion against World War I, had strong popular support and promoted many agreements against the use of military force in international affairs. In the Four-Power Pact of 1922, the United States, Great Britain, France, and Japan promised to respect the *status quo* in the Pacific region, and the Nine-Power Pact of the same year endorsed the Open Door in China. These efforts reached a climax in 1928 with the Paris Pact, sponsored by the American and French foreign ministers, Kellogg and Briand. It outlawed war as an instrument of national policy and was ratified by sixty-four nations.

The economic expansionists constituted an even more influential group. Composed of business leaders and key figures in the administration, including Hoover, they regarded economic expansion as essential for American prosperity and believed that it depended upon help from government. This policy did not mean free trade. The Fordney-McCumber Act of 1922 restored the high tariff policy against which Wilson had battled, rejecting the argument that the new creditor status of the United States obligated it to allow foreigners to sell goods in the American market. Economic expansion also did not mean the repudiation of war debts. The European nations who owed money to the United States proposed repudiation, and some Americans favored it, believing that forcing the Europeans to pay the debts would interfere with American efforts to sell goods in Europe, but most Americans, including the Presidents, regarded the debts as a firm obligation.

The policy of economic expansion meant aggressive behavior by American corporations. They expanded sales abroad and increased direct investments in other countries, raising the total from $3.9

billion in 1919 to $8 billion in 1930. The corporate giants were becoming multinational in scope, owning branch factories and raw materials in many other countries.

The program of economic expansion was facilitated by the large bankers, such as the House of Morgan. They had money to lend, were eager to float foreign loans and emphasized loans to foreign governments, including Germany. These lending policies enabled foreigners to obtain dollars they could use to pay on their debts and buy American goods.

The federal government promoted economic expansion. Hoover's Bureau of Foreign and Domestic Commerce worked hard at the task. So did the State Department, which battled for the repeal of foreign programs restricting American economic activities and pressed for the opening to American firms of areas under foreign control, such as the Middle Eastern oil fields.

The quest for economic opportunities abroad stimulated a search for a new policy in Latin America. The area seemed to offer an especially important market for American products, a major source of raw materials, and a place for the establishment of branches of American corporations. American businessmen at the expense of British and other foreign corporations expanded investments and sales there, but they also encountered growing hostility, especially from the revolutionary movement that had great strength in Mexico, and led to the seizing of American properties and restrictions on business activities. The federal government used loans to influence Latin American politics, and, coming to see the harmful consequences of a heavy-handed role, withdrew troops from Santo Domingo, sent Ambassador Henry Stimson to Nicaragua and Ambassador Dwight Morrow to Mexico in efforts to improve relations, and repudiated the offensive Theodore Roosevelt Corollary to the Monroe Doctrine. President-elect Hoover in 1928 made a goodwill tour of Latin America.

Why did Washington in the 1920s have such friendly relations with business leadership and the corporate giants? Part of the answer is found in the strength of the business system. It had the resources and know-how needed to influence public attitudes. The public-be-damned attitude had been discarded, at least by most large corporations. Although recognizing that their primary obligations were to their stockholders, up-to-date corporate managers insisted that they also had obligations to employees and the public. The larger companies established public relations departments that drew heavily on the experiences of World War I and the findings of modern psychology, and the evidence they supplied on the possibility of molding public opinion. The PR men attempted to improve the public relations of the business system and of individual businesses so that they would avoid the criticism that had characterized the Progressive Period, and the campaigns portrayed business as a warm, human institution with a conscience, affection for the workers and the public, and a great capacity for service. The campaigns sought to win the sympathy of the workers and the public for the labor policy of a firm and to promote favorable governmental policies.

Even more important, the business system backed up its public relations campaigns with impressive production records. Early in the century, Woodrow Wilson had mourned: "Nothing has spread socialistic thinking in this country more than the automobile . . . a picture of arrogance and wealth." By the 1920s, however, it became possible, a historian has observed, "to say that nothing has allayed the spread of 'socialistic thinking' as much as the spread of the automobile."

Public relations and production exerted an especially large influence on the urban middle classes who had been the major prop of prewar reform. They were over-represented in presidential politics because of their strong tendency to vote while less affluent groups did not. (Voter turnout, which had been as high as 79 percent in 1896, dropped below 50 percent in 1920 and 1924.) These people now deserted reform as they become more satisfied with American life. They no longer saw themselves and their culture as threatened by monopoly; they applauded a new set of business values: mass production and consumption, short hours, high wages, full employment, and welfare capitalism; and they saw—or thought they saw—government and business benefitting from excellent leadership.

Yet, this is not enough to explain the bias. Why did the middle classes not see the defects of their society, such as mass poverty, more clearly? And why did the millions of poor Americans not rebel? To understand the working of the federal government in the 1920s, one must also consider the critics of business leadership. Their weaknesses prevented them from educating the middle classes and mobilizing the lower classes so as to gain the strength needed to dominate politics and change America.

Critics of Business Leadership

Progressivism had not died out. The United States still contained individuals and groups who accepted capitalism but criticized business and advocated government attacks on social and economic problems. Congressman Fiorello LaGuardia, for one, spoke for working-class reform; social workers developed proposals for social insurance and other measures; the National Park Service added an aesthetic dimension to the conservation movement; and intellectuals such as John Dewey and Rexford Tugwell advocated social and economic planning.

Although alive, the Progressive Movement was plagued with troubles. It had been weakened by the war and the Red Scare, which had challenged the movement's belief in human progress and its confidence in government, and weakened still more by the divisive issues of 1919-1920—foreign policy, farm prices, and labor unions— issues that had restored the Democratic party to its pre-Wilson status as a weak minority. Progressivism had no strength in the Republican party, the majority party, since TR's bolt of 1912; the movement continued during the 1920s to be divided on foreign policy and economic issues like farm prices and labor unions, and it became very sharply divided on non-economic or cultural issues, such as prohibition, immigrants, and religion.

Weakened by problems, the progressives could not exert a large influence on politics, especially presidential politics, as much as they had before the war. The battle over the Tennessee River supplies an illustration of both the survival and the weakness of the movement. Progressives in and out of Congress fought the efforts of the Harding-Coolidge administrations to sell the federal hydroelectric and nitrate plants at Muscle Shoals to private interests and developed a proposal for federal development of the river valley. Senator George Norris of Nebraska spearheaded the campaign, which called for government ownership of electrical power facilities. Coolidge, however, defeated the efforts with a pocket veto in 1928. The episode indicated that the Progressives had substantial influence in Congress but none in the White House.

The health of American radicalism was much more precarious. It suffered chiefly from external pressures. Wartime hostility and the postwar Red Scare had damaged it severely, and anti-radicalism continued to inflict damage during the 1920s. Organizations like the Ku Klux Klan and the American Legion battled against radicals during the decade, and governments restricted civil liberties, passing new laws, including ones requiring teachers to take loyalty oaths, and obtaining Supreme Court decisions upholding convictions under state anti-radical laws.

A cause célèbre for radicals was the trial of Sacco and Vanzetti in Massachusetts. Their conviction for a payroll murder when the evidence of guilt was slight aroused many people. But they were anarchists and foreigners, and frightened people accepted the verdict of the jury.

Radicalism suffered also from an internal split. It was provoked by the Russian Revolution, which encouraged the left wing of the Socialist party to believe that revolution was a real and imminent possibility in the United States. Challenging the party's emphasis on evolutionary change and political democracy, the left lost in an effort to gain control of the party and make it part of a centralized, international organization, and seceded then, to the Communist party. It now competed with the Socialist party for support.

The Socialist party, once the main component of the American radical left, entered the 1920s in very weak condition and declined during most of the decade. Nominating its favorite candidate, Eugene V. Debs, once again, it gained only 3.5 percent of the popular vote in 1920, compared with 6 percent in 1912. Containing well over 100,000 members before the split, the party had only 11,000 by 1922. By 1924, it seemed to be "a political ghost stalking in the graveyard of current events seeking respectable burial."

Some radicals and progressives tried their hand at coalition politics in 1924 but failed. Socialists, reformers and some farm and labor groups backed Senator Robert LaFollette of Wisconsin for the Presidency in 1924. Promising various reforms, LaFollette was dominated by fear of "the control of government and industry by private monopoly." His efforts were hampered by conflict among his supporters and potential supporters over what to do about business power and the desirabilty of cooperation with Communists, and by the conservatism of the American Federation of Labor. LaFollette's efforts were harmed also by his radical image. The issue, according to one Republican, "is whether you stand on the rock of common sense with Calvin Coolidge, or upon the sinking sands of socialism with Robert M. LaFollette." He was more successful than the Socialists had been, gaining 16.5 pecent of the popular vote and the electoral votes of his home state. His showing reflected discontent, especially among the urban working classes and the farmers. Coolidge recognized the danger of his candidacy to Republican unity and directed the campaign as much against La Follette as against Davis.

The Socialist party showed a few signs of revival late in the decade. Norman Thomas took on the leadership role after Eugene V. Debs died in 1926. The party had less than 8,000 members by 1928 and its candidates held office only in a few small, scattered cities. Thomas provided vigorous leadership by championing a broad program, which called for various types of reforms but rejected the reformer's assumption that capitalism could be made into a workable system. Thomas's program advocated a peaceful revolution that would establish collective ownership and democratic management of the basic industries. In return for his labors, he received less than 1 percent of the popular vote in his bid for the Presidency in 1928.

The bias of the political system was not solely the result of the strengths of the business system and was surely not the consequence of lack of criticism. The critics were present and active. They were weakened, however, by a multitude of problems and could not gain the support of the politically active urban middle classes nor the millions of Americans who lived below the poverty line, most of whom did not participate in American politics.

Although seldom reformist and never radical, governments in the 1920s were not inactive. The dominant tendency was to assist the business system in areas where assistance seemed necessary to business and political leaders. Government spending, while well below wartime levels, was substantially higher than it had been before the war. The road- and highway-building programs, which involved all levels of government, were one of the major economic activities of the decade. In character and significance, these programs resembled the canal and railroad building activities of the nineteenth century. A much larger program than ever before, this economic activity was supported by a new form of taxation—the gasoline tax. No part of the country had such a tax in 1919; every state had one by 1929. The development reflected the eagerness of the public for highways. Their construction facilitated efforts by the automobile industry to sell cars; stimulated the growth of the busing, trucking, and other industries; and also made life more enjoyable for automobile owners. The programs seemed to their admirers to illustrate the harmony between business and public interests.

The Problems of Workers and Farmers

Growth and prosperity were conspicuous features of American life in the 1920s, but they were not the only features. For the labor movement it was a decade of decline. By 1920, more than five million workers had joined unions, and the American Federation of Labor had more than four million members. By the end of the decade, membership had dropped below three and one half million, and the AFL had fewer than three million members.

Why did the labor movement decline rather than grow? In the past, labor grew in numbers during periods of prosperity. Conditions in the 1920s, however, were strangely difficult for most wage earners as they tried to make pay checks meet expenses. Workers had grievances that could have resulted in organization. The answer to why they did not organize is found in the quality of leadership in the labor movement and the hostility to it in government and business.

Most workers failed to benefit from the economic progress of the period. Real income per capita increased by 17 percent from 1919 to 1929; Americans obtained more public services—more schools, libraries, hospitals and the like. The real income of non-farm workers increased by 11 percent from 1923 to 1929. Yet, working-class gains were limited largely to skilled workers who belonged to unions. Many workers suffered from monotonous and dangerous jobs, and many suffered from unemployment—5.5 million persons were unemployed during the recession of 1920-1922 (nearly 15 percent of the labor force); the number of unemployed persons ranged form 1.5 to 3 million from 1923 to 1929 (3 to 6 percent). And most Americans—nearly 60 percent—lived below the statistician's poverty line. Most wage-earners did so.

The labor movement failed to launch an attack upon the problem of poverty. Although the movement had accomplished much under the

Rural and Urban Population, 1850-1940

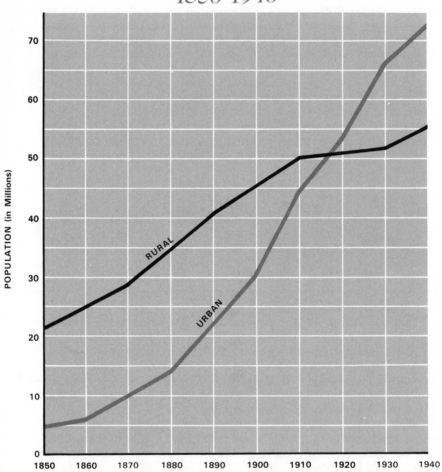

leadership of Samuel Gompers, it had major shortcomings. It focused its attention on skilled workers, when a growing percentage of industrial workers was unskilled or semi-skilled. William Green, who succeeded Gompers upon his death in 1924, held on firmly to his master's principles. Green and other labor leaders were quite uncritical of business and political leaders, and they refused to organize workers along industrial lines in spite of the many unskilled and semi-skilled workers in such important parts of the economy as the steel, rubber, textile, electrical appliance, and auto industries.

AFL leaders resisted efforts by the non-Communist left to enlarge the point of view of the labor movement. While the Communists attempted without success to organize industrial unions, the Socialists, the railroad unions, the needle trades, and several others battled for the nationalization of the railroads, mines, and water power; criticized imperialism; called for the abolition of the injunction in labor disputes; advocated recognition of the right to organize and bargain collectively; championed political action; and insisted that workers must be organized into industrial unions. AFL leadership made some concessions, as in endorsing the nationalization of the railroads and the candidacy of LaFollette, but did so without much enthusiasm, and contined to oppose social welfare legislation. Seeking to demonstrate their anti-communism, AFL leaders denounced the efforts by the Socialists and the progressives to swing labor to a more militant policy and curtailed the activities of the reformers in the labor press.

AFL leaders concentrated largely on preserving what had been gained in the past, but they failed for the labor movement had to contend with militant opposition to unionism. The federal administration, while taking some steps designed to benefit workers directly and expressing some sympathy for unions, did not provide as much protection and encouragement for them as Washington had done during the war and did not provide as much encouragement and help as the administration gave to business. Furthermore, Harding expressed a negative attitude toward unions when he intervened in the coal mine strike of 1922, and state governments in many places expressed anti-unionism by using frequently the militia in industrial disputes. The judicial branch of the government was especially important because almost no legislation had been passed on industrial relations and thus the common law (judge-made law) was supreme. Using their power to issue injunctions against strikes and labor's other weapons, the judges emphasized property rights, not the right of workers to organize, and defined property rights broadly. "Practically any normal action to convince management to agree to its proposals could be enjoined," one historian of labor has written, "and if the union failed to follow the court's orders, the union officials could be jailed or fined for contempt of court."

The anti-union efforts were accompanied by United States

Sources of Immigration and Quota Acts

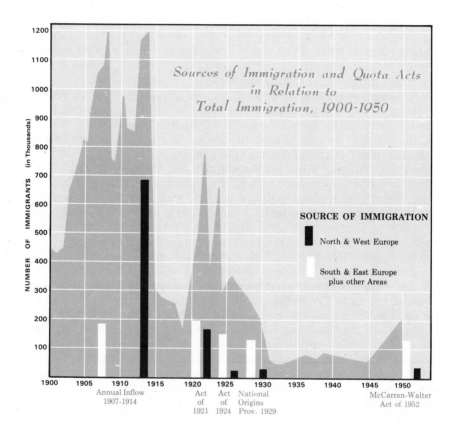

Sources of Immigration and Quota Acts
in Relation to
Total Immigration, 1900-1950

SOURCE OF IMMIGRATION

North & West Europe

South & East Europe
plus other Areas

Annual Inflow
1907-1914

Act   Act   National
of   of   Origins
1921   1924   Prov. 1929

McCarran-Walter
Act of 1952

Supreme Court decisions against efforts to use government to improve
the lot of workers. The Court invalidated a national anti-child labor
law and a District of Columbia minimum wage law for women. In
Adkins v. Children's Hospital (1923) Justice Sunderland spoke for the
Court in a five-to-three decision. He denounced special class legislation in the District of Columbia. Women, he said, have a right to bargain
their services without the interference of government. They can go
to another position if the terms of employment are unsatisfactory.
Society "cannot be better served than by the preservation against
arbitrary restraints of the liberties of its constituent members." This

case was but the most prominent of many decisions which invalidated social legislation.

Anti-unionism in business continued an old and very important theme. It was important, for business leaders were not only hostile to unions, but they also possessed the means required to make their hostility effective. To the typical businessman, unions and collective bargaining seemed to be irrational institutions that threatened the right of management to control the business and reduced industrial efficiency.

To combat unionism, businessmen used many devices. They expanded their use of old methods to destroy unions or prevent them from developing, including yellow dog contracts, labor spies, blacklists, strikebreakers, guards, and racial antagonism. They also developed new techniques, including more sophisticated employment of propaganda. The United States Chamber of Commerce and the National Association of Manufacturers conducted an "Open Shop" campaign, calling the open shop the "American Plan" and insisting that in America every man was free "to work out his own salvation." The propaganda also slandered labor leaders, portraying them as racketeers and Communists and the employers as fighting to free their workers from such people. Businessmen also stepped up their attention to human relations in industry, developing a system of "welfare capitalism" that included personnel departments, social science research, profit sharing, stock distribution, group insurance, retirement benefits, recreation programs, vacation pay, cafeterias, medical service, shop grievance committees and company unions. Although the motives behind welfare capitalism were complex, they included resistance to unions. Employers hoped that their workers would identify with their companies and feel no need for unions.

Thus, for several reasons, the labor movement declined in the 1920s. Along side the giant business organizations, labor was a puny force. American capitalism continued to move along a collectivist path, but the development was limited largely to the business sector of the economy. With help from government, business leaders developed their own organizations and combatted the not very vigorous efforts of union leaders to develop organizations for workers.

Rural America did not enjoy the prosperity of the 1920s, and one result was pressure for government action on behalf of the farmer. Many important politicians and business leaders recognized the existence of a "farm problem." They feared agrarian radicalism, so they helped farmers organize and endorsed government assistance to the farmer. They had a more positive attitude toward the farm movement than they had toward the labor movement. These business leaders and politicians joined with farm leaders who had a positive attitude toward the business system in efforts to make the farm business profitable once again, to fit the farmer into the system of collective capitalism, and to encourage him not to rebel against it. Little attention, however, was paid to the many rural people who lived below the poverty line.

The "farm problem" plagued a large but declining part of American life. In 1790, 90 percent of the work force was employed on the farm; by 1930, the percentage had dropped to 20. The farming community, as it was seen by many experts, suffered from low farm prices that meant little or no profit for the farm business. Farm income dropped from nearly $17 billion in 1919 to less than $9 billion in 1921 and did not reach $12 billion in any year during the decade. The situation resulted from the expansion of production, due largely to increased use of fertilizer and machinery, especially the tractor, and a fall in demand both at home and abroad. Encouraged by rising expectations as members of the American middle classes, commercial farmers added to their difficulties by borrowing money for the things they needed.

Rural people suffered also from a number of other problems that resulted in poverty for most of them. These problems included small farm units, poor land, and not enough machinery. Tenancy, insecure tenure arrangements, and unsteady work at low wages also plagued many farming areas.

Rural America contained a tradition of radicalism and protest, and that tradition was represented in the 1920s by such organizations as the Farmers Union and the Non-Partisan League, but these groups had to compete against an organization with a non-radical orientation that had taken shape from 1911 to 1920, the American Farm Bureau Federation. At first, it had been promoted by certain types of business people and public officials in the United States Department of Agriculture, the agricultural colleges, and their extension services who feared agrarian radicalism and hoped to make agriculture more prosperous by making it more scientific. The organization prospered, stabilizing at about 300,000 farm families in the 1920s, most of them in the Middle West, especially Iowa and Illinois. The members were the more substantial farmers, the rural businessmen. They seemed most capable of applying science, shared an interest in higher prices, and seemed likely to give the movement a non-radical bent. The organization also imitated rather than attacked urban business, organizing farmers as urban businessmen were organizing, forming marketing cooperatives, and engaging in political action which sought policies favorable to their interests.

The efforts to solve the farm problem produced a substantial amount of government action and demands for more. Research and education in the Department of Agriculture and the agricultural colleges were stepped up; the protective tariff was extended to agriculture; the meat packers, stockyards, and grain exchanges were brought under federal control; the government made loans to stimulate the export of farm products; legislation improved credit facilities for agri-

culture, and farm cooperatives were exempted from anti-trust pro-
hibitions. These moves reflected the strength of the farm bloc in Congress
as well as sympathy for the farmer in the Harding administration and
were designed to improve the farm business. They did not deal directly
with the problems of the rural poor, and, most troubling at the time,
they did not deal directly with farm prices.

An urban businessman, George Peek, tried to solve the price
problem. He had failed in his own busines, the Moline Plow Company,
during the farm depression, and he entered farm politics in 1921 for
both economic and political reasons. "You can't sell a plow to a
busted customer," he explained. And, fearing radicalism, he believed
that prosperous, independent, land-owning farmers would be a conservative force, and, rejecting trust busting and currency regulation, he devised a price-raising scheme that accepted the protective
tariff system and attempted to make it work for the farmer as it worked
for the industrialist. A government corporation would purchase
surplus farm products at the American price and dump them abroad
at the world price.

Congress endorsed Peek's plan, but the President defeated it. The
Farm Bureau and some businessmen endorsed the measure, and congressmen from rural areas voted for it, enabling it to pass in 1927 and
1928. It was opposed by most businessmen and by leaders in the administration, especially Hoover, and was vetoed successfully by Coolidge,
who charged that it violated economic laws and was class legislation.

The administration had its own farm plan, designed chiefly by
Hoover. It involved government promotion of cooperatives and efforts
by the cooperatives to establish "orderly marketing" and to encourage
farmers to bring production into line with demand. This plan, like
Peek's, encouraged farmers to behave like urban businessmen and was
put into operation with the passage of the Agricultural Marketing
Act and the establishment of the Federal Farm Board after Hoover
became President in 1929.

Cultural and Racial Tensions and Conflicts

Farmers felt threatened by more than inadequate farm prices.
They were also concerned about the destruction of their way of life
by the culture that they associated with the city. Thus, they fought
against urban culture in a variety of ways and were joined in the battles
by white, Anglo-Saxon Protestants who lived in the towns and suburbs.

According to the census taker, the city had become the home of
most Americans in 1920, and the urban areas continued to grow during
the Twenties. They no longer depended heavily on immigration from
Europe and depended much more on the migration of Southern blacks
and others from rural areas. By 1930, one-third of the population
lived in places over 100,000, 40 percent lived in communities of

Population Density, 1920

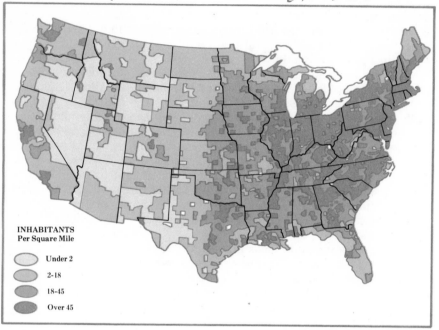

INHABITANTS
Per Square Mile

Under 2

2-18

18-45

Over 45

25,000 or more, and 57 percent lived in areas of more than 2,500.

The look and shape of the city changed during the decade. It became more congested with automobiles as well as people, and traffic jams, traffic cops, and traffic signs became familiar features. Cities grew upward at an accelerated pace with the building of many skyscrapers, climaxed by the construction of the Empire State Building; cities also grew outward at fast rate as people of means moved to the suburbs. Suburbia's growth owed much to the automobile and much also to middle class affluence, and its growth created problems for the central cities, such as the loss of taxable people.

While these population movements increased the segregation of American society along class, ethnic, and racial lines, other developments increased communication among people. Technological changes, especially the automobile, the truck, the radio, and the movies, drew people together, helping urban culture to influence rural life.

Cultural conflict took a variety of forms, including hostility toward immigrants. Congress, influenced in part by the coming of people

from Southern and Eastern Europe, passed highly restrictive and discriminating legislation. It used a quota system to separate national
groups, and the result was a sharp drop in immigration from Italy and
Greece in particular. But immigration from all countries was discouraged. The legislation marked the end of an era in which immigration
was a major theme in American history.

The revived Ku Klux Klan expressed similar conflicts. Founded
in Georgia in 1915, it spread beyond the South in the early 1920s and
had four to five million members by 1925. It appealed to groups with
a grudge against some minority group: Southerners and others who
wished to keep blacks in their places; political reactionaries who were
out to get liberals and radicals; "drys" (prohibitionists) who saw
"wets" to be in league with the Devil; nativists who resented the presence in the United States of recent immigrants; and intolerant Protestants who hated Catholics and Jews. Professing the deepest devotion
to Americanism, the Klan employed direct action to enforce its ideas.
It burned fiery crosses at night to make its presence known and in-
timidate its foes; it whipped blacks, aliens, and sinners, and participated in elections.

The centerpiece of cultural conflict was Prohibition. It had been
established before the 1920s, and the Eighteenth Amendment, which
outlawed the manufacture, sale, transportation, importation, and exportation of intoxicating liquors, went into effect at the beginning
of 1920. The amendment sought chiefly to dry up the cities where rural
youth, aided by the automobile, went to drink, and where drunken
and offensive behavior of city residents became a problem. State and
local efforts had been ineffective. Thus, Prohibition constituted an
effort by mostly rural, Protestant Americans to use the power of government to change the behavior of recent immigrants and Catholics who
lived in urban areas.

The experiment failed to achieve great success but managed to
hold on to much of its support. It did reduce drinking, especially
in rural areas and in small towns, but it was violated widely, especially
in the big cities where organized crime viewed the program opportun-
istically. The difficulties generated demands for repeal. They were
centered in the urban areas and led by Governors Alfred E. Smith of
New York and Albert Ritchie of Maryland. The foes of prohibition criticized it for enlarging the federal government, interfering with personal liberty and corrupting American life. Some people believed
that it justified civil disobedience and nullification, and many regarded it as generating contempt for the law. Yet, the experiment continued to have strong support, especially in the South and West and
among Baptists and Methodists. It was one of the major issues of the
decade.

Obviously, American life in the 1920s was more than economics.
It was also a period in which questions of culture or folk-ways and styles

of life meant very much to people and exerted a large influence on their political behavior. Representatives of an older America, living largely outside the big cities, felt threatened and employed many devices to defend their way of life. Representatives of a newer America, living mainly in the cities, fought back.

The racism involved in immigration policy also continued to influence relations between whites and blacks. But blacks were moving out of the South, where this form of racism was most prevalent and developing challenges to the American system of race relations. The system of Jim Crow that had been established well before the 1920s remained in place throughout the South. It involved the use of violence—lynching—as a system of control, laws that mandated segregation in nearly every area of life, virtually complete exclusion of Southern blacks from political life and discrimination against them in education and other public services. Nearly 90 percent of the black Americans lived in the South in 1910, but they moved out of the region in large numbers during the war and on into the 1920s, motivated by new economic opportunities due to the cutting off of immigration and by the hope of improving their political and economic conditions. Settling mainly in the central cities of the North and South, they obtained better educational opportunities and developed separate churches, businesses, banks, and other institutions. But they did not escape poverty because they were plagued by unemployment and job discrimination. They also encountered discriminatory practices in housing that contributed to their segregation into the poorer sections of the cities, and they did not find freedom from violence and Jim Crow. Segregation, in fact, was extended to transportation facilities in many communities and became widespread in Northern schools.

Yet, the migrants obtained a power base. As they could vote in the North, they increased their participation in politics, and in 1928, they elected the first black congressman in the twentieth century, Oscar De Priest, a Republican from Chicago.

Challenges to the system of race relations, which had emerged before the 1920s, continued to develop, but black protest was plagued by serious internal conflict. One group, the Urban League, emphasized economic problems, especially unemployment, and relied upon persuasion, seeking to urge employers to hire blacks, and unions to extend membership to blacks. However, the League enjoyed little success. The National Association for the Advancement of Colored People, composed of whites as well as blacks but with a black, W. E. B. Du Bois, as the key figure and representing the black middle class, protested against mob violence, segregation, disenfranchisement and limited job opportunities. The NAACP sought enforcement of the Fourteenth and Fifteenth amendments, gave much attention to the administration of justice, and battled for anti-lynching legislation but also achieved few victories. A. Philip Randolph emphasized working-class blacks, called for an alliance between white and black workers, advocated socialism, and formed the Brotherhood of Sleeping Car Porters; but he failed to mobilize many black workers. Marcus Garvey, on the other hand, who emphasized black pride, black solidarity and segregation, and who called for a return to Africa, gained support from many working-class blacks. And the New Negro Movement or Harlem Renaissance of Langston Hughes and others emphasized art, literature, and music—not economics and politics—and stressed race pride and enlarged black participation in American life. Dealing chiefly with themes from black life in America and protesting against materialism, racism, and repression, this movement received a significant amount of financial support and encouragement from whites and the black middle class but failed to make contact with the black masses.

The protests against racial prejudice, however, were not strong enough to win approval of the major civil rights proposal of the decade: an anti-lynching bill. Endorsed by Harding and passed by the House of Representatives, it was blocked by Southern filibusters in the Senate and was not pushed by Coolidge. No legislation or court decisions of the period attacked any parts of the Jim Crow system, contributing to the growth of black unhappiness with the Republicans, but blacks continued to distrust the Democrats.

The Rise of Women and Youth

The adoption of the Nineteenth Amendment in 1920 gave women the right to vote throughout the country, and the decade that followed gave them unusual, if frustrating, opportunities to find careers. More women than ever before challenged traditional ideas about woman's "place." Perhaps even more important, the widely endorsed idea of the moral superiority of women was challenged seriously. At least implicitly, many people argued that women are more like men than had long been assumed and thus could be permitted to behave like men in many different ways.

Most Americans continued to regard the home as the proper place for women, as the low voter turnout among women suggests, but women continued to increase their activities outside the home. They were encouraged to do so by the development of electrical appliances, the decline in the birth rate and the increase in the number of white collar jobs, as well as enfranchisement. Over two times as many women entered the job market as had done so from 1910 to 1920, bringing the total to ten million by 1929. Jobs were regarded as desirable for psychological as well as economic reasons. Employment gave women a degree of independence from men, and, by providing women with broader experiences, work experience enabled women to achieve greater self-confidence and higher aspirations. Yet, they encountered much discrimination, including lower wages and restrictions on entry into the professions, and their opportunities were limited also by competing demands of marriage and motherhood. They continued to be regarded as chiefly responsible for raising children. It was much more difficult to be both mother and worker than to be both father and worker.

Armed with the vote, women also stepped up their political activities. They joined political parties, voted, lobbied, and held office; they participated in reform movements like the League of Women Voters, the peace movement, and the social welfare movement; and they successfully promoted some reforms, such as child labor legislation. Yet, their efforts were weakened by internal conflict as women lost the unity provided by the suffrage battle and clashed along class lines, over the proposed equal rights amendment, and along partisan lines. Women's political efforts were weakened also by persistent discrimination. And, rather than use politics to produce major changes, women participated in a male-dominated political system; they did not develop an independent political movement with new goals for society. This suggested to some observers that women did not differ from men as much as many had assumed.

The attack upon the double standard had the same implication. The attack involved a demand by middle-class girls and women for a new freedom, comparable to that enjoyed by middle-class boys and men. The flapper symbolized the demand. She, according to Gilman Ostrander, "was the authentic personification of the twenties: a happily motherless child, smoking, boozing, petting, necking, joy-riding, doing the Charleston and Black Bottom; living for the moment; trying out every new thing and discarding every old thing." The demand for a new freedom could be seen in the sizable increase in public smoking and drinking by women and in the change in the sexual conduct of many of them. They talked more about sexual matters than in earlier decades, and necking was now regarded as normal. "None of the Victorian mothers," F. Scott Fitzgerald suggested, ". . . had any idea how casually their daughters were accustomed to be kissed." "The word 'neck'," a social historian observed, "ceased to be a noun; abruptly became a verb; immediately lost all anatomical precision." The use of birth control methods increased sharply; premarital and extramarital intercourse became more common; middle-class boys and men were more likely than in the past to have sexual relations outside of marriage with women of their own class.

Women's demand for a new freedom expressed itself in a number of ways. One was the dance craze that, according to one horrified observer, brought "the bodies of men and women in unusual relations to each other." The sharp change in female fashions, including the drastic reduction in the length of skirts, was part of the same phenomenon. The new styles provided greater freedom of movement and glorified youth and playfulness, not responsibility. The divorce rate also increased sharply, jumping from 100,000 in 1914 to 205,000 in 1929, and most divorces by then were initiated by women, reflecting unwillingness to tolerate situations they would have felt compelled to tolerate in the past.

Although propelled by several forces, the new freedom did not sweep all before it. The war, the new psychology, literature, movies, advertising, prosperity, and the automobile—often referred to as a "bedroom on wheels"—contributed to changing mores. The church did not resist these changes effectively, because for many people the church had been weakened by intellectual developments and by its own behavior, such as support of fundamentalism. The Scopes Trial in Dayton, Tennessee, advertised the conflict of traditional religious ideas with evolutionary doctrines. Two great men of the day, William J. Bryan and Clarence Darrow, opposed each other in a trial which had many notorious turns to it. Yet, most Americans resisted the pressures to change. As a result, the change in social behavior had the most influence on urban and suburban middle-class women.

For the history of youth also, a stage of life between adolescence and adulthood, roughly the years eighteen to thirty, the 1920s were significant. The decade's importance in the emergence of this stage of life is suggested by the great increase in enrollment in college and the style of college life. Less than 2 percent of the people 18 to 24 had been in college in 1890, but 4.7 percent were by 1920, and the percentage jumped to 7.2 to 1930. By then, total enrollment was more than 1.1 million while it had been only 157,000 forty years before. To middle-class youth, going to college seemed to be the thing to do. There, one could find the opportunities to "get ahead" and/or find a mate who was destined to succeed. Curricula emphasized preparation for a career and also invited the student to investigate many disciplines. The extracurricular activities seemed even more important to most of the students. They saw themselves as in a very important stage of life that deserved to be enjoyed before moving on to a place in a society that would differ greatly from the past and managed successfully only by people who were sensitive to and sympathetic with the new ways.

The greatest hero of the decade was Charles A. Lindbergh. A young man fascinated by machinery and skillful in handling it, he flew alone from New York to Paris in May 1927, the first person to do so. He was only twenty-five. Celebrated as both a representative of traditional American individualism and as a representative of the new America of the machine, he symbolized the new importance that technology gave to youth. Heroes and heroines, less real than Lindbergh, but almost as influential appeared on the screens of neighborhood theaters. Mary Pickford, Rudolph Valentino, and Bill Hart gave adventure, patterns of dress and conduct, and standards of art to an imitative public.

Mary Pickford: The Queen of the Silent Movies
(*University of Southern California*)

The Literary Rebellion

The 1920s was a very significant period in the history of American literature. It was a decade in which a substantial number of writers—F. Scott Fitzgerald, Ernest Hemingway, Sinclair Lewis, E. E. Cummings, John Dos Passos, Henry L. Mencken, T. S. Eliot, and Eugene O'Neill, among others, were at or near the peak of their powers. A striking feature of these literary intellectuals was their alienation from American society, their profound dislike for it or at least for what seemed to be its major features.

The alienation had several sources. It was influenced by prewar intellectual developments associated with Freud, Nietzche, Dostoevsky, Henri Bergson, William James, Henry Adams, and others that challenged the belief in the fixed character of moral values and the doctrine of progress. Instead, these intellectuals emphasized the dynamic character of life; the irrationality and lowliness of man; the importance of intuition and emotion; the relativity of values; and the decline of civilization. The war contributed by raising then dashing hopes; by discrediting ideas, leaders and institutions; by producing a sense of betrayal; and by strengthening and enlarging the ranks of the pessimists. And features of American life in the 1920s—hostility toward the intellectual and the artist, worship of the businessman, emphasis on money-making, and restrictions on drinking and on sex—offended the literary rebels.

Writers lashed out at the status of business in American life. Their criticism involved more than a protest against business power; it focused on values and expressed an unhappiness with the middle classes, both urban and rural. Middle-class Americans seemed to be corrupted by the business spirit and the closely related force of "Puritanism." They were loyal to the unworthy ideal of material success and were prone to legislate morality. They seemed to have rejected the value of individual freedom though they frequently paid lip service to it. The middle class had sacrificed individualism and embraced collectivism as a consequence of the temptations of material abundance. They had placed restrictions on themselves and others in order to get the material benefits of industrialism, by embracing certain habits of work requiring a concentration of energy and certain restrictions on speech and writing—on discussions of sex and socialism—that threatened the system.

The literary rebels represented a small but very discontented minority. They were prominent and quite widely read and did exert some influence, especially on young members of the middle classes, but they did not write best sellers. Their sales fell far below such writers as Gene Stratton Porter, Zane Grey, Edgar Rice Burroughs, and Harold Bell Wright who produced many best sellers and conveyed an old fashioned image. Their popularity suggests that many Americans were clinging to rather than rejecting traditional values, seeking certainty in a confusing, bewildering, fast-moving time.

The Triumph of Herbert Hoover

The triumph of Herbert Hoover in the presidential election of 1928 suggests that by the end of the decade Americans hoped that they could somehow get the best of both worlds, both the old and the new America. A champion of the new era, he also embodied some of the nation's traditions, and he opposed a candidate who seemed, in the eyes of many, to represent some of the worst features of the new society.

Hoover triumphed over a weak opposition party. The Democrats had become the minority party in the 1890s and had failed to hold on to the gains made under Wilson's leadership from 1912 to 1916. They had lost badly in 1920, receiving only 34.5 percent of the popular vote in the presidential election, losing every state in the Northeast, the Midwest and the Far West and carrying only eleven states, all of them in the South. The party suffered losses of record proportions in the congressional elections, and 1924 had been a disaster for the party had been torn apart by cultural conflict.

Al Smith was the leading Democrat candidate that year. Born and raised in a poor Irish Catholic neighborhood on New York City's East Side, he had turned to politics as his best opportunity for advancement, was sent to the New York Assembly by the Tammany Hall political machine. He became the Democratic leader there and was a champion of social welfare legislation. Elected governor in 1918, he served four two-year terms in the next ten years. He was supported by Tammany and other Democratic machines and by urban progressives and immigrant groups who viewed government as having obligations to enlarge opportunities and looked upon him as a symbol of what new Americans could accomplish and contribute. Concerned with protecting the individual against the hazards of industrial society and not seeking fundamental change or the redistribution of wealth, he championed a broad series of reforms and made himself into a strong candidate for the presidency as the governor of the most populous state and a sharp contrast with Coolidge.

Smith, however, encountered strong opposition in the South and West and failed to get the nomination. Anti-urban, anti-Catholic, anti-immigrant and anti-Tammany sentiments and the KKK were strong in the regions that opposed Smith. Speaking for the Bryan wing of the party, William Gibbs McAdoo opposed Smith, attacked Wall Street and monopolies, supported Prohibition and refused to criticize the Klan. The last issue split the party badly as the Northeast wing wanted to explicitly denounce it in the platform while the South and the West wanted to remain silent as the Republicans had and they won by a single vote. Then the party split over the presidential nomination as Smith and McAdoo refused to withdraw until after the ninety-fifth ballot. After nominating John W. Davis, the party suffered a major defeat in November when Davis picked up only 29 percent of the popular vote.

The controversial Al Smith became Hoover's opponent in 1928. The New Yorker obtained 41 percent of the popular vote, the best showing by a Democrat since 1916, but he obtained only eighty-seven electoral votes. Hoover, in short, won by a wide margin.

Hoover carried all of the Middle West and Far West. He did so in spite of Coolidge's vetoes of the farm plan. The strength of Republican traditions in the Midwest helped him and so did Smith's weaknesses. Many farmers could not believe that the New Yorker could understand their problems, and Hoover took advantage of this by representing himself as an Iowa farm boy steeped in the traditions of rural America. Many Midwesterners also feared Smith's Catholicism.

Hoover also broke the solid South, carrying Virginia, Texas, Tennessee, North Carolina, Florida, Kentucky, and Maryland. He accomplished this in spite of the strength of the Democratic tradition in the region. To many Southerners, the party seemed to be the guarantee of white supremacy. Hoover benefited from Smith's association with features of urban life that most Southerners did not like, including recent immigrants, hostility to Prohibition, and Catholicism. Hoover, in contrast, had been born in an Iowa village of old stock, Protestant parents and he endorsed Prohibition.

The Republican carried all of the urban industrial East except Massachusetts and Rhode Island. He benefited from middle-class prosperity and the consequent popularity of Republican policies. His admirers portrayed him as a great businessman and a great engineer who was to a significant degree responsible for that prosperity, and he associated himself and the Republican administration with the prosperity, promised to continue the beneficial policies, and warned that the Democrats would bring prosperity to an end. As he predicted in his acceptance speech, "given a chance to go forward with the policies of the last eight years, we shall soon, with the help of God, be in the sight of the day when poverty shall be banished from the nation." The new material abundance, he claimed, was a consequence of Republican adherence to the old principles of "free enterprise" and defense of "the American system" as compared with Democratic promotion of socialism.

Hoover, however, did not do as well in the nation's twelve largest cities as earlier Republicans had and failed for the first time to gain a Republican victory in Massachusetts. The Republican margin in those cities had been 1.5 million votes in 1920 and 1.3 million in 1924, but Smith now enjoyed a 200,000 vote margin. In Massachusetts, a vigorous campaign brought out 95 percent of the registered voters. It emphasized cultural factors as well as economics, with most Protestants battling for Prohibition. The Irish-Americans and recent immigrants, however, rejected Prohibition as an invasion of privacy and expressed their unhappiness about the heavy unemployment in the textile ills and shoe factories. Old stock people in the Bay State feared Smith as an uncultured politician and favored Hoover as a representative of an older America. The Irish regarded Smith as a folk hero, and the recent immigrants rallied behind him because of the opposition's attacks on Catholicism and immigrants, Prohibition, Smith's programs for urban workers, and the way in which he symbolized the ability of non-old stock groups to make valuable and positive contributions. Hoover failed to win because the Irish supported the Democrats as they had since the mid-nineteenth century and people of recent immigrant background deserted the Republicans.

Massachusetts, however, was not the nation, and Hoover carried it by a wide margin, receiving 58 percent of the popular vote. His victory seemed to suggest that the new era would continue to develop but that not all features of American life that had emerged in recent years would receive equal emphasis. Important elements from the past would remain important.

Hoover represented rule by a cultural group. The strongest element in it was business leadership, but the group included the whole of WASP America. Some elements in it, especially the farmers, were unhappy with the power of business leaders and the economic policies of the national government, but they were even more fearful of other groups and the policies that they might enact. Farmers yearned for leadership of a different sort, more sensitive to their values and needs, while the outsiders were unhappy not only with business rule but with WASP rule generally.

SUGGESTIONS FOR FURTHER READING

Allen, Frederick Lewis, Only Yesterday. New York, Harper, 1931.

Bernstein, Irving, The Lean Years: A History of the American Worker 1920-1933. Boston, Houghton Mifflin, 1960.

Burner, David, The Politics of Provincialism: The Democratic Party in Transition, 1918-1932. New York, Alfred A. Knopf, 1967.

Freedman, Estelle B., "The New Woman: Changing Views of Women in the 1920s," Journal of American History, LXI, 372-393.

Fite, Gilbert C., George N. Peek and the Fight for Farm Parity. Norman, University of Oklahoma Press, 1954.

Hawley, Ellis W., "Herbert Hoover, the Commerce Secretariat, and the Vision of an 'Associative State,' 1921-1928," Journal of American History, LXI, 116-140.

Heald, Morrell, The Social Responsibilities of Business: Company and *Community, 1900-1960.* Cleveland, Case Western Reserve University Press, 1970.

Higham, John, *Strangers in the Land: Patterns of American Nativism, 1860-1925.* New Brunswick, Rutgers University Press, 1955.

Hoffman, Frederick J., *The Twenties: American Writing in the Postwar Decade.* New York, Collier Books, 1962.

Leuchtenburg, William E., *The Perils of Prosperity 1914-1932.* Chicago, University of Chicago Press, 1958.

Margulies, Herbert F., "Recent Opinion on the Decline of the Progressive Movement," *Mid-America,* XL, 250-268.

McCoy, Donald R., *Calvin Coolidge: The Quiet President.* New York, Macmillan, 1967.

Murray, Robert K., *The Politics of Normalcy: Governmental Theory and Practice in the Harding-Coolidge Era.* New York, W. W. Norton & Co., 1973.

Nash, Roderick W., *The Nervous Generation: American Thought, 1917-1930.* Chicago, Rand McNally and Co., 1970.

Nevins, Allan and Frank B. Hill, *Ford.* New York, Charles Scribner's Sons, 1954, 1957, 1963.

Ostrander, Gilman M., *American Civilization in the First Machine Age: 1890-1940.* New York, Harper & Row, Publishers, 1970.

Pease, Otis, *The Responsibilities of American Advertising: Private Control and Public Influence, 1920-1940.* New Haven, Yale University Press, 1958.

Prothro, James W., *The Dollar Decade: Business Ideas of the 1920's.* Baton Rough, Louisiana State University Press, 1954.

Shannon, David A., *The Socialist Party of America: A History.* New York, Macmillan Co., 1955.

Sinclair, Andrew, *Prohibition: The Era of Excess.* Boston, Little, Brown & Co., 1962.

Williams, William Appleman, *The Tragedy of American Diplomacy.* Cleveland, The World Publishing Co., 1959.

Wilson, Joan Hoff, *Herbert Hoover: Forgotten Progressive.* Boston, Little, Brown & Co., 1975.

15

The Great Depression
and The New Deal

VERY QUICKLY IN THE FALL of 1929, the new era came to an end, at least the prosperity that had been its major feature did, and soon thereafter a New Deal took its place. The decade of the 1930s was dominated by a crisis, the Great Depression, and it was a time of change, although not revolutionary change. Above all, the 1930s experienced significant structural changes in American capitalism. It became much more highly collectivized. Big business, the strongest element in the structure by the end of the 1920s, survived the crisis but found itself dealing with a much larger and stronger government and a much larger and stronger labor movement by the end of the 1930s. Government and labor became much bigger under the pressures of the decade. These were significant changes, but even greater ones that often seemed possible during these tense years were not made. The apparent possibilities included anti-capitalistic revolutions. Traditions, business power, and reform, among other forces, stood in their way, blocking pressures from left and right.

The Coming of the Great Depression

At the outset, two questions face the student of the 1930s: Why did the economy turn downward late in 1929? Why did the downturn become a great depression? Experiences before and since 1929 indicate that business downturns need not become depressions. That is, they need not result in unemployment of the magnitude of the early 1930s. Several factors were involved; a simple explanation will not do.

The structural weaknesses in the economic system that had developed by 1929 contributed significantly to the depression. The system was composed of powerful businessmen, weak workers and farmers and a biased government. As a consequence, the economy depended heavily on the behavior of upper-income groups. To keep the economy moving forward, they had to buy luxury items and raw materials, provide jobs, invest in new or expanded enterprises, and lend money at home and abroad. They had to lend money in order to compensate for the inadequate purchasing power of workers, farmers, and foreigners relative to the tremendous productive power of the American economic system.

Although important, the structural weaknesses were not enough to produce depression. They left the economic system highly vulnerable to shocks. A major one hit in October 1929, the stock market crash. It was the triggering mechanism in the development of the crisis and resulted from a loss of confidence that stock prices would continue to spiral upwards as they had been for several years. Apparently, cuts in production earlier in the year by some important industries, including automobiles, produced the psychological change. The industries had decided that their production capacities were significantly greater than the market for their products, and their decisions to cut back communicated their concern about the future to careful observers among the many participants in the stock market. The crash, in turn, had a severely damaging impact on the key people in the economic system. Heavily involved in the market, they now lost both money and confidence and stopped playing the roles upon which the economy was so dependent. Rather than continue to stimulate economic growth, they cut wages, prices, production, employment, investment, and loans.

The stock market and the business cycle need not have continued their downward spirals but did so for more than three years because of a new shock in 1931. This was the economic collapse in Europe. It came largely because of the troubles in the United States because the economies on both sides of the Atlantic were closely linked. Americans, reeling under the impact of troubles at home, had cut back on the loans that had been so important to the European economy during the 1920s. The European collapse promoted further economic decline in the United States, for the Europeans, now with few dollars to spend, had to cut back on their purchases from the United States.

Still, the dismal conditions of the winter of 1932-1933 might have been avoided had the American government functioned more ef-

Economic collapse, 1929-1939			
	1929	1933	1939
Population (millions)	122	126	131
GNP (billions of dollars, 1929 prices)	104	74	111
Per capita GNP (dollars, 1929 prices)	857	590	847
Wholesale commodity prices (1926 = 100)	95	66	77
Farm products price index (1926 = 100)	105	51	65
Wheat price (current dollars per bushel, received by farmers)	1.04	0.38	0.69
Realized gross farm income (billions of current dollars)	13.9	7.1	10.6
Average weekly earnings for production workers in manufacturing (current dollars)	25.03	16.73	23.86
Unemployed (millions, followed by percent of labor force) (estimates only)	1.6(3)	12.8(25)	9.5(17)
Common stocks price index (1941-43 = 100)	260	90	121
Volume of sales on the New York Stock Exchange (millions of shares)	1,125	655	262
Bank suspensions	659	4,004	72

From Cole, *Handbook of American History*, p. 211.

fectively as the crisis took shape. The federal government, headed by President Hoover, was dominated by confidence in business, a willingness to use government for economic purposes and a fear of big government. Officials moved upon the problem but did not do so quickly and massively. They were unable quickly to fill the gap created by the retreat of businessmen from boldness in the economic arena. Instead, the Hoover Administration enlarged the role of government slowly and reluctantly. The President emphasized voluntary cooperation and the restoration of business confidence, and the Democratic Congress voted only modest sums of money for these purposes and a small public works program. It empowered the Administration, however, to set up a new agency in 1932, the Reconstruction Finance Corporation (RFC), which made some substantial loans to industrial and financial institutions, regarding them as corporate bodies of fundamental importance that must be preserved, and also made loans to the states. Hoover, although under some pressure from Congress to do so, did little to enlarge purchasing power for he did not regard it as crucial, and he tried to balance the federal budget, regarding that as necessary to revive business confidence. Businessmen, he believed, were convinced that the federal government must conduct a cautious fiscal policy. To balance the budget, he resisted major pressure for the expansion of government, pressures aimed in part at relief for the unemployed, and he even pressed successfully for an increase in federal taxes in 1932. His budget balancing efforts failed, due chiefly to the decline in federal revenue as the economy declined, and he resorted to deficit financing, but he kept the deficit very small.

Thus, the economy lost vigor because of structural weaknesses in the American economic system and the stock market crash. The downturn became a major depression as a result of the collapse of the European economy and the inadequacy of the recovery efforts by the federal government. The most obvious result was massive unemployment, as high as 15 million or 25 percent of the labor force in the winter of 1932-1933. Unemployment, often for long periods, afflicted white-collar as well as blue-collar workers and people who had been trained or educated for their jobs as well as those who had not. The Depression meant the loss of savings, investments, businesses, and homes as well as jobs. It meant inadequate food, clothing, and even shelter for many people. For farmers, it meant a sharp drop in farm prices, even sharper than the drop in prices of the things that farmers needed to buy. For more than a few, it means the loss of their farms and a decline in status from owner to tenant or from tenant to wanderer. For many, the Depression was a time of troubles psychologically as well as economically for it weakened or shattered confidence in themselves or in others. For nearly everybody, the Depression shattered confidence in traditional values and beliefs and in institutions and people, including the business system, business leaders, and Herbert Hoover.

Depression Politics

The Depression stimulated intense political debate, and the fundamental issue was: "How much change should be made?" Should the American economic system be maintained essentially as it was? Should it be modified in significant ways? Should a new system be substituted for it? Three of the major participants in the debate were President Hoover, the leading representative of American conservatism at the time, and two challengers, Norman Thomas, the leading spokesman for American radicalism, and Franklin Roosevelt, the leading spokesman for liberalism or what was then more often called progressivism. Their importance in 1932 as presidential candidates indicates that American voters then had a very significant choice to make. The differences among the candidates were real differences.

Hoover's confidence in the American economic system had not been shattered by the Depression. He still assumed that it was superior to all others and basically sound, although in need of some changes. It needed more cooperation in order to become more efficient, but it did not need the massive infusion of government that the Socialists, the Fascists, the Communists, and even the progressives seemed to desire. He disliked and feared them. America's troubles, he maintained at first, resulted from the misdeeds of speculators. As the Depression deepened, he found a new explanation: the Europeans. They had exported their weaknesses to the United States in 1931. In these explanations, he would not admit that there were fundamental defects in the American economic system. Rejecting the views of extreme conservatives like Andrew Mellon, he believed that the Depression demanded some government action, but he continued to emphasize voluntary cooperation, seeing it as the solution to business, farm, unemployment, and banking problems, and he resisted the pressure for a rapid expansion of the government's role and cost. He was forced by the seriousness of the crisis to accept more government action than he desired, first the RFC and then a small program of federal relief for the unemployed. By election time, he had expanded the role of the federal government in economic affairs, a development that reflected some confidence in government as well as great confidence in business, but he had done so hoping to prompt the recovery of the system, not to change it, and he now stressed the dangers of additional expansion. That would mean confidence-shattering spending, the loss of liberty, and the destruction of the American character. Americans, he insisted, must continue to rely upon themselves and upon one another, not upon the federal government in distant Washington.

Thomas used the crisis of 1932 to press forward with his call for socialism. He had begun his adult life as a Protestant clergyman and had moved from religion to pacifism and then to socialism while remaining more of a Christian than a Marxist. The Depression did not surprise him. It seemed to be the logical product of the workings of the capitalist system, and it surely helped his party to grow. By 1932, he was the leader of the largest radical organization in the country, the Socialist party. His platform was linked to the progressives in the calls for relief and reform, differing in no more than a degree in these areas, but socialism differed from progressivism in its call for revolution. The Socialists insisted upon public ownership and democratic control of the major industries. They had no confidence in the business system. Thomas and his associates differed from the Communists, who were also active in 1932, in their call for peaceful change. Socialists assumed that the forces of resistance were not so strong that they could not be overcome by the people using their power in the polling places, and the Socialists assumed that peaceful change would create a more desirable society, a liberal and democratic society rather than an autocratic and authoritarian system.

In contrast with Hoover and Thomas, Franklin Roosevelt called for a "New Deal," a somewhat vaguely defined system of reformed capitalism. FDR differed significantly in background from both Hoover and Thomas, having been born and raised in aristocratic circumstances. He had been influenced heavily by participation in Progressive politics and the Woodrow Wilson administrations. It had shaped his point of view, giving him definitions of both the desirable and the possible. The desirable seemed to be the use of the power of government for social and economic reform; the possible seemed to demand caution in the promotion of change, careful calculation of political realities, and efforts to maximize support. Politics had also provided an outlet for his ambitions, which early on reached to the White House and were not destroyed by a crippling bout with polio early in the 1920s. In 1928, he was elected governor of New York, and he served in that important office for the next four years.

Roosevelt differed from Thomas and resembled Hoover in his commitment to capitalism and his determination to preserve it, but he differed from Hoover in his willingness to make necessary changes in the system. He was more critical of big business than the President was, and he blamed the United States rather than Europe for America's troubles in the early 1930s. He argued, for example, that inadequate purchasing power in the United States was largely responsible. By 1932, he believed in many types of government programs: regulation of big business, conservation, public power, farm relief, old-age pensions, unemployment insurance, relief for the unemployed through public works and planning. Yet, he did not call for large-scale government spending and deficit financing, in part because he wanted the support of conservative Democrats but even more because he personally shared the fears that many people had of deficit spending.

In political philosophy Roosevelt was essentially a Progressive. He believed that government should become more important, but that business must not become unimportant, in national life. He believed that the role of government needed to be enlarged to make the economic system function successfully. And he believed that the system needed to be reformed in order to avoid a revolution. His New Deal, as defined in 1932, amounted essentially to a call for significant change in the structure of American capitalism. He would not destroy big business. He had little to say about labor unions. He emphasized the enlargement of government in the operations of the economy.

Roosevelt stood at the center of the American political spectrum in 1932. To the right was Hoover who had more confidence in business, less confidence in government and thus advocated less change. To the left stood Thomas, who had less confidence in business, more in government and thus advocated more change, revolution rather than

reform. And Thomas and Hoover were not at the poles. To the right
of Hoover were people like Andrew Mellon who had even less confidence in government; to the left of Thomas were the Communists
who insisted that only violence could destroy the established order.
Yet, the differences among these three presidential candidates were
discernible to the voters.

With significant alternatives available to them in November,
1932, American voters chose the center. They rejected both the right
and the left and did so by a wide margin in an election that generated rather wide interest.

Roosevelt won in a landslide. Fifty-seven percent of the voters
endorsed him; only 40 percent endorsed Hoover, a major change from
1928; only 2 percent voted for Thomas. Fifty-eight percent of the
adults voted, a rather high turnout, not high relative to the late nineteenth century, but higher than it had been throughout the 1920s.

FDR won by a wide margin in spite of the traditional strength of
the Republican party and the traditional weakness of the Democratic
party. The Democrats had won only two presidential elections since
1892, and those victories had come only after a major split in the Republican party. And the Democrats had lost by a wide margin as
recently as 1928, failing that year even to carry some traditional
Democratic states.

Roosevelt won also in spite of the predictions of the left. For years,
radicals had been predicting that capitalism would collapse and then
the masses would turn sharply to the left. Now, capitalism was close
to collapse, yet the voters had supported one of the pro-capitalist
candidates for the Presidency.

The victory had come because most farmers and workers backed
Roosevelt's candidacy. Their support for him was greater than it had
been for earlier Democratic candidates for the White House and was
substantial in spite of the cultural differences between farmers and
workers that had been such an important part of the politics of the 1920s.
Those differences had been submerged by the economic problems that
both groups now faced. Roosevelt's strength among farmers and workers
enabled him to be more successful than his predecessors in the Middle
West, Far West, and East. He added great strength in the Middle West
and Far West and substantial strength in the East to traditional Democratic strength in the South. He had added strength to the Democratic
cause outside the South while restoring the latter to solid support for
his party's presidential candidate.

Voter behavior in 1932 suggests that many people had given serious
thought to politics that year. Obviously, they were not dominated by
habit because many had voted differently than they had in 1928 and
many had broken with long-standing traditions. Apparently, most
voters wanted change, more change than Hoover would produce. They
wanted relief, jobs, higher farm prices, and the like. Apparently also,

An Evicted Sharecropper in New Madrid, Missouri *(Library of Congress)*

the desire for radical change was very weak. Even when one adds the votes for the Communist and the Socialist Workers parties to those for Thomas, the total is less than 3 percent. Some traditions had maintained great strength. In fact, 40 percent of the voters were so heavily influenced by tradition that they voted for Hoover.

Most voters, apparently, had great confidence in the political system and substantial confidence in the economic system. They did not want to scrap the latter and substitute something radically new for it. Instead, they assumed that the political system could make the economic system work successfully and serve their interests.

A disturbingly large number of people had no confidence or interest in either of the established systems or in their critics. Over 40 percent of the adults in the country did not vote. Some, especially most Southern blacks, were barred from doing so, but most of the non-voters made their own decisions. Lack of knowledge no doubt barred some from voting as effectively as anti-black voting laws barred others, but many, it would seem, knew about the candidates and issues and could vote but did not have enough confidence or interest to do so.

Roosevelt could ignore the non-voters for they seemed incapable of being mobilized for political action. He could conclude with confidence that he had a mandate for non-radical change. He was obligated both to maintain capitalism and make changes in it. He was obligated to give the American people a New Deal. If he did not, he assumed, then most of the politically active people would demand radical change.

The Development of the New Deal

With financial disaster visible, Roosevelt opened his first term on March 4, 1933, in the traditional place before the East portico of the United States capitol. His powerful address, warning of the emergency confronting the nation, set the tone of his administration:

> It is to be hoped that the normal balance of executive and legis-
> lative authority may be wholly adequate to meet the unprece-
> dented task before us. But it may be that an unprecedented demand
> and need for undelayed action may call for temporary departure
> from that normal balance of public procedure. I am prepared under
> my constitutional duty to recommend the measures that a stricken
> nation in the midst of a stricken world may require.

On that day Roosevelt gave the people a preview of his personality. Probably no President had a better grasp of the English language, and none had the charm, humor, and enthusiasm that he possessed. He was both a cultured person and tenacious leader, who seized opportunities as they presented themselves and who had a sense of drama. Inspiring loyalty, he gathered around him educated people, created a "Brain Trust," and welcomed any one with ideas.

President Hoover and Roosevelt en route to the Inauguration Ceremony
(*Franklin D. Roosevelt Library*)

His first act in office was the declaration of a national bank holiday. Congress met soon after in special session and passed An Emergency Banking Law, providing for an early end of the holiday but granting him power to regulate banking practices. The drama of these critical days, with an address on radio, the President speaking before Congress, and the closing of the banks, gave the people a feeling of hope.

Roosevelt was of course deeply committed to the preservation and reform of American capitalism, and these events surrounding the banks emphasized his concern for the safety of deposits and availability of credit. Banks had been failing at a record rate, and confidence in them was low, but Roosevelt did not press for nationalization of them, as Norman Thomas surely would have done. He advocated instead quick restoration of normal banking, succeeded in getting the banks back into operation, keeping only a few unusually weak ones permanently closed, and restored public confidence in the banking system.

The centerpiece of the early New Deal, the National Recovery Administration, also testified to the commitment to capitalism.

Dominated by the assumption that big business was here to stay, this program relied heavily on the trade associations, those institutions in which Hoover had such great confidence, and it emphasized price raising, production control, and the enlargement of profit. Far from a complete success, NRA did help to check the downward spiral of the economy.

The main program for the farmer, the program administered by the Agricultural Adjustment Administration, supplied similar evidence. The Triple-A emphasized production control as the means of raising farm prices and making the farm business profitable once again. It employed the powers of government to help farmers regulate production the way industrial corporations regulate their production, and it did help the farm business become more profitable.

Other features of the New Deal also testified to the pro-capitalistic bent of the New Deal. The laws establishing federal regulation of the stock market and creating a new agency, the Securities Exchange Commission, for this purpose were based on the assumption that the stock market was an essential part of the system and sought to strengthen rather than destroy the market. The Tennessee Valley Authority, perhaps the closest to socialism that the New Deal moved, stimulated business and industrial development in the region by supplying cheap electrical power but waiting for non-government groups to take advantage of it. The Reciprocal Trade Program, which battled against the barriers to international trade that had developed in recent years, aimed at the opening of markets, especially for the products of American industry. And the Motor Carrier Act attempted to stabilize the trucking industry by controlling entry into it and regulating rates.

This emphasis upon helping capitalism recover its vitality raises an interesting question. Why was the preservation of capitalism such an important goal of government at this time? The system had, after all, performed rather badly. Part of the answer is the power of businessmen. Their prestige had declined under the impact of the Depression, but they had held on to much else. Many of them were already in Washington when Roosevelt arrived. Some of them, carryovers from the Hoover administration, contributed significantly to the development of the banking program. Also, business leaders knew how to operate in politics and had the money and organization required to do so. Thus, a president of the United States Chamber of Commerce, Henry Harriman, played a large role in the development of NRA and in other areas, and a major representative of the rural businessmen, the American Farm Bureau Federation, participated actively in the development of the farm programs. And businessmen were widely regarded as important and knowledgeable. Thus, for example, Roosevelt turned to Joseph Kennedy, an active participant in the stock market, to serve as first chairman of the SEC, confident that he could gain the support for it that it needed. Furthermore, other groups, such as consumers, workers, and tenant farmers, were quite weak in 1933. They did not have substantial amounts of money to devote to politics, were poorly organized and had, except for a few labor leaders, no more than a small amount of political experience.

The administration's point of view was also important. It held that capitalism was superior to the alternatives in spite of its obvious weaknesses. And administration leaders believed that they must have the cooperation of businessmen in order to succeed with recovery efforts. They tried especially hard to gain the cooperation of the automobile manufacturers.

In addition, the point of view of nearly all Americans contributed to the result. Most of them were disillusioned with business leaders and blamed them (and/or Hoover) for the Depression. Yet, the people were not ready to scrap capitalism. They had demonstrated that in the 1932 elections.

Obviously, the New Deal was not a revolution. Its strong commitment to capitalism is a massive fact that contradicts suggestions that it was. The New Deal, instead, sought to preserve capitalism in a crisis situation that seemed to threaten its existence. The New Deal functioned to preserve capitalism because most Americans desired its preservation, not just because economic and political elites did.

Roosevelt and the New Deal did not, however, try merely to preserve American capitalism as it had developed by 1929. That system seemed inherently unstable and unjust, incapable of operating successfully very long and of serving adequately the interests of the various groups of Americans. Capitalism had to be reformed in order to survive. It also had to be reformed in order to serve the interests of the American people more satisfactorily. Thus, from 1933 to 1936, New Dealers worked quite effectively to reform capitalism, chiefly by altering its structure, enlarging the role of government substantially and providing a basis for the growth of organized labor.

The expansion of government can be illustrated by contrasting New Deal policies with those of Hoover. The New Deal gave the federal government more power than Hoover favored. The force of law, not merely voluntary cooperation, governed the relations between NRA and the trade associations. The AAA used the taxing and spending powers of the federal government, not merely verbal appeals, to persuade farmers to cut back on their production. Also, the New Deal spent more money. In fiscal 1933, Hoover's last and most extravagant year, the federal government spent $4.6 billion. Three years later, the Roosevelt Administration spent $8.5 billion.

Some of the new powers and dollars were used to change the behavior of American business. NRA sought to affect production, prices and the treatment of workers and, among other results, reduced the amount of child labor in the nation. The Securities Act and the Securities Exchange Act forced businesses issuing securities to supply potential customers with more information about the business and established a regulatory agency to look after the job. The Wagner or National Labor Relations Act established another agency, the National Labor Relations Board, and empowered it to force industrialists to stop what were defined as "unfair labor practices."

The federal government was also enlarged so that it could do things that business could not do, or at least would not do. Some of the New Deal agencies—the Public Works Administration, the Federal Emergency Relief Administration, the Civil Works Administration, the Civilian Conservation Corps, the Works Progress Administration and the National Youth Administration—could invest and supply jobs. Others, including the AAA, the TVA, the CCC and the Soil Conservation Service, had the power to conserve and improve the use of natural resources. The TVA and the Rural Electrification Administration, among others, supplied customers with inexpensive electrical power. The Social Security program provided workers with unemployment insurance and old-age pensions, and the Resettlement Administration, more than any other part of the early New Deal, had as its assignment the improvement of the lives of the rural poor, a largely neglected group in the past.

Other New Deal programs sought to reduce the power of business through direct legislative attacks upon it. The tax legislation of 1935-1936 had this as an announced aim, although it was very mild legislation and its efforts to tax the wealthy were offset by the taxes designed to support the Social Security program because they hit workers rather hard. The Banking Act of 1935 reduced the power of the large banks by increasing the power of the Federal Reserve Board in Washington.

Finally, a few leaders of the New Deal in these years wanted to empower the government to reduce the size of large business organizations. The most notable of these people was Louis Brandeis, who was still a member of the United States Supreme Court but had close ties with some members of the Roosevelt Administration. A Public Utilities Holding Company Act was passed in 1935 that gave the SEC some power to break up large holding companies, but the legislation was ineffectual. The government, however, was not ready to launch a large scale anti-trust campaign at this time.

In addition to enlarging the federal government in various ways, the New Deal also affected the structure of the economic system by providing a legal basis for the growth of the labor movement. The National Industrial Recovery Act of 1933, which established NRA, included a provision guaranteeing workers the right to form unions and bargain collectively, and it stimulated some growth of the labor movement but was resisted by business leaders and not effectively enforced by the administration. The Guffey-Snyder Coal Act of 1935 sought to increase collective bargaining in the coal industry. Much more important, the Wagner Act of that year declared that workers had the right to bargain collectively in organizations that they, rather than their employers, controlled, outlawed "unfair labor practices" by employers that violated that right and established the National Labor Relations Board to enforce the law. The law constituted a big change in policy. Usually hostile or at best indifferent to the labor movement, the national government had never before offered it so much help.

Why was there such an active reform movement from 1933 to 1936? The answer lay largely in the popular convictions shared by Roosevelt and Congress that capitalism must be reformed and that the federal government could remove the defects from the economic system. These convictions were not merely the product of the Depression, but were the essence of the progressive tradition. The Depression, however, made capitalism's defects more obvious and reduced the prestige of business leaders. Roosevelt and other New Dealers had endorsed them for years, and more people did so now.

The performance of the economy and the behavior of the businessmen after Roosevelt came to power strengthened the influence of progressivism. The economy began to recover but recovered only slowly, a fact that suggested to many that purchasing power needed to be enlarged much more rapidly. Most business leaders resisted reform, a pattern of behavior that seemed foolish and shortsighted to Roosevelt and others and suggested that businessmen should not be so powerful.

Reform in these years was a popular movement, not just something imposed by elites. Elites were at work, including the people who clustered about the President, but they had popular support and responded to popular pressure. In fact, the Democratic party strengthened its hold on Congress in the 1934 elections, which was a major achievement. Customarily, the party in power lost ground in the congressional elections, but the people rallied to the cause of reform in 1934.

The possibility of undesirable political developments also stimulated reform in this period. If reforms were not made, Roosevelt reasoned, the revolutionaries might gain widespread support, and he might be defeated in 1936. These possibilities suggested to him, especially in 1935, a year of great importance in the history of American reform, that he must strengthen himself and his party with lower income groups.

For reasons already given, the New Deal did not promote even more change in these years. The opponents of change had strength and Roosevelt and other New Dealers recognized it and concluded that they must make compromises. Furthermore, the New Dealers were committed to capitalism and other parts of the American past. Roosevelt's persistent fears of large-scale deficit spending illustrated this dramatically. He would tolerate only small deficits in the federal budget. (The deficit for fiscal 1936 was only $3.5 billion.) Roosevelt's fears

The New Deal President (Franklin D. Roosevelt Library)

persisted in spite of the presence in his administration of "Keynesians" like Marriner Eccles who advised that large-scale deficit spending was the way to move the economy out of the Depression. This was the policy area in which the President worried most about "business confidence," and he assumed that most people opposed such advice.

Roosevelt and the New Dealers were cautious and restrained, but they were promoting change. They did not stress the scaling down of the size of big business, but they did reduce its power, chiefly by enlarging the federal government and its power and also by encouraging the growth of labor unions. The New Deal was thus changing the structure of American capitalism, moving it farther down a collectivist path. The goal was change in the performance of the system—a higher standard of living, a better distribution of the products, and the avoidance of depressions—a type of capitalism that would function satisfactorily from a democratic point of view.

The Triumph of the New Deal

As it developed, the New Deal became very controversial, but it triumphed impressively over its opponents in the 1936 elections. It was criticized from both right and left. One group of critics stressed the changes that it made; another emphasized the changes that were not made; each deplored what it saw. Most voters, however, supported Roosevelt and his party.

Conservatives charged that the New Deal was producing too much change. They were represented at the time by established organizations like the United States Chamber of Commerce, the American Bankers Association and the National Association of Manufacturers and new groups, including the Liberty League. They charged that the New Deal was a revolution. It was "un-American;" it was creating absolutism or totalitarianism, also bureaucracy and socialism; it was spending too much. Conservatives called for sharp cuts in government activities and for a positive attitude toward business. They suggested, for example, that Roosevelt should substitute businessmen for the intellectuals and politicians who seemed so important in the development of the New Deal. They insisted that recovery depended upon the development of a more positive attitude toward business in Washington. They hit the "business confidence" theme very hard. The concerns of conservatives included status and power as well as economics. All of them—the power, status, and profit of the businessmen—seemed to be threatened by the New Deal. The conservatives held on to and propagated a long-established intellectual tradition in order to recover what they seemed to be losing.

Radicals, on the other hand, insisted that the New Deal was not producing nearly enough change. Thomas was not the only advocate of this point of view. A diverse group, including an intellectual, Alfred Bingham; a Catholic priest, Charles Coughlin; a Southern senator, Huey Long; and a California doctor, Francis Townsend, saw short-comings of this sort in the developments in Washington. Such people insisted that the New Deal was not socialism, was dominated by and serving capitalists, international bankers and the like, was not doing enough for the unemployed workers and the farmers and was harming tenant farmers and consumers. They called for the expansion of government in various ways, all designed to solve the problems of lower income groups. Some called for the establishment of a cooperative commonwealth or socialism, insisting that business power must be destroyed and rejecting the reformer's basic assumption about the ability of government to make capitalism work satisfactorily. The views of Coughlin, Long, and Townsend in this area were less clearly defined. They called for specific changes, seeming to regard them as enough. Coughlin emphasized the nationalization of the banks and government management of the money system; Long called for a redistribution of wealth, and Townsend advocated the payment of $200 per month to each person over sixty who would retire and spend the money during the month. Perhaps they should not even be classified as radicals, for they did not call for the destruction of business power, but they did insist that not enough change was taking place under Roosevelt's leadership.

Thus Roosevelt remained in the middle just as he had been in 1932. Seeking both to preserve and to reform capitalism, he alienated both those who believed that capitalism did not need to be changed and those who wished to discard it.

In 1936, the American people once again had several choices available, and once again, they chose the center, doing so, in fact, by an even wider margin than they had in 1932. Once again, they rejected the candidate of the right and the candidates of the left. Their political behavior suggests that most politically active Americans were pleased that Roosevelt had changed American capitalism but had not substituted another system for it.

Alfred M. Landon, the governor of Kansas and the Republican candidate for the Presidency, represented the American right. He did not identify with the Liberty League, but he was supported by it, and he clearly did not favor as many changes as Roosevelt had made. He received less than 37 percent of the popular vote and was supported by most business leaders and professional people and most old stock, middle class, Protestant Americans in the towns and suburbs. They were influenced by strong attachments to the Republican party and/or dislike for the changes that had been made since 1932.

Once again, Thomas spoke for the radical left. Indicating clearly that he would destroy business power and substitute socialism, he received less than 1 percent of the popular vote, an even smaller amount than in 1932.

William Lemke, a North Dakota congressman and the candidate of the Union party, represented a less clearly defined form of radicalism. Supported by Coughlin and others, he called for changes that were spelled out in rather vague and confusing terms. About 2 percent of the voters backed him.

Faced with this diverse battery of opponents, Roosevelt enjoyed a landslide victory. In his campaign, he appealed to non-Democrats as well as Democrats for he recognized that most Americans were not Democrats by tradition. He pointed with pride to the changes that had been made since 1932 and promised more of the same. His reward was nearly 61 percent of the popular vote.

Roosevelt had the support of a complex coalition of voters. They included people who had not voted before and people who had voted for others, including both Thomas and Hoover. He was more attractive than his opponents to people who had not been inclined to vote, and turnout increased, although it did not return to the level of the late nineteenth century. His coalition included more workers than it had in 1932 and more blacks. For the first time, most black voters supported a Democratic candidate for the Presidency. His coalition also included more union members than it had in 1932 and most farmers, most women and most intellectuals.

Several influences affected voter behavior. Those who voted for Roosevelt were not influenced only by the attractiveness of the changes that had been made since 1932. Some Southern Democrats voted for him in spite of their dislike for those changes and were affected mainly by the hold of the Democratic tradition on them. Those who had greater enthusiasm for him and his policies were not influenced only by the attractiveness of the economic changes. Ethnicity, religion, race, status, and patronage also exerted influence. And Roosevelt supporters were not swayed only by enthusiasm for the changes that the New Deal had made in the structure in the economic system. Many farmers who voted for him did so in spite of their unhappiness with the enlarged role of government in their lives. Above all, the Roosevelt voters were influenced by the results of the structural changes: jobs, higher farm prices, greater security, and the like.

With alternatives available, the American people had obviously given some thought to politics. They admired Roosevelt as a person, were impressed with his radio appeals, and appreciated his pledges of help in times of need. Many people wanted changes, but not revolution, and favored his programs. By their votes, they had produced a change: the Democratic party was now stronger than before. Even more important, they gave new encouragement and strength to the builders of big government and big labor.

The Troubles and Triumphs of the Late 1930s

Roosevelt's second term has often been interpreted as a failure, and his effectiveness as a reformer did decline somewhat after 1936. This was the period, however, in which the United States Supreme Court changed its ways and the labor movement grew rapidly, partly as responses to pressures from the New Deal. It was also a period in which Roosevelt became more of a Keynesian than he had been and in which he made his strongest attack upon the size of business organizations. It was also a period of accomplishment in the development of the welfare state and of agricultural planning. Yet, the President did have more trouble with Congress than earlier, and he did not accomplish as much as his spectacular victory in 1936 had led people to expect. A new force placing limits on the change that FDR could promote emerged in this period: the Conservative Coalition in Congress.

The new enthusiasm for Keynesianism, with its emphasis on fiscal policy as the means of controlling the performance of the economy, grew out of the recession that hit the economy in the fall of 1937. This abrupt interruption in recovery seemed to result from sharp cuts in federal spending and was not ended by a continuation of a cautious fiscal policy. Harry Hopkins, the head of WPA, a program of work relief for the unemployed, pushed the Keynesian position most effectively at this juncture, and his arguments were officially and publicly endorsed by Roosevelt in April 1938, when he called for an increase in federal spending and explicitly embraced fiscal policy as a way to promote recovery. Congress responded both by cutting taxes and increasing spending, and the economy quickly moved upwards once again, thereby strengthening the reliance on fiscal policy.

The attack upon business size also resulted from the recession. While some blamed it on faulty fiscal policy, others blamed business power, arguing that businessmen had damaged the recovery efforts by administering prices and refusing to invest. In response, the government established the Temporary National Economic Committee to investigate the distribution of power in the economic system and make recommendations for changes and employed the anti-trust laws with new vigor in a campaign headed by Thurman Arnold, a lawyer recruited from the Yale Law School to serve as Assistant Attorney General. These efforts, although strenuous, did not accomplish nearly as much as the simultaneous use of fiscal policy.

The development of the welfare state also moved forward during this period. To Social Security, the WPA, and other welfare programs, the administration and the Congress added the Wagner Housing Act and the Fair Labor Standards Act. The first authorized the construction of a small number of public housing units, and the latter attempted to place a floor under wages, and a ceiling over hours and to cut back still more on the employment of children. At the same time, Congress substituted a Farm Security Administration for the Resettlement Administration in an effort to strengthen and redesign the attack upon rural poverty.

The administration also made a significant effort to improve agricultural planning. The Secretary of Agriculture, Henry A. Wallace, made the department's Bureau of Agricultural Economics the Central planner for the farm programs, and the BAE embarked upon a vigorous campaign to coordinate the several farm programs and to draw various groups, including farmers as well as physical and social scientists and government officials, into the planning process.

Much of the New Deal irritated members of Congress, who joined with newspaper critics to assault the administration. In the late 1930s a Conservative Coalition was drawn together by many grievances, irritations, and suspicions. Roosevelt's attack upon the United States Supreme Court and the intense labor-management conflict of the period influenced this development, as did the recession and the recovery from it. The recession damaged Roosevelt's prestige, while recovery reduced the sense of emergency. The growing importance of urban groups in American politics contributed significantly, and so did the growth of the federal government and of organized labor. The New Deal's apparent threats to class and race relations influenced congressional behavior, as did resentment of the growing power of the Presidency relative to the power of Congress.

The coalition produced troubles for Roosevelt but could not defeat him on every issue. Opposed to most of the New Deal, it was composed of many Southern Democrats and most Republicans in the Congress. The members had secure holds on their congressional posts and thus did not believe that they needed to support the President in order to succeed in politics, and most of them represented rural areas. They had the support of and were influenced by the United States Chamber of Commerce, the National Association of Manufacturers, many of the leading bankers, representatives of the private electrical power companies, local businessmen and the American Farm Bureau Federation. They defeated Roosevelt in 1938 on taxes and on reorganization of the executive branch, were helped by urban-rural tensions in the reform coalition but were weakened by their own conflict over issues and party affiliation that weakened their ability to cooperate. Two of Roosevelt's failures in 1938, his failure to bring about the defeat of some conservative Democrats in the primary elections—the "purge"—and the Republican comeback in the congressional elections that fall, strengthened the coalition.

It exerted a substantial influence on Roosevelt. In 1939, he relaxed his pressure for new programs and emphasized preservation of established programs, a strategy that led to a mixture of victories and defeats. Although not completely unsuccessful in his dealings with Congress, he was much less successful than he had been in his first term, especially in obtaining legislation to benefit urban groups. His troubles contributed to his decision to run for an unprecedented third term in 1940 for he feared the triumph of a conservative in the presidential election, and the outcome, while a victory for him, revealed that he had become more dependent than before on urban support—on the workers, the new Congress of Industrial Organizations, and the big city political machines.

Although there were important New Deal-type changes during Roosevelt's second term, there were not as many as seemed to be forecast by Roosevelt's spectacular victory in 1936. His efforts as a reformer were limited effectively by the conservatives. Their ranks grew, and they offered more effective resistance in Congress than they had during the first term. The conservatives did not stop change in the country at large, but they made it increasingly difficult for Roosevelt to persuade Congress to give the federal government new power to alter American life.

Roosevelt had greater success with the United States Supreme Court. For four decades before the 1930s, it had hampered significantly the efforts to develop a collectivistic type of capitalism. It had not interfered in important ways with the development of big business, but it had created major problems for people who tried to develop strong labor unions and large roles for government in economic affairs. The Court continued to function in this way during the early years of the New Deal.

In 1935-1936, it invalidated the National Industrial Recovery Act, arguing that it involved an unconstitutional delegation of power and an unconstitutional effort to regulate intrastate commerce, and the Agricultural Adjustment Act, maintaining that it used the taxing power in an unconstitutional way and made an unconstitutional effort to regulate production. The Court also overturned the Guffey-Snyder Act, seeing it as an improper effort to regulate intrastate commerce, and a state minimum-wage law for women, insisting that it violated the "liberty of contract" that was protected by the Fourteenth Amendment. It seemed likely that as soon as it had the chance, the Court would destroy the Social Security program and the Wagner Act, and the prospect encouraged Roosevelt to ask Congress in 1937 to empower the president to enlarge the Court, adding one member for each one over seventy who chose not to retire, a request that brought a battle of words in Congress and a denial of legislation.

A new Court emerged after 1936 and began to do so even before any changes were made in personnel. Two justices, Charles Evans Hughes and Owen Roberts, desiring to protect the Court and other institutions that seemed to be threatened by Roosevelt, the popular mood, and the labor movement, changed their voting position. This shift created a new majority and permitted the Court to uphold a state social welfare

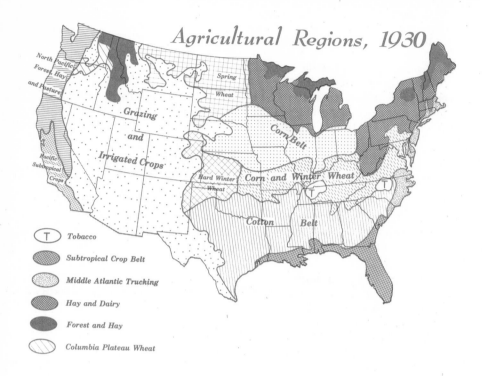

Agricultural Regions, 1930

North Pacific Forest, Hay and Pasture

Spring Wheat

Grazing and Irrigated Crops

Corn Belt

Pacific Subtropical Crops

Hard Winter Wheat   Corn and Winter Wheat

Cotton Belt

(T) Tobacco

Subtropical Crop Belt

Middle Atlantic Trucking

Hay and Dairy

Forest and Hay

Columbia Plateau Wheat

law, the Wagner Act, and Social Security.

From 1937 to 1941 Roosevelt had many opportunities to make appointments to the Court, thus enlarging the new majority. One appointee, Hugo Black of Alabama, caused much public anger and public criticism, because of his former connections with the Ku Klux Klan. Otherwise, the Court gained prestige with its new membership.

The new Court emphasized judicial restraint in economic affairs. Not dominated by fear of government action as their predecessors had been, the new majority assumed that economic legislation was constitutional. They assumed that the state and national governments had the power to act in economic affairs as they had decided to act, and thus the Court must permit them to do so. They accepted New Deal legislation and similar laws passed by the states, often overturning doctrines to reach this result. As a consequence, economic policy was now largely in the hands of elected officials. They could enlarge the role of government if they believed they should do so. The new tendency in the Court also facilitated efforts to build unions and to use the power of unions. The Justices, for example, interpreted peaceful picketing

Unemployed Squatters During the Depression *(Chicago Historical Society)*

as a form of speech and thus as protected by the United States Constitution.

A major obstacle in the path of the development of collective
capitalism had been removed, and the New Deal, to a significant degree,
was responsible for the change. The New Deal reflected and generated
the pressures that produced it.

Perhaps the most important development of the late 1930s was
the emergence of a large and strong labor movement. When Roosevelt
came to power, organized labor had only 2.8 million members. By
1941, the number had jumped to 8.4 million. The chronology suggests
that the New Deal was responsible for the change, and it was very important, but it was not the only force at work.

The Depression contributed significantly but is far from the total
explanation. It reduced the confidence that workers had in business
leaders and suggested to workers that they should not depend so
heavily on their employers. Yet, at the beginning, the depression promoted decline of the labor movement. Membership dropped from 3.5
million in 1929. If the Depression had been the only force affecting

unions during the decade, organized labor might have been destroyed in spite of the disillusionment with business leadership experienced by many workers. The movement was so weak by 1932-1933 that it did not contribute significantly to Roosevelt's victory, and he chose a social worker, Frances Perkins, rather than a labor leader, as Secretary of Labor and she emphasized social welfare legislation rather than the growth of unions as the way to improve the lives of wage earners.

The New Deal, in a sense, came to the rescue of the labor movement, passing pro-union legislation, especially the Wagner Act of 1935. In this, Senator Robert Wagner of New York was much more influential than Roosevelt, who did not have a strong interest in unions. The strong champions of the Wagner Act believed that unions were essential for both political and economic reasons. They could offset the political and economic power of the corporations. The legislation seemed necessary in order to force a change in the behavior of employers and thereby give unions a chance to come into existence, grow and function.

The legislation stimulated organizing efforts that enjoyed some success but was not enough to produce a large and effective labor movement. The administration did not enforce it vigorously at first, fearing that efforts to do so might hamper recovery, and employers resisted, refusing to conform to its requirements after failing to prevent its enactment. Hoping to avoid dealings with independent unions, employers continued to use anti-union weapons: company unions, spies, force, strikebreakers, propaganda, the dismissal of workers who joined or tried to organize unions, the eviction of such people from company houses and the denial of credit to them at company stores. And the employers received help in many places from state and local officials who, fearing that the companies might move away, made use of police and National Guard units and injunctions to check organizing drives. Those who defied the Wagner Act assumed that the Supreme Court would declare it to be unconstitutional.

Other people, however, backed up the legislative efforts. New Dealers such as Senators Wagner and La Follette (son and namesake of the distinguished Wisconsin governor and senator) defended the Wagner Act and the National Labor Relations Board and publicized anti-union activities.

The New Deal was important, and so was the United States Supreme Court after Hughes and Roberts joined the new majority. They had voted against the NIRA and the Guffey Snyder Act, but now upheld the Wagner Act, even declaring that it was a rational response to the existence of big business. Then the new majority upheld the work of the NLRB, enabling it to function more effectively as a foe of traditional anti-union practices, and assisted the labor movement in other ways. The Court's actions put great pressure on businessmen to behave in accord with the law of the land.

Decline and Recovery of the National Economy, 1925-1945

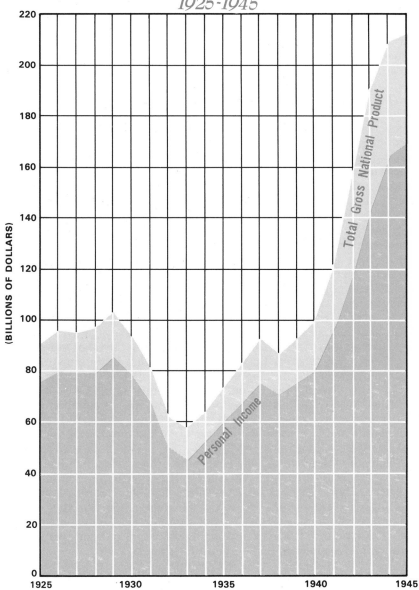

Economic recovery also contributed to the growth of the labor movement. It meant an increased number of jobs for workers, thereby enlarging the pool of potential union members, giving workers the dollars needed to pay union dues and enabling the workers to feel less vulnerable and capable of thinking about more than survival. Recovery also increased the willingness of buisnessmen to recognize unions and bargain with them because they did not want strikes to prevent them from seizing the new opportunities.

Leadership in the labor movement was important. Especially after 1936, its leaders were functioning in an unusually favorable situation, much more favorable in important ways than had been available to them earlier. Some of them, such as John L. Lewis, David Dubinsky, and Sidney Hillman, had much experience with union activity before the 1930s and accepted the New Deal as a great opportunity, making great organizing drives, spending money and conducting strikes. They altered the structure of the labor movement in a very important way. This was resisted by top people from 1933 to 1935, leaders like William Green, but Lewis and others persisted, rejecting the traditional emphasis on organizing the skilled workers into trade or craft unions and pressing for the formation of industrial unions. They formed a new organization—the CIO—for this purpose. The structural change enlarged the movement's potential by opening the doors to the unskilled and semi-skilled. Their success forced the AFL eventually to respond to the challenge, becoming more receptive to organization along industrial lines and making large-scale organizing efforts that enabled it to continue to be the largest part of the labor movement.

Finally, the workers themselves contributed to the growth of the labor movement. Expressing much greater interest in unions than ever before, they joined unions in ever larger numbers as soon as the New Deal went into operation, and they participated in strikes and other forms of protest, including the sit-down strikes of 1936-1937 that alarmed so many people but brought some employers, including General Motors, into line.

Labor's new power by the beginning of the 1940s involved more than numbers of members. The movement was more powerful than ever before not only because it had more members but also because it had organized the major firms in the basic industries and the leading industrial cities. It had moved itself into parts of the economy that had been closed to it earlier and that were very important, parts such as automobiles and steel, Detroit and Pittsburgh.

While labor developed a strong economic base, it did not forsake political power. Politics seemed more important than it had been in the past, and the political system seemed more responsive to demands from the workers. The movement became more closely allied with the Democratic party, largely deserting the Republicans and the Socialists, because the Democratic party seemed to be the movement's most effective friend. Unions supplied Democrats with funds, compensating for the large-scale withdrawal of business support from the national Democratic party, and encouraged their members to vote and to vote for friends of labor.

The series of changes meant a decline in the power of business leaders. They could not treat workers just as they had treated them in the past, and they lost their monopoly of decisions governing the conduct of their firms; they could not exert as much influence in politics for they had more effective competition. The changes, troubled many businessmen as profit, power, and status seemed to be affected. Increasingly, business leaders concluded that they had no alternative to conforming to the trend. Although nearly all of them remained unhappy with unions, most stopped using the old anti-union devices.

Very significant changes had taken place. The economic system had become more highly collectivized; business power had been reduced; while labor power had increased. Although several factors were important, the New Deal, which functioned as a promoter of labor power, was one of them.

The Limits of Change

Although the New Deal promoted many changes, it did not bring the country out of the Depression. The gross national product, which had been $103.1 billion in 1929 and had fallen to $55.6 billion in 1933, had reached only $99.7 billion in 1940. Unemployment, which averaged 3.2 percent of the work force in 1929 and nearly 25 percent of the work force in 1933, remained at 8.1 million in 1940, which was 14.6 percent of the labor force.

In part, the New Deal was excessively timid in using governmental power to promote recovery. In spite of the growing influence of Keynesian economics, the government pursued a timid fiscal policy. That is, it was a timid investor, consumer and employer. Federal expenditures grew from $4.7 billion in fiscal 1933 to only $9.6 billion in fiscal 1940. The deficits were small, rising from $2.6 billion in Hoover's last year to only $3.5 billion at the peak (fiscal 1936), nearly disappearing two years later, and rising back only to $2.7 billion in 1940. The development of fiscal policy was inhibited by fears that declined somewhat but did not disappear.

The state and local governments actually interferred with recovery by counteracting New Deal fiscal policy. Influenced more heavily by conservatism and by fears of deficit financing, they moved expenditures from $8.4 billion in fiscal 1932 to $11.2 eight years later but increased revenue even more, raising it from $7.9 billion to $11.7 billion, thereby moving from a deficit to a surplus. Given this pattern of behavior on the lower levels, the federal government would have

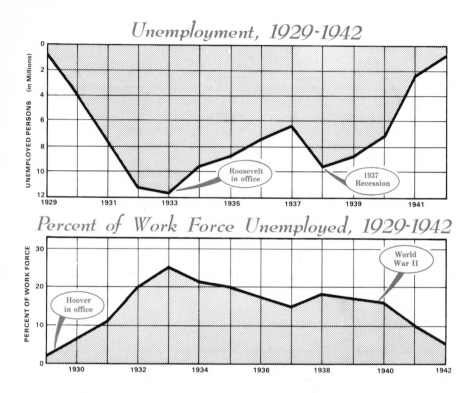

Unemployment, 1929-1942

Percent of Work Force Unemployed, 1929-1942

had to be very bold to have had a massive impact on the business cycle.

Businessmen were also timid. They increased investment cautiously. It had dropped from $16.2 billion in 1929 to $1 billion in 1932, rose to $11.8 billion in 1937, dropped to $6.5 billion the following year and moved only to $13.1 billion in 1940, remaining well below the 1929 level. Strong doubts about the possibilities for profit obviously afflicted the mind of the businessman. The New Deal generated some of them. Conservatives emphasized that. The Depression itself was even more to blame. It suggested to businessmen that they had expanded production too much in the 1920s.

The American people actually faced some difficult dilemmas during the 1930s. They were trying to do something that was very difficult. They were trying both to reform capitalism and to bring about its recovery, and in pressing for reforms, they alarmed a group—the businessmen—upon whom they were dependent for recovery. The nation was intellectually incapable of producing rapid recovery. Most people believed that the economic system had to be reformed, yet reform alarmed people upon whom a capitalistic system is dependent, but the nation could not rely totally on government when many people hesitated to use its powers.

If the New Deal had advocated much bolder efforts involving massive government spending, it would have encountered severe resistance. Its efforts at recovery would have been hampered by the fears in the state and local governments and even more by the fears of the businessmen. They did not believe in massive spending. Instead, they feared it and thus would have been even more frightened by a bold New Deal than they were by a cautious one.

And the nation would not have succeeded if it had relied upon the conservative approach to recovery. It emphasized almost exclusive reliance on businessmen, but they were inhibited by fears that they had expanded production beyond the limits of the American market. This approach seems more likely to have produced revolution than recovery, but, if the people had been patient and recovery had come about, the experiences of the 1920s suggest that the new prosperity would not have lasted very long.

More than the shortcomings of the New Deal, then, were involved in the economy's failure to recover completely from the Depression during the 1930s. The situation was so complex that no way out of the Depression actually was available to the American people. The forces that were at work, including the distribution of ideas, were incapable of producing complete recovery. Something new was needed.

The New Deal focused on the economic system, not the racial system and promoted a new type of capitalism, not a new system of race relations. Furthermore, New Deal programs were affected by racial prejudice. Nevertheless, black voters supported the New Deal and did so in spite of the strength in the past of the Republican party in black communities. As black voters changed their ways in the 1930s, the New Deal gained their respect and admiration. For many, Roosevelt became a hero.

Most black voters supported the Republican party as late as 1932. They did so in spite of high unemployment and in spite of the appeals for support by Communists and Socialists. They did give the Democrats more support than ever before, but their voting behavior was dominated by traditional views of the Republican party as the party of emancipation and the Democrats as the party of white supremacy.

From the point of view of black Americans, the New Deal had several negative features. The agricultural adjustment program discriminated against black and other sharecroppers, and discrimination and segregation existed in the CCC, the FSA and other programs.

Also, the main attack made upon the race system failed. The attack focused on lynching, which had long afflicted blacks and was revived by the Depression, although lynchings were not nearly as numerous as they had been in earlier and the number began to decline again after

1932, but lynching was a very persuasive form of social control, and protest against it was a way of dramatizing the plight of blacks. A new effort on behalf of anti-lynching legislation began in 1934, pressed by the NAACP and Wagner, and the House passed the measure in 1937. Most senators endorsed it, but a Southern filibuster prevented the measure from being brought to a vote in the Senate in 1938. The opposition prevented Roosevelt from endorsing the bill, fearing that endorsement would alienate the Southern Democrats and believing that an anti-lynching law was less important than some other measures, especially economic ones. He did criticize black disenfranchisement and call for the repeal of the poll tax during the 1938 primaries, but the New Deal did not produce any civil rights legislation.

Nevertheless, black voters changed their ways. For the first time, they sent a black Democrat, Arthur Mitchell of Chicago, to Congress, doing so in 1934, and they gave Roosevelt three-fourths of their votes in 1936 and they continued to reject the radical parties.

How can the change be explained? Disgust with the Republicans, who seemed to have little interest in the problems of blacks, played a part. Help from the New Deal contributed even more. Blacks benefited because the New Deal helped the unemployed, including the unemployed blacks, who were very numerous. And New Deal labor policies helped the Brotherhood of Sleeping Car Porters, the most significant black union, and the CIO, which organized blacks as well as other unskilled workers. And the equalitarianism that appeared in the rhetoric of some New Dealers and affected New Deal appointment policies also influenced black voters. Also, the Democratic party, at least part of it, seemed to have become the party of change, and blacks were very eager for change.

The change in black voting behavior was, of course, a change in the behavior of only a minority of blacks. Most Southern blacks were not voters; only 5 percent of them were registered in 1940, and Southern blacks were the ones most affected by sharecropping and lynching. The change took place in the North and West where blacks could vote. Only about 20 percent of the blacks in the United States lived outside the South.

On the other hand, bases for future change were being constructed in the 1930s. Black voters, recognizing that they had become more important in American politics, had a new sense of power. Northern Democrats, recognizing their need for black votes, were sensitive to black problems and willing to work for civil rights legislation. The NAACP gained experience and new allies and pressed for change in a number of areas. And the Supreme Court was more receptive to the NAACP's arguments and in the Gaines Case in 1938 enforced for the first time the equal protection clause of the Fourteenth Amendment on behalf of black claims in the field of education.

Yet, white Southerners, especially, remained highly resistant to change in race relations. They were increasingly alarmed by pressure for it and very determined to maintain the established system. And they had allies among Northern Republicans as well as strength of their own, especially in the Senate.

The 1930s was a period of change in race relations but not a period of revolutionary change. Jim Crow remained in place. Yet, black voters changed their political behavior because of benefits they derived from the New Deal and pressed for additional changes, encountering strong resistance as they did.

The fact that the 1930s was not a revolutionary period in race relations and other major aspects of American life indicates, not that the New Deal failed, but that the radical left failed, both as prophet and politician. Marxism, the most important form of radicalism in the Western World, involved predictions that capitalism would produce a major depression and then an anti-capitalist revolution would occur. These developments seemed inevitable, and this confident interpretation of history gave Marxism some appeal in the early 1930s, especially among intellectuals. Throughout the 1930s, radicals worked hard to make the inevitable happen, seeking to give leadership to the discontented. Yet, in spite of the seriousness of the Depression and the shortcomings of the New Deal, the revolution did not occur.

Division and diversions contributed to the left's failure. The left divided into a number of different types: Communists versus Socialists, Marxists versus Christians, Marxists versus Native Radicals, advocates of cooperation with reformers v. opponents of cooperation, etc . The disagreements, often profound, made cooperation among the foes of capitalism impossible. Their problems were complicated still more by features of American life—the large farm population and the large black population—that produced theoretical difficulties as well as organizational problems. The genuine revolutionaries had to compete against Coughlin, Long, and the like, who were more attractive and diverted some of the discontented away from Norman Thomas and others.

The alienated and the disenfranchised, while seemingly an opportunity for the left, turned out to be a problem. About 40 percent of the population, most of them were poor. For some, legal barriers blocked them from participation in American politics. For many, their own attitudes, their lack of interest in politics, stood in the way. Efforts to draw them into revolutionary movements, as well as any political activity, were hampered by educational deficiencies and scattering. They could not be mobilized.

Traditions also worked against the left. Some were embodied in institutions—the police and the military forces, the church, the schools, the press, advertising—that worked against revolution. Others, including religion, nationalism, and party loyalty, restrained the discontented, encouraging them to fear the radicals and desire only moderate changes.

The New Deal was a powerful anti-revolutionary force. It promised and then produced change, thereby suggesting that the nation did not need a revolution. It captured and held the support of a key group in revolutionary theory, the workers. And it captured the support of the other major groups upon whom the American left counted for support: the blacks and the farmers. Also, the New Deal drew some people, including Hillman, Dubinsky, and Walter Reuther, three important labor leaders, away from radical parties. Even more important, it prevented many people from joining them, people who might have done so if conservatism had been the only alternative.

The labor movement, closely associated with the New Deal, played a similar role. As the 1930s progressed, this movement gained the support of many workers. There were radicals in the unions, but they had only a small amount of strength. The movement was dominated by a pro-capitalist point of view that suggested the workers did not need to overturn the economic system. Instead, they should use the power that organization supplied to gain a larger share of the benefits of American capitalism.

Finally, the importance of mass culture should be recognized. Throughout the Depression, the American people continued to be supplied with many forms of entertainment: sports, music, dancing, radio, movies. The movies, for one, were dominated by non-revolutionary points of view; all forms diverted attention away from problems and politics and consumed time. All of them significantly added to the attractiveness of the established order.

Several factors produced the Left's failure. The New Deal's role seems especially important because it provided direct benefits, revived hopes, assisted the growth of the labor movement, constructed recreational facilities, and supplied funds that could be used for recreational purposes. Without the New Deal, other forces, including the police, might have been overwhelmed. They might not have been able to preserve major institutions if desires for moderate change had been frustrated.

As it was, the 1930s was a period of significant but not revolutionary changes. Above all, capitalism survived, but changes were made in its structure, changes that made the system more complex and collectivized. At the beginning of the decade, big business was clearly the strongest element; at the end, it remained strong, but it had to deal with a much larger and stronger government and a much larger and stronger labor movement. The American people entered the 1940s with their economic system dominated by three sets of large organizations, not just one.

SUGGESTIONS FOR FURTHER READING

Bellush, Bernard, The Failure of the NRA. New York, W. W. Norton, Inc., 1975.

Bernstein, Irving, Turbulent Years: A History of the American Workers 1933-1941. Boston, Houghton Mifflin Co., 1969.

Bergman, Andrew, We're in the Money: Depression America and Its Films. New York, New York University, 1971.

Braeman, John, et al., eds., The New Deal. Columbus, Ohio, Ohio State University Press, 1975, 2 vols.

Burns, James MacGregor, Roosevelt: The Lion and the Fox. New York, Harcourt, Brace and Co., 1956.

Conkin, Paul K., The New Deal. New York, Thomas Y. Crowell, 1967.

Freidel, Frank, Franklin D. Roosevelt. Boston, Little, Brown and Co., 1952, 1954, 1956, 1973, 4 vols.

Fine, Sidney, Sit-Down: The General Motors Strike of 1936-1937. Ann Arbor, Mich., University of Michigan Press, 1969.

Hawley, Ellis W., The New Deal and the Problem of Monopoly: A Study in Economic Ambivalence. Princeton, N.J., Princeton University Press, 1966.

Huthmacher, J. Joseph, Senator Robert F. Wagner and the Rise of Urban Liberalism. New York, Atheneum, 1968.

Kennedy, Susan Estabrook, The Banking Crisis of 1933. Lexington, Ky., The University Press of Kentucky, 1973.

Kirkendall, Richard S., Social Scientists and Farm Politics in the Age of Roosevelt. Columbia, Mo., University of Missouri Press, 1966.

_____, ed., The New Deal: The Historical Debate. New York, John Wiley & Sons, 1973.

_____, The United States 1929-1945: Years of Crisis and Change. New York, McGraw-Hill Inc., 1974.

Kyvig, David E., FDR's America. St. Louis, Forum Press, 1976.

Leuchtenburg, William E., Franklin D. Roosevelt and the New Deal 1932-1940. New York, Harper & Row, 1963.

Patterson, James T., Congressional Conservatism and the New Deal: The Growth of the Conservative Coalition in Congress, 1933-1939. Lexington, Ky., University of Kentucky Press, 1967.

Salmond, John A., The Civilian Conservation Corps, 1933-1942: A New Deal Case Study. Durham, N.C., Duke University Press, 1967.

Schlesinger, Arthur M., Jr., The Age of Roosevelt. Boston, Houghton Mifflin Co., 1957, 1959, 1960, 3 vols.

Williams, T. Harry, Huey Long. New York, Alfred A. Knopf, 1970.

Wolfskill, George, Happy Days are Here Again! A Short Interpretive History of the New Deal. Hinsdale, Ill., Dryden Press, 1974.

16

The Global War

BY 1941, AMERICAN LIFE WAS dominated by a new crisis, international in scope and political and military in nature. This crisis was the Second World War, an event of global magnitude involving savage, destructive fighting in Asia and Africa as well as Europe and both the Atlantic and the Pacific oceans. The war promoted many changes in American life, especially in the nation's relations with other countries and in its power, converting the United States into a global power, a nation able and willing to influence developments in remote places and no longer confining its attention largely to events within its own borders or its own hemisphere. At the same time, the nation avoided other possibilities. Just as it had avoided revolution during the 1930s, so it now avoided defeat and subjugation, by developing alliances and expanding its own strength. The U.S. emerged from the experience, or at least its leaders did, persuaded that it must continue to function as a global power. That realization seemed to be the greatest lesson of this bloody experience in international affairs.

American Intervention

The United States was drawn into World War II by programs of militaristic imperialism—aggression—conducted by Japan, Germany, and Italy. Relying heavily on military force, they gained control of vast areas in East and Southeast Asia, North Africa, and Europe by 1941. Their programs attacked the international system that had been constructed from 1919 to 1929 in the Versailles Treaty, the Washington arms limitation treaties and the Kellogg-Briand Pacts outlawing war.

The pattern of expansion involved a movement from north to south on the Asian mainland by the Japanese. They began with an attack on Manchuria in 1931 and then moved into China, engaging in numerous skirmishes at first, waging war from July 1937 on and gaining control of the coastal areas and establishing a puppet regime. Next, the Japanese moved into Southeast Asia, invading Indochina in September 1940 and controlling that French colony by July 1941.

The pattern also involved an attack on Ethiopia by Italy in 1935 and a series of moves by Germany from 1936 to 1941. The Germans remilitarized the Rhineland in 1936, seized Austria in March 1938, and then invaded Czechoslovakia, and took control of the German-populated parts in September 1938 as a consequence of the appeasement of Adolf Hitler by the British at Munich; Germany gained control of the rest of Czechoslovakia the following March. In September 1939, Germany attacked Poland and soon divided it with Russia. After a lull, the German war machine moved once again, and from April to June 1940 it seized control of Denmark, Norway, Belgium, Holland, Luxembourg, and much of France. Shifting attention to England, the Germans pounded the country from the air as a necessary preliminary to invasion; early in 1941, they seized control of the Balkans and moved into North Africa, hoping to acquire Libya and Egypt. Finally, in June, Germany invaded Russia.

The three countries were linked together in various ways. In 1936, Italy and Germany formed an alliance; soon thereafter, they cooperated by supporting Franco in the Spanish Civil War, and when Germany attacked France, Italy declared war on that country. Germany and Japan formed the Anti-Comintern Alliance in 1937, aimed at the Russians, and Germany, Italy, and Japan came together in September 1940 in the Tripartite Pact that divided the world into spheres. The three powers hoped that the United States would be satisfied with its position in the Western Hemisphere and would tolerate expansion by others. Furthermore, German activities in Europe, by commanding the attention of the colonial powers, Great Britain, France, and Holland, created opportunities for the Japanese in Southeast Asia.

Economic and other considerations influenced the development of these programs of expansion. The expanding nations wanted markets, raw materials such as oil and rice, space, and jobs for their people. The aggressors were also interested in military bases and security. A desire for revenge affected the Germans significantly. Their country had been weakened during and following World War I; having been defeated, they were forced to disarm, pay reparations, and surrender some territory. Their program included efforts to regain control of lost territories in Czechoslovakia and Poland, and propaganda to support the German leader, Adolf Hitler, and his Nazi party. Anti-communism also contributed and so did the desire for greater prestige. The Italians hoped to establish a new Roman Empire, and the Japanese talked of displacing white rule in Asia.

The economic interests underlying this expansion, however, were not narrowly economic. The desire for personal profit did not exert a significant influence upon policy makers. Businessmen were not in control of the politics of any of the expanding nations. The army was the strongest force in Japanese politics, and political men controlled Germany and Italy. The three nations sought power for economic and other purposes. For example, the raw materials desired by the Japanese military were desired chiefly as a source of national strength.

The programs of military expansion stimulated a revival of an old American faith, isolationism, which drew much support from the people until late in 1941. Isolationism encouraged Americans to avoid involvement in the gigantic developments outside the Western Hemisphere, to think of their nation as no more than a regional power, and to stress the dangers involved in becoming a global power. The United States, according to the isolationists, did not need to play a global role and would be harmed seriously if it attempted to do so.

The behavior of foreign nations was not the only source of the revival of isolationism. The Depression also contributed by focusing attention on domestic problems, at least for people with a strong commitment to reform, and Roosevelt himself gave priority to national and hemispheric problems. Disillusionment with World War I suggested to many that war was a source of problems rather than a solution. The decline in the prestige of the business leaders also played a part.

Isolationism in the 1930s was a package of beliefs. The essentials included the idea that the power and influence of elites, especially big business and the military, were the sources of an ambitious foreign policy; overseas economic activity and the military establishment must, therefore, be kept small to curb the elite. Isolationism also involved a refusal to make commitments to other nations in advance, hostility toward involvement in foreign wars and warnings about the bad domestic consequences of involvement. Isolationism encouraged doubts that developments abroad threatened the United States. The two broad oceans provided security. Also, isolationists insisted that the United States should devote its time and energy to domestic problems which seemed a rational position for many years in the 1930s.

Several measures, above all, the Neutrality Acts of 1935, 1936, and 1937, testified to the strength of isolationism. Those acts placed restrictions on American economic activities, declaring that no loans or arms sales could be made to belligerents, warring nations must pay cash for

American goods and carry them away in their own ships, Americans must not travel on the ships of belligerents, and American merchant-men must not carry arms for their own defense. These laws also tied the hands of the President, requiring him to impose all of these restrictions once he declared that a war existed and thus preventing him from using American economic power to help one side in the war.

As the international situation deteriorated, isolationism still maintained considerable strength. A proposed constitutional amendment to require a popular referendum prior to a declaration of war was defeated in the House of Representatives by a narrow margin in 1938; and many people battled against Roosevelt's efforts to repeal the Neutrality Acts from 1939 to 1941 and to establish Lend-Lease and continue the draft in 1941. During these years, the isolationists had a litany of arguments to confront opponents. They contended that the battles in Europe and Asia did not pit good against evil; the United States could not promote desirable developments in those parts of the world; the programs of expansion did not threaten the United States; sales and aid to belligerents would weaken the United States and lead to war; an excessive military buildup would lead to war; intervention would damage the United States and distract it from efforts to improve itself; and the United States had no economic need to get involved. The isolationists also maintained that international bankers, munitions makers, Jews, and Roosevelt were responsible for the mounting pressure to intervene.

Isolationism faced, however, a mounting challenge from people who argued that the United States must assume responsibilities for peace and order in world affairs. Many business leaders, Hoover, Roosevelt, and his Secretary of State, Cordell Hull, challenged isolationism from an economic point of view, stressing the importance of foreign trade and investment, denying that they would lead inevitably to political involvement and war, and asserting that American prosperity, due to the productivity of the system, depended on them. They also insisted that democracy and peace depended on trade and investment for the alternatives were a tightly controlled economy and war for needed markets and resources. This point of view was involved most significantly in the Reciprocal Trade Program. Established in 1934, it enabled the State Department to cut tariffs as much as 50 per cent in exchange for reductions in economic barriers by other nations.

The isolationists were also challenged by a point of view that stressed political considerations. Roosevelt, the Committee to Defend America by Aiding the Allies, Henry Stimson, Wendell Willkie, most Democrats by 1940, Polish- and Jewish-Americans, and people with ties to Great Britain and China, emphasized the importance of power, feared the domination of Europe and Asia by a hostile and aggressive power, and interpreted Germany and Japan as threats to the United States. German power seemed especially threatening, and the ties between Germany and Japan and the dependence of Great Britain on

Asia added to the danger. The anti-isolationists denied that security was a gift of God to the American people and a built-in feature of American life, insisting that it depended on efforts by the United States and others. They argued that France and Great Britain were too weak to protect the United States and could become a threat to the United States if Germany and Japan gained control of them and their colonies. Contrary to the claims of the isolationists, the oceans did not offer protection, for they were more likely to function as highways than as moats. Germany, especially, if she was victorious in Europe, was capable of invading the Western Hemisphere.

The anti-interventionists called for a military buildup, economic aid to Great Britain and other victims of aggression and restrictions on sales to Japan. They insisted that naval and military power could protect rather than threaten peace and democracy, and they argued that a military buildup and economic aid would exert desirable influence, restraining aggressors and strengthening their foes. Aid to Great Britain was especially crucial. The United States must prevent the fall of Britain and the conquest of the areas upon which she depended. These were basic requirements of American security.

In addition to emphasis on the threats to American security, the foes of the isolationists interpreted the war in moral terms. German totalitarianism, especially, threatened democracy and Western Civilization.

During 1941, many of the interventionists moved away from the argument that their programs would enable the United States to stay out of war. To most Americans, the defeat of Germany became more important than staying out of the fighting. And a few participants in the debate, including the Century Group, Walter Lippmann, Henry Stimson, and Henry Morgenthau, called for American military intervention. They assumed that the United States could produce a British victory.

Three major ways of looking at foreign affairs were available to the American people by the beginning of the 1930s. The isolationist point of view came to the front by the middle of the decade, but the political alternative to isolationism was by 1940-1941 the most influential way of interpreting foreign affairs. By then, the behavior of Germany, Italy, and Japan was clearly perceived as a threat to the United States that could not be ignored and must be resisted.

As concern grew, Americans realized that they did not have much power. They had refused to develop a large military establishment. The nation did have great military potential for it was one of the most populous countries and the most productive, but the size of the armed forces had been cut by the Democratic Congress during the Hoover years from more than 255,000 to less than 244,000, reflecting dislike for both military power and government spending, and they were not enlarged significantly before 1940. Roosevelt had a positive attitude toward military power, but he was sensitive to anti-military feeling, having been defeated by a Democratic Congress in an early effort to expand the Army and the National Guard. Military spending was increased, but slowly, rising from slightly more than one-half billion dollars in 1934 to somewhat more than one billion in 1938. By the late 1930s, the United States was far behind Germany and Japan. It turned out slightly more than 2,000 military planes in 1939 while Germany and Japan produced nearly 13,000.

On the international stage, the United States also suffered from economic weaknesses. It had great potential, given its great capacity for production, but had imposed restrictions on the use of economic power by passing the Neutrality Acts. These laws made it impossible for the United States to shape the course of events by discriminating among belligerents, helping some nations by sending supplies to them and hurting others by depriving them of supplies.

Deprived of stronger methods, Roosevelt relied chiefly upon words in the late 1930s. His now famous address in Chicago on October 5, 1937, called for a quarantine of aggressors. "When an epidemic of physical disease starts to spread, the community . . . joins in a quarantine of the patient in order to protect the health of the community against the spread of disease." But his words failed to produce the desired results. Americans criticized Germany, Italy, and Japan, refused to recognize the results of their expansion and made appeals to them and others. Germany and Japan, however, continued their aggression. Many Americans were alarmed, but they could do little to check the expanding nations.

Highly sensitive to American weaknesses and convinced that developments abroad threatened the United States, FDR devoted most of his time and energy from the fall of 1939 to the fall of 1941 to the development and use of American power. Hoping to move events abroad in ways that benefited the United States, he achieved some successes, but ultimately failed. His radio addresses to the American people, nonetheless, made them aware of the serious crisis abroad.

The development of American military power began immediately after the German attack on Poland and accelerated again following the fall of France. Military spending jumped to $5 billion by 1941. The increase in defense spending stimulated the defense industry. The rapid German advance in the spring of 1940 prompted Roosevelt in May to call for the production of 50,000 planes per year, which was five times the current capacity of the industry and equal to its entire output since 1903. Roosevelt's goal forced rapid expansion, most of it financed by the federal government, and encouraged the administration to draw the automobile industry into aircraft production. It took time to convert and

World War II, European Theater

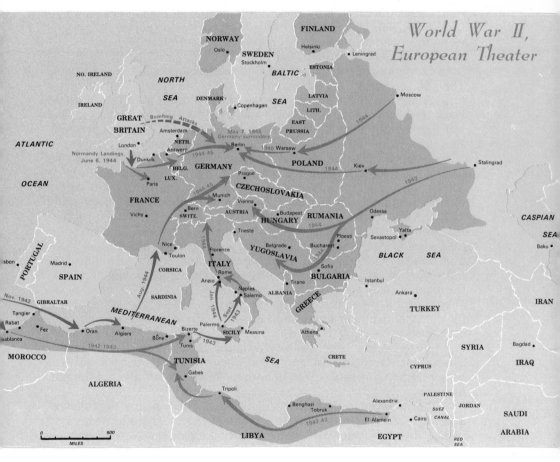

expand existing facilities and build new ones, and industry did not reach the goal overnight; but the production of military aircraft jumped from less than 4,000 in 1940 to nearly 20,000 in 1941. The armed forces grew from less than 335,000 in mid-1939 to 1.8 million in two years, a feat made possible by nationalizing some National Guard and Organized Reserve units and by drafting manpower through a system of Selective Service.

Yet, many problems hampered the progress of preparedness. Strikes, ineffective administration, and resistance to conversion by some industries, including auto makers, slowed the development of the defense industry, preventing it from supplying the many demands on it from Latin America, Great Britain, Russia, and China as well as American forces. The armed forces, staffed largely by inexperienced people, were unprepared for combat outside the Western Hemisphere.

During 1941, American leaders continued to worry about the threats from Germany and Japan, but the German threat seemed more serious. The administration hoped to be able to devote more of its resources to it. A portion of the Pacific fleet had been shifted from California to Pearl Harbor in 1940, and, in the summer of 1941, a part of that fleet was transferred to the North Atlantic. Given their appraisal of realities, American leaders were especially eager to avoid war with Japan.

As the military preparedness program moved forward at its unsatisfactory pace, officials relied chiefly on American economic power to help Britain. This forced Roosevelt to seek to free the nation from the restrictions that had been imposed by the Neutrality Acts. In November 1939, he obtained repeal of the arms embargo and the substitution of the cash and carry principle for it, a change that favored the British for they needed American weapons and had a navy to protect the transport of arms. In September 1940, however, the President traded fifty destroyers for British bases in the Western Hemisphere, believing that the British navy needed to be strengthened in order to protect the flow of supplies. In March 1941, Congress accepted Roosevelt's request for the establishment of a Lend-Lease program that bypassed the ban on monetary loans by permitting the President to loan or lease supplies to countries whose defense were vital to the defense of the United States. The initial appropriation and a supplement in October totaled $13 billion, and Russia became one of the beneficiaries soon after the German invasion.

The President supplemented economic aid with the deployment and use of American forces in the North Atlantic. These moves, made as a result of presidential orders, not congressional action, illustrated how the crisis strengthened the Presidency.

In November, Congress, in response to Roosevelt's pressure, repealed provisions of the Neutrality Law governing American merchant ships. They could now carry arms for their own defense, and they could enter the combat zones, including England.

Related programs took shape for the other side of the globe. From July 1940 to July 1941, Washington embargoed American sales of a growing number of commodities to Japan, including scrap iron and oil,

The Attack on Pearl Harbor *(Library of Congress)*

believing that the restrictions would restrain the Japanese and force them to stop before they seriously damaged British interests. The United States also supplied aid to Chiang Kai-shek, the Nationalist leader in China.

Most advocates of these economic moves hoped that nothing more would be demanded of the United States, that it would not be forced to intervene militarily. Washington employed negotiations as well, conducting them with Japan from February through November 1941 with an end to limiting Japanese expansion and gaining time. The military chiefs were especially enthusiastic advocates of negotiations. American negotiators hoped to persuade the Japanese to endorse American anti-expansionist principles. Acceptance of expansion had been one of the great mistakes of the past, especially at Munich.

American officials could not halt, however, the programs of expansion or obtain endorsement of their ideas. In fact, the Japanese tried to get the United States to accept their imperialist goals. Instead of halting their moves, the Germans and the Japanese attacked American forces, seeing them as threats to their ambitions. German attacks began in September 1941 and were made upon the American Navy in the North Atlantic; the Japanese launched a massive, well coordinated strike on December 7 against American forces at Pearl Harbor and other places in the Pacific.

Prior to the Japanese attack, Roosevelt had been in an extremely difficult situation. Seeing Hitler as the greater threat, he planned to deal with him first if drawn into the war, but he feared that the Japanese would attack British and Dutch territories in East Asia. That would be serious for it could not be resisted effectively by the British and Dutch and would deprive the British of valuable resources. Thus, the United States would be forced to resist, but, because most Americans would not regard the situation as serious, the resistance would come from a divided and hence rather ineffective nation. Thus, Roosevelt hoped at least to postpone the Japanese moves and was encouraged by his military advisers, for they believed that the United States needed three to six months to build its defenses in the Philippines and elsewhere in the Pacific.

Other pressures, however, encouraged Roosevelt to take a firm stand in China and elsewhere. They came from the British Prime Minister, Winston Churchill, influenced by the failure of the Munich agreement and by the desire for American military intervention. They came also from Chiang and from three members of the Cabinet — Hull; Morgenthau, the Secretary of the Treasury; and Harold Ickes, the Secretary of Interior. Public opinion was growing increasingly hostile to the Japanese.

The Japanese were determined to obtain resources from both Southeast Asia and the United States. While willing to pull back from much of Indochina but not to surrender their position in China as the United States demanded, Japanese leaders decided that they would go to war in December if diplomacy failed. Their supply of oil was running short and could be replenished in the East Indies, which now seemed to be a more reliable source than the United States. They had begun preparations for an attack on the naval base at Pearl Harbor, believing that they must severely damage the U. S. Pacific Fleet there to succeed with a program of further expansion, and a carrier force began to move toward Hawaii on November 26. At the same time, they moved other and much larger forces into Southeast Asia so as to be able to attack at many points and gain the resources and bases that they needed.

Officials in Washington had a large yet inadequate amount of information on the Japanese moves. Intelligence agents had broken the Japanese top diplomatic code and several lesser diplomatic codes and had good observers in China and Southeast Asia. They also had evidence from the Japanese press of hostility toward the United States and Japan's determination to expand farther in Southeast Asia. Yet, they had not broken the Japanese military codes and could not observe Japanese military preparations closely. They did not know about technical developments that would permit bombing in the shallow waters at Pearl Harbor; they could not monitor the messages to commanders; and they did not know the location of the carriers. The U.S. had no observers in the Pacific region through which the Japanese came because the Navy had ordered merchant ships to stay out of the area so as to avoid incidents. Just before the attack, Americans received a number of false alarms in Hawaii.

As tension mounted, American attention focused on Southeast Asia. Officials assumed that Japan would proceed as Hitler had and attack weaker nations first so as to keep the risks as low as possible, and officials assumed the Japanese would follow their own line of advance that had begun in Manchuria and would move beyond Indochina to obtain the resources they needed.

The Japanese hit the British and Dutch positions in Southeast Asia, but they also hit other places, including the Philippines and Pearl Harbor. On December 8, an angry Congress declared war on the Japanese. The people, shocked by the suddenness of events, listened on their radios for direction from their leaders.

The amazing fact of Pearl Harbor was the unprepared state of American defenses. The commanders were uninformed of the serious crisis in American-Japanese relations, and Roosevelt also was not ready. He had, in fact hoped to delay a showdown between Japan and the United States since he regarded Hitler as a much more serious threat and recognized the weaknesses of American forces. The attack, while it solved Roosevelt's political problem by uniting the American people behind him, enlarged his military problem by damaging seriously the Pacific Fleet. The United States had not developed the strength needed to exert the influence it desired in Europe and Asia. Rather than restrain and limit Germany and Japan, the United States had provoked them into attacks on American forces, and the Japanese attacks had weakened those forces.

The Impact on American Life

As a giant event, global in scope, the war that followed imposed enormous pressures on American life. It was obvious to nearly everyone by the end of 1941 that America must change in major ways to avoid defeat and accomplish its objectives in the world, and change moved forward at an unusually rapid pace in the next three and one-half years. Many of the most significant developments were economic. The war affected both the structure and the performance of the system, which became even more collectivized and much more productive.

Each of the three major components of the system felt the war's impact. The federal government grew very rapidly. Several of the welfare programs that had been developed during the 1930s were cut back or dismantled, but a new welfare program for returning veterans—the "G.I. Bill"—was established in 1944. The anti-trust program of the late New Deal was also discarded. Yet, the federal government grew enormously in size and cost, much more so than it had under the New Deal. To accomplish wartime purposes, Washington became a major planner, investor, regulator and consumer. At the same time, big business grew once again, chiefly because the large firms received most of the government contracts for the production of things needed by the war machine. Also, the relations with government, including the military, and business became more harmonious as Roosevelt and his aides concluded that they must have the help of businessmen to win the war. The labor movement also grew in size. Roosevelt, backed by an enlarged and politically active labor movement, resisted most anti-union pressures during the war; wartime agencies enforced pro-union legislation, regarding good labor relations as essential for the expansion of production. Unions benefited from the expansion of industrial employment. More industrial workers meant more people who could be drawn into the movement.

The performance of the system changed in even more spectacular ways. Defects did appear, including shortages in important materials from time to time, less-than-perfect cooperation among the representatives of the different parts of the system, and inflation, but they were more than offset by accomplishments. The economy moved from depression to boom. This change resulted in part from the federal government's fiscal policy, which involved a massive increase in spending and large-scale deficits that dwarfed the record of the New Deal. Widespread acceptance of the policy also contributed, as most Americans including most businessmen, emphasized the need for, rather than the dangers of, large-scale deficit financing in wartime. The war helped also by weakening, at least for the moment, the fears among businessmen and farmers of American productivity. Thus, as time passed, both industry and agriculture expanded production enormously, enlarging and constructing factories, increasing the use of science and technology and enlarging the industrial work force. The move from depression to boom involved the virtual disappearance of unemployment. The standard of living increased sharply; the number of poor shrank significantly; the middle classes grew rapidly; and the American people paid off debts from a less prosperous past. The economy had never performed so successfully. In 1929, the gross national product had been $103.1 billion; in 1945, it was $211.9 billion.

The economy's performance strengthened confidence in the system. Many people feared that the nation might slip back into depression after the war as the government slashed spending and foreign markets disappeared. Many others, however, believed that the American system would enjoy permanent prosperity if the federal government pursued a wise fiscal policy and/or reformed the international economy.

The war also had a powerful impact on American society, pressing nearly everyone into its service and purging those who threatened the war effort. The Socialists did not have the trouble they had had in World War I, for the group was small and offered little criticism. The Communists, while criticized by many Americans, also had little difficulty, for they were zealous supporters of the war. While German-Americans and Italian-Americans suffered some harassment in a

A Wartime Poster *(National Archives)*

few localities, they did not suffer as German-Americans had in World War I, for the nation's hostility focused on the German and Italian governments, not the people, and German and Italian-Americans were assumed to be loyal to the United States. On the other hand, the government moved against a small group of people who seemed to sympathize with the Fascists and jailed about 5,000 Conscientious Objectors who refused to enter military service or work in civilian public service camps. Most significantly, officials early in 1942, influenced by a sense of national weakness at that moment and a well-established brand of racism, moved the more than 100,000 Japanese-Americans from their homes on the West Coast and placed them in concentration camps in the interior, and with few exceptions, keeping them there until 1945.

The people drawn into the service of the nation were not limited to the 14 million who served in the armed forces. The recruited included nearly everyone to some degree. Those encouraged to do something served in civilian defense, participated in scrap drives or bought war bonds. More demanding jobs were available in the war plants. Many rural and small town people left their home communities to take such jobs. Teenagers entered the work force in large numbers, reversing a twenty-year decline in child labor. Blacks found many more jobs open to them and received help in their job-seeking efforts from the Fair Employment Practices Committee, established in 1941 as the first federal civil rights program since Reconstruction. The FEPC sought to integrate blacks into the defense industries and achieved some success, although its powers were weak and it encountered resistance from people who did not believe in racial integration. The FEPC was defended as necessary for the war effort as well as just because the nation needed all available workers.

Educators and scientists participated in the war effort in large numbers, providing training and conducting research, as on the secret project to develop the atomic bomb. This $2 billion project was not solely a scientific enterprise. Roosevelt placed the Army in charge in 1942, regarding military control as a way of maintaining secrecy as well as managing a big project, and major corporations, including Du Pont, Union Carbide, and Tennessee Eastman, made major contributions. But scientists, benefiting from work done in Germany and spurred, as were the other participants, by fear that Germany would develop an atomic bomb before the United States, played major roles, working in teams at Columbia University, the University of Chicago, the University of California, Oak Ridge, Tennessee and other places. The participants included Vannevar Bush, James Conant, Harold Urey, Arthur Compton, Enrico Fermi, Glen Seaborg, Ernest Lawrence, J. Robert Oppenheimer, and many others.

The war produced a great increase in job opportunities for women. Jobs for women had declined during the Depression but increased rapidly after Pearl Harbor as the male labor force dwindled and the total number of jobs increased. The number of working women rose by over 50 percent, increasing the percentage of women who worked outside the home from 25 to 36. The number of married women who worked doubled, bringing the percentage to 24, and the number of women in unions moved from 800,000 in 1939 to three million in 1945. Encouraged by government and the media, the employment of women was at least accepted by most people as necessary. Wages and working conditions for women improved, although they did not achieve equality in the job market. They continued to face discrimination based on concepts of women's work and to receive less pay in many industries for comparable work. Moreover, women were supplied with only a small number of child care centers, a fact that placed a major limit on job opportunities for women. But, although the war did not produce a revolution in the status, place and role of women in American life, it did promote significant changes.

To encourage people to participate in the war effort, the nation employed various devices. They included patriotic and economic inducements and exemptions from the draft for certain types of workers. Some officials even proposed, although not successfully, a National Service Law that would tightly control the work force. All of these efforts were accompanied by militant nationalism. Americans had no doubt that the United States was right and its enemies were wrong. The type of nationalism that prevailed was not uncritical as the black leaders demonstrated, but even they were nationalistic, relying on a conception of Americanism to appraise the nation's race relations and the need for enlarged opportunities for blacks to move into the mainstreams of American life. They were, in fact, encouraged by the war to press their claims, and black protest not only grew but gained more support from whites who shared the belief that the prevailing system of race relations was incompatible with the nation's democratic values. Their foes, on the other hand, insisted that the critics of the race system were affected by alien ideas and threatened the American way of life. Working to maintain a segregated society, the foes of change in race relations maintained most aspects of the established order, including segregation in the armed forces.

Some racial tensions disturbed the cities as blacks, Mexican-Americans and others found employment. In Los Angeles race riots, caused by engagements between police and Chicanos were extremely serious. Many people were hurt and a few imprisoned.

The Emergence of a Global Power

Most important, the war converted the United States into a global power. In late 1941 and early 1942, the United States was involved in a global war, but it was not yet a global power. The economy had not yet been effectively converted to war production, and the armed forces remained in an early stage of development. Several undesirable consequences flowed from the persistent weakness of the United States.

In the Pacific, the United States could not check Japanese expansion. The nation's limited state of preparations, the conviction that the European theater of war demanded priority and the size of the Pacific all worked to Japan's advantage; consequently, the Japanese gained control of the vast areas its leaders had in mind on December 7. The area was rich in resources and bases and brought the Japanese close to India and Australia, and their expansion forced the United States to pay more attention to the war against Japan than had been planned.

The United States faced comparable problems in Europe. Its forces could not deal effectively with the German submarines or set up a second front in Western Europe. American forces were not ready for that task; any invasion in 1942 would be largely a British operation, and the British opposed such at move at that time.

Roosevelt decided instead to invade North Africa. His decision reflected British pressure and a desire for better relations with Britain, as well as desire for some action against the Germans. Such a move could be managed by the small forces then available and would help FDR resist pressure to switch the emphasis to the war against Japan. His top military advisers, however, Secretary Stimson and General George C. Marshall, opposed such a move as diversionary, believing it would not contribute significantly to victory, would delay the essential invasion of Europe and would postpone a large-scale move against Japan. The decision also angered Joseph Stalin, the Russian leader, for it seemed to mean that Russian suffering would be prolonged. It also meant that the Russians would have large opportunities for expansion in Europe, but that was not seen by either side at the time. Stalin pressed for the quick opening of a British-American front in Western Europe, but the United States was too weak and its resources were spread too widely to be able to agree with him at this time.

The armed forces, however, grew very rapidly. Military spending jumped from nearly $23 billion in fiscal 1942 to nearly $75 billion two years later; the armed forces, which had fewer than 4 million members as late as June 30, 1942, had 11.5 million by 1944 and added more than another half million during the following year. Consequently, the Army, which had 8.3 million members in mid-1945, was the second largest in the world, and the Navy, which with its Marine Corps had nearly 3.9 million, was the largest.

The United States did not concentrate only on the development of the armed forces. Soon after Pearl Harbor, the administration decided that the United States would make a giant economic contribution to the war effort and to do so would limit the Army to only ninety divisions, reserving a substantial amount of manpower for economic purposes. During the course of the war, the United States did not give all of the economic output to military affairs for administration leaders were concerned about civilian morale, too concerned the military leaders believed. The American people enjoyed a much higher standard of living than other belligerents could.

Nevertheless, the nation devoted better than 40 percent of the output of the economy to military purposes. It produced more military goods than its allies and its enemies, including 45 percent of the world's supply of arms and ammunition by 1944.

The automobile industry became the largest producer of goods for war. This constituted a major change as the industry had not been involved significantly in military production prior to the war. After Pearl Harbor, it stopped producing private automobiles, and in the years that followed, it manufactured nearly $30 billion worth of military supplies, 20 percent of the nation's total. General Motors, the nation's biggest war contractor, produced military supplies valued at $12 billion. The industry played its large role because it had more know-how in large-scale production than any other industry. Its output included trucks, jeeps, and tanks. It also turned out many things with which it had previously been unfamiliar, including airplane engines, airplane parts, and entire planes; it turned out nearly all of the armored cars, scout cars, and carriers, most of the helmets and aircraft bombs, more than one-half of the carbines and tanks, nearly one-half of the machine guns, 10 percent of the torpedoes and land mines, and 3 percent of the marine mines, and it produced over 4 million engines, nearly 6 million guns, nearly 3 million tanks and trucks, 27,000 aircraft and substantial quantities of more than fifty other items.

The aircraft industry drew heavily upon government funds to expand production after Pearl Harbor and continued to expand facilities and labor force until the end of 1943. It emphasized the production of bombers but also turned out large numbers of fighters and transports. It suffered some failures, such as the failure to get the new Ford plant at Willow Run into full production, but it produced nearly 100,000 military planes in 1944 while Germany and Japan were turning out less than 70,000. The industry also improved the quality of its product. The B-17 bomber of 1944 was far superior to the B-17 of 1939; the B-29 of the last year of the war was better than the B-17, and American fighter planes—the P-38, the P-39, the P-47 and the P-51—were as good as the German fighters during the last two years of the war.

The aircraft industry moved into first place in terms of dollar value of output of American industries. The firms that had been in the business before the war—North American, Convair, Douglas, Curtis-Wright, Lockheed, and Boeing—were transformed into giant corporations. In engine production, the industry was composed largely of the automobile manufacturers. Aircraft firms enjoyed good profits and provided a large number of jobs.

In addition to supplying American forces with large amounts of advanced equipment, American industry provided aid to the nation's allies. Lend-Lease functioned throughout the war, spending over $50 billion. It was designed to affect the behavior of other nations and thus to shape international affairs.

The employment of the growing power of the United States was influenced by conflicting strategies. The dominant American conception was that first attention must be given to the war in Europe. Most of the resources must be concentrated there because Hitler was the most dangerous force, Europe was more important than Asia, and transport problems were smaller on the Atlantic than they were on the much larger Pacific. The leading strategists also assumed that Western Europe was the place where American forces could be used most effectively, and they considered an invasion of Western Europe as the best way to maximize Western political influence in Europe. The advocates of such ideas included Stimson, Marshall, and General Dwight Eisenhower; they argued against diversions and for a rapid buildup and the earliest possible invasion; and their ideas made sense to FDR for political as well as military reasons.

American military men, however, clashed over the forces that should be employed and some challenged the Europe-first strategy. Marshall and others emphasized land warfare, while General H. H. Arnold and others emphasized strategic bombing of German industry. General Douglas MacArthur, who was based in Australia after his forces were defeated by the Japanese in the Philippines early in 1942, Admiral Ernest J. King, the Chief of Naval Operations, and Admiral Chester Nimitz, the Commander of Allied Forces in much of the Pacific, advocated an emphasis on Japan, viewing it as the special responsibility of the United States and stressing the importance of Asia and the need for the United States to enlarge its influence there. Emphasizing operations in the Pacific, they pictured the islands as objectives and called for movements west from Hawaii and north from Australia that would converge on Japan, involve both the Army and the Navy and substantial use of air power and be comparable in size to the war in Europe.

America's allies had still other ideas. China wished to emphasize the war against Japan and, hampered by internal conflict between the Nationalists and the Communists, wanted the United States to play large economic and military roles on the Asian mainland. The Russians, who had done most of the fighting against Germany in 1941 and 1942, had been invaded through Eastern Europe and faced German forces close to Moscow by the time the United States entered the fighting, favored the emphasis on Europe and called for the quick opening of a Western front in Europe that would reduce the pressure on Russia. The British, who were being hit from the air and were fighting in Egypt and Southeast Asia, also advocated the Europe-first policy but feared a premature move onto the continent and German-Japanese control of the area from India to North Africa. As time passed, British leaders feared Russian military strength in Europe where they could upset the balance of power. Recognizing the political significance of the movement of armies, they called first for an emphasis on the Mediterranean theater and then for an invasion of Southern Europe.

As American power grew, U.S. political leaders developed an elaborate set of postwar objectives rather than the simple objective of victory. These leaders sought to use American power and wartime opportunities to promote major changes in the world. It seemed to them that one of the greatest mistakes of the recent past had been the American effort to play a small role in the world. The United States must function in the future as a global power and create an international situation in which Americans and others could find peace and prosperity.

One American objective was unconditional surrender. Announced by Roosevelt early in 1943, it was not a simple military objective. Instead, it involved the effort to use military means for a political purpose: to guarantee a lasting peace. That would be accomplished by the transformation of the "war makers." The United States and its allies would fight until they were in a position to demand unconditional surrender and would not be satisfied with any other type of victory.

The reduction of economic barriers constituted another goal that was necessary for political as well as economic purposes. It would guarantee worldwide prosperity and peace by enabling people to satisfy freely their economic needs.

American leaders also talked of the destruction of imperialism, regarding it as desirable for economic and political reasons. The dismantling of colonial empires would provide opportunities for American businessmen, remove a source of instability among restless colonial peoples and extend American principles to other parts of the world. FDR pressed this objective until restrained by opposition from Churchill and others.

The designs of the Left also figured in the calculations of American leaders. Roosevelt and others feared that the Left, dominated by Russia, would achieve successes, due to the war's destructiveness. They feared also that the triumphant Left would harm the United States, seizing American property in the countries brought under its control and closing them to American trade and investment.

Finally, American leaders hoped to use the war to bring about the establishment of an international organization as Wilson had tried to use World War I. Influenced by his failure and the failure of the League of Nations, Roosevelt did not press this issue at first, stressing instead international control by the "Big Four" after the war. Pressure groups, some Congressional leaders and members of the State Department, however, urged Roosevelt to consider the matter, seeing an international organization as a substitute for unsuccessful ways of conducting international affairs and as an application of American principles to those affairs. In time, Roosevelt came around, although he envisioned an in-

The Big Three: Stalin, Franklin D. Roosevelt and Churchill at the Teheran Conference

fluential position for the big powers, and the idea was endorsed widely in the United States by 1944.

As American power grew, the nation pursued the conflicting strategies, although not in ways that fully satisfied their proponents, and laid the military basis for the accomplishment of at least some of its postwar objectives. American forces invaded Morocco and Algeria in November 1942, as the British desired. By May 1943, victory over the Axis armies had been achieved in North Africa. American and British forces invaded Sicily in July, again as the British desired. Victory there came quickly and was followed by the overthrow of Mussolini, the Fascist leader of Italy, and the surrender of that country. After rejecting Churchill's plan for an invasion of the Balkans, a rejection that reflected growth in American strength relative to the British, American and British forces invaded Italy. It was occupied by the Germans, and movement against them proved very difficult. Allied forces advanced slowly but captured Rome in June 1944 and then moved farther north. With British cooperation they purged Fascists from places of power, frustrated Communists who hoped to gain power and favored the Italian center.

By June 1944, the United States and its allies crossed the English channel and invaded Western Europe. Several earlier developments had made this second front possible. Victory in the battle of the Atlantic, which was achieved before the end of 1943, enabled the United States and its allies to transport the necessary goods and men across that ocean. They had also gained control of the air over Europe, a success that reduced the risks involved in the invasion and enabled the flyers to destroy the transportation facilities of northern France. The Russian offensive contributed indirect help because it forced Hitler to keep most of his forces on the eastern front. Finally, the American build-up was, of course, very important. As a result of it, the American forces in Great Britain were much larger than the British, and the United States, not Great Britain, was now the most powerful nation in the Atlantic community.

Supplementing the invasion of northwestern Europe with an invasion of German-controlled southern France in August, Allied forces moved effectively against the Germans. By fall, France, Holland, and Belgium had been freed from German control. In early winter, the move toward victory was delayed by the Battle of the Bulge—a last desperate battle of the Nazi troops, but the Allies invaded Germany early in the new year. They had continued to pound it from the air, and they had victory within grasp by late March 1945.

The United States obtained great but not unlimited political influence in the liberated areas. They cooperated with others to remove Nazis from office but encountered some resistance to other efforts from popular national leaders, especially Charles de Gaulle in France, and competed as well as cooperated with the British. Yet, the Americans produced frustrations for the revolutionaries. The American military presence encouraged them to behave cautiously. As in Italy, the Americans helped the politicians of the center.

The American effort in the Pacific expanded more rapidly than most Washington leaders had planned and also achieved success. The American military force there did not become as large as that deployed in Europe or as large as MacArthur and others desired, but it did enable the United States to check the Japanese effort to complete the destruction of the United States Navy and seize additional territory, doing so in the battles of Midway and the Coral Sea in the spring of 1942, although failing to prevent the Japanese from gaining a foothold in the Aleutians. Later in the year, American forces took the offensive, attacking Guadalcanal and New Guinea and gaining control of them by February 1943. Then, during 1943 and 1944, Allied forces, led and composed mainly of

Americans, moved against Japan from Hawaii and Australia, seizing control of many islands and gaining dominance of the central Pacific by the summer of 1944. The advance enabled the United States to hit Tokyo and other major Japanese cities with B-29s based in the Marianas that focused their attack on Japan's industry and inflicted heavy civilian casualties, especially in the fire-bomb raids of March 9 and 10, 1945. Allied forces invaded the Philippines in October 1944 and captured Manila the following February. Thus, the United States had virtually complete control of the Pacific, and it moved very close to Japan with victory at Iwo Jima in March and the invasion of Okinawa in April. The strength and location of allied forces made it very difficult for Japan to obtain supplies.

These military successes indicate that a change of great significance had taken place. The United States had become a global power. It had become a nation capable of functioning effectively far from its own borders.

Areas of Weakness

The United States could not operate effectively everywhere. One part of the world that the new power of the United States did not reach significantly was China. Although great by 1944, the power of the United States was not unlimited, and thus choices had to be made. The choices that were made favored other areas over the vast and populous country on the Asian mainland.

The China tangle involved more than war with Japan. It also involved a contest for control between the Nationalists and the Communists. Moderated somewhat by the war against Japan, it was only postponed, not ended. American leaders were interested in the outcome of that contest as well as the war against Japan, but they did not feel capable of supplying large amounts of support to the party they preferred. They preferred Chiang because he was anti-Communist as well as anti-Japanese, and they hoped that China under Chiang's leadership would become a great and democratic power, capable of promoting stability in Asia and friendship with the United States. Yet, Americans had long feared military involvement on the Asian mainland, and they now felt that other areas where American forces could be engaged more easily and effectively were more important.

The United States tried to influence developments in China but failed. They supplied several billion dollars in Lend-Lease, but not nearly as much as they gave to Great Britain and Russia; they deployed approximately 30,000 troops and two generals, Claire Chennault and Joseph Stilwell. Washington resisted pressure for more supplies and

World War II, Pacific Theater

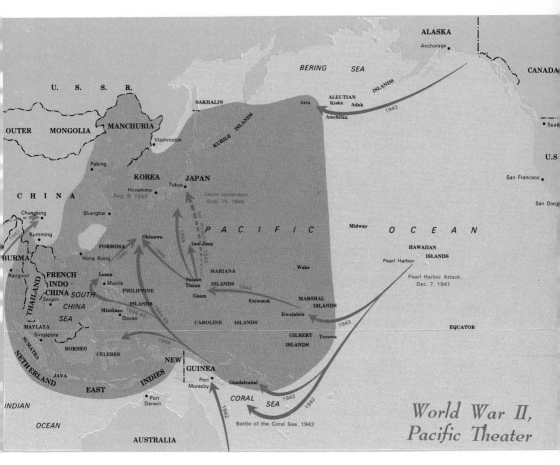

World War II, Pacific Theater

troops that came from Stilwell as well as Chiang. The United States had
only so much of each, and China was difficult to supply because of its
distance from the United States, Japanese control of the coast and

high mountains which separated China from Western-controlled parts
of Asia. Furthermore, China did not seem as important as some other
parts of the world. Not only did Germany seem to be more important
than Japan, but the United States preferred to fight the war against
Japan in the Pacific. It seemed to be a better place than China for the
employment of American forces, and American efforts in the Pacific
seemed more important than depending on Chiang's forces. In addition, in 1944 the United States gained air bases in the Marianas that
were better than bases in China because they were nearer both to the
United States and the most important Japanese cities.

Thus, rather than make a major American effort in China, Americans pressed Chiang to make reforms and take strong action against the
Japanese but did so without success. The pressure came chiefly from
Stilwell and was resisted by Chiang who wanted to reserve his strength
for the civil war and preferred to rely on air power rather than war on
the ground. Chiang made some moves, but they were ineffective, and he
persuaded Roosevelt to recall Stilwell in October 1944. Stillwell's
successor, Patrick J. Hurley also failed to persuade Washington officials
to make a greater effort in China. Consequently, the Japanese, who met
stronger resistance from the Communists in northern China, were able
to expand in southern China until the Americans moved close to their
homeland, and the Communists benefited more from the war than the
Nationalists did.

The United States also functioned ineffectively in Eastern Europe.
There, the Russians enjoyed significant victories for their power had
also grown and American power had limits.

Roosevelt was neither very enthusiastic about nor very fearful of the
Russians. He saw Russia essentially as a regional power, not as ambitious as Germany or Japan and not interested in communizing the world
through military means, and Russian-American cooperation as possible
in spite of differences in ideologies. He had considerable confidence in
his own ability to promote cooperation and assumed that the Russians
would come to see it as the best way to achieve peace. He also saw such
cooperation as necessary because of Russian power. The United States
needed Russian help to win the war and achieve lasting peace. Several of
his moves—Lend-Lease to Russia, the promise of an early invasion of
Western Europe, and the unconditional surrender policy—were influenced by his desire to improve relations between Russia and the
United States.

The Russians had ambitions of their own and took advantage of the
opportunities that the war supplied. Russian leaders were dominated in
their foreign policies by security considerations, not ideology, and
hoped to secure their nation against another invasion from the West,
especially Germany. They assumed that the West was unable or unwilling to assure Russian security and were convinced that failure to invade
Western Europe in 1942-1943 was a betrayal motivated by a desire that

Russia suffer very heavy losses. The Russians feared also that the West, especially the British, would try to control Eastern Europe. Thus, they concluded that they must rely on their own efforts to obtain security. After stopping the German offensive, they moved onto the offensive in 1943, liberating western Russia and then entering Eastern Europe in 1944. Determined to use military force to establish friendly regimes, they achieved dominance in Poland, Romania, Bulgaria, Hungary, and much of Czechoslovakia by February 1945. Soviet intentions were revealed by allowing a Communist-dominated group to come to power in Poland, brushing aside representatives of the old ruling groups that had quite negative attitudes toward communism and Russia. The Russians were willing to tolerate non-Communists but only if they were friendly toward the Soviet Union.

Roosevelt hoped to minimize Russian influence in Eastern Europe. He recognized that Russia would enlarge its influence there but hoped that she would not establish tight and permanent control. His views were influenced by ideological considerations for he believed that such control would conflict with American principles, lead to other violations, and provide ammunition for opponents of administration plans for the postwar role of the United States. Economic and political concerns also affected him. He had some interest in American trade and investment in that part of the world and strong interest in the opinions of Polish-American voters in the United States.

Several considerations restrained Roosevelt in his handling of the Eastern European issue. He wanted Russian cooperation in the war against Japan and in the establishment of an international organization; he wanted to avoid war with Russia, and he did not want to make commitments to an extended American military presence in Europe. Thus, he rejected Churchill's proposals for military action to influence the Soviets. In the summer of 1944, Churchill called for an enlargement of the Italian campaign, and early in 1945, he proposed a quick thrust to Berlin and other places led by a British general, Montgomery. He believed that such moves could both contain Russia and strengthen Great Britain. Rather than endorse these suggestions, FDR expressed his unhappiness over British behavior in Southeast Europe where the British worked out an agreement with the Russians defining spheres of influence for the two countries and then, following the German withdrawal, moved troops into Greece and used them to influence politics.

Roosevelt also declined to use American economic power to influence the situation in Eastern Europe. He rejected proposals for the tightening of Lend-Lease and did not make a significant effort to negotiate a reconstruction loan. Advocates of such plans believed that to change Russian behavior the U.S. should take advantage of its economic strength and Russian needs.

Instead, Roosevelt relied chiefly on words. He preferred efforts at persuasion and conciliation to reliance on military and economic pressures. The former seemed more likely to produce good relations. His efforts came to focus on proposed agreements that free elections would determine the politics of Eastern Europe. He also argued that the Russians should rely upon the international organization and other means and not the control of Eastern Europe to obtain security.

If Roosevelt had been a simple-minded man, the last months of his life would have been much easier. As it was, he had a complex set of objectives that did not harmonize fully with one another and with Russian objectives and thus demanded even more power than the United States had. He hoped not only to win the war, which he was doing, but also to reshape the world in certain ways. Stalin also wanted to win the war, which he also was doing, and to reshape the world on Russia's borders, especially in Eastern Europe.

The two men came together, along with Churchill, at Yalta in the Russian Crimea in February 1945. Both attempted to use diplomacy to further their objectives and had to compromise with one another because neither had enough power to dominate the conference and dictate its terms. For Eastern Europe, they reached agreements on the Polish government, promising that it would be reorganized by adding outsiders and free elections and on "Liberated Europe," assuring that they would help solve its problems by "democratic means." For Roosevelt, these agreements for Eastern Europe constituted an attempt to make the most of a difficult situation involving domination by Russian armies and no desire to move American armies into the region. As to Germany, the conference agreed that the regime and its military power would be destroyed, the country would be carved into four occupation zones (including one for France) and it would be forced to make rather substantial reparations. A Far Eastern agreement, heavily influenced by desire for Russian participation in the war against Japan so as to shorten it and save American lives, involved Stalin's promise to participate and also to support Chiang in China and promises to him that Russia would be given territory at the expense of both China and Japan. And on the international organization which the powers had already agreed to establish, agreements were reached on some important details. It would be permitted to discuss all issues but to take military or economic action only if the big powers agreed.

Roosevelt did not discard his optimism upon his return from Yalta, but he looked tired and fragile. He spoke optimistically, nonetheless, about the conference to the Congress, assuring them that the old ways of conducting international affairs were being discarded and new ways, including decisions by elections and control by an international organization, would take their place if Congress supported the administration. He rejected a new proposal from Churchill for the use of military moves to force Russia to live up to the agreements, hoping to maintain the military focus on the defeat of Germany and to shift forces to the Pacific as soon as possible, to use other methods of influencing the

Russians and to avoid a military confrontation with them. Yet, he recognized that the Yalta agreements had defects and grew more alarmed as the Russians maintained Communist control in Poland and formed a pro-Communist government in Romania. Thus, he joined Churchill in criticism of the Russians. Nevertheless, he had not surrendered confidence in the possibility of Russian-American cooperation.

The United States had become more powerful and effective in world affairs but it had not become capable of accomplishing all that it desired. Roosevelt recognized that while his nation had become a global power it had not become the only nation with power in its hands and thus it must accept compromises. He could talk of a new order in world affairs, and he had promoted change, but a new way of conducting international affairs had not yet come into existence. Power politics remained very important. What was new were the leading participants in the game. The United States and the Soviet Union had become the strongest nations in the world as a result of the impact of the war upon them and upon other countries.

Change in Command

On April 12, 1945, death and provision of the U.S. Constitution transferred control of the enormous power of the United States from Franklin D. Roosevelt to Harry S Truman. Much of that power was new, a by-product of the war that had been raging in the world since the 1930s. Truman's move to the top had been influenced by this change in the nation, and he brought to his task a point of view that encouraged him to appreciate this new power and also to recognize that it would not permit him to realize all of his hopes.

Truman held the Vice-Presidency in 1945 because he had been substituted for Henry A. Wallace in the 1944 convention. The change was made possible by the badly divided condition of the Democratic party and Truman's prestige as chairman of a special Senate committee that had investigated the economic side of the war effort. The change was affected by foreign policy concerns, for the two men disagreed in this area as Wallace was an "idealist" and Truman was a "realist." Both were hostile toward isolationism and believed in vigorous foreign trade and the establishment of an international organization, but they disagreed on military power, with Wallace eager to dismantle it and Truman convinced of its permanent importance. The change was affected also by differences on the New Deal, for Wallace was a leader and a crusader on its behalf while Truman was only a faithful supporter. Differences in personalities also affected the outcome. Wallace was aloof while Truman was gregarious; Wallace seemed to many to be impractical while Truman seemed to be a very practical man. And Roosevelt's health affected the outcome for doubts about it generated large interest in the Vice-Presidency and health problems dissuaded him from battling for his first choice, Wallace.

Unlike Wallace, Truman could cut across intraparty lines. He seemed more capable of uniting the faction-ridden organization. His nomination was engineered by a representative of the urban machine wing of the party, Robert Hannegan. The effort benefited from Truman's acceptability to Roosevelt, who recognized the Missouri senator as a loyal supporter whose popularity could win him reelection. The effort also benefited from Southern hostility to Wallace that encouraged Southerners to move behind Truman after they realized their own candidates could not get the nomination. And the efforts on behalf of Truman profited from his acceptability to the New Deal or liberal wing of the party, although most liberals preferred Wallace.

In addition to experience in several areas of American life and politics, Truman carried strong convictions to the White House. He endorsed the New Deal and the plans for reviving it as a reforming force; he also emphasized the need to avoid the mistakes of the past in international affairs. By the past, he meant the interwar period, and by mistakes, he meant isolationism and pacificism. Troubled by the evidence of isolationist strength and the possibility that it would grow, he believed that the United States must establish and join an international organization and maintain a substantial military establishment.

Emphasizing power in his analysis of international affairs, Truman regarded the United States as very powerful but not omnipotent. He was impressed with the new economic strength of the nation and its large military machine. He recognized, however, that the United States had only some of the power in the world and thus needed help from other nations in order to win the war and avoid another one.

Truman's point of view on Russia and Eastern Europe resembled Roosevelt's. He was influenced by the same concerns that had affected Roosevelt, including beliefs in national self-determination and the importance of Polish-Americans. He did have a link with Eastern Europe that Roosevelt had not had; it came from music and Truman's admiration for Chopin and Paderewski. And he did have a different personality. But he also believed that he had an obligation to continue Roosevelt's efforts, and he was advised on Russia and Eastern Europe by the same people who would have advised Roosevelt, including Ambassador W. Averell Harriman, Admiral William Leahy and Secretary of Navy James Forrestal. They feared Russian ambitions, regarding them as very great and extending beyond Eastern Europe. Convinced that the Russians were violating the Yalta agreements, these men urged Truman to be firm, and their advice made sense to him for weakness had been a mistake of the past and might now play into the hands of the isolationists.

Truman, during his early months as President, pursued a Russian policy that did not differ much from Roosevelt's. He did criticize Molotov, the top Russian diplomat, quite harshly, more harshly, it

seems, than Roosevelt would have, but the difference was only a difference in tactics. And Truman did not move farther along that line. He
rejected Churchill's suggestions that American forces should seize
Prague and remain east of their occupation zone until Russia changed
its ways, for Truman felt restrained by the need for Russian help in the
war against Japan, a desire to avoid war with Russia, hopes for shifting
troops to the war against Japan, the wish to live up to an agreement that
Roosevelt had made and his conviction that he must not set a bad example. He did not give much more support than Roosevelt had to the
ideas about using economic pressure, and he relied chiefly upon words,
including negotiations with Stalin at Potsdam in mid-summer.

Truman's efforts on behalf of Eastern Europe had little impact.
The Polish government was broadened somewhat and then promised
free elections, but the Communists retained control of the military and
the police. Russia rejected an American-British proposal for the reorganization of the governments of Bulgaria, Romania and Hungary
and the supervision of elections. Rather than behave as the Americans
desired, the Russians strengthened their political control of and economic ties with Eastern Europe, defended their moves on security
grounds and criticized British and American behavior in Greece and
Italy.

The End of the War

In other areas, the new President enjoyed more success. Germany,
almost defeated by the time Roosevelt died, surrendered on May 8. And
Truman both completed Roosevelt's work and avoided Wilson's failure
in obtaining Senate confirmation of the proposal for American membership in the new international organization, the United Nations. During
the interwar period, Truman had emphasized military power, rather
than an international organization, as the best means of controlling
international affairs, but during the war, he had been caught up in the
Wilsonian revival and had come to see the defeat of Wilson's plans as
one of the great mistakes of the past and to see himself as personally
obligated to battle against a repetition of it. As soon as Truman became
President, he assured the American people that he would carry forward
Roosevelt's plans. After the Americans enjoyed considerable success
at the San Francisco conference to work out the final details for the
new organization, Truman moved on to victory at home. The cultivation of Republican senators, which had been started by FDR and continued by Truman and which focused on Arthur Vandenberg of Michigan, contributed to the outcome. On July 28, the Senate ratified the treaty
by a vote of 89 to 2. One of the great mistakes of the past, it seemed,
had been avoided.

Truman moved on to victory over Japan. The war ended as it had
begun: very suddenly as a result of a surprise attack. By mid-summer,

Victory in Europe *(National Archives)*

Japan was severely damaged, and many people in Japan (including the leaders) were eager to end the war, although not on the American terms of unconditional surrender. Some American leaders, including top members of the Army and the President, contemplated an invasion of Japan itself and believed that the Japanese army was still determined and able to resist the American advance and inflict heavy casualties. By August, however, a possible alternative to invasion seemed to be at hand. The atomic project had triumphed over difficulties and succeeded; the first test of the new weapon at Alamogordo, N. M., on July 16 had, in fact, demonstrated that it was even more powerful than anticipated, and two bombs were soon available in the Marianas for use against Japan. For Truman and some of his top aides, the development opened up an opportunity for a quick victory on American terms and, at the same time, strengthened the ability to the United States to build the kind of world it desired even though Russia had different ideas. Thus, the decision to use the bombs was made without difficulty, influenced chiefly by the desire to obtain unconditional surrender, a surrender that would

Destruction Wrought by the Atom Bomb *(Library of Congress)*

enable the United States to reshape Japanese life, but affected also by the hope of affecting Russian behavior. Used first against Hiroshima and then against Nagasaki, the bombs, coupled with the entry of Russia into the war against Japan on the Asian mainland, produced the surrender of the surprised and stunned Japanese on August 15 on terms acceptable to American leaders.

The United States had fought a global war effectively and the country had been transformed by it in significant ways. Most important, the nation had become a global power. The experience had persuaded American leaders that the United States must continue to function as such a power. Although somewhat uncertain about the future, they hoped that the American people had learned the same lesson and were encouraged by the Senate's vote on American participation in the United Nations. That vote might mean, however, some officials feared, that the people would place too much confidence in the United Nations and not recognize the importance of the nation's own strength.

SUGGESTIONS FOR FURTHER READING

Ambrose, Stephen E., *The Supreme Commander: The War Years of General Dwight D. Eisenhower.* Garden City, N.J., Doubleday, 1970.

Blum, John Morton, *V Was for Victory: Politics and American Culture during World War II.* New York, Harcourt, Brace Jovanovich, 1976.

Buchanan, A. Russell, *The United States and World War II.* New York, Harper & Row, 1964, 2 vols.

Burns, James MacGregor, *Roosevelt: The Soldier of Freedom.* New York, Harcourt Brace Jovanovich, Inc., 1970.

Chafe, William H., *The American Woman: Her Changing Social, Economic, and Political Roles, 1920-1970.* New York, Oxford University Press, 1972.

Clemens, Diane Shaver, *Yalta,* New York, Oxford University Press, 1970.

Dalfiume, Richard M., *Desegregation of the U.S. Armed Forces: Fighting on Two Fronts 1939-1953.* Columbia, Mo., University of Missouri Press, 1969.

Daniels, Roger, *Concentration Camps USA: Japanese Americans and World War II.* New York, Holt, Rinehart and Winston, Inc., 1971.

Davis, Lynn Etheridge, *The Cold War Begins: Soviet-American Conflict over Eastern Europe.* Princeton, N.J., Princeton University Press, 1974.

Divine, Robert A., *Roosevelt and World War II.* Baltimore, The Johns Hopkins University Press, 1969.

Donovan, Robert, *Conflict and Crisis: The Presidency of Harry S Truman, 1945-1948.* New York, W. W. Norton & Company, Inc., 1977.

Feis, Herbert, *Churchill, Roosevelt, Stalin: The War they Waged and the Peace they Sought.* Princeton, N.J., Princeton University Press, 1957.

————, *The China Tangle: The American Effort in China from Pearl Harbor to the Marshall Mission.* Princeton, N.J., Princeton University Press, 1953.

Gaddis, John Lewis, *The United States and the Origins of the Cold War, 1941-1947.* New York, Columbia University Press, 1972.

Gardner, Lloyd C., *Economic Aspects of New Deal Diplomacy.* Madison, Wis., University of Wisconsin Press, 1964.

Hewlett, Richard G., and Oscar E. Anderson, Jr., *A History of the United States Atomic Energy Commission, Vol. 1 1939/1946: The New World.* University Station, Pa., Pennsylvania State University Press, 1962.

Jonas, Manfred, *Isolationism in America 1935-1941.* Ithaca, N.Y., Cornell University Press, 1966.

Kirkendall, Richard S., *The United States 1929-1945: Years of Crisis and Change.* New York, McGraw Hill Book Co., 1974.

Kolko, Gabriel, *The Politics of War: The World and United States Foreign Policy, 1943-1945*. New York, Random House, 1968.

Perrett, Geoffrey, *Days of Sadness, Years of Triumph*. Baltimore, Md., Penguin Books, Inc., 1973.

Pogue, Forrest, *George C. Marshall*. New York, The Viking Press, 3 volumes, 1963, 1966, 1973.

Polenberg, Richard, *War and Society: The United States 1941-1945*. Philadelphia, J. B. Lippincott Co., 1972.

Sherwin, Martin J., *A World Destroyed: The Atomic Bomb and the Grand Alliance*. New York, Alfred A. Knopf, 1975.

Wohlstetter, Roberta, *Pearl Harbor: Warnings and Decisions*. Stanford, Calif., Stanford University Press, 1962.

The Cold War and Containment

AS HARRY S TRUMAN AND MANY OF his presidential aides had hoped, the United States continued to function as a global power in the postwar years. It did so because of the "lessons" that had been learned and because a "Cold War" quickly moved into the place once occupied by the very hot war of 1939-1945 as the dominant feature of world affairs. The Truman people had, of course, the opportunity to shape the initial American response to the postwar situation because the war did not bring their power to an end. The striking fact is that the response they developed—the Containment Policy—continued to be the American foreign policy after a Republican administration replaced the Democrats. A very active foreign policy, Containment was established rather than isolationism, and it triumphed over the challenges to it from Henry Wallace, from Joseph McCarthy, and from "Liberation" to become the bipartisan foreign policy of the United States.

The Emergence of the Cold War

The Cold War emerged in 1945 and 1946 as the shooting war came to an end, doing so as a process of interaction between the United States and Russia, both governed by men convinced they had learned the

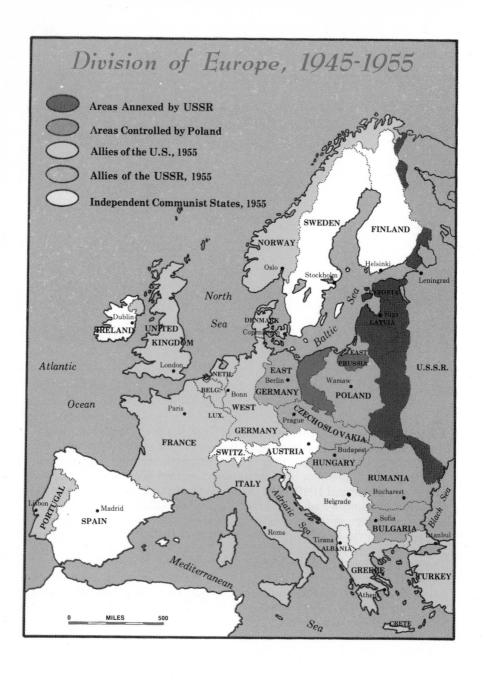

Division of Europe, 1945-1955

Areas Annexed by USSR

Areas Controlled by Poland

Allies of the U.S., 1955

Allies of the USSR, 1955

Independent Communist States, 1955

SWEDEN

FINLAND

NORWAY

Oslo

Helsinki

Stockholm

Leningrad

North

Sea

ESTONIA

Baltic

Riga

Sea

LATVIA

Dublin

IRELAND

UNITED

KINGDOM

DENMARK

Copenhagen

EAST
PRUSSIA

U.S.S.R.

Atlantic

London

EAST

Berlin

Warsaw

NETH.

GERMANY

POLAND

BELG.

Bonn

Ocean

Paris

WEST

LUX.

GERMANY

CZECHOSLOVAKIA

Prague

FRANCE

SWITZ.

AUSTRIA

Budapest

HUNGARY

RUMANIA

ITALY

Bucharest

PORTUGAL

Belgrade

Black

Lisbon

Adriatic

Sea

Sofia

Madrid

Sea

BULGARIA

Istanbul

SPAIN

Rome

Tirana

ALBANIA

Mediterranean

GREECE

TURKEY

Athens

0   MILES   500

Sea

CRETE

lessons of history and that the relevant lessons were those taught by World War II and the background to it. The Cold War involved Russian-American conflict, but that had been present in varying degrees since the Communist revolution of 1917. It involved non-violent conflict, a feature that distinguished the Cold War from what is customarily meant by war. It was intense conflict, so intense that conflict was the dominant feature of the relationships between the two countries. And it was significant conflict, so important that it affected virtually all other nations and imposed pressure on them to take sides.

Both ideological differences and economics contributed to the emergence of the Cold War but did not fully explain it. It involved a struggle between communism on the one side and capitalism and democracy on the other, but they had long been present in the relations between Russia and the United States and had not prevented the two from cooperating in some important ways during World War II. The struggle involved a clash between those who believed they must control and exploit the economies of their neighbors and those who preached the "open door" and hoped to penetrate the economies of all parts of the world. Yet, similar disagreements between Great Britain and the United States did not produce a Cold War between them. They frequently disagreed on international economic policies, but the British were inclined to give in, although they frequently looked for ways around the concessions made to American demands for the open door. Obviously, ideological differences and economics were not the only forces responsible for the Cold War.

Of the others, World War II was especially important. It had destroyed the power of the nations that had separated Russia and the United States, thereby providing them with new opportunities to clash with one another. It had increased the power of both nations. There can be no doubt about the war's impact on the power of the United States, but the Russian evidence is more ambiguous. The war did inflict serious damage on the Soviet Union, taking many more lives than it took in any other country and inflicting heavy economic losses, but it also gave the Russians new opportunities, especially in Eastern Europe and Germany, and they seized them. They separated their allies and satellites by an "Iron Curtain" that had the impact of isolating them from the Western powers. The war also increased the self-confidence or sense of power of both nations for they had triumphed over strong adversaries. Finally, the war reduced the influence of isolationism in both countries, convincing American leaders of the folly of it and persuading Russian leaders that they must control Eastern Europe and Germany to be secure.

The Cold War emerged and escalated when it did (late 1945 and on through 1946) for several reasons. The ending of the Second World War reduced pressures on both nations to cooperate with one another. The atomic bomb increased the American leaders' sense of strength, alarmed the Russians, and also alarmed some Americans who worried about the day when Russia as well as the United States would have this awesome weapon. Russian behavior in Eastern Europe and Iran, where they maintained their military presence and sought to shape political developments, troubled Americans. It violated their theory of what the world should be like, seemed to violate the Yalta agreements, and suggested that Russia might expand farther, as Hitler and Japan had. Russian pressure on Turkey in 1946 also contributed and so did the rivalry over Germany. There, the two nations were locked into a system of joint control; they had promised reunification, but they disagreed over terms.

The Cold War did not involve the use of military force by the competitors, at least not against one another. The Russians used troops in Eastern Europe and Iran but not beyond, while the United States used them in Italy, western Germany, Japan, and a few other places but not in the areas in which the Russians were present. In fact, the United States reduced its military forces in Europe very rapidly after the fighting stopped and carried through a major program of demobilization at a rapid pace. The United States did continue to develop the atomic bomb but did not threaten to use it. It did establish and then enlarge a naval presence in the Eastern Mediterranean during 1946.

Also, the Cold War did not involve a large use of American economic power during this period. The United States had great economic strength; Russia needed outside aid for reconstruction purposes, although she had alternatives in Eastern Europe and Germany to American aid; some American officials believed that economic power might be used to exert an influence on Russian behavior, and occasionally they hinted at changes that the Russians must make in order to get American economic help. Yet, the United States did not attempt to bargain over a reconstruction loan to Russia and provided the funds for the United Nations Relief and Rehabilitation Administration, an agency that distributed its resources without regard for politics. The United States did use its economic strength at the time to influence politics in Italy, France, Great Britain, and western Germany. The U.S. wanted to find ways to use its economic strength more effectively, but it did not bring economic pressure to bear directly on the Soviet Union.

The Cold War in its early months was largely a war of words. Each side employed verbal pressure against the other. They clashed verbally over Eastern Europe, Italy, Germany, Turkey, and atomic energy, seeking liberation or control in Eastern Europe, trying to prevent control of Germany by the other side, and hoping to protect themselves from destruction by atomic weapons. While the United States maneuvered to prevent the Russians from developing atomic bombs, the Russians tried to get the United States to destroy the atomic weapons that it had.

The Cold War had some consequences in its early months, but the

United States failed to achieve most of its objectives. The Russians removed their troops from Iran and relaxed their pressure on Turkey, but did not agree to the American proposal for a system of international control of atomic energy. The two sides moved toward the permanent division of Germany; the Russians, concerned but not controlled by American power, tightened their control of Eastern Europe, and the Truman Administration achieved unity on foreign policy in September 1946 with the removal from the cabinet of Henry Wallace, an advocate of toleration of Russian behavior in Eastern Europe and renewed efforts at cooperation.

The Cold War had clearly emerged by late 1946. Russian-American conflict had reached a point where it deserved a special label. Neither side had confidence in the possibility of cooperation with the other. The Cold War had emerged as the consequence of the interaction between two powerful and ambitious nations, both of whom were convinced that history proved that they must behave as they were behaving. The Russians believed that they must exert a large influence in Eastern Europe and Germany, while the Americans believed that they must challenge Russian behavior in those places. Each side, in a sense, saw the other as having moved into Hitler's shoes and was convinced that it must not repeat the mistakes of the 1930s.

The Emergence of the Containment Policy

In 1947, the Truman Administration's attention shifted from efforts to liberate Eastern Europe from Russian control to efforts to contain further expansion in Europe by Russia and Communists. The interaction between the situations in Southern and Western Europe and American conceptions of Soviet intentions produced the new policy of Containment. The situations in Southern and Western Europe included the persistence of economic depression and Communist pressure. The latter came from guerrilla warriors in Greece who had outside support and from large Communist parties in France and Italy. The possibility of renewed Russian pressure on Turkey also loomed over the scene, and British weaknesses were an important part of it. Early in 1947, the British announced that they must soon withdraw their troops and economic support from Greece and Turkey.

By now, the Truman Administration had a well-defined way of looking at such developments. American leaders saw Russia as ambitious and powerful and Europe as important to the United States for economic and political reasons. They assumed that economic conditions exerted a powerful influence on politics, and they believed that the United States had the capacity and responsibility to tackle problems such as those that were developing on the other side of the Atlantic. The old concept of the "American Mission" reinforced the

President Harry S Truman *(National Park Service-Abbie Rowe)*

new idea of the "lessons of history" to produce this sense of responsibility.

Interpreting developments as it did, the Truman Administration formulated the Containment Policy in 1947-1948, with the Truman Doctrine and the Marshall Plan as its major features. The policy was unilateral in character. Although the United States did call upon the Europeans to develop a plan that the Americans would try to support, the United States acted largely on its own at the outset and made no effort to work through the United Nations. The new policy relied upon American economic power, supplemented by the atomic bomb but not explicitly. Containment also, at this time, emphasized military and economic development. The policy was ambitious, although not as ambitious as Lend-Lease, calling as it did for nearly one-half billion dollars in aid for Greece and Turkey and additional billions of dollars per year for several years to carry out the Marshall Plan or the European Recovery Program. Yet, Containment also had limits. It focused on Southern and Western Europe and did not extend to Eastern Europe, at least after Russia refused to participate in the Marshall Plan, or to Asia.

The objectives, while partially economic, were chiefly political. Containment sought mainly to check Russian expansion. It sought to safeguard the political consequences of the movement of Western armies during World War II, not to undo the political consequences of the movement of Russian armies, at least not immediately. The policy did, as was suggested by one of its architects, George Kennan, have liberation as a long-run goal. He argued that liberation of Eastern Europe and even Russia would come after Containment frustrated Russia and communism and demonstrated the strength of the United States and capitalism.

One of the most striking aspects of the Containment Policy is that is succeeded in the United States. The Truman Administration persuaded the Congress to support it with appropriations in spite of opposition to it. Some of the opposition came from those, represented most significantly by Wallace, who were clinging to the hopes for cooperation with Russia and reliance upon the U.N. Opposition came also from leaders, such as Republican Senator Robert A. Taft of Ohio, who wanted to reduce government expenditure sharply. The Republicans controlled Congress in 1947-48. The Administration's success resulted in part from its own efforts, which included dramatic rhetoric about the international situation, impressive evidence on Europe's needs and America's abilities, and the cultivation of friendly Republicans. The success owed something also to the work of some Republicans, especially of Senator Arthur A. Vandenberg of Michigan. The Russians also made contributions, first by refusing to cooperate with the recovery program and then by contributing to a coup in Czechoslovakia that drove liberals from a coalition government and put the Communists in control.

Consequences flowed immediately from the new policy. It strengthened anti-Communist groups in Southern and Western Europe and
stimulated progress toward the establishment of a West German Republic. It also encouraged the Russians to tighten still more their
control of Eastern Europe, a process that persuaded Yugoslavia to
rebel and establish itself as an independent Communist country.
Progress toward the establishment of a West German Republic convinced the Russians to impose a blockade on land and water traffic
into Berlin, a city jointly controlled by Russia, the United States, Great
Britain, and France. The United States responded to the blockade by
airlifting supplies into the western sectors of Berlin and expanding
American air power in England and Germany. This alarming series of
events, which aroused in Western leaders, bitterness and determination, led to the building of a defense alliance.

The Cold War, quite obviously, was escalating rapidly in 1947-
1948. Again, this resulted from a process of interaction. The process
began with the possibility of further progress by the Communists;
it encouraged an American reaction that in turn produced a Russian
reaction; the latter resulted in new American moves. The Cold War,
in other words, spiralled upwards. If the United States and Russia
had not had so much power relative to other nations, they would not
have been able to behave as they did. Yet, they became more powerful; Russia tied Eastern Europe more closely to it and the United
States tied Western and Southern Europe more closely to it.

By late 1948, the United States was playing a very large role in
Europe. It was relying on its economic power, although that was
supplemented by one form of military power, the atomic bomb and with
the B-29. To administration leaders, the development was quite
satisfying, not because they were grasping men, but because they
were convinced that history dictated that they should behave as they
were. They believed that they were demonstrating that they had
learned the lessons of history and were avoiding the mistakes of the past.

By 1949, reliance on American economic power, supplemented
by American air power, seemed inadequate to some American leaders,
and they pressed for the expansion of military power. The United
States had reduced in strength most of its military power that had
been developed during the war, although it had not returned to the low
prewar level. The nation's military policy emphasized the new weapons
—atomic bombs and long-range bombers, and the government continued to develop and test bombs while establishing tight civilian control over them by the President and the new Atomic Energy Commission. The policy also involved a strict limit on military spending. The
armed forces were unified, although not very effectively, in hopes
of making them more efficient, and the Congress turned down the Ad-

ministration's proposal to build strength through a system of Universal Military Training.

A combination of factors produced the policy. One was a widespread, emotional desire in 1945 to "bring the boys back home" as rapidly as possible, a desire that was shared by nearly all members of the armed forces. Traditional American hostility toward military service and a large military establishment also contributed, as did confidence that the U.N. could guarantee American security. Fear of large-scale government spending was very important and was related to a sense of the limits on American power, particularly by the strength of the American economy. A conception of the importance of the economic recovery of Europe also exerted an influence, suggesting to many that it should consume funds that might otherwise be used for military purposes. And confidence in air power played a major role. As the United States had a monopoly on atomic bombs and long-range bombers, air power seemed capable of guaranteeing American security and doing so at a lower cost than would be involved in the development of a large army and navy.

Other forces of some strength, however, competed with at least some of these during 1948 and into 1949. One was the fear of Russian armies, although they too had been cut sharply since the war. Stimulated by the Czech coup and the Berlin blockade, the fear did not subside after the Russians lifted the blockade in May 1949. The armies seemed to threaten hopes for economic growth; Western European businessmen, it seemed, would not be very enterprising if they assumed that the Russian armies might roll into their countries and seize their properties. Declining confidence in the United Nations also suggested to some that the West should develop more military strength. The decline resulted largely from the Russian use of the veto power. Dean Acheson, who became Secretary of State in 1949, had long been very skeptical about the U.N.'s potential. To him, military power was especially important in international affairs.

These various pressures led to the establishment of the North Atlantic Treaty Organization. It was a Western institution and a defense alliance. The member nations on two sides of the Atlantic promised to cooperate militarily if Russia moved against one of them, and they assumed that their cooperation would maximize their strength. It was only a limited arrangement. It did not include the West German Republic, which was established in May 1949, or Greece and Turkey, and it did not involve a military buildup. It meant mainly that the United States would use its atomic power. That became more explicitly involved in the Containment Policy. The planners assumed that NATO would exert a restraining influence on the Russians, thus keeping the peace rather than provoking war, and the establishment of the new organization constituted a new stage in the elaboration of

Containment. Senate acceptance of the treaty by a wide margin of bi-partisan support indicated that opposition to the policy had ceased to be significant. Support for Containment was so strong through the na-tion that the people willingly rejected its tradition against "entangling alliances" in peacetime.

Further militarization of Containment followed quickly after the establishment of NATO, due chiefly to the Russian atomic bomb, which was secretly tested in August 1949, but publicized by Truman the following month. The Russian atomic program had succeeded more quickly than had been anticipated, and the success challenged the basis of American military policy: its dependence on the American monopoly of atomic weapons. Widespread emotion in the United States arose over the Russian success, and orators calculated how the atom bomb could be used to devastate American cities. Congress responded by accepting an Administration request for the establishment of a Mili-tary Assistance Program that used American economic power to pro-mote the military development of the nation's allies. This supplemented use of that economic power for economic purposes and was linked to the European Recovery Program in political objective. Also in re-sponse to the Russian atomic bomb, the Administration decided early in 1950 to build an even more powerful weapon, a hydrogen bomb, and thereby guarantee that the American Air Force would continue to be more powerful than its Russian counterpart.

The Administration also developed a plan—NSC-68—for a vast buildup of American forces. The plan called for a great increase in the defense budget, including a substantial expansion of the Army. Widely endorsed inside the Administration by the late spring of 1950, the plan assumed that the Russian capacity to expand had been in-creased significantly by the success of its atomic program and would become even greater if the United States and its allies did not develop much more military power. The plan also assumed that the United States could afford to spend much more money on its military forces. Truman did not, however, decide to implement NSC-68.

Thus, as the European Recovery Program was going into operation, the United States moved toward heavier reliance on military power. The objective remained the same—containment and eventually liber-ation, but the means were being changed. Containment was being militarized. By June 1950, however, Truman had not yet decided to press for a vast program of military spending and the development of a complex military establishment involving a large army and a large navy as well as a powerful air force.

Triumphs and Troubles at Home

Chiefly significant for its role in the history of American foreign policy, the Truman Administration did not accomplish nearly as much at home. Yet, it did enjoy some victories there. Among other accomplishments, Truman and his aides avoided postwar depression and extended Democratic control of the White House beyond 1948. Truman also tried to be an innovator in some areas, above all in civil rights, but desires to protect established institutions against internal and external threats dominated the politics of the period. Before the end of his years as President, Truman was spending much of his time defending himself against charges that he was not doing enough to safeguard the nation.

Whatever may be written of the years from 1945 to 1953, the personality and presence of Harry S Truman must be evaluated. Truman succeeded the popular and sophisticated Roosevelt, whose voice, manner, habits, and prestige gave the new President a high standard of conduct to match. Truman's qualities of plain speaking and honesty in political dealings were not always appreciated. His voice, background, opinions, and presence often aroused much criticism and satire. He seemed to many people rustic, uncultured, and unsuited for the presidency. His spontaneous remarks on the military, opponents, and political issues often injured his image.

The American people entered these postwar years with considerable tension. With millions of men returning from the service, their reentry into civilian life often was traumatic, and they found themselves not only older but forced to take up life that they had left as boys or as young men. Returning to school or old jobs was an ordeal, and they reacted to regulations, shortages, and inflation by condemning the administration and officeholders generally. Many ex-servicemen turned to politics; others joined unions in strikes for better wages and working conditions. Many Americans moved from farms to cities, and some to the western states.

The Truman administration faced these postwar conditions with much skill. It avoided a postwar depression which many anticipated. Pessimists recognized that the Great Depression had not ended until 1941 and that only the war, not the New Deal or private enterprise, had brought it to an end. They had feared that the war's end, by stopping massive government spending and reducing the size of foreign markets, would bring depressed conditions similar to those of the 1930s.

The postwar depression, however, did not arrive and did not do so, in part, because of the work of the Truman Administration. Had it blundered seriously in the handling of economic affairs, the economy would surely have gone into a tailspin because the federal government had become an important part of the economic system. The government did cut its spending very sharply, and the Administration did have difficulties in trying to establish a domestic economic program as a consequence of conflicts over economic policies within the Administration and between the Administration and Congress. Also,

Washington failed to create an open-door world. But federal spending remained well above prewar levels, and Washington administered programs estabished during the Roosevelt years, especially Social Security and the G.I. Bill of Rights, that gave the unemployed dollars to spend and kept many people out of the job market. Also, the Administration and the Congress agreed on a tax cut immediately after the war; the government maintained foreign sales at a high level through relief, loans, and aid and helped American firms gain access to raw materials abroad, especially oil. Legislation in 1946, the Employment Act, defined the government's basic responsibility in economic matters and established a new agency, the Council of Economic Advisers, to help it fulfill its responsibility.

Private forces contributed even more to the level of prosperity enjoyed in the second half of the 1940s. Business firms and consumers had the funds needed to invest and spend as a consequence of the profits and incomes they had enjoyed during the war, and they were eager to use those funds for many opportunities and things they wanted had not been available during the war. Furthermore, the business firms could make the transition from war to peace quite easily because it involved only a return to activities they knew how to perform.

Although not free of economic problems, the postwar years were quite prosperous. During the first year after the war, the economy suffered from many strikes, shortages of things that people wanted to buy, and an increase in unemployment and inflation, but the nation avoided large-scale unemployment. After a brief transition period, the economy grew again and continued to do so until 1949.

In spite of the economic accomplishments of these years, Truman experienced many political troubles that made his election victory in 1948 seem very dramatic and significant. He appeared to face a reviving Republican party when it regained control of Congress in the 1946 elections. And his own party seemed to be disintegrating, losing groups on the left to Henry Wallace, due chiefly although not exclusively to unhappiness with Truman's foreign policy, lost support in the South as a consequence of his efforts to promote change in race relations. These efforts were influenced by the interest in the issue that he brought to the White House, his concern about violence against blacks after the war, his interest in the black vote, and his concern about the American image in the world. By the spring of 1948, Truman appeared to be quite unpopular, a fact that encouraged several groups of Democrats to try to substitute Eisenhower for Truman as the party's candidate, and by the summer, the pollsters agreed that the Republican candidate, Thomas E. Dewey of New York and his popular running-mate Earl Warren of California, would win the election.

But Truman won! This accomplishment resulted largely from the basic strength of the Democratic party and from Truman's campaign. Most of the strength had developed under Roosevelt's leadership, and Truman's campaign which was colorful and vigorous, sought to rally Democrats by describing the benefits that different groups had derived from Democratic rule and warning against Republican threats to them, threats that were illustrated by the Republican-controlled Congress. As campaigner, Truman also portrayed Wallace, who was running for the White House as the candidate of the Progressive party, as Communist-dominated and as a threat to effective liberalism. Truman represented the Dixiecrats, the party representing the most discontented Southerners, as a threat to Democratic control and thus to Southern development and prosperity. Moreover, Truman's success resulted from the fact that the Republicans were not effective campaigners. Dewey seemed overconfident and cold, and neither he or the party had much that was new to offer the nation.

Truman also helped himself to victory by the ways in which he used presidential power. In May, he recognized the new state of Israel. In July, he issued two executive orders calling for changes in race relations in the armed forces and the federal government. At the same time, he called Congress into special session. And throughout the campaign period, he clashed with the Russians over Berlin and promoted negotiations with them.

Truman held on to most but not all Democratic strength. He was somewhat weaker in the East and South than Roosevelt had been. He was slightly stronger in the Midwest and Far West than Roosevelt had been in1940 and 1944.

Although the campaign was waged chiefly on domestic issues, the outcome was especially significant for foreign policy. Truman's victory maintained Democratic control of the White House but did not demonstrate great popular support for Truman himself. He received less than 50 percent of the popular vote, won by the narrowest margin since 1916, and drew a much smaller percentage of voters to the polls than had voted in the presidential contests of the 1930s. The congressional elections that accompanied the presidential contest reestablished Democratic control of Congress, and the two sets of Democratic victories strengthened the New Deal by providing evidence of popular support for established domestic programs. The outcome did not demonstrate great support for new proposals, except among black voters, and it strengthened Containment even more than it strengthened the New Deal. Three of the four presidential candidates—Dewey and Strom Thurmond as well as Truman—endorsed Containment. The only one who challenged it—Wallace—was destroyed politically, for he received less than 3 percent of the popular vote.

After his victory in 1948, Truman battled for change in American life. He battled for what he called a Fair Deal, which was based upon the New Deal with its assumption about the ability of government to promote desirable social and economic developments but involved more than a continuation of the New Deal. The Fair Deal involved a restoration of one of the features of the New Deal by calling for repeal of the Taft-Hartley or National Labor Relations Act of 1947 that had amended the Wagner Act in ways that the labor movement found highly undesirable. The Fair Deal involved the enlargement of the New Deal by calling for greater benefits from and wider coverage by Social Security, a raise in the minimum wage, more public housing, slum clearance, public power and reclamation, federal aid to education, and national health insurance. Fair Deal proposals included a departure from the New Deal's farm programs with the Brannan Plan that paid greater attention to the interests of consumers and envisioned the establishment of a farmer-labor alliance. And the Fair Deal paid much more attention to civil rights than the New Deal had. Truman pressed for the implementation of his executive orders of 1948, called once again for broad civil rights legislation and emphasized an attack on discriminatory employment practices.

Truman enjoyed some victories but also suffered some defeats. His accomplishments were topped by the Housing Act of 1949, which included a public housing provision and was passed with bipartisan support over opposition from realtors and most conservative congressmen, although not from Robert A. Taft. As the President proposed, Congress expanded public power and reclamation, which, while opposed by private power companies and many farmers, had strong support in the West and South. Congress also strengthened the Social Security programs and raised the minimum wage. Congress did not, however, enact the Brannan Plan or the civil rights proposals or repeal the Taft-Hartley Act.

The Administration did influence Supreme Court decisions in the area of civil rights. Cooperating with the National Association for the Advancement of Colored People, the Justice Department submitted "friends of the court" briefs that helped to persuade the Court to hand down decisions in 1950 attacking segregation in interstate commerce and higher education. And before Truman left office, his Justice Department decided to join in an attack on segregation in secondary and elementary schools.

Truman also successfully promoted the desegregation of the armed forces. Resisted by the Army and by Southern congressmen, it was pressed by the President and by a presidential committee as well as the leaders of the Air Force and the Navy, and the pressure forced the Army to change its policy early in 1950. Then the Korean War forced a change in practice as well, when commanders were compelled to send in black soldiers to fight alongside whites and discovered that integration worked well.

While Truman wanted to accomplish more reforms, his own shortcomings as a reformer limited him. He was not as interested in domestic matters as he was in foreign affairs because problems in the latter area seemed much more pressing, and he was not as articulate and skillful as FDR. He worked, however, in a situation that posed major difficulties for a reformer. He did not benefit, as Roosevelt had in the 1930s, from widespread demand for a broad program of reform, and he had to contend with a Conservative Coalition in Congress that had demonstrated that it could even frustrate FDR and that had not been destroyed by the 1948 elections. As an advocate of change in race relations, he had to contend with the filibuster, which was used by Southern senators who took advantage of the interest that Truman and other advocates of civil rights legislation had in other issues. Because of that interest, they could tolerate inaction by the Senate for only so long. Powerful pressure groups, such as the American Medical Association, which opposed national health insurance, and the American Farm Bureau Federation, which fought against the Brannan Plan, also produced problems for Truman. And religious divisions got in the way, for Protestants battled against Catholics over federal aid to education.

The Korean War, which began late in June 1950, became a giant obstacle in the path of the Fair Deal. It distracted the President and the Congress, encouraging them to think that nothing was more deserving of their time and energy than the war. It elevated the Southern Democrats, for many of them, such as Senator Richard Russell of Georgia, occupied important positions in the congressional committees concerned with military and foreign affairs. And, as a far from popular war, Korea helped the Republicans strengthen themselves in Congress in the 1950 elections.

The rising Red Scare was another obstacle. It distracted attention from reform, completed the destruction of the radical left, thereby depriving reformers of helpful pressures from that direction, and raised doubts about the loyalty of liberals. Anyone who suggested that the United States needed to be changed seemed "unAmerican" to many people in the early 1950s.

The Red Scare came to be called McCarthyism during the years of the Korean War, and McCarthyism owed much to the frustrating course of that war. McCarthyism was the thought and behavior of a Republican senator from Wisconsin, Joseph R. McCarthy. It was an intense version of the Red Scare, that widely held belief that Communists inside the United States constituted a serious threat to the nation. McCarthyism was an interpretation of recent history that ignored American successes, focused on discouraging developments, explained them as results of Communist influence, especially in the State Department, and assumed that had that influence not been present the United States would have succeeded. McCarthyism also involved a reckless attitude toward the truth. The Wisconsin senator moved from attack to attack and did not bother to supply the evidence needed to support his charges.

Some historians have blamed the Truman Administration for the rise of McCarthyism. The administration had, in 1947, established a Loyalty Program that assumed Communists in the United States did constitute a threat of some kind. Truman and many of his supporters had used anti-Communist rhetoric to sell Administration programs and defeat Henry Wallace. The Justice Department did prosecute the leaders of the Communist party in the United States. Truman did come to see some features of the anti-Communist crusade in the United States as a threat to freedom, but he realized the seriousness of the crusade only after it turned against him.

These activities by the Truman Administration, however, were but parts of a very complex picture and hardly the crucial factor in the rise of McCarthyism. It seems likely to have become even more important if Truman had not pressed his anti-Communist activities for they provided an answer to charges that satisfied many people. Fear of the radical had long been a feature of American life, and that fear had focused on Communists after the Russian Revolution and had gained new strength after World War II, promoted by the House Committee on UnAmerican Activities, many Catholics, business groups, Republicans and others, including anti-Communists in the liberal and labor movements fighting for control of those movements. By the late 1940s, the fear affected almost all parts of American life, especially the schools and colleges, labor unions, and the entertainment industry. A series of frustrating developments after 1948, including the Communist victory in China, the development of the Russian atomic bomb and the Korean War, added mass hysteria to an already emotional situation. The nation was then engrossed in various spy cases, especially the conviction of Alger Hiss for perjury in January 1950, after this former government official denied that he had been a member of the Communist party and had passed on secret documents. Congress, at the height of this emotion passed the McCarran Act, which provided for registration of Communist and Communist-front organizations and internment of Communists during national emergencies.

The frustration of many conservatives and the needs of Republicans were also important parts of the picture. Conservatives were distressed by many of the policies that had been adopted since 1932, and Republicans, after a series of defeats, including the unexpected defeat of 1948, needed an issue to help them return to power. Thus, conservatives, especially conservative Republicans, and Republicans of all kinds, used the anti-Communist issue frequently in their efforts to return to power.

The timidity and ineffectiveness of its opponents also contributed to the rise of McCarthyism. Many people held back, refusing to express their opposition, because they feared McCarthy's apparent power. Truman spoke out but failed to rally much support.

McCarthy's needs plus his skills of invective and slander were im-

"Injuns" Follow the President *(Library of Congress)*

portant in this "disease" that he spread. Faced by 1950 with possible defeat in 1952, he needed an issue at the time he appropriated anti-communism, and he seized the opportunity that circumstances supplied. He used the press effectively, exploited resentments that many people felt, including resentments against Eastern private schools and the military, and provided a simple explanation for discouraging events and an easy solution to the nation's problems, suggesting that the United States needed only to remove traitors from power in the State Department and other places and substitute loyal Americans for them. And he identified closely with conservative Republicans.

In addition to completing the destruction of radicalism and weakening liberalism, McCarthyism was important for other reasons. It demoralized the State Department and encouraged it to become quite inflexible in order to prove its loyalty. The movement also weakened the Truman Administration by suggesting constantly that it was "soft" on communism and insensitive to the dangers from Communists in American life and government, and McCarthyism helped the Republicans regain control of the White House and Congress. The Red

Scare and McCarthy, while not the most important factors, figured prominently in the successful Republican campaigns of 1950 and 1952.

Troubles in Asia

The frustrating course of American foreign relations in Asia contributed significantly to McCarthyism. One frustration was the Communist triumph in China in 1949.

The Chinese civil war escalated after the defeat of Japan, and the American government tried to influence the outcome. Fearing that the war would result in the expansion of communism, the enlargement of Russian power, and the closing of China to American missionaries and businessmen, the United States made a small military effort there, an effort that was especially small after 1946, and a more substantial economic effort. The latter, although much smaller than the program of aid to Europe, was larger than the Truman Administration regarded as desirable but it yielded to Republican pressure. American efforts also involved the use of diplomacy in 1945-1946, aimed at ending the civil war and establishing a coalition government and based on the assumption that Nationalists and Communists could behave like Democrats and Republicans. The United States also pressured Chiang, seeking to persuade him to make reforms that would increase his popularity and effectiveness.

These efforts, while not insignificant, were small compared to the efforts being made in Europe during the late 1940s. Traditional American fears of military involvement on the Asian mainland exerted a restraining influence, as did the nation's postwar military policy. As the civil war reached a crisis state, the United States did not have a large military establishment that could provide the basis for military action in China. And conceptions of the limited scope of American power and the superiority of Europe also restrained decision-makers. Believing that they had but a limited number of dollars that could be devoted to foreign policy objectives, the leaders of the Truman Administration also believed that Europe was more capable than China of using American aid. Europe seemed more important also because it was highly industrialized and hence a more powerful area and was an area in which the Russians had more interest. Also, American leaders doubted that anything but a massive effort in China could succeed. They did not think in terms of a limited war for a limited objective, say the preservation of Chiang's control over southern China.

Thus, with the United States making a relatively small effort to assure the defeat of the Chinese Communists, the Communists gained control of mainland China. Their victory did not result from the numerical superiority of Communist forces, for they had a smaller number of troops and less equipment as the civil war began to rage. The

Communist victory was not a consequence of Russian aid, for the Russians supplied the Chinese Communists with even less aid than the United States gave to the Nationalists. The outcome was determined largely by the ineffectiveness of Chiang's regime and forces. Chiang failed to rally the support of the Chinese people, and his troops surrendered easily, enlarging the Communist forces and their supply of arms when they did. The skill of Mao Tse-tung and his lieutenants also contributed because they were more effective militarily and demonstrated greater appeal to the masses.

Mao's victory came in 1949. Chiang and many of his followers fled to the island of Formosa, giving Mao control of the mainland and enabling him to substitute an effective dictatorship for an ineffective one. The outcome led to closer ties between China and Russia and greater conflict between China and the United States. The Chinese denounced the Americans harshly for their intervention, and the United States refused to recognize the new regime or to permit it to become a member of the U.S. Some United States Senators, such as William F. Knowland of California, used the collapse of China for political advantages. They accused the Democrats of bungling, and pressed for the nonrecognition of the new regime.

The United States, in spite of the collapse of China, maintained a presence in Asia. America had bases and economic strength in the Philippine Islands, although they had been granted independence in 1946. The United States also had an interest in South Korea because it had occupied this former part of the Japanese Empire after the war, influenced political developments there, and maintained some influence after withdrawing its troops in 1949, doing so chiefly by supplying economic assistance. And the American presence in Asia was especially important in Japan. There, the United States monopolized the occupation, refusing to allow any other nation to participate, and used its new power in the country to reshape Japanese life, destroying military power and the political role of the military, exalting the Diet, and promoting economic growth and other changes. At the same time, Americans worked against Communist influence in Japanese life. Although Japan was the most productive and the most powerful part of Asia, most Americans derived little comfort from their nation's accomplishments in that country, while developments in China gave many Americans a sense of great frustration.

In the last week of June 1950, the United States embarked upon a new adventure in Asia that would add to the sense of frustration. The nation intervened in a war in Korea that resulted from the interaction of four nations. The Korean peninsula had been divided by the United States and Russia for occupation purposes, and the division had been strengthened by their individual efforts to shape the politics of their occupation zones. North Korea began the war in hopes of reunifying the peninsula and of preventing South Korea from doing so; the North

The Shifting Front in Korea

June 25, 1950

U.S.
S.R.

CHINA

Vladivostok

Tumen R.

Mukden

Yalu R.

NORTH
KOREA

Wonsan

Pyongyang

North Korean Invasion

Sea

Japan

of

38°

Seoul

SOUTH

KOREA

Yellow

Sea

Pusan

QUELPART

Sasebo

JAPAN

September 15, 1950

U.S.
S.R.

CHINA

Vladivostok

Tumen

Mukden

Yalu R.

Chosan

Wonsan

Pyongyang

Inchon

Seoul

Inchon
invasion

Yellow

Sea

Pusan Perimeter

Taegu

U.N. Forces
counterattack

Pusan

Sea

of

Japan

38°

JAPAN

November 24, 1950

U.S.
S.R.

CHINA

Vladivostok

Chinese intervention

Tumen R.

Mukden

Yalu

Chosin
Resv.

Chongjin

Battle line
as of Nov. 1950

Hungnam

U.N. evacuations,
Dec. 1950

Sinanju

Pyongyang

Wonsan

38°

Seoul

Yellow

Sea

Taegu

Pusan

JAPAN

July 27, 1953

U.S.
S.R.

CHINA

Vladivostok

Tumen

Mukden

Yalu R.

NORTH

KOREA

Pyongyang

Wonsan

Armistice line,
July 27, 1953

Panmunjom

Seoul

Nov. 12, 1951

Yellow

Sea

SOUTH

KOREA

Pusan

38°

JAPAN

was encouraged to move by military weaknesses in the South. The Russians contributed to the outbreak of war, for they had supplied arms and training for North Korean forces and believed that the Korean situation provided an opportunity to strengthen their influence in Asia. They were persuaded that the United States was not sufficiently interested in Korea to intervene militarily and the risks of a large war were minimal. The frequently provocative acts of the South Koreans, who hoped to bring the entire peninsula under their control but were restrained by their weaknesses, also formed an important part of the background to the war. And American actions in Asia constituted another part. The United States had not made a giant effort in Asia, had withdrawn its troops from South Korea and defined the country as beyond the American defense perimeter and had given aid to the South Koreans but not offensive weapons. On the other hand, the United States seemed to be planning to turn Japan into a permanent American base.

The decision to intervene was not dictated by a belief that South Korea was an area of great strategic or economic significance. Americans believed that North Korea was only a puppet of the Russians, and that belief encouraged Truman and his advisers to see the Korean situation as similar to ones in the 1930s, such as the Japanese invasion of Manchuria. They were firmly convinced that they must avoid the great American mistake of the 1930s: the refusal to get involved significantly early in the development of aggression. If they intervened, they would halt aggression, discourage Communist moves in other places, reassure America's allies about the reliability of the United States, and avoid a larger war. And the Administration was not inhibited by the fact that postwar United States had not avoided the mistake of military weakness. The President and others believed that only a little effort would be required to succeed in Korea.

Although Korea was small in territory and population, the war was significant. It involved the largest military effort that the United States had yet made in Asia. The war became large in a step-by-step fashion and inflicted very heavy losses on both sides. Beyond this significant military activity, the war encouraged other developments in Asia. During the war, the United States sent large amounts of aid to the French in Indochina who faced a Communist-led revolution. Relations between the United States and China deteriorated still more under the impact of the war, as the United States intervened once again in the Chinese civil war by placing a fleet between Formosa and the mainland, the Chinese intervened in the war in Korea as American forces drove close to the Chinese border and Washington continued to refuse to recognize the Chinese government and to keep it out of the U.N. Furthermore, the Korean War accelerated the development of peace and security treaties with Japan that freed that country from occupation but enabled the United States to hold on to bases there.

In addition to these important developments in Asia, the war constituted and promoted the further militarization of Containment. Soon after the fighting began, the United States rapidly developed its military power, doing so along the lines that had been laid out in NSC-68. The war had not destroyed the theory of the primacy of Europe, so the United States sent additional troops there and an American commander, General Eisenhower, to take charge of NATO forces, increased the Military Assistance Program and pressed, although unsuccessfully, for the rearmament of the West German Republic. By 1952, Containment had become almost completely dependent upon military power for the American-financed European Recovery Program had been completed.

The war also produced the most important civil-military conflict in American history. It pitted the President against his top commander in Asia, General Douglas MacArthur. The conflict focused on the size of the war because MacArthur wanted to extend it beyond Korea into China, and the Administration regarded any extension as an enormously dangerous proposal. The conflict involved a challenge by a general to the authority of his commander-in-chief, for MacArthur tried to force a change in policy by appealing to Republicans and the American people. As a consequence, the President removed the general from command.

The war also promoted some changes inside the United States. It stimulated an economic boom with only mild inflation, except for the fall and winter of 1950-1951. It strengthened presidential power, for Truman had made the decision to intervene and also sent troops to Europe on his own authority, refusing in both cases to seek authorization from Congress. Yet, the Supreme Court rebuffed him when he seized the steel mills in order to avoid a strike and keep steel production moving. The Senate debated for weeks the argument that the Constitution limited presidential power over troop movements. The war also weakened Truman and his Administration with the public, chiefly because the fighting became stalemated in 1951 and efforts at a negotiated settlement were unsuccessful.

One's definition of the war as a victory or a defeat depends on one's definition of those terms. MacArthur and his admirers regarded it as a defeat because it did not free North Korea from Communist control nor seriously weaken China. The Administration, however, regarded it as a victory for it had accomplished the original and the final objective of the American effort—containment, had avoided other undesirable developments that seemed possible, especially Russian expansion in Europe and World War III, and demonstrated American strength and determination. The war did check a Communist effort at expansion, maintaining the independence of South Korea from Communist control, but the effort did not persuade everyone that the United States could or should make a similar move when faced with similar situations in the future. In fact, the great unpopularity of the war and

Old Soldiers Never Die: General Douglas MacArthur Addressing Congress.
(Library of Congress)

of Truman during the war period was interpreted by many to mean that the United States would never make such an effort again.

To Truman, the significance of the war was even greater than the militarization and expansion of Containment that it involved and promoted and the frustration of the North Koreans that it produced. To him, the American effort proved conclusively that he had learned the lessons of history and had avoided the mistakes of the past.

The Survival of Big Government

The elections of 1952, affected by intense unhappiness with Truman and Democratic rule, especially the frustrating course of the Korean War, restored Republican control of both Congress and the White House for the first time since 1930. The figure of Eisenhower as military hero gave strength to the presidency, but the years of Republican rule to come were dominated by continuity, not change. One of the most important illustrations of this was the continuation of the large role of the federal government in economic affairs.

The prospects for significant change seemed rather good when the Republicans came to power in January 1953. Many of them had been criticizing big government since 1933, and that criticism encouraged expectations of change even though Robert A. Taft had been turned down in his bid for the Republican presidential nomination in 1952. The presidential candidate who spoke for those most eager for change, he had suffered from his foreign policy views as well as from the unattractiveness of his personality relative to Dwight Eisenhower's. The advocates of change had not been totally defeated in 1952, however, for another one of their spokesmen, Senator Richard Nixon of California, had been nominated and then elected to the Vice Presidency, and Eisenhower made promises to Taft to cut the size and cost of the federal government. The rhetoric of the Republican campaign also encouraged observers to believe that the federal government, or at least large parts of it, would come tumbling down, and the size of Eisenhower's victory in November suggested that his party would surely have the power to produce such results. He won by a large margin in a high turnout election in which many Democrats defected and voted for him. Republican victories in the congressional elections gave the party control of Congress, and the selection of conservatives, including Taft, to leadership positions there, strengthened still more the assumption that changes were at hand.

Furthermore, much about the new administration encouraged those who disliked what the New Deal and Fair Deal had done to relations between government and the economy. The new President, in line with Republican tradition and his own great confidence in businessmen and doubts about the economic abilities of the federal government, appointed many businessmen to positions of power in Washington, and the new men of power there, including the President, spoke often of the need to scale down the size of the federal government. And they did not stop with words. They pressed a program that emphasized sharp cuts in government spending, and they achieved some victories at the outset, including a substantial reduction in government spending.

Big government, however, did not disappear. The weaknesses of the Republican party limited change. It controlled Congress by only a small margin, for millions of voters still feared the party's domestic politics. Republican victories in 1952 resulted largely from unhappiness with the course of the Korean War and Eisenhower's popularity.

The economic recession of 1953-1954 also interferred with Republican plans. Triggered by the cut in government spending, the downturn generated pressures for government action. They were resisted by the administration, which insisted that the calls for a massive increase in spending and a large cut in taxes were dangerous, but the Administration also promised to do whatever became necessary to avoid a depression. Eisenhower and his aides stopped their efforts to cut spending and made other moves that assumed that the economic role of the federal government was of some importance. Also, the recession provided fresh evidence of the value of Social Security, which, while it did not seem as important to the Administration as private actions in bringing the recession to an end, did seem to have some significance as a means of supplying purchasing power to unemployed people. Thus, the Administration pressed successfully for expansion of this New Deal program in 1954 and 1956.

The strengthening of the Democratic party also restricted efforts to reduce the size and cost of the federal government. The Democrats regained control of the Congress in the 1954 elections as a consequence of the recession, and this emboldened advocates of the expansion of government and gave power to people, above all Senator Lyndon Johnson and Representative Sam Rayburn of Texas, who wanted to preserve programs that their party had established. Under their leadership, Congress enacted a New Deal-type farm program, the Soil Bank, as well as other measures of economic significance.

Pressures from the society also favored expansion rather than reduction of government. By the mid-Fifties, to cite a major illustration, the nation's highways, which had not been improved significantly for many years, were inadequate for the rapidly growing number of cars and trucks that used them. Republicans had, of course, long favored government action to develop the nation's transportation system; Eisenhower now called for the development of a system of interstate superhighways, and Congress appropriated even more money than he requested.

The embarrassment of businessmen also contributed. Several cases, such as the Dixon-Yates affair, involving business efforts to shape policy in ways that would benefit them came to public attention. The publicity defeated specific proposals and kept alive the notion that businessmen were not completely reliable and thus the nation should not become too dependent on them.

Eisenhower's leadership played a role in this story. Plagued by health problems in 1955-56 that restricted his activities, he was heavily influenced throughout his first term by theories of government and politics that made him reluctant to participate as vigorously in the affairs of Congress as Roosevelt and Truman had and persuaded him to do very little to build his party. In other words, he did not work as actively on behalf of his ideas as he would if he had enjoyed better health and had endorsed other theories. He enjoyed an impressive personal victory in 1956 in his bid for reelection, but it was accompanied by the strengthening of Democratic control of Congress.

Big government did not wither away. Many wanted to reduce the size and cost of the Federal government, but they lacked the power to do so.

The Continuation of Containment

The foreign policy of the first Eisenhower Administration also reveals the importance of continuity in the history of these years. The Administration expressed desires for change, but they were not strong enough to triumph. The foreign policy that had been created by the Truman Administration continued to be the foreign policy of the United States. Weakness of the desires and the moderation of the President prevented any drastic reforms.

A basic change in American policy seemed likely by 1953. Containment was criticized for both costing too much and not accomplishing enough. Change seemed likely even though Robert A. Taft as a major critic, failed to get the Republican nomination. Taft's stand on foreign policy affected Eisenhower's champions and his own decision to seek the Presidency. Involved in the development of Containment, Eisenhower feared Taft as an isolationist.

The Republican platform and campaign, however, promised change. They criticized Containment as immoral and dangerous and called for "Liberation." The Truman Administration had regarded that as an inevitable product of Containment, but the Republicans seemed to promise an earlier freeing of the people under Communist control. Influenced by hopes of uniting Republicans and shattering the Democratic coalition, the rhetoric of Liberation alarmed some people, including Eisenhower, forcing its champions to insist that they did not intend to use force and encouraging the campaigners to give less attention to it than to the Korean War in the late stages of the election contest.

Nevertheless, the new Administration seemed determined to change American foreign policy. Eisenhower appointed the architect of Liberation, John Foster Dulles, as Secretary of State, and the Administration employed the rhetoric of Liberation, threatening a MacArthur-like policy to end the Korean War and announcing that the American Navy would no longer prevent Chiang from moving back to the mainland. Dulles also proposed a "roll back of the Iron Curtain" in Eastern Europe, telling the people, "you can count on us."

The Eisenhower Administration, however, did not change American foreign policy. The new team concluded the Korean War on Truman's, not MacArthur's, terms and then kept an American force in Korea to discourage a new attack from the north. Washington did not intervene in the 1953 uprising in East Berlin or in an even more substantial effort in 1956 by the people in Hungary to free themselves from Russian control. Two new NATO-like defense alliances were established, one for Southeast Asia and one for the Middle East, and the United States began to support Diem in South Vietnam, doing so after Eisenhower rejected a plan for military intervention to save northern Vietnam from Communist control and after the French withdrew their forces from the region. Washington concluded a defense pact with Chiang that reimposed restrictions against his efforts to move back onto the mainland and offered assurances of American support if Mao attempted to gain control of Formosa. The Administration did hope that political change would take place on the mainland, but continued the policies of the Truman Administration, including nonrecognition, as the means of moving toward that goal. In Europe, Dulles carried to completion Acheson's plans for the rearmament of West Germany as a part of NATO, and throughout the world, the Administration continued the policy of military assistance to its allies, regarding that as cheaper than spending dollars on American forces and assuming that these allies would be responsible for any military actions on the ground that became necessary. Washington encouraged the use of force on behalf of liberation only in Iran and Guatemala, and in those places, the American role was played mainly by the Central Intelligence Agency, not American troops. The Administration checked efforts by three of its closest allies—Israel, France, and Great Britain —to use force against Egypt following the failure of American efforts to use economic aid to gain influence in Egypt after the British had withdrawn.

Strong desires to cut government spending and avoid war stood in the way of change from Containment to Liberation. The desire to cut spending affected military policy and encouraged the administration to return to the emphasis on air power. The United States now had the hydrogen bomb, which had been successfully tested before Truman left office, but so did the Russians. A real policy of Liberation, involving, say, forceful intervention in Eastern Europe, could have triggered a nuclear war. In contrast with Containment, Liberation was, in other words, beyond the real power of the United States. It was also outside the limits of American needs. The United States could survive and even prosper in a world that included Communist control of Russia, Eastern Europe, China, North Korea and North Vietnam.

Before the end of Eisenhower's first term, the Administration retreated from Liberation in theory as well as in practice. Realizing that it had generated unrealistic expectations of American help, it stopped talking about Liberation after the Russians crushed the Hungarian uprising. All along, the policy had only been rhetoric. Dulles had assumed that a combination of that rhetoric, Containment and the force of human nature would liberate the people controlled by communism. Assuming that the drive for freedom was man's strongest drive, he believed that the United States was obligated to encourage that drive with its words. Now, however, the Administration made all

President Eisenhower Makes His Last Campaign Speech Over National Television *(Dwight D. Eisenhower Library)*

but an explicit return to the policy of the Truman Administration. It had assumed that the combination of Containment and human nature would produce liberation eventually and had been willing to be patient.

Rather than scrap Containment, the Eisenhower Administration had made it even more clearly global in scope by developing new alliances. By 1957, the policy was more firmly in place than ever before. It had triumphed over both Henry Wallace and John Foster Dulles as well as the shocks of the Communist triumph in China, the success of the Russian atomic program and the Korean War. It now had few if any critics of political significance.

Containment had also triumphed over the challenge from Senator McCarthy. His influence had largely disappeared while the Administration made Containment more explicitly global and scrapped the rhetoric of Liberation. He was, after all, a champion of change, profoundly dissatisfied with major features of American policy, especially the foreign policy of the Truman Administration, while the Eisenhower administration promised continuity.

McCarthy's decline did not begin with the beginning of the Eisenhower Administration. In fact, his influence continued to rise for some months after January 1953. Because his party now controlled the Senate, McCarthy was elevated to chairman of the Subcommittee on Investigations of the Committee on Government. With this new power he launched abusive attacks on many groups and individuals in American life as infiltrated by Communists and their sympathizers. These included the Protestant clergy, the Voice of America and the Army. He also attacked the nation's European allies as soft on communism. He continued, in other words, to threaten the foreign and military policies of the United States.

McCarthy's decline began in the spring of 1954, and was moved along by his censure by the United States Senate in December of that year. Following censure, his influence declined rapidly and so did his health. He died an early death in 1957.

McCarthy's influence waned mainly because he had become a threat to many people and useful to only a few. Eisenhower was not a major force propelling the downward course of his fortunes, for Eisenhower tried to get along with him and was reluctant to attack him. A new industry, television, played a large role by providing many people in the Army-McCarthy hearings during the spring of 1954 with an opportunity to see the man and to learn why his foes found him so offensive. The Senate also played a major role. It had been timid in its dealings with him, but during 1954, the majority of Senators threw off their timidity and then censured him for behavior unbecoming a senator and damaging the reputation of the Senate. By then, he had become a threat to the Senate, the Army, American foreign policy and the Eisenhower Administration, and he seemed useful only to those who were very dissatisfied with established policies. These were the most conservative Republicans. Only they called upon him for help in the 1954 elections, and only they voted against the censure resolution.

McCarthy's decline ended a major threat to Containment. His decline did not mark the end of the Red Scare. In fact, some of his foes contributed significantly to new anti-Communist legislation in 1954. Regarding Containment as an ineffective way of combatting communism, he portrayed the policy as soft and as a product of Communist influence. Well before his death, however, he had ceased to be an influential critic of what had clearly become the foreign policy of the United States.

By 1957, Containment occupied a very secure position. The United States was still functioning as a global power as the Truman Administration had believed it must, and the nation was playing its global role in the way the Truman Administration had defined. That way assumed that the United States had substantial responsibilities and power but that they had limits on them. The United States must be very active in international affairs, but the nation should not expect to accomplish all that it might desire.

SUGGESTIONS FOR FURTHER READING

Alexander, Charles C., *Holding the Line: The Eisenhower Era, 1952-1961*. Bloomington, Ind., Indiana University Press, 1975.

Bernstein, Barton J., ed., *Politics and Policies of the Truman Administration*. Chicago, Quadrangle Books, 1970.

Dalfiume, Richard M., *Desegregation of the U.S. Armed Forces: Fighting on Two Fronts: 1939-1953*. Columbia, Mo., University of Missouri Press, 1969.

Davies, Richard O., *Housing Reform During the Truman Administration*. Columbia, Mo., University of Missouri Press, 1966.

Gaddis, John L., *The United States and the Origins of the Cold War, 1941-1947*. New York, Columbia University Press, 1972.

Goldman, Eric F., *The Crucial Decade: America, 1945-1955*. New York, Alfred A. Knopf, 1956.

Griffith, Robert, *The Politics of Fear: Joseph R. McCarthy and the Senate*. Lexington, Ky., The University Press of Kentucky, 1970.

_____ and Athan Theoharis, eds., *The Specter: Original Essays on the Cold War and the Origins of McCarthyism*. New York, New Viewpoints, 1974.

Hamby, Alonzo L., *Beyond the New Deal: Harry S Truman and American Liberalism*. New York, Columbia University Press, 1973.

Hartmann, Susan M., *Truman and the 80th Congress*. Columbia,

Mo., University of Missouri Press, 1971.

Haynes, Richard F., *The Awesome Power: Harry S Truman as Commander in Chief*. Baton Rouge, La., Louisiana State University Press, 1973.

Hewlett, Richard G. and Francis Duncan, *A History of the United States Atomic Energy Commission: Volume II 1947/1952. Atomic Shield*. University Park, Pa., Pennsylvania State University Press, 1969.

Kirkendall, Richard S., ed., *The Truman Period as a Research Field*. Columbia, Mo., University of Missouri Press, 1967, 1974.

_____, *Power and Prosperity: The United States in the Truman Period*. Bloomington, Ind., Indiana University Press, 1979.

Kolko, Joyce and Gabriel, *The Limits of Power: The World and United States Foreign Policy, 1945-1954*. New York, Harper & Row, 1972.

May, Ernest R., *"Lessons" of the Past: The Use and Misuse of History in American Foreign Policy*. New York, Oxford University Press, 1973.

McCoy, Donald R. and Richard T. Ruetten, *Quest and Response: Minority Rights and the Truman Administration*. Lawrence, Kan., University Press of Kansas, 1973.

Parmet, Herbert S., *Eisenhower and the American Crusades*, New York, The Macmillan Co., 1972.

Paterson, Thomas G., *Soviet-American Confrontation: Postwar Reconstruction and the Origins of the Cold War*. Baltimore, The Johns Hopkins University Press, 1973.

Patterson, James T., *Mr. Republican: A Biography of Robert A. Taft*. Boston, Houghton Mifflin Co., 1972.

Reichard, Gary W., *The Reaffirmation of Republicanism: Eisenhower and the Eighty-Third Congress*. Knoxville, Tenn., University of Tennessee Press, 1975.

Smith, Gaddis, *Dean Acheson*. New York, Cooper Square Publishers, 1972.

Rising Confidence

By 1957, A MAJOR ISSUE had been settled. It seemed clear not only that the United States was to continue to play a major role in the world but that it was to play it largely as the Truman administration had designed it. With that decision out of the way, the nation was, in a sense, free to turn to other matters. The biggest issue of the postwar decade had been settled.

The next decade was dominated by rising confidence. The nation did not turn away from Containment and try to accomplish more, but endeavored to conduct that policy more effectively. It became increasingly convinced that it could do so on a global scale. Americans also became more confident of their ability to attack domestic problems.

Mounting Pressures for Change at Home

One early illustration of rising confidence was the liberal revival of the second half of the 1950s. Liberalism of the fifties was an intellectual as well as a political movement. It was linked to earlier liberalism in its belief that the American system was fundamentally sound, its sensitivity to the existence of problems in American life and its confidence in government, especially the federal government and the President. Yet, it had some new features, including militant hostility toward Marxism. To the liberal of the period, Marxism had failed as a philosophy of history by predicting falsely the collapse of capitalism and the triumph of the proletariat and not anticipating the rise of totalitarianism and other evils of modern life. Marxism also provided an inadequate analysis of American life by failing to appreciate the strength of American capitalism, by emphasizing oppression by the ruling class while missing the pressures of mass opinion and by providing an overly simple view of social reality. Stressing two-class conflict, Marxism missed the pluralism of American life, the importance of many groups.

More than in the past, liberals now called attention to the positive qualities of American life. They admired the nation for the strength it had demonstrated since 1932; they saw it as much more than an extension of Europe, as unique and superior, surely worthy of preservation and imitation and the antithesis of Russia. And America's pluralism seemed to be one of its most valuable qualities. Power was distributed rather than concentrated; the nation was dominated by a multitude of groups that were led by elites who participated more actively in politics than most people did, were subject to popular pressure for they competed with one another for support, were open to ambitious and talented people and represented group interests quite effectively. The groups had different points of view but were united by basic beliefs or unconscious attitudes, and thus they tolerated and compromised with one another.

These liberals placed heavy emphasis on civil liberties, civil rights, and economic growth. Respect for civil liberties seemed an essential feature of American life and one that was threatened in the modern world by totalitarianism abroad and McCarthyism at home. The nation's record in civil rights appeared to be its greatest shortcoming, and reforms needed to be made in order to bring the nation into conformity with its ideals and make it more open and pluralistic. Constant economic growth seemed possible if all parts of the economic system functioned satisfactorily, and an adequate rate of economic growth would reduce the size of all problems, facilitating, for example, efforts to integrate blacks into the mainstream of American life.

The liberals of the fifties did not expect to promote rapid change in order to create a perfect society. That object was well beyond man's somewhat limited capacities. The nation, modern history seemed to suggest, would be harmed by the efforts of zealots and revolutionaries for they led to the loss of freedom.

Liberalism revived during the second half of the 1950s in spite of the lack of pressure from the radical left. That part of the political spectrum did not have a political party capable of running a candidate for the Presidency in 1956. The Socialist party decided not to nominate a candidate after its dismal showing in 1952 when Norman Thomas's successor picked up only 20,000 votes. And the Communist party neither sponsored nor supported a candidate in 1956. Dwindling away, it had only 3,000 members by 1958. The new Russian leader's revelations of the crimes of Stalin as well as harassment in the United States were largely responsible. The radical left had only a few representatives, like C. Wright Mills and William Appleman Williams, in American intellectual life.

Liberalism also revived in spite of the persistence of the Red Scare. Its campaigns of fear were blunted by the rising optimism. No one emerged to take McCarthy's place, and the Supreme Court under the new Chief Justice, Earl Warren, placed restrictions on the consequences of the Red Scare. Yet, it remained a source of trouble for liberals, kept alive by the House Un-American Activities Committee, among others.

Nevertheless, liberalism gained strength and did so for several reasons. People such as Senator Hubert Humphrey of Minnesota supplied forceful leadership. Stimulus came also from the emergence into view of several social problems, including costly medical care and inadequate education. These problems were not new and were not even larger than before, but perceptions of them were changing. Humphrey and others were convinced that the United States should be able to do better. The recession of 1958 also affected their thinking about the economy. Increasing unemployment, the recession generated pressures for government action and affected the congressional elections of 1958, weakening the conservatives and strengthening the liberals. The slow rate of economic growth in the United States also stimulated the liberal revival. The rate had slowed following the Korean War, and the rate of growth was less than in the economies of Western Europe and Japan.

The liberal revival did not produce much action of the sort the liberals desired. A new system of federal aid to education was established by the National Defense Education Act, but it owed at least as much to the international difficulties of the period as to liberal pressure. The liberals had to contend against the still popular Eisenhower who feared large-scale spending and inflation and became increasingly vigorous in reaction to liberal demands, employing rhetoric and the veto power. The Conservative Coalition, although reduced in size by the 1958 elections, remained influential, producing, for example, new restrictions on the labor movement with the Landrum-Griffin Act. Divisions among liberals also reduced their effectiveness. They fought, for example, over whether or not desegregation provisions should be attached to federal aid for education. Congressional leadership, headed by Johnson and Rayburn, also limited liberal accomplishments because they sought to unite Democrats and to cooperate with the President and refused to identify with the liberals. As a result of their frustrations, they became increasingly eager for a different kind of President, one who would use his power on behalf of their causes.

The liberal revival, while reflecting growing concern about domestic problems, also expressed confidence in the ability of established institutions and traditional methods to reduce their size. Congress and the Presidency, working together, influenced by pressure groups and responsible to popular demands expressed in elections and other recognized ways, could, liberals assumed, promote progress.

The development of black protest provided additional evidence of the rising interest in attacking domestic problems. The movement, which had been gaining momentum for many years, changed in significant ways from 1956 to 1960. Affecting the changes were doubts about established institutions and traditional methods but confidence that there were methods that could be employed successfully to improve American life.

In the Brown case of 1954, the civil rights movement had enjoyed its greatest victory in the judicial arena. Unanimously, the Supreme Court had declared that segregated schools violated the Fourteenth Amendment to the United States Constitution. The reasoning behind the decision stressed the psychological consequences of segregation.

The champions of the legal approach expected great progress. They assumed the Court's decision would be obeyed and thus legal change would result in social change. They assumed that the decision dealt with an area of major importance. Desegregation of the schools would provide opportunities for social contact between whites and blacks in a crucial period of life and would provide blacks with better opportunities for social and economic advancement.

The decision, however, encountered massive resistance. Although accepted rather quickly in the urban areas of the border states from Maryland to Missouri, it was resisted in the states farther South. Southerners denounced the Court and worked openly to prevent the decision from being implemented. They pressured blacks not to try to integrate the schools and changed the school laws. These efforts to get around the decision forced black leaders to seek new decisions from the Court and restricted the rate of change so that by 1960 only slightly more than 10 percent of the Southern school districts were integrated and little or no integration had taken place in the deep South. The resistance continued until late in the 1950s when moderate Southerners, convinced that the region was being damaged economically by the image projected by massive resistance, relaxed the pressure against school desegregation.

President Eisenhower provided little support for desegregation efforts. He gave no more than mild, cautious support for civil rights and did not offer leadership and support to facilitate the progress of desegregation. Social and economic theories as well as desires for Southern support restrained him. He warned frequently against trying to move too fast and to attempt the impossible. Yet, he was forced to intervene massively in September 1957. The Governor of Arkansas, Orval Faubus, had used the National Guard to block court-ordered integration of Central High School in Little Rock, and mob violence had erupted following the court-ordered removal of the troops. In response, the President federalized the Guard and used it and the 101st Airborne to enforce the Court order.

Congress, restrained by the power of the South, did not provide large-scale support for the civil rights movement. Congress rejected legislative solutions to the crisis in the schools. It did pass civil rights legislation in 1957 and 1960, forced to do so by liberal and black pressure; the legislation created a Civil Rights Commission to investigate and report on race relations and focused on voting, assuming that an increase in black voting would give Southern blacks power that could be used to accomplish other goals. In response to the laws and other pressures, however, black voting in the South increased very slowly, moving from about 20 percent of the adult blacks in 1952 to 25 to 30 percent eight years later.

In spite of massive resistance from white Southerners and the cautious efforts of President and Congress, blacks experienced rising expectations and growing confidence. They were nurtured by the progress that was taking place. It involved improvements in education for blacks, economic advance and the desegregation of the armed forces as well as Supreme Court decisions and congressional legislation. Outside support also contributed. Help came from former President Harry S Truman and from liberals in and out of politics; help that was reassuring in a hard battle. The support revealed to blacks that they could count on others for aid, and it strengthened their conviction that they were right in calling for change in race relations.

The combination of massive resistance, cautious efforts by Eisenhower and Congress, rising expectations and growing confidence encouraged a growing number of blacks to experiment with ways of producing change. Non-violent, direct action had been tried in the past and was emphasized by a small civil rights group in the 1940s and 1950s, the Congress for Racial Equality, and it had been used by Gandhi in his campaign against British rule in India. Blacks in Montgomery, Alabama employed the technique in 1956. In protest against segregated seating arrangements, they boycotted the city's bus system and produced change in racial practices. The effort also produced a new leader and a new organization, Rev. Martin Luther King, Jr. and the Southern Christian Leadership Conference. Their techniques of protest spread quickly to other Southern cities.

Non-violent, direct action took on new size in 1960. In February, black college students in Greensboro, North Carolina sat-in at a lunch counter where service had been denied them and their example was quickly copied in other parts of the South. Relying chiefly on young blacks but gaining support from adults and some whites, the efforts focused on lunch counters and other areas of importance in daily life and encountered violent resistance, but the blacks did not retaliate in kind. These efforts enjoyed victories in the upper South and led to the formation in June of another organization, the Student Non-violent Coordinating Committee.

Developments in the civil rights movement in these years illustrated the rising interest in domestic problems and also the growing confidence that they could be solved or reduced in size. The change in methods was influenced by frustrations, but the advocates of direct action had confidence in their ability to produce change in America. This involved a degree of confidence in whites and in American institutions. American life seemed capable of being reformed in significant and desirable ways. And the goal was an integrated society, a society in which blacks would participate on equal terms with whites. Such a society seemed both desirable and within reach.

Rising Demands for More Effective Foreign and Military Policies

The liberals and the black militants were not the only groups calling for change in American life in the second half of 1950s. Another group of importance was the one Eisenhower would label the "military-industrial complex." It shared the confidence of the liberals and the civil rights activists but saw America and its needs in a very different way.

This group was a complex, not a solid power bloc. In fact, it had even more parts than Eisenhower's terminology suggested. Military officers formed a part of it. They were much more numerous and prominent than they had been before World War II, yet they were not the only component of the group and not even its most powerful component. They participated in politics rather cautiously, restrained by the principle of civilian supremacy.

Businessmen exercised even more power in the complex. Many of them had defense contracts, which continued to go chiefly to the giant corporations but were often distributed by them to smaller firms functioning as subcontractors, and the contracts linked the firms closely to the military services. Businessmen held leadership positions in the military establishment as Eisenhower turned to them, including the top man at General Motors, Charles Wilson, to serve as Secretary of Defense. And businessmen had another important way of influencing military men. They could give them jobs after retirement from the armed forces and did so in large numbers.

Nevertheless, the businessmen in the complex did not have unlimited power there. They were weakened by divisions because they competed with one another for defense contracts, and they did not have the only jobs to which military officers looked forward. Individual firms lost as well as gained ground as time passed. General Motors, in fact, declined as a defense contractor while Wilson served as Secretary of Defense, and the aircraft manufacturers rose in importance as a consequence of the influence of the air power theory. Depending on the government for most of their sales, these firms competed with one another for this lucrative business.

Many congressmen also participated in the complex. They desired contracts and bases in their states or districts, and they were especially important in the complex and especially successful in the quest for bases and contracts if they occupied high positions in Congress concerned with the armed forces. Two Georgians, Senator Richard Russell and Representative Carl Vinson, held commanding posts during the 1950s.

Some universities also formed a component of the group. Many of them obtained contracts for military research. Even more of them supplied the armed forces and the defense industries with trained people.

The complex also had a mass base. It was composed of veterans organizations, labor unions active in the defense industries and defense communities that were heavily dependent for their prosperity on defense contracts and bases.

The military-industrial complex was a loosely organized pressure group. Its members agreed on the importance of military power. They disagreed on the best form of military power and the best place to obtain it. Some championed air power; others backed the ground forces or the Navy. Some regarded Boeing in Seattle as the best supplier; others endorsed Lockheed in Burbank.

In the second half of the 1950s the complex functioned as an advocate of change. The members publicized conceptions of American weaknesses and of the need to build up the armed forces. They argued that the nation could afford to spend much more money. In fact, they insisted that the economy would be stimulated by such an increase. During this period, the armed forces spent most of the federal budget and a much larger part of the gross national product than they had before World War II.

Yet, the complex was not completely effective. Weakened by internal conflicts, it also had to compete with people with other priorities, including businessmen who were not defense contractors and wanted to cut government spending and taxes. The group's effectiveness was also limited by the President. The Eisenhower Administration did spend much more on the military than Truman's had before the Korean War, but the administration kept such spending below Korean levels. Even the aircraft companies experienced a decline in sales in spite of the influence of the air power theory and the development of jet aircraft and missiles. Eisenhower warned frequently of the dangers of spending too much on the armed forces and, drawing on his great prestige as a soldier, he assured the people that they had an adequate defense system. His efforts frustrated members of the complex, especially Army leaders. Three Army Chiefs of Staff resigned in order to protest against Eisenhower's policies.

Many of the demands for change in the late 1950s were rooted in domestic interests; others owed much to foreign events. A sense of international crisis developed, gripped manyAmericans and generated demands for change, although not a departure from the Containment Policy. The demand instead was for more effective application of Containment which critics felt was not being applied with the vigor and imagination that the United States was capable of producing.

The sense of crisis resulted from the progress being made by Russia and communism. Russian progress in the development of the new weapons contributed significantly. By the late 1950s, Russia not only had atomic and hydrogen bombs; she also had a superior delivery system, which was demonstrated when a powerful Russian rocket launched an earth satellite, Sputnik, in October 1957. To some Americans it seemed that the Russians would soon move far ahead of the United States in the number of long-range missiles.

Russian progress in the Middle East also alarmed Americans. Russia had had almost no influence there as late as 1955 but gained ground rapidly thereafter, especially in Egypt, using foreign aid and trade and supporting nationalistic anti-Westerners like Egypt's Gamal Abdel Nasser.

A Communist breakthrough in Latin America also generated alarm. The rise of Fidel Castro to power in Cuba in 1959 aroused anxieties in the United States. Cautious toleration gave way quickly to hostility when he employed authoritarian policies and nationalized properties, put Communists in his government, and received help from Russia.

Communist activity in Southeast Asia contributed to the growing sense of crisis. It included guerrilla warfare against the American-backed government of South Vietnam.

The apparent renewal of Russian efforts at expansion in Europe also contributed to the feeling of crisis. Beginning in November 1958, the Russians put new pressure on Berlin. They hoped to cut off the flow of people from East Germany to the West. They also seemed eager to force the United States to withdraw from that city, a move that would surely weaken the confidence that other nations had in the Americans.

In response to these developments, pressures for changes in American policies mounted rapidly in the United States. They came from Republicans as well as from Democrats and from people outside the military-industrial complex as well as people inside it. The pressures reflected more than partisanship and self-interest.

The pressure took two major forms. Some advocates of change called for much more American economic aid for economic development, while others emphasized a military buildup. Proposals for expansion of the armed forces included the acceleration of the missile program, other ways of strengthening American air power and redevelopment of the Army.

To the proponents of changes, their proposals seemed practical as well as necessary. They assumed that the changes would make Containment more effective. They assumed also that the United States could afford the changes. Although the advocates of change suggested that the United States might fail to respond adequately, they assumed that the nation need not fail.

Eisenhower responded to these pressures from home and abroad. He continued the surveillance of Russia with high-flying U-2 planes. He sent troops into Lebanon, hoping to check the spread of Nasser's influence. He increased spending on defense, space exploration and foreign aid. He imposed economic and diplomatic pressure on Castro and authorized the preparation of a military force to invade the island and remove Castro from power. He enlarged the American advisory force in South Vietnam. He reasserted American determination to remain in Berlin and sought to negotiate a settlement of it and other issues. And he made ceremonial visits to several countries.

The President, however, tried very hard to deflate the sense of crisis. Repeatedly, he offered assurances about American defenses and warned about the dangers of large-scale spending. It could wreck the American economy, he insisted, and the anti-Communist effort in the world depended upon the strength of that economic system. And as a major part of his campaign, he called attention to the military-industrial complex in his farewell address as President. To him, the complex was an essential part of American life, but it also was a threat because it had such grandiose notions about government spending. Thus, his speech was an effort to keep the complex under control so that the nation would benefit from it but not be damaged by it.

Pressures for change were mounting, but Eisenhower was resisting them and thereby reducing the amount of change taking place. The President remained extraordinarily popular, and few critics dared assail him in the newspapers on on radio. Many people, nonetheless, hoped for a different kind of President who would use the powers of the office to promote change. Some hoped for a President who would make changes in foreign and/or military affairs. Others were interested chiefly in domestic matters. Some were eager for changes in both areas. All of Eisenhower's critics assumed that the nation had the capacity to be much more effective and successful.

The Dynamic Leaders

Fortunately for the Democrats, Eisenhower could not run again, and thus the Democrats were able to regain control of the White House in the election of 1960. The new President, John F. Kennedy, an Irish

John F. Kennedy Campaigning in California
(University of Southern California)

Catholic, the son of an enormously successful businessman and a former Representative and Senator from Massachusetts, represented and reflected many of the pressures for change that had been building up. Unlike Eisenhower, Kennedy used the power of the Presidency to promote rather than resist change. His youthful appearance, boyish determination, and crisp voice attracted a host of friends who gave him a loyal and dedicated following.

Kennedy's leadership style differed from Truman's as well as Eisenhower's. The new man was more sophisticated and articulate than the Missourian had been. And, unlike his immediate predecessor, Kennedy enjoyed the exercise of presidential power and regarded it as essential. He also had confidence in his capacity to use it effectively.

At the same time, Kennedy agreed with the liberals, and also with Catholic tradition, about the limits on power and the impossibility

Candidate Nixon in 1960
(University of Southern California)

of creating the perfect society. His sense of limits was reinforced by the unusually narrow margin of his victory over Richard Nixon, the strengthening of the Conservative Coalition somewhat by the 1960 congressional elections and his own lack of experience as a legislative leader. Although a member of Congress for fourteen years, he had not been a strong, effective person there.

The promotion of economic growth occupied a high position on Kennedy's agenda. He was influenced by economists of Keynesian persuasion, especially Professor Walter Heller of the University of Minnesota who became chairman of the Council of Economic Advisers. These scholars argued that many of the nation's problems were the result of a slow growth rate. Kennedy accepted the appraisal and urged a reversal of the trend.

His hopes for a harmonious and powerful society also encouraged

Gross National Product in Constant Dollars

Year	In Billions of 1972 $	Year	In Billions of 1972 $
1946	477.6	1961	755.3
1947	468.3	1962	799.1
1948	487.7	1963	830.7
1949	490.7	1964	874.4
1950	533.5	1965	925.9
1951	576.5	1966	981.0
1952	598.5	1967	1,007.7
1953	621.8	1968	1,051.8
1954	613.7	1969	1,078.8
1955	654.8	1970	1,075.3
1956	688.8	1971	1,107.5
1957	680.9	1972	1,171.1
1958	679.5	1973	1,233.4
1959	720.4	1974	1,210.7
1960	736.8	1975	1,186.1

(Source: Bureau of Economic Analysis, Department of Commerce)

him to emphasize economic growth. The health of the economy seemed to him to be a matter of basic importance. Economic growth could reduce social conflict and tension by satisfying more material needs. It could also provide the basis for the expansion of power by supplying the resources needed to give more foreign aid and expand the armed forces.

The Administration relied upon fiscal policy to stimulate growth. At the beginning, it increased government spending. Soon it applied a conservative form of Keynesianism. It was Keynesian in that it stressed the importance of deficit financing; it was conservative in that it emphasized a cut in taxes rather than an increase in spending. Kennedy hoped that businessmen and congressional conservatives would support this approach. It relied heavily upon private action, would not supply jobs directly and assumed that the private sector of the economy, responding to the stimulus of a tax cut, would expand employment.

In pursuit of his economic objective, Kennedy was not completely successful. He obtained passage of various anti-recession programs in 1961 and 1962 and, making use of his oratorical skills, persuaded more people to accept the Keynesian approach. He also built support for his major proposal, which he made in January 1963 and which called for a $10.2 billion tax cut without a cut in spending. He failed, however, to obtain passage of the measure. Passage was hampered by conflicts among those who endorsed reliance on fiscal policy but disagreed about the type that should be employed. In addition, the measure encountered strong resistance from conservatives who rejected

President Kennedy Meets the Leaders of the March on Washington
(*United Press International*)

Keynesianism of any type. Here Democratic Senator Harry Byrd of Virginia was especially important. He insisted that spending as well as taxes must be cut, and he held the tax cut bill in the Senate Finance Committee. Thus, Kennedy's proposal remained only a proposal at the time of his death, and unemployment remained above 5 percent.

Civil rights was also high on Kennedy's domestic agenda, but there too his accomplishments fell short of his aspirations. His attention to the issue did not result largely from a personal interest in it. He had not been a champion of legislation in this area, although he had supported the efforts of others. He did have somewhat more interest in it than Eisenhower had, in part because he did not share Eisenhower's philosophy on the promotion of social change, but he did not bring to the job as much interest in civil rights as Truman had had. Before entering the White House, Kennedy had not had as much experience with black people.

Kennedy's political experiences in 1960 influenced him on this issue. He benefited from Nixon's eagerness for support from Southern whites and from his own support for King. Kennedy owed his victory largely to the large size of the black vote for him.

The pressures from the civil rights movement after he entered office exerted an even larger influence on Kennedy. The movement continued to escalate. The Congress for Racial Equality conducted "freedom rides" through the deep South in 1961; a large and growing number of blacks protested from 1961 to 1963 against disenfranchisement and segregated public facilities; the protests spread into the North and West, and the movement reached a new high with the March on Washington in August 1963 that illustrated both the demands and the complexity of the protest movement. As the movement escalated, it encountered violence in Birmingham and other places. No earlier President had faced as much pressure on this issue.

Kennedy's interest in foreign affairs reinforced these other considerations. To play the role in the world that he envisioned, the United States, he believed, needed social harmony and needed to give other people a good example. The widespread publicity given to violence in the South seemed to him to be extremely harmful.

Kennedy's approach during his first two years in the White House ranged over a wide area but emphasized voting. He pressed for the desegregation of transportation facilities and made some other moves on behalf of civil rights, but he did not call for civil rights legislation, and he disappointed the champions of civil rights in other ways. The emphasis on voting appealed to him in part because it did not require major new legislation. He feared alienating Southern Democratics for he wanted their support in other areas—economics and foreign policy—that seemed even more important to him than civil rights. Also, the attention to voting was in harmony with his own background; he recognized what politics had meant to Irish-Americans and assumed that voting power would enable blacks to make the same advances. Furthermore, the emphasis on voting harmonized with his hope for peaceful change and by emphasizing voting he could rely on his brother, Robert, now serving as Attorney General. Although he often disappointed the civil rights movement by failing to provide protection for demonstrators, Robert F. Kennedy had a stronger commitment in this area than the President did, and he brought a large number of suits under the voting rights legislation and promoted voter registration drives.

The President switched his emphasis to broad civil rights legislation in 1963. He was alarmed by the growing violence and now assumed that a new law could produce an orderly as well as a just society.

Kennedy's accomplishments in civil rights were not insignificant. The number of Southern blacks who were registered to vote increased substantially. The proposed civil rights law had several important features, including desegregation of public accommodations, authority for the Justice Department to support efforts to desegregate schools, and authority for the federal government to withhold federal funds from certain types of segregated facilities. Kennedy worked hard and with some success to build support for this proposal. But Kennedy failed, nevertheless, to obtain passage of his proposal. It moved close to passage in the House but encountered stronger opposition in the Senate where Senator James Eastland of Mississippi bottled up the bill in the Senate Judiciary Committee.

Kennedy was more active on behalf of civil rights than any of his predecessors had been, but his accomplishments fell short of his aspirations. The situation was not ideal for nearly all Southern whites and their representatives in Congress opposed his efforts. Perhaps, he should have been bolder. Above all, however, he needed more time. The problem was not only that he was not permitted to serve a full term. It was also that other problems consumed much of the time that he did have. Most of those problems were international.

Foreign policy topped Kennedy's agenda, and his ambitions in foreign affairs (and his conception of international realities) compelled him to develop a new military policy. That policy came to a focus in the McNamara strategy of flexible response.

This strategy had several sources. One was the principle of the subordination of the military involved in the Constitution and in the tradition of the American officer corps and that had been reaffirmed by both Truman and Eisenhower. NSC-68 and American military policy during the Korean War were other sources, as was criticism of Eisenhower's policies, especially the criticism of the emphasis on air power and on budgetary limitations. Kennedy as senator and campaigner had participated in the criticism, arguing that Eisenhower's policies gave the United States only two alternatives—all-out nuclear war or surrender, and he appointed several of the critics to office, including General Maxwell Taylor and Walt Whitman Rostow.

The practices of modern management also contributed. They involved systems analysis, cost effectiveness and long-range forecasting and were applied by the new Secretary of Defense, Robert McNamara, a recruit from the auto industry. Not an engineer and not primarily a car maker or a salesman, he was an expert in organization and represented a new type of business leader. He had been educated at Harvard's Graduate School of Business, which emphasized scientific management, had gained an opportunity to apply those techniques as an Air Force officer during World War II, had gone to work at Ford Motor Company after the war and had become its president in 1960. He was fascinated by the intellectual problems of administering large organizations, convinced that by subjecting any enterprise to rigorous analysis it could be brought under control, and he drew heavily on mathematics and the social sciences and relied heavily on computers.

Selected because of his reputation as a manager, McNamara accepted the cabinet post in spite of the financial sacrifice involved. He was attracted by the challenge of managing an organization that had more than 3.5 million employees, consumed over 50 percent of the federal budget and nearly 10 percent of the gross national product and was centered in the largest office building in the world. Kennedy's assurances of strong support, as well as the strengthening of the office in the late 1950s, also attracted him.

McNamara assumed that managerial principles could be used to evaluate military spending proposals. His principles involved the

consideration of alternatives, such as bombers versus nuclear submarines versus intercontinental ballistic missiles, and the definition
of options in quantitative terms. He hoped to make the military as
efficient as business and to increase the amount of security obtained
for each dollar spent. His efforts resulted in frequent conflicts with
the professionals in the armed forces and their allies in industry and
Congress and were not always successful, even though he had strong
support from Kennedy.

The strategy that McNamara championed rejected the emphasis
on bombers and missiles and expressed confidence in the ability of the
United States to develop a militarized but relatively peaceful world
controlled by civilians rather than soldiers. Bombers and missiles
seemed capable of deterring the first strike if the supply were adequate
to survive such a strike and thus inflict damage on the Russians, but
they could not deter all types of aggression: Thus, the United States
must be ready and willing to respond to a variety of challenges: large-
scale nuclear war, limited nuclear war, limited war of a pre-nuclear
type and guerrilla war. The United States must be ready to fight two
and one-half wars at the same time; one in Europe, one in Asia and a
small one elsewhere, and the American response must be escalated
as necessary but kept as small as possible. The strategists assumed that
the Communists would expand if the United States was not prepared
and willing to use its power and that the ability and willingess to act
militarily would make military action unnecessary or keep it at a low
level. The strategy also implied civilian supremacy. McNamara and
his associates looked upon the military as an instrument to be used
as political leaders determined.

This strategy guided the development of military policy. The
administration enlarged and redesigned the armed forces, increasing
the military budget sharply and expanding spending on both non-
nuclear and nuclear forces, the Army as well as the Air Force. Washington also encouraged its European allies to increase their spending on
conventional or non-nuclear forces. The development of the American armed forces was facilitated by the existence of the draft which
supplied the men needed to serve in conventional forces and did so
more satisfactorily than either the Reserves or the National Guard could.
The draftees could be trained as the strategy required and kept in the
national service for extended periods.

The Kennedy Administration devoted much of its time and energy
to the development of a larger and more complex military establishment. The development of the military (guided by the McNamara strategy) gave the Administration a sense of ability to act effectively. Kennedy enlarged and reformed the armed forces because he assumed that
international problems were very serious and that military power was
very important.

Two of the most troublesome areas were Cuba and Berlin, and

they produced major episodes—and both successes and failures—in the Kennedy years. The United States has always had a strong interest in Cuba not only because of its proximity to the Florida mainland but because of its fertile lands and friendly people. In the Cold War, however, Cuba became a threat to security and peace and became the Soviet's link to Latin America. The other strategic area, Berlin, raised different problems of defense, but equally serious ones nonetheless. Berlin was not only the traditional center of German life but a divided city located inside the Russian sphere and a city that provided means of escape from Russian control and a symbol of American determination. In both areas, the Russians pressed for change and attracted the attention of the Kennedy administration.

Very early in Kennedy's Presidency, the United States backed an unsuccessful invasion of Cuba. This curious affair was inspired by the CIA and the military chiefs who believed that Castro was unpopular and an invasion would encourage revolution. Their plans were put before Kennedy, who also hoped to topple Castro, and he approved the enterprise. Special forces invaded Cuba in April 1961, encountered some opposition, and aroused no local support. At this point of crisis, Kennedy refused to commit United States air and ground support, and pondered why he had become involved. The project failed quickly, and the failure strengthened Castro in Cuba and throughout Latin America and led to stronger ties between Russia and Cuba. The failure also reinforced Kennedy's conviction that he must not appear to be weak.

Berlin also supplied dramatic moments in 1961. Kennedy and the Russian leader, Nikita Khruschev, clashed verbally in June over Russian support for "wars of national liberation" and the American presence in Berlin; the Russians followed with new demands for change there; the Americans reaffirmed their determination to stay in the city, and both sides strengthened their armed forces. Then, suddenly, in August, the Russians constructed a wall dividing east from west Berlin so as to check the flow of people from east to west, and Kennedy responded rather like Eisenhower had to the crushing of the Hungarian uprising. He enlarged American forces in Berlin, but he relied chiefly on words to express his displeasure with what the Russians had done and made no effort to dismantle the wall. He was restrained by fear of provoking a war. The wall must be regarded as a failure by both sides, but this was the last Berlin crisis.

A new crisis, the Cuban missile crisis, erupted in October, 1962. It involved Russian efforts to place short and intermediate range missiles in Cuba. Several considerations influenced the Russians. The shortcomings of their missile program was one. It was behind the American program, and missiles in Cuba could increase the effectiveness of Russian missiles by increasing the number that could hit American cities. A Russian desire to strengthen ties with the Cubans, who feared invasion from the United States, also exerted an influence, as did hopes of embarrassing the United States and obtaining a bargaining counter.

The political implications of the move affected Kennedy's response more than the military implications did. He believed that the United States could not permit the Russians to succeed with such a move so close to it. The nation would appear very weak and that would embolden the Russians and discourage America's allies.

Thus, Kennedy moved but did so cautiously, fearing nuclear war as well as a demonstration of weakness. He turned down a suggestion, pressed only by the nation's ambassador to the UN, Adlai Stevenson, for reliance on diplomacy and concessions. He also rejected the suggestion of the military chiefs for an air strike. Instead, he accepted advice from Robert Kennedy, McNamara and others that the U.S. should blockade Cuba. This seemed less risky than an air strike and would rely on naval power, an area of American superiority. The move benefited from geography for the United States could function more easily on Cuban waters for they were close to the United States. Latin America's importance to the United States resembled Eastern Europe's importance to Russia.

Supplemented by preparations for an attack on Russia and Cuba and a warning to Russia, the blockade persuaded the Russians to pull back. They ordered the ships that were carrying more missiles to Cuba to turn around and promised to withdraw the missiles that had already been placed there. They also asked the United States to dismantle its missile bases in Turkey, a request that Kennedy rejected, and asked the United States to promise not to invade Cuba, a request that Kennedy accepted. Soon, the Russians withdrew their missiles. After the pressure had been relaxed, the administration removed its missiles from Turkey both as a gesture of peace and as an admission of the fact that the missiles were obsolete.

The missile crisis strengthened Kennedy's confidence in his power and skill; it also supplied fresh evidence of the dangers of nuclear war. That enlarged sense of danger, as well as the growing evidence of the dangers of fallout from the testing of atomic weapons, encouraged him to press for a treaty banning testing. The evidence that the resolution of the missile crisis supplied of United States and Russian ability to reach meaningful agreements helped the cause along. And Kruschchev's response was influenced by his need to strengthen himself at home and his growing fear of China.

In July 1963, the United States, Russia, and Great Britain signed a Test Ban Treaty. It promised that these nations—the nuclear powers— would not test nuclear weapons in the atmosphere, outer space and under water. The treaty did not establish a system of inspection; because there was no need for inspection to detect such tests.

The treaty was easily ratified by the United States Senate in September even though extreme conservatives in the United States cam-

paigned against it. The opposition was bitter and included businessmen, scientists, and military men. The reception abroad was also
mixed. Many nations endorsed it, but the French and the Chinese, the
two groups most interested in developing nuclear weapons, refused
to sign.

Another highly significant illustration of Kennedy's attention to
foreign affairs was his enlargement of the American role in Vietnam.
He could have rejected Eisenhower's personal commitment to Ngo
Dinh Diem and carried out a policy of disengagement. But he regarded
Vietnam as a vital area and the struggle there as one that had more than
local significance. Endorsing what has been called "the domino theory,'
he believed that developments in South Vietnam would influence situations elsewhere. Vietnam seemed to him to be a test, as Korea had been
for Truman or Manchuria had been for Hoover. His interpretation of the
lessons of history influenced him and so did his reading of the proponents of Communist revolution by means of guerrilla warfare. Thus,
he maintained the American commitment to Diem and hostility to
the Viet Cong in South Vietnam and Ho Chi Minh in North Vietnam.
He could see no virtues in domination of Vietnam by Ho and saw Russian and Chinese influence in revolutionary movements and victories
for them as victories for Russia and China.

Kennedy did recognize the non-military dimensions of the conflict that was growing in intensity in South Vietnam. Some of his advisers insisted that Diem must make reforms in order to become more
effective, and some American officials encouraged him to do so. The
Americans, however, did not apply much pressure for reform because
they could see no alternative to him, and he did not make many reforms
because he was not interested in doing so. Heading a corrupt, repressive
and incompetent regime, he had not gained popular support.

Kennedy's most influential advisers encouraged him to see the
military problem as basic. The Department of Defense, the most influential bloc in the Administration, pressed this point of view. So
did the Secretary of State, Dean Rusk, a man heavily influenced by the
lessons of the 1930s.

Thus, the President decided to apply the McNamara strategy. He
assumed that Eisenhower's objective had been correct but that his
method had been faulty. He had not made a sufficiently large effort and
had not paid enough attention to guerrilla warfare. Kennedy increased
the number of American troops in South Vietnam from about 600 to
somewhere between 16,000 and 25,000. He had the troops, including
a new group of special forces, the Green Berets, and he had a theory to
guide them. The Americans emphasized advice and training, including
training for guerrilla warfare, but they also engaged in some combat
and many intelligence operations. In addition to troops, the United
States sent dollars and supplies, and Kennedy brushed aside signals
from the revolutionaries, the National Liberation Front, for a nego-

tiated settlement for he was not willing to allow the NLF a role in the government of South Vietnam.

Kennedy enlarged substantially the American role and, by doing so, encouraged the revolutionaries to seek more support from North Vietnam, but he hoped and expected to keep the American role a secondary one. Fearing the consequences, he rejected advice to send in combat troops. He insisted that the South Vietnamese must remain chiefly repsonsible for the fighting, and he had confidence that his method would work. He rejected pessimistic reports from journalists and the CIA, embraced optimistic ones, including McNamara's quantitative analyses, and tried to stop the flow of critical news accounts. The situation deteriorated during 1963 and included numerous demonstrations by militant Buddhists against repression, but Kennedy refused to consider getting out. He continued to regard the American effort as essential, compared it with earlier efforts in Europe, warned of dangers from China and expressed fear that Americans would grow impatient and withdraw. In the meantime, he renewed the pressure on Diem for reform and more effective military operations but failed, and then offered no opposition and some encouragement to a military coup that took place at the beginning of November and resulted in Diem's death. He hoped that a more effective regime would be established.

In enlarging significantly the American role in Vietnam, Kennedy was influenced by the same interpretation of history that had affected the thinking of the Truman Administration. He had, after all, been the author of an anti-appeasement book, *Why England Slept*, written as a very young man before World War II, and had fought in that war. He was influenced also by the theory that the United States had a special mission in the world and by a conviction that the nation faced a very serious crisis there. He did assume that there were limits on American power; he did try to keep the American role small in Vietnam, but he was determined to succeed. He was comforted by the assumption that the United States could do so without major sacrifices.

The Johnson Presidency

An assassin's bullets brought Kennedy's efforts to a sudden end on November 22, 1963, and brought to power one of the most active and skillful Presidents in American history. Lyndon Johnson, the tall Texas schoolmaster who went to Washington in 1932 and became a New Dealer, had acquired unusually rich experience in the capital, chiefly as the majority leader in the Senate, and he moved from triumph to triumph in domestic affairs during his first year and a half as President.

Johnson quickly obtained passage of Kennedy's major domestic proposals. Influenced by a desire to prove himself to the doubters as well as his own interest in reform, he obtained passage of the tax cut

President Johnson Signs the 1964 Civil Rights Act
(United Press International)

and civil rights proposals and also of plans that had developed before Kennedy's death for a war on poverty. Johnson's triumphs owed much to Kennedy's preparations, the mood created by his assassination, the civil rights movement, the liberals, students of poverty, and congressional leaders, especially Senators Hubert Humphrey and Everett Dirksen, but the Texan made his own contributions. He used the talents he had developed as the leader in the Senate—pressure, negotiation, and compromise—and he moved with confidence, feeling more powerful than ever before and convinced that the United States could do what was needed. And his triumphs involved the collapse of the Conservative Coalition. It frustrated Johnson on some issues, but he obtained crucial Republican support on civil rights and the votes of most Southern Democrats for the anti-poverty program.

Johnson moved on from his triumphs on Capitol Hill to victory by a landslide in the presidential election of 1964. He desired such a victory for psychological as well as political reasons; he wanted a convincing demonstration of his right to rule. He benefited from his record since entering the White House and from his selection of Hubert

Humphrey as the vice presidential candidate, for they weakened distrust of him among liberals and civil rights activists.

Johnson also drew strength from the ultra-conservatism of his Republican opponent. Senator Barry Goldwater of Arizona was identified with the "Radical Right." As a successful businessman and military expert, he was known for his honesty and wisdom, but also for his desire to make major changes in domestic and foreign policies. He advocated sharp cuts in the size and cost of government, except the police power, and at the same time called for a more forceful American role in the world, one that would produce victories rather than defeats. (He did not dissent from the confidence of the period.) His specific proposals included the topling of Castro and the bombing of North Vietnam. His stands on the issues alarmed many people, including many Republicans who deserted their party.

Johnson's own efforts also contributed to his victory. He campaigned vigorously, identified with both the desires for stability and the desires for change and presented himself as an advocate of cautious, restrained firmness in foreign affairs. He suggested, for example, that he would both prevent a Communist victory in Vietnam and avoid a wider war. He was, he maintained, very different from Goldwater.

Both Johnson and his party enjoyed great success. He carried all of the nation but the deep South and Arizona and obtained more black votes than any of his predecessors and more business votes than Democratic presidential candidates had been getting for many years. His victory was accompanied by Democratic victories in Congress that strengthened the liberal bloc there. The Democrats received sixty-two percent of the popular vote.

From his triumphs in 1964, Johnson moved on to new victories in 1965. He obtained passage of Medicare—a system of health insurance for the aged, federal aid to education, new immigration legislation departing from the discriminatory program of the past and laws attacking urban problems and pollution. Congress continued and enlarged the war on poverty and passed new civil rights legislation attacking the discriminatory practices of Southern registrars. These accomplishments owed much to the elections that had suggested that Johnson had broad popular support and created an unusually favorable situation in Congress. Johnson continued to benefit from the work of others, including Truman who had battled for health insurance years before, King who continued to lead demonstrations on behalf of change in race relations and Dirksen, the Republican leader in the Senate who cooperated once again with a Democratic President. But Johnson made his own contributions by employing his own talents.

Not since 1935-1936 had a president been such a successful reformer. The situation was favorable. Johnson's triumphs were, in a sense, triumphs for the liberal and civil rights movements, and the victories benefited from Truman's preparations. Yet Johnson accomplished what Truman and Kennedy had failed to do; he routed legislation through Congress with speed and precision unlike any of his predecessors.

The Warren Court

Johnson was also fortunate to have Earl Warren and a group of responsible judges on the Supreme Court. Their decisions were not always popular with the people, but they worked consistently for the causes of the common people and for racial justice. The court had never been particularly popular at any time in history, and in the 1960s Warren was harassed in New York by pickets and conservatives who called repeatedly for his impeachment.

The court aroused some bitterness when it reluctantly heard a case from the federal district court in Tennessee. Several residents of the state challenged the distribution of seats in the assembly where the five urban centers of the state were seriously underrepresented. In *Baker v. Carr* (1962) the court urged states to develop guidelines for rational distribution of seats without a "crazy quilt" of "invidious discrimination." Within a year twenty-five of the fifty states had their systems of legislative representation challenged as a result of this case. The overrepresentation of rural areas, their most consistent characteristic, was generally destroyed by additional court cases.

Decisions relating to the criminal law caused more opposition. A series of cases defined rights to counsel in criminal cases. In *Gideon v. Wainwright* (1963) the Court decided that paupers charged with felony must be provided a counsel, and in *Miranda v. Arizona* (1966) the court ordered police officers to inform arrested persons of their civil rights. The criticism levied against the court as a result of this decision has been harsh and persistent: the court is too lenient toward criminals at a time when society is pressed on all sides by crime. The answer of liberals is that the police have consistently violated the spirit of these cases, and that crime arises from other sources.

Life in America

Johnson's aim, as he defined it, was a Great Society, and American life in the mid-sixties was more prosperous than ever before. He, of course, was not solely or even chiefly responsible for that for the American economic system was complex. Since World War II, it had continued to be a system of collective capitalism composed of big government, big labor and big business, but it had developed in important ways as each component of the system had grown, relations among them had become more harmonious and the system had enlarged its operations outside the United States.

The federal government moved above its World War II size during the 1960s after shrinking following the war, expanding during the

Korean War, declining slowly right after it, growing slowly in the second half of the 1950s and growing rapidly in the 1960s, and it functioned in a variety of ways. It remained very active in transportation, regulating and promoting the development of the transportation network. It continued to regulate various economic activities, including the food and drug industry, the stock market, radio and television, but the regulators tended to be promotional more than critical in their relations with the regulated. Washington continued and expanded the welfare and agricultural activities of the New Deal and added new ones and became more active in science and education, supplying funds to institutions, faculty, and students. Government agencies guaranteed home loans and purchased commodities, especially for defense and war, serving as the chief customer for some firms, including the aircraft companies. The government used taxation in various ways to encourage economic activities, such as the exploration for oil, and promoted overseas expansion by battling against trade barriers and employing foreign aid, tax benefits, and diplomacy and enjoying great success in its efforts to penetrate the oil fields of the Middle East. And the federal government's heavy and growing involvement in the operations of the economy also included efforts to avoid depression and promote growth.

The labor movement did not grow as rapidly as it had from 1935 to 1945, but it did grow. It grew rapidly only during the Korean War and encountered difficulties following the war as a result of the decline of some industries like coal, the advance of automation, opposition in the South and West and poor leadership. Labor leaders tended to be fairly well paid and quite secure, and during the 1950s, they made little effort to organize white collar workers, women and blacks. In spite of automation and other problems, unions grew again in numbers during the 1960s as some leaders made a greater effort to organize the expanding segments of the urban work force. In California, beginning in 1962, Cesar Chavez fought for the organization of farm workers. Fierce opposition hampered his efforts, but by the late 1960s, 17,000 Chicanos and others had joined his union and several companies had signed contracts with it. And throughout the years after 1945, the movement made other efforts to strengthen itself—purging Communists, merging the CIO and the AFL, and expanding political activities.

Labor's political record was spotty, with more successes in the 1960s than in the 1950s, but its record in the economic arena featured successes. No longer forced to concentrate on achieving recognition and establishing collective bargaining, the movement emphasized higher wages and more fringe benefits. Achieving better relations with management, labor felt less need to use the strike. Most business leaders learned to live with unions and found it possible to pass increased labor costs on to consumers.

By the 1960s, the American labor movement was a widely accepted

Cesar Chavez: A Champion of the Rural Poor
(*United Press International*)

part of American life and also a participant in the world-wide activities of the United States. The movement did not enjoy great prestige.
Many Americans regarded it as corrupt, undemocratic and too powerful, but there was no significant inclination to destroy it. Quite secure
at home, union leaders tried to help workers in other countries develop
non-Communist labor movements on the American model.

Major business organizations grew more impressively than unions
did. The practices of the federal government facilitated this growth.
Washington did use its anti-trust powers from time to time and gave
some help to small firms, but it relied very heavily on the large firms,
especially for defense and war and in efforts to enlarge the American
presence in other parts of the world. The availability of opportunities
in a growing economy also encouraged the expansion of business
organizations. Economic growth stimulated growth in the size of

business firms and encouraged mergers, which occurred at a record-setting rate in the 1960s. Business organizations continued to grow in traditional ways with both horizontal and vertical mergers bringing together firms involved in different parts of a particular industry, but they increasingly emphasized the development of conglomerates, which combined firms active in very different economic activities.

As the firms grew, they became more sophisticated. Controlled by managers rather than owners—at least in most of their operations —they decentralized, expanded research programs, and paid more attention than ever before to public and employee relations. They also made greater use of advertising.

The corporations became more active outside the United States as they pursued markets, investments, and raw materials. They did not rely only on trade, although it was expanded substantially. They relied more heavily than before on "direct investment" and developed more and larger "multinational" corporations, purchasing oil, mining, and other properties, and establishing plants and other facilities that enabled them to penetrate markets in spite of tariffs and other barriers.

Although many American corporations were very large, few were free from competition. It was conspicuous in certain areas, such as style, advertising and retailing. The giants, however, tried, usually with considerable success, to avoid price competition.

American business had quite good relations with the public, government and labor. Those relations were not perfectly harmonious, but they were much better than they had been during the 1930s. The presence of many corporation executives and corporation lawyers in top spots in Washington symbolized the prestige as well as the power of the business system. They were present during Democratic administrations as well as during the Eisenhower years.

The economic system did not function perfectly, but, measured in terms of the dominant values of the period, functioned more successfully than ever before and more successfully than any other economic system. It did produce recessions in 1949-1950, 1953-1954, 1957-1958 and 1960-1961 and grew only slowly in the second half of the 1950s, but it avoided depression. Unemployment was never one-third of what it had been in 1932-1933 and never more than one-half of what it had been at the end of the 1930s. Furthermore, the system set a new record for growth from 1961 to 1969. It had grown for six and one-half years during World War II, and now it grew for eight and one-half years.

Several industries grew at especially impressive rates. Agriculture increased its output enormously in spite of a sharp drop in its labor force, doing so because of an increase in the size of farms and greater use of science and technology. Construction boomed as Americans built office buildings, factories, stores, homes, schools, churches, etc., in very large numbers. Electricity and the industries allied with

	GNP	Percent Change from GNP of Preceding Year (+ or −)	National Income	Disposable Personal Income	Per Capita Disposable Income (in current dollars)
Economic growth, 1950-1960: National Product and Income (in billions of current dollars)					
1950	284.8	+11.0	241.1	206.9	364
1951	328.4	+15.3	278.0	226.6	469
1952	345.5	+ 5.2	291.4	238.3	518
1953	364.6	+ 5.5	304.7	252.6	683
1954	364.8	+ 0.1	303.1	257.4	585
1955	398.0	+ 9.1	331.0	275.3	666
1956	419.2	+ 5.3	350.8	293.2	743
1957	441.1	+ 5.2	366.1	308.5	801
1958	447.3	+ 1.4	367.8	318.8	831
1959	483.7	+ 8.2	400.0	337.3	905
1960	503.7	+ 4.1	414.5	350.0	937

From Council of Economic Advisers, "Annual Report, January 1975" in *Economic Report of the President* (Washington, D.C., 1975), pp. 249, 267, 289.

it, such as home appliances, grew rapidly. A new industry, television, developed at a spectacular pace. The chemical industry turned out plastics, synthetic rubber, detergents, and other products in tremendous quantities. The aircraft and then the aerospace industries grew, largely because of the expansion of the military system and the development of the space program, and the airline industry, helped by technical developments, especially the introduction of the jet engine, became the nation's number one commercial carrier of passengers by the late 1950s. The automobile industry, which was operating above the 1929 level by the beginning of the 1950s, turned out the chief means of passenger travel and the buses and trucks that moved freight, as the airlines did, at the expense of the railroads. Several of the growth industries stimulated the development of the petroleum and natural gas industries, which moved forward at the expense of the coal industry in both transportation and heating.

The boom was accompanied by and facilitated many other elements in American life, including a population explosion. The nation grew from less than 149 million people in 1945 to nearly 195 million by 1965. It did so even though immigration was no longer a large feature of American life. This growth resulted in part from a baby boom that had begun during the war, reversing a downward trend in the birthrate, and continued until the late 1950s. It was not explained by ignorance for it occurred among that segment of the population—the middle classes—that was well informed about birth control. The explanation involved more than economics, although the economic boom did contribute by encouraging people to believe they could

The American Urban Sprawl of the 1970s'
(Department of Transportation, State of California)

afford larger families, but the baby boom ended as the economy moved into its most prosperous period. The baby boom may have involved a reaction to major features of the period, including the pressures that military service placed on the people, for this boom seemed to reflect a reaffirmation of family life and private life in a period when they were under attack. Growing interest in other forms of satisfaction and rising concern about over-population brought the boom to an end. The population continued to grow, however, for the explosion resulted from increase in the length of life as well as an increase in the birthrate. Improvement in diet and advances in medical science were responsible for the increase in the life span.

The American people continued to be a mobile people as they had been since the beginning of their history. The mobility patterns now included movements to the South and the West, especially to California, Arizona, Texas, and Florida. Helped by spending for defense and war, the South and West industrialized and grew rapidly. The patterns also included a large movement from farm to city. One feature here was a large movement of blacks out of the South, a development that made the population of the big cities increasingly black. In the Southwest hundreds of thousands of Mexican workers flocked across the border. Many chose to settle in Los Angeles, El Paso, and Houston. Still another pattern was the movement from the central cities to the suburbs, which were the most rapidly growing area of American life. The suburban immigrants sought to flee some but not all features of big city life, and their mobility was social as well as geographical. It reflected the rapid expansion of the middle classes, including the blue-collar middle class. And the rapid growth of suburbia provided abundant evidence of the scope of the economic boom. Suburbia's growth meant that millions of people had the money as well as desire to live outside the central city but to hold on to the latter's opportunities.

A sharp increase in travel added to the evidence that mobility remained a major theme. Domestic travel increased from 508 billion passenger miles in 1950 to 971 billion in 1966, and this development was accompanied by a spectacular change in the number and quality of motels and camp grounds. Foreign travel by Americans increased even more rapidly as the number of overseas travelers jumped from 676,000 in 1950 to nearly 3 million in 1966. Travel clubs, airplane charters, and special rates helped to make European trips available to increasingly larger numbers of people.

Poverty, while remaining a substantial part of American life, was a declining part. By 1968, as many as twenty-five million Americans lived below the poverty line. Poverty affected whites as well as non-whites, rural areas as well as the central cities. Poor land, the lack of skills, old age, racial discrimination, and unemployment were responsible for most of the poverty. Yet, it was not nearly as large a part of American life as it once had been. It had dropped rapidly during

Transcontinental Travel Time

New York - San Francisco

COVERED WAGON	5 MONTHS
PANAMA STEAMER	30 DAYS
OVERLAND STAGE	23 DAYS
RAILROAD 1875	7 DAYS
RAILROAD 1900	4 DAYS
RAILROAD 1945	2½ DAYS
PROPELLER PLANE	7½ HOURS
JET PLANE	4½ HOURS

World War II, as it afflicted well over half of the population in 1940 but less than 40 percent in 1945. It continued to decline but at a slower pace from 1945 to 1960, dropping to less than 25 percent, and then declined at an accelerated pace during the boom of the 1960s so that 12 percent of the population lived below the poverty line by 1968. The decline resulted chiefly from economic growth, which created a large number of jobs, dropping unemployment close to 3 percent of the labor force by the end of 1968, and increasing civilian employment to seventy-eight million as compared with the fifty-four million of 1945. The growth of the economy both forced and made possible increases in salaries and wages.

The decline in poverty and the other forms of social mobility were not accompanied by a levelling trend. The top 5 percent of the families had 17.5 percent of the before tax income in 1947 and 15.6 percent in 1966 while the lowest 20 percent moved from 5.1 to 5.6 percent of the income. The nation had emphasized enlarging the pie, not cutting it in new ways.

The increasingly prosperous nation experienced a religious revival. Many developments testified to this: the increase in church membership from 64.5 million in 1940 to 123.8 million in 1966, the widespread tendency of people to define themselves in religious terms and endorse basic religious doctrines, the popularity of the writings of Fulton J. Sheen, Norman Vincent Peale, and others, and of religious films, the success of evangelists like Billy Graham, and the frequent references to religion by politicians. Roman Catholics changed more than any group. Their use of vernacular in the mass, lay persons in the liturgy, and modern forms of music, art, and vestments represented unusual departures from past practices. Their willingness to carry on dialogues with other religious groups opened up possibilities of larger cooperation and unity discussions. The revival was not concentrated in any one religious group; the nation continued to be pluralistic in religion; the different religious groups became more tolerant of one another, but religious conflict did not disappear. The election of John F. Kennedy in 1960 testified to both the growth of tolerance and the survival of conflict.

The messages of America's religious leaders in these years contained both optimism and pessimism. Peale, for example, gave millions a religious base for optimism, while the less popular but intellectually influential Reinhold Niebuhr expressed a darker view of life.

The revival is not easily explained. Some commentators have offered a crisis hypothesis, emphasizing the possibility of mankind's destruction in atomic war and other grim features of modern life. Others have presented a political hypothesis that stresses the importance of religion for a people involved in a Cold War with communism. And a social hypothesis maintains that highly mobile people, uprooted from their families and ethnic groups, turned to religion in order to find a sense of identity and an organization to which they could belong. As the movement was large, it seems likely that all of these factors contributed to it; and as most of the participants were also beneficiaries of the economic boom, it seems unlikely that lack of confidence in the possibility of finding a rather good life in this world, at least in the American part of it, dominated the revival.

America also became in these years a "leisure society." As a consequence of the short work week and the vacation with pay, as well as the increase in income, leisure was not the monopoly of a small class. And most Americans, no longer dominated by old beliefs in hard work and saving, placed a high value on having a good time. The increase in personal expenditures for recreation from $8.5 billion in 1946 to $26.3 billion in 1965 illustrates the growing importance of leisure.

Leisure-time activities took a variety of forms. Spectator sports were very important. Attendance at major league baseball games increased from 18.5 million in 1946 to only 22.5 million in 1965, but attendance at other types of games, especially profesisonal football and basketball, grew even more rapidly than baseball. Participation in sports also increased as the number of golfers grew from 2.5 million in 1948 to 7.8 million in 1965, the number of bowlers from 1 million in

Sports and Politics: Stan Musial and President Kennedy
(*Wide World Photo*)

1946 to 7.6 million in 1965 and the number of hunting and fishing licenses more than doubled in the same period, moving from 20.9 million to 44.4 million. The mass media filled many of the hours away from work. Attendance at movies dropped from 90 million a week in 1946 to 44 million in 1965, a drop that encouraged the industry to become more experimental. Households with radios increased from 34 million to 55.2 million in the same period, and that industry switched its emphasis from entertainment for the entire family to teenagers and motorists as it, like the movies, adjusted the the development of television. In 1951, TV could be found in only 10.3 million homes but in 1965 over five times that number had television. Its quality was uneven, but great theater, absorbing sports and good music were regularly available. In addition to TV, Americans had a rich variety of music available to them, facilitated by the advent of long-playing records and great improvement in the equipment for playing them, and they purchased paperback books in huge numbers. These and other leisure-time activities combined to strengthen the conviction of most Americans that their way of life was a good one and superior to other ways.

There were skeptics who insisted that the nation should not have such a lofty view of itself. C. Wright Mills, for example, maintained that conformity and elite rule were the main features of American life, while William Appleman Williams insisted that American foreign policy was nothing more than an effort to find and protect economic opportunities for American businessmen. Some intellectuals, such as Ralph Ellison, portrayed racism as the major feature of American life, and Michael Harrington focused the spotlight on mass poverty. Scattered groups of students formed the Students for a Democratic Society, the Free Speech Movement, and other groups to protest against a number of features of American life in the early Sixties, and many urban blacks rioted in 1964 and 1965 in protest against the aspects of American life that seemed most distasteful to them. And prominent literary figures, including William Faulkner, Jack Kerouac, William Styron, Norman Mailer, Tennessee Williams and Edward Albee, lacked enthusiasm for the American scene and optimism about human prospects.

These skeptics, however, did not set the tone of American life in the 1950s and the first half of the 1960s. The rapid expansion of higher education more accurately reflected the dominant mood. This development was made possible by the economic boom, which supplied the required funds, and expenditures on higher education moved from $675 million in 1940 to $12.5 billion in 1966. The number of students in the same period jumped from 1.5 million to 5.9 million, in part because of the baby boom but also because of a spectacular increase in the percentage of the population 18 to 24 that attended colleges and universities. Only slightly more than 9 percent did so in 1940, but nearly 28 percent did so in 1966. And the expansion of higher education was backed up by comparable developments at all educational levels.

The boom in education reflected American confidence. With widespread public and private support, the educational system assumed that the capacity to benefit from higher education was widespread, that the nation could supply such education for millions of people, and that both the individual and the society would benefit. The universities contributed to the spectacular development of American science, sought to serve all aspects of American life, not just the learned professions, and had a problem-solving emphasis.

Americans generally had confidence in their way of life and its capacity for improvement. They assumed that their economic system was functioning very successfully and was capable of becoming even more successful. They had seen it move from long-term depression to an even longer boom and produce great changes in their daily lives. They had more "things" than ever before and than any other people had. They did not expect to create a perfect society, but they did expect to create a better one through the use of reason. The rapid development of higher education testified to their faith.

Escalation and Americanization in Vietnam

In 1965, the dynamic leader of a confident people escalated the war in Vietnam and shifted the major burden of the anti-Communist effort there to American fighting men. President Johnson had not rushed eagerly to these decisions, for he had hoped to concentrate his energies on the improvement of life inside the United States. He was convinced that he was in a better position to promote change at home than any President had been since the late 1930s, and he feared the diversion of resources from domestic to foreign concerns. During 1964, he had warned against Americanization of the war and the bombing of North Vietnam, talking much like Kennedy had. Other factors, however, led him to the decisions of 1965.

One was the deteriorating situation in Vietnam. The situation there deteriorated rapidly in 1964 for the overthrow of Diem had not led to the establishment of a strong regime in South Vietnam. Hoping to take advantage of the situation, the Viet Cong enlarged their efforts, although they still received only a small amount of aid from North Vietnam. By the beginning of 1965, they were moving rapidly toward victory.

The advice from Kennedy's former advisors also influenced Johnson. He had kept on the top figures from the Kennedy administration, including McNamara, Rusk, Rostow, Taylor and MacGeorge Bundy, for he had great confidence in them, especially McNamara. He relied upon them even more heavily than Kennedy had, perhaps because of a sense of insecurity. He recognized the contrast between their backgrounds and his and shared their lack of confidence in his ability in foreign affairs, which encouraged them to feel he was very dependent on them and encouraged him to avoid any appearance of weakness. They did share his confidence in his ability to get things done. In advising him, they stressed the importance of the war, portraying it as a test of America's ability to combat "wars of national liberation" and warning, as the "Munich Analogy" and the "Domino Theory" suggested, that if the anti-Communist effort failed there, Communists elsewhere would be encouraged to strike. These advisers also expressed confidence in the nation's ability to do what was required and to succeed quickly. During 1964, they pressed for further application of the McNamara strategy, and they were not challenged significantly. The new American commander in South Vietnam, General William Westmoreland, had confidence in what American forces could do, and George Ball, the Undersecretary of State who doubted that escalation would work, had no important allies in the Administration.

Johnson's own sense of responsibility also affected him. He had been a consistent supporter of an ambitious foreign policy backed up by military power since entering Congress in 1937. He had learned the "lessons of history." He had strong convictions about the dangers of communism, the value of Containment and the importance of the global commitments of the United States, including the commitment to South Vietnam. He commented frequently that he was determined not to lose Vietnam as Truman had lost China, and he feared that if he lost he would suffer attack as Truman had, his entire program would be damaged and he would not be regarded as a great president.

Furthermore, by 1965, Johnson had a sense of great personal and national power. He had a large and complex military machine and a theory to guide its use, and that machine was supported by an economy that was growing rapidly and being stimulated rather than harmed by government action. He seemed to have strong popular and congressional support, and the people and the Congress seemed to believe in the dangers of communism and the responsibility of the United States to contain it. Congress, after all, had passed with only two dissenting votes the Tonkin Gulf Resolution in August 1964 that gave him the authority to act in Vietnam in the ways that seemed necessary to him. And he faced a small, seemingly weak nation, North Vietnam, that was led by just another man similar to the ones with whom he had dealt successfully in Washington. Surely, the application of a specific amount of power would quickly bring Ho into line.

A sense of great responsibility and power overwhelmed the doubts in Johnson's mind, and he escalated and Americanized the war in a series of decisions in the first half of 1965. First, the United States began to bomb North Vietnam, and then it enlarged greatly the number of American troops in Vietnam and their role in the fighting. The process moved forward in a step-by-step fashion as dictated by the McNamara strategy.

The process of escalation and Americanization in Vietnam expressed the confidence that had been growing in the United States for a decade. By 1965 it seemed possible, if not to create a perfect society, at least to create a Great Society and, at the same time, to function effectively as a global power.

SUGGESTIONS FOR FURTHER READING

Alexander, Charles C., Holding the Line: The Eisenhower Era, 1952-1961. Bloomington, Ind., Indiana University Press, 1975.

Bartley, Numan V., The Rise of Massive Resistance: Race and Politics in the South During the 1950s. Baton Rouge, La., Louisiana State University Press, 1969.

Burner, David, Robert D. Marcus and Thomas R. West, A Giant's Strength: America in the 1960s. New York, Holt, Rinehart and Winston, Inc., 1971.

Diggins, John P., The American Left in the Twentieth Century. New York, Harcourt Brace Jovanovich, Inc., 1973.

Halberstam, David, The Best and the Brightest. New York, Random House, 1972.

Heath, Jim F., Decade of Disillusionment: The Kennedy-Johnson Years. Bloomington, Ind., Indiana University Press, 1975.

————, John F. Kennedy and the Business Community. Chicago, University of Chicago Press, 1969.

Lewis, David L., King: A Critical Biography. New York, Praeger, 1970.

Meier, August and Elliott Rudwick, CORE: A Study in the Civil Rights Movement, 1942-1968. New York, Oxford University Press, 1973.

O'Neill, William L., Coming Apart: An Informal History of American Life in the 1960s. Chicago, Quadrangle, 1971.

Parmet, Herbert S., Eisenhower and the American Crusades. New York, The Macmillan Co., 1972.

Purcell, Edward A., Jr., The Crisis of Democratic Theory: Scientific Naturalism and the Problem of Value. Lexington, Ky., University Press of Kentucky, 1973.

Roland, Charles P., The Improbable Era: The South Since World War II. Lexington, Ky., The University Press of Kentucky, 1975.

Rostow, W. W., The United States in the World Arena: An Essay in Recent History. New York, Harper & Row, Publishers, 1960.

Schlesinger, Arthur M., Jr., A Thousand Days: John F. Kennedy in the White House. Boston, Houghton Mifflin Co., 1965.

Shannon, David A., *The Decline of American Communism: A History of the Communist Party of the United States Since 1945*. New York, Harcourt, Brace, 1959.

Stein, Herbert, *The Fiscal Revolution in America*. Chicago, The University of Chicago Press, 1969.

Sundquist, James L., *Politics and Policy: The Eisenhower, Kennedy, and Johnson Years*. Washington, The Brookings Institution, 1968.

Trewitt, Henry L., *McNamara*. New York, Harper & Row, Publishers, 1971.

Walton, Richard J., *Cold War and Counter-Revolution: The Foreign Policy of John F. Kennedy*. New York, The Viking Press, 1972.

Woodward, C. Vann, *The Strange Career of Jim Crow*. New York, Oxford University Press, 1974.

Troubled Times

THE CONFIDENCE OF 1965 soon came to seem quite unrealistic. The war in Vietnam proved much more difficult than anticipated and contributed decisively to the growth of discontent at home. The economic system functioned less effectively, and confidence in American leadership, especially the Presidency, declined sharply. Two talented but flawed Presidents, although achieving some impressive accomplishments, failed in ways that had damaging impacts upon public attitudes.

Revival on the Left

The escalation and Americanization of the war in Vietnam generated an enormous amount of discontent in America, especially among young people, and much of that discontent was given focus and direction by a "New Left" that had emerged before 1965 and now flourished for a moment in the new political climate in the United States.

The New Left was not just a repeat of the old. It was less influenced by Marx, more by Freud; had less admiration for Russia and placed less emphasis on the role of the working classes in the historical process. And, less convinced than theorists of the old left had been that capitalism would automatically and inevitably produce the revolution that destroyed it, the New Left paid great attention to the process by which groups became radicalized.

Some of the roots of the New Left could be traced to men and movements of the postwar years; some to conditions of American life. It owed debts to radical pacifists such as David Dellinger and A. J. Muste, to the civil rights movement of Martin Luther King, Jr., and others, to the beat generation represented by Allen Ginsberg and Jack Kerouac, among others, and to radical intellectuals, especially Paul Goodman, William Appleman Williams, C. Wright Mills, and Herbert Marcuse. Poverty and racism in America also supplied stimuli.

The New Left owed even more to the special experiences of upper-middle-class young people. They composed and led the movement. Unlike their parents, they had not experienced depression and war and the triumph over them, and they had been raised in boom times. Many of them now found the life that was expected of them quite unsatisfying. They also found college life quite unattractive. They sought and often found satisfaction in involvement in "the movement."

The unexpected revival on the left also owed something to student participation in a series of protests from 1960 to 1964. The series included protests in 1960 against the execution of Caryl Chessman at San Quentin and against the hearings conducted by the House Un-American Activities Committee in San Francisco. The protests also included the civil rights movement of the early sixties and the efforts in 1963-64 of a new group, the Students for a Democratic Society (SDS), to educate and organize poor whites in the slums. Participation radicalized many of these people, moving them away from critiques of aspects of American life that seemed capable of being reformed to thorough-going alienation.

The upheaval on the Berkeley campus of the University of California in the fall of 1964 provided the first substantial evidence of the development of discontent among young whites of the upper middle class. The upheaval took place in a unique situation that included an attractive location, a distinguished faculty, and an institution that was proud of its record of public service and open only to students of high ability. It was also a large and impersonal place that regulated the student's social lives, but gave them a high degree of political freedom. It had a tradition of political activism and housed in 1964 a small group of radical students who now demanded large and rapid changes in the University. Triggered by new restrictions on the use of the campus as a base for off-campus political action, the protest attracted a large number of students, led to the formation of the Free Speech Movement, and involved civil disobedience, demonstrations and the occupation of the administration building. The police were called in; the students staged a strike; the campus debated and restrictions were relaxed.

The Berkeley upheaval was a significant event. It suggested to some people that universities as well as other institutions were coercive and students were an oppressed class that should create a revolution for themselves as well as for others. The experience also suggested that the campus provided good opportunities for recruitment and training of revolutionaries.

The crisis at Berkeley erupted only a short time before the escalation and Americanization of the war in Vietnam, and those developments had a profound impact on young people. The war became the focal point of student protest in 1965, 1966, and 1967. The war drew radical groups together, stimulated the growth of SDS, provided an important basis for cooperation with non-radical groups and produced widespread support for protest. And the left had an interpretation of the war that contributed to the radicalization process. The war was portrayed as an inevitable consequence of American racism and imperialism, an obstacle to change at home, and evidence of the need for a thorough-going revolution in America.

Under the pressures of the period, the most prominent New Left group, SDS, changed in important ways. It removed the Communist exclusion clause from its constitution and absorbed the students affiliated with the Progressive Labor party. Its official line, which had been essentially reformist, became more consistently radical. And by 1967, SDS had shifted its attention from the poor and the blacks to the college students. SDS theorists rejected the Marxist theory about the role of the proletariat, emphasized the "new working class," the white-collar workers who were viewed as exploited and oppressed, although affluent, and argued that these people must be politicized and radicalized while they were on campus. These aims could be accomplished by seizing upon matters of interest to students and demanding major and quick changes, thereby creating major clashes with administrators. The universities, which oppressed students and served the larger system, would be revolutionized, and that change would pave the way for revolution in other places.

Large-scale protest hit many campuses from 1966 to 1968. Not limited to the war, protest extended to on-campus recruitment by the military, the defense industries and the CIA, higher education's cooperation with the draft, the research being done in university laboratories for the Defense Department, the racial practices of the schools, and the ways in which they were governed.

By 1968, protest was a very large and prominent part of American life. There were more than 3,000 campus demonstrations in the spring of that year. Columbia University in New York City experienced one of the major ones. Promoted by SDS, the protest focused on Columbia's membership in the Institute for Defense Analysis and plans to build a gymnasium on the east side of campus, near Harlem. This upheaval included the seizure of several buildings, the holding of three administrators, police action, many injuries and arrests, and disruption of the class schedule. Changes were made in the governance of the University, and the plans to build the gym were scrapped.

By the fall of 1968, SDS had more than 100,000 members, but the New Left had become much more than a young people's movement. It involved radical caucuses in professional societies and radicals in the media—some working in established firms and others in "underground" newspapers. Prominent intellectuals expressed radical views in the New York Review and other places; one group, the Yippies, sought to fuse cultural and political radicalism, and many groups, led by the Resistance, participated in mass protests against the war, making use of draft resistance and other methods. Activity reached a new high in the protest against the Democratic National Convention in Chicago.

The New Left involved a challenge to the fundamentals of American life, an insistence that the nation was a failure and a demand for revolution. It challenged not only the business and military leaders and their institutions but also the leading intellectuals, the universities, and the labor unions. It challenged not only the conservatives but the liberals and the reformers as well. Arising after an age of confidence, the New Left was unexpected and surprising. Although not merely the product of Vietnam, the war made it a prominent part of the American scene.

While the New Left gained strength, a related development took shape in black America. "Black Power," expressed by Stokely Carmichael of the Student Nonviolent Coordinating Committee, among others, came to the front, reflecting rising discontent over the pace of change and questioning the reliance on nonviolent methods and broad coalitions. Young blacks in the civil rights movement had been growing increasingly resentful of the use of violence by their foes, tension and conflict had been developing between whites and blacks in the movement, and concern had been mounting about its failure to reach the social and economic problems of the poorest blacks. A product of these experiences, Black Power was influenced also by the tradition of black nationalism expounded by Booker T. Washington, W. E. B. DuBois, Marcus Garvey, Malcolm X, and others.

One of the most publicised features of Black Power was criticism of Martin Luther King, Jr., and liberalism. King was criticized as too close to white leaders and too quick to compromise. His philosophy, with its emphasis on nonviolence, cooperation between whites and blacks, and integration, was rejected as inadequate. Carmichael and others accepted the fact that the Civil Rights Acts of 1964 and 1965 had achieved major social and political changes. But these affected largely the middle class. Needed economic gains for the benefit of the masses had not come and this fact demanded a new emphasis.

Black Power involved an attack upon class exploitation as well as white racism. Carmichael and his associates argued that attention should shift away from the concerns of the middle class and focus on the impoverished blacks in the rural South and the urban ghettos. Programs should be established that would provide more and better jobs, education, housing, and food and also provide family allowances and a guaranteed annual income. These must be government programs, for private enterprise could not serve the needs of the poor.

Lacking King's degree of confidence in whites, the advocates of Black Power insisted that blacks must draw together and rely chiefly on their own efforts. There was a strong psychological dimension, an emphasis on black identity and pride. Coalition politics was criticized as certain to produce compromises and only small, insignificant changes when blacks were weak. Black Power rhetoric was addressed primarily to black people for the purpose of building group unity.

Related to this plea for self-determination was a critique of integration. Emphasis on it ignored the big problems and also insulted blacks because it implied that white society was superior. Theorists for Black Power argued that just the opposite was true. Integration meant assimilation of blacks by an evil way of life. Prime interest, however, was in a united power base for black action and not in racial separation per se.

These theorists regarded violence as an important force. Some regarded nonviolent forms, such as voting and boycotts, as better, but most if not all insisted that acts of violence by blacks were permissible if whites did not change their ways. The radical wing of the Black Power movement, the Black Panthers, placed especially heavy emphasis on violence. It was founded in Oakland in October 1966 by two young blacks, Huey Newton and Bobby Seale; Carmichael and Eldridge Cleaver soon joined the organization and contributed to its ideological development, and it spread to other urban centers. The Panthers emphasized the importance of the gun as a means of self-defense, a symbol of manhood and courage, and an instrument of revolution. They regarded the police as a symbol of oppression of blacks by whites, labelled them "pigs," and sought to protect ghetto blacks from them. One consequence was frequent "shoot-outs" in which both Panthers and police were killed. While the organization did engage in non-revolutionary activity, such as providing breakfasts for black children, the Panthers were a revolutionary group. As Newton explained, "our one goal is to crush American capitalism and American imperialism."

Although the Panthers endorsed violence, they opposed the unsystematic rioting in the black ghettos that took place during the decade. The first riots erupted in 1964. In July, there was a large one in Harlem, the biggest episode of its kind since 1943. In August 1965, an even larger riot exploded in the Watts section of Los Angeles.

There were still more in 1966, and then the rioting reached a peak
in the summer of 1967 when about seventy cities were hit by large-
scale disorders that produced 85 deaths and more than 3,000 injuries,
most of them black, damaged property, and forced governments to
spend large sums trying to halt the death and destruction. In April
of the following year, the assassination of Martin Luther King, Jr.,
in Memphis triggered riots in urban centers throughout the nation.

The chief objects of attack were the representatives of white society in the black ghettos. White-owned businesses and the police
were hit especially hard. Symbols of white power, white racism, and
white repression felt the force of black resentment and frustration.

The riots were unorganized acts of protest against slum conditions
and white power. They were political acts, and agitators preaching
violence were involved in them. But the chief force at work was the
contrast between ghetto and surburban life. The typical rioter was a
young black male who had always lived in the city, had attended but
not graduated from high school, had a poor job, was proud to be black
and extremely hostile toward whites, and hoped for a better life. He
did not want to destroy the capitalistic system; he wanted a larger
share of its benefits. Television had an important influence on him,
supplying a picture of an alternative way of life: the life lived by whites
in the suburbs. That was the type of life he desired. Migration from the
South, the civil rights movement, and the war on poverty had stirred
hopes in his community, but they were not being realized. He seemed
incapable of breaking out of the life he was in, and he doubted that the
political system would solve his problems. Thus, he lashed out. White
violence seemed to justify his own acts.

The Frustrations of LBJ

The change in the situation, combined with Lyndon Johnson's
refusal to change, altered the course of his career abruptly and surprisingly. He had been enormously successful in 1964 and 1965. From
1966 to 1968, however, he failed repeatedly.

Vietnam supplied the President's basic frustration. He continued
to escalate the war throughout 1966 and 1967, increasing the number
of targets until virtually all of North Vietnam was open to attack from
American bombers, and increasing the number of American troops until
more than 500,000 were participating in the war. At the same time, he
refused to invade North Vietnam or to authorize use of atomic bombs,
fearing that such moves would lead to larger problems. His goal was
a settlement that would bring the fighting to an end and keep the Viet
Cong out of power in South Vietnam.

Johnson failed to bring the Viet Cong and their allies to the bargaining table. The Viet Cong received increasing amounts of support
from North Vietnam, China, and Russia. The combatants recognized

War in Vietnam

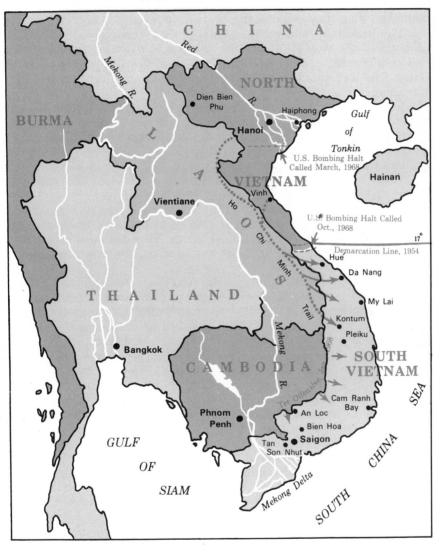

CHINA

Red

NORTH

Mekong R.

BURMA

Dien Bien
Phu

Haiphong

Gulf
of
Tonkin

Hanoi

U.S. Bombing Halt
Called March, 1968

L A O S

VIETNAM

Hainan

Vientiane

Vinh

Ho Chi Minh Trail

U.S. Bombing Halt Called
Oct., 1968

17°

THAILAND

Demarcation Line, 1954

Hue

Da Nang

My Lai

Kontum

Pleiku

Bangkok

Mekong R.

CAMBODIA

SOUTH
VIETNAM

Tet Offensive, Jan. 1968

Cam Ranh
Bay

SEA

Phnom
Penh

An Loc

Bien Hoa

SOUTH

Tan
Son Nhut

Saigon

CHINA

GULF

OF

SIAM

Mekong Delta

SOUTH CHINA SEA

his reluctance to accept them as at least a part of the governing group in South Vietnam and believed they could accomplish more on the battlefield than they could at the bargaining table.

The President held on tenaciously to his conception of the importance of the war. He likened it to earlier challenges from fascism and communism. He stressed the dangers to the United States from China. The war, in other words, was more than an effort to defeat the Viet Cong or even the North Vietnamese.

Johnson also maintained his confidence that the United States would succeed by continuing the existing methods. General William P. Westmoreland and others assured him that success lay ahead. The Defense Department's quantitative analyses of casualties and control of territory backed up the optimistic words.

Much to Johnson's surprise and dismay, the Viet Cong and the North Vietnamese embarked upon a major offensive early in 1968, the Tet offensive. It contradicted the optimistic appraisals that American officials had been making. It also persuaded Westmoreland to ask for more than 200,000 additional troops. That degree of escalation would, he was convinced, bring the war to an end on terms that Washington could accept.

While his troubles mounted in Southeast Asia, Johnson also experienced frustrations at home. As the war became more expensive, he felt compelled to make smaller, less costly efforts to promote change in the United States than had been planned when programs like the war on poverty had been initiated. The massive and mounting protests and riots on campuses and in the central cities posed major problems for him, and the Republican victories in the 1966 congressional elections, although they did not give the Republicans control of the Congress, did weaken his position there. The coalition that he had formed disintegrated as many members became criticial of him, especially his policies in Vietnam. He suffered several defeats in Congress and encountered mounting inflation as federal spending soared in response to the escalation of the war. The riots encouraged liberals to press for a massive attack on poverty, but he felt compelled to resist their pressure, convinced that the federal government could not spend more money. He tried to quiet his critics by explaining the war but failed to accomplish his aim. And his popularity dropped sharply.

Discontent with Johnson became so widespread that he was challenged by members of his party for renomination. One challenge came from Senator Eugene McCarthy, a liberal from Minnesota, and McCarthy surprised the nation—and the President—by a strong showing in the New Hampshire primary. Then Senator Robert Kennedy of New York announced that he too would run for the Democratic nomination for the White House. The Wisconsin primary lay ahead, and Johnson seemed likely to lose there.

In this frustrating situation, Johnson surrendered the power that remained in his hands, and his party in the coming election lost control of the White House. On March 31, 1968, he announced two surprising and significant decisions, informing the nation that he would reduce the bombing of North Vietnam and would not run for another term. He feared the domestic consequences of further escalation such as Westmoreland proposed and hoped that his decisions would strengthen him at home and abroad.

Johnson did not regain enough strength to accomplish his major objectives. The Congress continued to rebuff him on important issues. He did achieve the nomination of his choice for the Presidency, Hubert Humphrey, but did so in part because of Senator Kennedy's assassination in June, an act that removed the strongest challenger from the scene and added to the evidence that America had become a deeply troubled society. Nominated in spite of liberal opposition, Humphrey depended upon support from Democratic organizations, Southern Democrats, and organized labor.

Johnson's decision to de-escalate did not bring the war to an end. While he got the negotiations started, he failed to achieve success through negotiations as both South Vietnam and North Vietnam caused difficulties. Late in the presidential campaign, he felt compelled to end all bombing of North Vietnam, hoping that this would both assist the negotiators and help Humphrey.

Johnson's efforts, however, failed to produce a victory for the Minnesota Democrat. His association with and loyalty to LBJ destroyed much of the support that liberals once had given him. Of these groups labor remained most loyal, and the unions worked hard for the Democratic candidate. He benefited also from the established strength of his party as ties to the party pulled many unhappy Democrats into the ranks of Humphrey supporters by election day. Johnson's decision to halt the bombing also helped Humphrey to gain ground rapidly. Yet, he failed to catch up and lost by a narrow margin to former Vice President Richard Nixon even though the latter received much less than 50 percent of the popular vote. A large bloc of voters supported a third-party candidate, George Wallace of Alabama.

The situation that had emerged so abruptly and surprisingly after 1965 had proved too tough for LBJ. Though he had demonstrated that he was a very skillful politician, he was not skillful enough to master the enormous difficulties that developed after 1965. His failure should not obscure the fact that he was more than a politician. He was not only interested in his own power. He was influenced also by a doctrine—a doctrine that owed much to the historical experiences of the 1930s and 1940s. A product of that era, he could not accept a victory for the "forces of aggression." The lessons of the past, as he and others defined them, controlled his behavior in Southeast Asia and prevented him from behaving in ways that might have enabled him to achieve more success at home, perhaps holding on to the power of the Presidency for another term. Yet, surrender of his convictions might not have worked, for many people as late as 1968 interpreted the war as he did and supported the American effort.

The situation was very complex. A new crisis had emerged—a leadership crisis characterized by wide and deep lack of confidence in American officials.

The Triumphs of Richard Nixon

The new President's basic task was to end the leadership crisis, but he failed to do so. In fact, it was more severe at the end of his Presidency than at the beginning. He enjoyed some triumphs during his years in the White House, but in the end, he failed more dramatically than any of his predecessors had.

For Kennedy and Johnson, the big problems of American life had seemed to be slow economic growth, racial discrimination, and poverty. For Nixon, the big domestic problems seemed to be inflation and disorder. The differences reflected change in both situation and values. Inflation and disorder had not only emerged as problems, but they were the kinds of problems that appeared to be especially important to Nixon.

By 1969, when Nixon took office, inflation had been rising for nearly three years, and the situation worsened after he became President, causing him to feel compelled to act. The consumer price index had mounted only 1 or 2 percent a year throughout much of the 1950s and during the first half of the 1960s, but prices jumped 3 percent in 1966 and again in 1967 and 4 percent in 1968. Then, they moved up 5.6 percent in 1969, 6.5 percent in 1970 and 7 percent in 1971. Nixon felt compelled to intervene massively in the summer of 1971 and imposed a system of economic controls.

The demand for "law and order" had also been building for several years. It had been a major theme of Barry Goldwater's campaign in 1964, and two other prominent figures, George Wallace and Ronald Reagan, the governors of Alabama and California and active presidential candidates, had also emphasized it. Nixon hit it hard in 1968, blaming liberals and the United States Supreme Court as well as radicals for the disorder.

Nixon's personality affected his use of this theme. Having a strong drive for power, he assumed that the world was a dangerous place and his own life was a series of crises. He lacked the liberal's confidence in the ability of social and economic reform to create an orderly society and emphasized the need to be tough in dealing with the dangers that surrounded him.

In his efforts to reestablish order, Nixon tried without success to relax pressure for change in race relations. The Senate rebuffed his effort to weaken the Voting Rights Act of 1965, and the Supreme Court

President Richard Nixon in a Happy Moment
(*University of Southern California*)

frustrated his attempt to slow desegregation.

Nixon's efforts to change the Supreme Court did not accomplish much more. He regarded its liberal decisions on race and criminals as sources of disorder, and he nominated two conservative Southerners —Clement F. Haynsworth, Jr., and G. Harrold Carswell—for positions on the Court, hoping that their votes would force it to behave in more sensible ways, but the Senate rejected these nominations, brushing aside his claim that he alone had the power of appointment to the Court. These defeats persuaded him to turn to Warren E. Burger and Harry A. Blackmun of Minnesota, less conservative men with spotless records that made them invulnerable to attack. These changes in personnel did not result in as much change in Court behavior as the President desired.

Still other efforts to restore order emphasized repression. Here, Nixon relied heavily on his Attorney General, John Mitchell, who obtained from Congress tough anti-crime legislation and expanded authority to tap telephones. Members of the Justice Department investigated, infiltrated, and prosecuted the New Left. National efforts were backed up by some state and local officials, including Mayor Richard Daley of Chicago and President S. I. Hayakawa of San Francisco State University. National Guard units were deployed against demonstrators, including those at Kent State in May 1970. Most Americans approved of these tactics.

At the time, however, the public did not know about other efforts being made by the Nixon Administration to suppress the critics, which included the development of an elaborate system of domestic intelligence and espionage. Nixon was convinced that the security of the Republic and the life of his Administration were threatened by radicals. Under his authority, officials tapped telephones of several members of the staff of the National Security Council and several newsmen. This practice, conducted from 1969 to 1971, was done without warrants and resulted from unhappiness about news leaks concerning B-52 raids over Cambodia, a military operation that the Administration wanted to conceal. In 1970, the President endorsed a scheme for a vast enlargement of domestic intelligence operations involving a number of illegal techniques, but this was cancelled as a result of opposition from the director of the FBI, J. Edgar Hoover. In 1971, a special investigation unit, called the "Plumbers" because stopping leaks was one of its functions, was established inside the White House following the publication of some secret documents, the "Pentagon Papers." The unit was headed by Egil Krogh and included E. Howard Hunt and G. Gordon Liddy. It burglarized the office of the psychiatrist of Daniel Ellsberg, the former official responsible for the leaking of the Pentagon Papers, and broke into Democratic National Headquarters at the Watergate in Washington. The White House also developed an "enemies list" composed of prominent critics of the Administration and planned to use federal power, such as the Internal Revenue Service, to punish its "enemies."

Nixon believed that the existence of a national emergency forced him to act in these ways and justified his actions. The system of domestic intelligence and espionage was developed and operated secretly. The President did not explain what was being done, encourage debate about it, or seek approval for his moves.

Nixon's most effective move on behalf of a more orderly society was the winding down of the American role in Vietnam. It was, after all, the chief source of disorder in American life. His move away from military involvement was part of a larger effort to adjust to new realities in international affairs as well as partly to reestablish order in American life. Also important were his surprising negotiations with China and Russia. What made them so surprising was that, while they amounted to a waning of the Cold War, he had been an unusually militant cold warrior.

Militant anti-communism had been a major feature of Nixon's record in American politics. It figured prominently in his first campaign for Congress, the campaign of 1946, and his campaign for the Senate in 1950. He had come to national attention as a leader in the attack on Alger Hiss, and he had been a leading proponent of the theory that Communists influenced the policies of the Democratic administrations. While serving as Vice President, he had used such themes frequently, and they had continued to be a significant feature of his life in the first half of the 1960s when he promised the voters of California "the best Communist control of any state in the United States," criticized the Kennedy-Johnson policies as weak and "doomed to failure" and insisted that the American goal must be "nothing less than a free Russia, a free China, a free Eastern Europe, and a free Cuba."

Several forces moved Nixon to a new position, although he never surrendered his conviction that American life was threatened from within. After his bitter defeat for governor of California in 1962, he had moved to New York City to join a law firm and had gained an opportunity to improve his relations with the "Eastern Establishment." Troubled by his feeling that he was an "outsider," he had blamed his poor relations with the establishment for his political troubles, and he now concluded that he must develop a more sophisticated image. His new position also involved a new relationship for him with corporate leaders, the heads of the multinational companies. They suggested to him that the United States should reduce the costs of its foreign policies and that American corporations should be able to operate anywhere, including Russia and China.

The new international situation also affected Nixon's thinking. The world was no longer dominated by two powers as it had been after World War II. American troubles were reducing its power. They included the difficulties in Vietnam, were illustrated by the refusal of many nations to behave as the United States desired, and were underscored by the weakness of the dollar and inflation and turmoil in the United States. At the same time, the economic progress of Western Europe had affected the distribution of power in the world, giving France and West Germany especially a new sense of independence. And the development of conflict between Russia and China meant that Russia was not as strong as it once had been.

The man chosen as top adviser on foreign affairs—Henry Kissinger —also influenced Nixon. This social scientist from Harvard emphasized power and its distribution, argued that the postwar era of bilateral confrontation was over and maintained that multipolar world had emerged with five centers of powers: the United States, Russia, China, Japan and Western Europe. Maintaining that the relative power of the United States had declined, he insisted that the nation could not continue to depend so heavily on its own efforts. He also recommended that the United States should take advantage of the conflict between Russia and China. "The deepest international conflict in the world today," he suggested, "is not between us and the Soviet Union but between the Soviet Union and Communist China." International stability, he recommended, should be the American goal, and an equilibrium should be the means of achieving it.

Finally, the situation inside the United States affected Nixon profoundly. It included great dissatisfaction with American policy in Vietnam and had given him an unexpected political opportunity by destroying Johnson's career and seriously damaging Humphrey's. He believed that, while he must avoid a retreat to isolation and military weakness, he must find a way out of the war. The costs of the American role in the world had to be reduced, the limits on American power had to be recognized and a negotiated settlement of the war had to be obtained.

Influenced by these forces and considerations, Nixon and Kissinger devised a strategy that sought accommodation with Russia and China within the five-power system. The American leaders hoped to play the five powers off against one another, taking advantage of the strengths that the United States had and of the conflicts among the others. The strategy's aim was coexistence, not liberation. "The United States is confident that tension can be eased and the danger of war reduced by patient and precise efforts to reconcile conflicting interests on concrete issues," the President declared in 1970. "Co-existence demands more than a spirit of good will. It requires the definition of positive goals which can be sought and achieved cooperatively. It requires real progress toward resolution of specific differences."

For Asia, including Southeast Asia, the President defined a "Nixon Doctrine." In Vietnam, the bombing had been halted and negotiations had begun, but the United States had not made much progress toward a settlement because both sides were clinging to hopes for victory. The Nixon Administration continued to supply aid to the South Vietnamese and to negotiate with the North Vietnamese and the Viet Cong, but the President announced a new approach in Guam during the summer of 1969. Designed to lower the risks of future Vietnams, the Nixon Doctrine promised that the United States would supply a nuclear shield against big power aggression but insisted that countries threatened with "other types" of aggression must supply the necessary manpower. The doctrine meant that the American role in Asia would be reduced and the United States would rely heavily on others to check the spread of communism. The announcement of the doctrine was followed by the withdrawal of nearly 60,000 American troops from South Korea, Thailand, Japan, and the Philippine Islands by June of 1971.

Sharp reductions in the number of American troops in Vietnam also followed the announcement of the Nixon Doctrine. Nixon cut the number from more than 540,000 in January 1969 to only 255,000 by May 1971 and to about 50,000 by late 1972. He hoped to conduct the withdrawal in a way that would not appear to be an American defeat and would not destroy "confidence in American leadership." He hoped that a modernized South Vietnamese army supported by American air power and Russian pressure on the North Vietnamese to accept a negotiated settlement would produce the desired results: a compromise peace. Thus, the United States increased the fire power of the Americans that remained in Vietnam and provided the South Vietnamese government with the aid required to enlarge its army.

Nixon also supplemented these moves with several others. American and South Vietnamese forces invaded Communist "sanctuaries" in Cambodia in the spring of 1970; American planes bombed Cambodia and also hit North Vietnam from time to time, and South Vietnamese forces supported by American aircraft invaded Laos. These moves triggered new protests in the United States, especially in the spring of 1970, and were defended as necessary to safeguard American troops, permit the program of withdrawal to go forward and bring the war to an end. The President also argued that as commander-in-chief, he had the authority to act in these ways and did not need to obtain the consent of Congress. He assumed that the President had virtually a monopoly on the war-making power.

In addition, Nixon defeated efforts by liberals to place geographical and time limits on American military operations in Southeast Asia. Such limits would, he insisted, prevent him from achieving a satisfactory settlement of the war and encourage the forces of "totalitarianism and anarchy" throughout the world.

As these developments moved forward, Nixon tried to improve America's relations with Russia and China. Early in his administration, he had negotiated with the Russians on arms and other issues, and he spoke of the "People's Republic of China" rather than "Red China." He announced in 1970 that "No nation need be our permanent enemy"; American officials conducted formal talks with the Chinese in Warsaw, and the Administration eased trade restrictions against the Chinese.

Soon, the President decided to make a major effort. Influenced by the situation in Vietnam as well as the larger international situation, he decided to visit China. He hoped that it would "play its appropriate role in shaping international arrangements," that the development of a "connection" between the U.S. and China would encourage Russia to negotiate seriously on a broad range of issues and that the Chinese would restrain the Japanese as the United States reduced its role in Asia. He hoped also that a spectacular move would increase his chances of reelection. A change in the Chinese attitude also contributed to the decision. They invited an American table tennis team to visit China in April 1971 and allowed many other Americans to visit their country. The new attitude amounted to a significant retreat from the harsh criticism of the United States as a "capitalist-imperialist aggressor" and an enemy of the Chinese people. The change was influenced by fear of war with Russia and the American policy of military withdrawal from Asia.

Prepared by Kissinger, the visit was made in February 1972, the first by an American President, and involved a round of festivities and meetings with Chinese officials. The President proclaimed that there was "no reason for us to be enemies" and even quoted Mao on television. The spectacle caused a disgruntled conservative journalist to complain: "He would toast Alger Hiss tonight, if he could find him." The event shocked the left as well as the right, for China had been the country most admired by the New Left and China now seemed to be betraying the world revolution. Nixon and the Chinese reached an agreement on Taiwan, agreeing that it was an integral part of the People's Republic but that the change would be peaceful; they expressed opposition to "foreign domination" of "any independent country" and efforts by any nation to establish "hegemony in the Asia-Pacific region". The Chinese soon after the visit agreed to buy ten American passenger planes, and the two sides made additional progress toward resumption of formal diplomatic relations. Most Americans applauded.

Soon after the China trip, in May, Nixon visited the Soviet Union. While he and his Russian hosts could not agree on a joint Vietnam policy nor reach a trade agreement, they were willing to work on some joint projects. They agreed to limit strategic arms in the hope of avoiding an arms race that would upset the nuclear balance and they reached a settlement of Lend-Lease that paved the way for new loans from the United States. The visit was followed by a large sale of

American wheat to the Russians and increased Nixon's popularity significantly.

In Vietnam, the United States moved toward a negotiated settlement. Nixon authorized the bombing of North Vietnam once again in the spring of 1972 and the mining of Haiphong harbor in response to an advance by Communist forces, but negotiations continued, with Kissinger as the chief American negotiator. They were deadlocked over the demand for the removal of the South Vietnamese leader, Thieu, a move that was necessary if free elections were to be held but one that would symbolize defeat for the United States. Progress began to be made, however, after the Russians did not cancel Nixon's visit in response to the bombing and mining. Russia's behavior meant that it was not giving as much support to the North Vietnamese and the Viet Cong as they expected and needed. Late in October, the two sides agreed to a cease fire, a development that encouraged Kissinger to announce that "peace was at hand." The negotiators had agreed that the "two present administrations of South Vietnam" would "hold consultations" and schedule general elections, agreements that meant the North Vietnamese had given up their demand for the resignation of the Thieu government and the United States had surrendered its opposition to recognition of the Viet Cong as the equal of the Thieu regime. The negotiators also agreed that North Vietnam could keep its troops in South Vietnam during the truce period, thereby gaining an opportunity to influence the elections.

Nixon's major moves at home and abroad put him in a strong position as the election approached. This was so even though some efforts had failed, including the effort at party realignment. He had hoped to strengthen and reestablish the Republicans as the majority party. He saw bases for optimism in two parts of the Democratic party—the South and the white workers in the North. Both seemed concerned about the "Social Issue," a combination that included worries about drugs, race, sex, and protest. To accomplish his aim, he relied heavily on the talents of Vice President Spiro Agnew, who employed dramatic rhetoric against the news media, liberals, and protestors and who helped Nixon draw some support away from George Wallace. The President also participated in the congressional campaigns of 1970, focusing much of his attention on the defects of the liberals as he interpreted them, including their contributions to disorder. He failed to produce a big Republican victory, however, for efforts by the Democrats and organized labor frustrated him.

Nixon's battles against inflation and disorder achieved more success. His anti-inflation program slowed the price rise to 4 percent in 1972, and, although his campaign against disorder had not reduced crime, other forms of disorder—demonstrations and riots—had come to an end by 1972, in part because of his policies.

The New Left collapsed as a political force as a result of the pressures on it and its own defects. It experienced intense internal conflict as radical movements always had. It included challenges from blacks, women, gays, Indians, Mexican-Americans, and Puerto Ricans to the white middle-class males who dominated the movement as each of the challengers concluded that they needed movements of their own. The emphasis on political action was challenged by those champions of instant cultural revolution, the Yippies, led by Jerry Rubin and Abbie Hoffman. Two groups quarrelled with the established SDS emphasis on a nonviolent revolution led by students allied with the new working class. One was the Progressive Labor party, which saw the blue-collar workers as the key, assumed that they could become revolutionaries, gained control of SDS in 1969, but could not hold on to the support of its members. An SDS faction that emphasized violence also clashed with the old leaders. Led by Mark Rudd and Bernadine Dohrn, among others, these people called for identification with and support for world-wide revolution based chiefly in the underdeveloped countries and the underdeveloped parts of the United States and aided by the young white revolutionaries here. Rudd and his associates assumed that working-class youth would rally behind them as they demonstrated their toughness and bravery but felt no need to gain the support of white workers generally, seeing them as corrupted by the goods supplied by imperialistic capitalism. These SDS advocates of violence formed the Weathermen in 1969 and engaged in a series of demonstrations and bombings that were criticized by other radicals as adventuristic, insane, and cruel. Weathermen themselves became disillusioned with violence because it failed to accomplish their aims and led to police hostility and bloodshed.

Although some people in the New Left hoped to gain working-class support, the movement, as had earlier radical ones, failed to do so. Workers were antagonized rather than attracted, offended by disruption and violence and by the life style of many radicals. In seeking working-class support, the New Left, as many of its theorists recognized, had to compete against the attractions of the material things the system made available. Rather than support the New Left, some workers attacked demonstrators.

The New Left also lost its ability to rally college students. They were influenced by the winding down of the war and the draft. The downturn in the economy weakened the economic position of young people and forced many to be more concerned about personal economic matters than they had been in the 1960s and encouraged many to be more careful about political activities. By 1972, the left had lost its ability to stage demonstrations on college campuses.

The left suffered also from disillusionment among many of its members with all forms of radical political action. Learning it was difficult to produce large-scale changes, many dropped out of the movement. Some joined communes; others moved back into the mainstreams of American life. Some of the latter, including the Panthers, turned to conventional politics.

In November 1972, Nixon won by a wide margin over his Democratic opponent Senator George McGovern in a low-turnout election. He obtained nearly 61 percent of the popular vote and 521 of the 538 electoral votes. His support included many traditional Democrats, especially the white workers, Catholics and Southerners. Yet, only 55 percent of the eligible people voted.

Nixon won in spite of the weaknesses of his party and partly because of his own accomplishments. The party failed to gain control of Congress. He, however, had promoted political stability, slowed inflation, reduced sharply the number of Americans fighting in Vietnam and improved relations with Russia and China. Those accomplishments influenced many voters.

The Democrats also helped Nixon. Their nominee Senator McGovern of South Dakota, was supported chiefly by reformers and foes of American foreign and military policies. McGovern was nominated over the opposition of the labor movement, the city bosses, and the Southerners. Calling for a sharp reduction of the American role in the world and for an emphasis on domestic problems, he alarmed many people. He was hurt by the forced resignation of his running mate, Senator Thomas Eagleton of Missouri, and he disillusioned some of his supporters by making concessions to his foes in a quest for party unity. He failed also in his effort to persuade people that the Nixon administration was corrupt.

Nixon's campaign also contributed to his victory. He moved cautiously and spent a record amount of money. He also denied that the White House had been involved in the break-in at Democratic headquarters at the Watergate in June. Most voters found his denials persuasive.

Soon after his victory, Nixon ended American participation in the Vietnam war. Thieu resisted the agreement that had been reached in October and the North Vietnamese also delayed the final settlement, hoping that the United States would abandon Thieu. In response, Nixon authorized heavy bombing of North Vietnam late in December and also put pressure on the South Vietnamese government. The final settlement came in January, and it enabled Thieu to stay in power and the North Vietnamese and Viet Cong to hold on to recent territorial gains, recognized the existence of two South Vietnamese "parties," obliged them to organize "free and democratic general elections" and agreed that each side would return its prisoners of war. The settlement amounted to a significant retreat by North Vietnam and the United States from earlier positions and was followed by the exchange of prisoners and the final withdrawal of American forces.

These developments did not end the fighting, but they did end

American participation in it. Fighting was resumed in a large way in the fall of 1973, but Congress prevented Nixon from reintroducing American forces into Vietnam or Cambodia. He wanted to use air power, but even he would not have sent in American ground forces. Doing so could have overturned the results of his efforts to recreate an orderly society in the United States.

The Nixon Tragedy

At home, however, Nixon's position was deteriorating rapidly. Unhappy with controls, the President relaxed them after inflation slowed, and prices soared by nearly 8 percent in 1973 and almost 15 percent the next year. Even greater troubles emerged from Watergate.

Pressures against the President came from several directions. Papers like the New York Times and the Washington Post, not satisfied with official explanations of the break-in, had been probing Watergate. The men caught in the break-in were prosecuted early in 1973, and the trial revealed that they had received money from the Committee to Re-elect the President and that two had been officials in the committee. The Federal District judge involved in the case, John J. Sirica, encouraged those who were convicted or pleaded guilty to tell all they knew, and one of them, James McCord, Jr., charged that Mitchell and two members of the White House staff, Jeb Stuart Magruder and John Dean, had been involved in the planning. Dean, Magruder, and Mitchell then testified about their own activities and those of others, including H. R. Haldeman and John Ehrlichman, the top men on the White House staff. An investigation by a special Senate Committee headed by Democratic Senator Sam J. Ervin of North Carolina produced such spectacular episodes as Dean's charges that Nixon had been involved in the coverup of the White House role, Ehrlichman's reliance on national security to defend the Administration's actions, and the revelation that conversations in the White House had been recorded. Additional pressure came from a special prosecutor, Archibald Cox, who ranged beyond Watergate to investigate campaign finances and Nixon's personal finances.

These efforts produced disclosures of irregularities in the financing of the campaign, the use of political espionage and "dirty tricks" by campaign workers, the burglarizing of the office of Ellsberg's psychiatrist, and the offer of the directorship of the FBI to the judge in the Ellsberg case. They also included insufficient tax payments by the President, large government expenditures on his personal homes, the secret bombing of Cambodia, and the development of an enemies list and of plans to use the Internal Revenue Service against the President's enemies.

Embarrassed by these disclosures, the Administration soon crumbled. The process began in April 1973 with the resignations of Haldeman, Ehrlichman and Dean, and they were followed quickly by many other resignations, the reshuffling of the people who remained, and difficulties in finding replacements. In October, Agnew resigned after he had been accused of taking bribes and pleaded no contest to charges of income tax evasion. The "Saturday Night Massacre" took place when Nixon called upon his Attorney General, Elliott Richardson, to fire Cox because of his refusal to back down in efforts to gain access to the tapes and other sources. Richardson and his Assistant Attorney General, William Ruckelshaus, resigned rather than fire Cox, and the President had to turn to a third official to accomplish that task. By the summer of 1974, thirty-eight former officials had either pleaded guilty to charges or been indicted.

As the Administration disintegrated, the President's effectiveness declined. Nearly 70 percent of the people had approved of his conduct of the office early in 1973, but only 27 percent did so a year later. He tried but failed to regain his popularity and to turn attention away from Watergate and became increasingly ineffective in national and international affairs. Congress, for example, passed a War Powers Act over his veto in August 1973 that reduced the President's authority over the use of troops.

In response to mounting demands, the question of impeachment was turned over to the House Judiciary Committee, headed by Peter Rodino, a Democrat from New Jersey, and the committee dealt with the question from May to June 1974. Several Republican members defended the President, admitting that members of the Administration had behaved unethically or illegally, but arguing that the offenses were not impeachable and that Nixon's guilt had not been established. A bipartisan majority endorsed articles of impeachment charging that the President had "prevented, obstructed, and impeded the administration of justice," "repeatedly engaged in conduct violating the constitutional rights of citizens, impairing the due and proper administration of justice in the conduct of lawful inquiries, and contravening the law of governing agencies of the executive branch and the purposes of those agencies" and "failed without lawful cause or excuse to produce papers and things, as directed by the Committee on the Judiciary ..., and willfully disobeyed such subpoenas." The majority concluded that Nixon had "acted in a manner contrary to his trust as President and subversive of constitutional government, to the great prejudice of the cause of law and justice, and to the manifest injury of the people of the United States" and thus he warranted "impeachment and trial and removal from office." The articles had strong public support and seemed certain to be passed by the full House.

Before the House had an opportunity to act, Nixon encountered difficulties with the United States Supreme Court. He had frequently relied on the doctrine of "executive privilege" to resist requests for tapes and documents and had responded to pressure by releasing some tapes and edited transcripts of others. Even the materials he released

President Richard Nixon announces his resignation.
(Wide World Photo)

damaged him by revealing that he used coarse language and "hush money," but the new special prosecutor, Leon Jaworski, needed more evidence and turned to the judiciary to gain access, arguing that the rule of law was involved but encountering arguments about the separation of powers and executive privilege. On July 24, the Supreme Court, by a vote of 8 to 0 ordered Nixon to turn tapes over to Judge Sirica. He would make the relevant portions available to Jaworski who, in turn, could make them available to Congress.

Pressed by his aides to comply with the Court's ruling and admit complicity, Nixon on August 5 made public his conversations with Haldeman and Dean just after the break-in, and these revelations destroyed the President's support. They contradicted not only his initial denial of White House involvement but his subsequent insistence that he had not known of it until March 1973 and had made every effort to obtain the facts and punish the guilty. The tapes proved that he had promoted the coverup from the beginning and had lied repeatedly. His defenders in the Judiciary Committee now announced that they favored impeachment, and several Republican congressional leaders, including Senator Goldwater, advised Nixon that removal from office was a certainty.

Under these pressures, Nixon announced his resignation on August 8. He admitted only to "errors of judgment," denied that the acts revealed by the tapes justified "the extreme step of impeachment," called attention to his accomplishments, especially in foreign affairs, and explained that he was resigning because he "no longer [had] a strong political base in Congress."

Nixon was the second President in a row to fail in spite of some impressive accomplishments. Both Johnson and Nixon had behaved in unexpected and shocking ways. Johnson had promised restraint and then had escalated and Americanized the Vietnam War. Nixon had promised law and order and then had encouraged the breaking of the law and had protected law breakers. Such experiences were enormously disillusioning for the American people and seriously damaged the Presidency and other institutions. By the summer of 1974, the leadership crisis was extremely severe.

SUGGESTIONS FOR FURTHER READING

Barber, James D., *The Presidential Character: Predicting Performance in the White House.* Englewood Cliffs, N.J., Prentice-Hall, Inc., 1972.

Burner, David, Robert D. Marcus and Thomas R. West, *A Giant's Strength: America in the 1960s.* New York, Holt, Rinehart and Winston, Inc., 1971.

Heath, Jim F., *Decade of Disillusionment: The Kennedy-Johnson Years.* Bloomington, Ind., Indiana University Press, 1975.

Hoopes, Townsend, *The Limits of Intervention (an inside account of how the Johnson policy of escalation in Vietnam was reversed)*. New York, David McKay Co., Inc., 1969.

Gardner, Lloyd C., *The Great Nixon Turnaround: America's New Foreign Policy in the Post-Liberal Era*. New York, New Viewpoints, 1973.

Schlesinger, Arthur M., Jr., *The Imperial Presidency*. Boston, Houghton Mifflin Co., 1973.

Unger, Irwin, *The Movement: A History of the American New Left, 1959-1972*. New York, Dodd, Mead & Co., 1974.

White, Theodore H., *Breach of Faith: The Fall of Richard Nixon*. New York, Atheneum Publishers, 1975.

White, Theodore H., *The Making of the President 1972*. New York, Atheneum Publishers, 1973.

20

A New America

SINCE 1974 NIXON'S SUCCESSORS have restored some of the Presidency's lost prestige. Ford and Carter profited from the contrast between their personalities and those of Johnson and Nixon. Largely because of their personal qualities, both men gave the people the promise of honest, constructive, and devoted leadership. Though Ford nearly won the election of 1976, Carter as the candidate of the majority party gained the confidence of most Americans.

Gerald Ford succeeded to the Presidency in a time of crisis. A veteran congressman from Michigan who had risen to the post of minority leader, he had been appointed Vice President after Agnew's resignation. Soon after entering the White House, he weakened himself by pardoning Nixon, a move that many regarded as unfair and that caused his popularity to drop sharply. A short time later, he suffered from the damage that Nixon had done to his party as the congressional elections enlarged already substantial Democratic majorities. And throughout his period as President, he suffered from the damage Nixon had done to the Presidency. A strong desire for the reassertion of congressional authority affected the nation's politics.

Ford had little success in foreign affairs. A deteriorating situation in Vietnam greeted him when he took office. The fighting continued, Congress refused to appropriate the aid advocated by the administration, and the Communists gained complete control of Vietnam in the spring of 1975. By then, they had also triumphed in Cambodia. With doubts about the value of the American connection growing elsewhere in Southeast Asia, Ford sent Marines in May 1975 to rescue a merchant ship, the *Mayaguez*, and its crew that had been seized by a Cambodian naval vessel, but the episode had a positive impact only on the American public. The President continued to rely heavily on Kissinger, who had become Secretary of State in 1973, and to pursue the policies that he and Nixon had developed. The Secretary tried without success to mediate the Arab-Israeli conflict and produce a final settlement. He contributed to the development of a European Security Treaty in 1975—the Helsinki Treaty—that endorsed the boundaries established by World War II and Soviet imperialism in Eastern Europe without gaining concessions beyond promises to respect "human rights." His performance was criticized by those who remained concerned about Russian power and ambitions and/or the rights of people in Russian-dominated areas, but Kissinger insisted that American policies were in accord with realities. The Administration made no progress in negotiations with Russia on arms or with China on Chinese-American relations and expressed concern about the use of Cuban mercenaries in Angola and the possibility that the French and Italian Communists would gain places in their governments. Kissinger did work out an agreement promising black rule in Rhodesia, an African country in which most people were black but whites monopolized political power, but the agreement did not seem firm.

Ford's domestic policies enjoyed limited success. At home, his attention was dominated by three difficult and conflicting problems: growing unemployment as the economy slipped into another recession, severe inflation, and a shortage of energy sources. Stressing the second and third problems, he advocated conservative fiscal and monetary policies and higher prices for oil, gas, and other sources of energy. The latter, it seemed, would encourage both conservation and exploration and reduce the nation's dependence on foreign oil. The Democrats who controlled Congress, however, emphasized unemployment as the problem and government spending as the solution. They also opposed high gas prices. Using the veto power with unusual frequency, Ford defeated many of the spending proposals, but still the federal deficit mounted. Under pressure from the recession, he felt compelled to accept both an increase in overall spending and a tax cut in 1975, and he could not defeat the demand for low prices for domestic crude oil. By 1976, the economy was recovering slowly, and inflation had moderated, dropping to 5 percent, but unemployment, which had moved above 9 percent in 1975, did not fall much

President Ford on the Campaign Trail *(University of Southern California)*

below 8 the following year, and the nation's dependence on foreign oil continued to grow.

Nevertheless, many people liked Gerald Ford. He did not have Nixon's sense of insecurity and distrust of people; he pulled back from his predecessor's grandiose conception of the Presidency, and he seemed to be a modest, open, candid, honest, and hard-working person, not a genius or a man of vision but a good American. One of his heroes, he suggested frequently, was Harry Truman. The Michigan Republican had a calming effect after the trauma of Watergate and Nixon's forced resignation.

Yet, Ford had difficulty obtaining his party's nomination. He was challenged quite effectively by the ultra-conservative Ronald Reagan and won by only a narrow margin. He had to compromise with Reagan's faction on the platform and selected one of the faction's representatives, Senator Robert Dole of Kansas, for the Vice Presidency.

In midsummer, 1976, Ford seemed likely to lose the election by a wide margin, but he gained ground rapidly as had his hero, Truman. He took advantage of his position as President, spending much of the campaign period in the White House. He attacked his foe as inexperienced, inconsistent, unclear, and misguided, and he attacked the Democratic Congress as a big spender and the major source of inflation. He pointed with pride to his record, arguing that no Americans were fighting a war, employment was increasing and inflation was declining. Several blunders, including a statement about freedom in Eastern Europe, and Reagan's less than full support, hampered his progress.

In the end, Ford lost but by only a narrow margin. The winner, Jimmy Carter, was a Southerner, a devout Baptist, a former naval officer, a former governor of Georgia, a farmer, and a business man. He had surprised the nation by gaining the nomination with ease at the Democratic National Convention after strenuous and successful participation in primaries throughout the nation and a campaign that stressed Washington's defects and his personal honesty, not specific issues. Against Ford, he stressed government reorganization, the reduction of unemployment, the continuation and expansion of government services, tax reform, fiscal responsibility, his own virtues and freedom from the sins of the past, and Ford's shortcomings as a leader. The Georgian benefited from the strengths of his own party relative to the opposition and from the weaknesses of the economy, but he was hurt by doubts about him as a Southerner and a "born again" Baptist, and an unfortunate interview with Playboy. On election day, the liberals preferred him to Ford; his fellow Southerners gave him more than half of their votes; Catholics and the organized workers gave him more support than they had given McGovern; most Jews stayed with the Democratic party, and more than 90 percent of the black voters voted for Carter, offsetting the white majority for Ford. Carter carried nearly every southern state and split the North and the West,

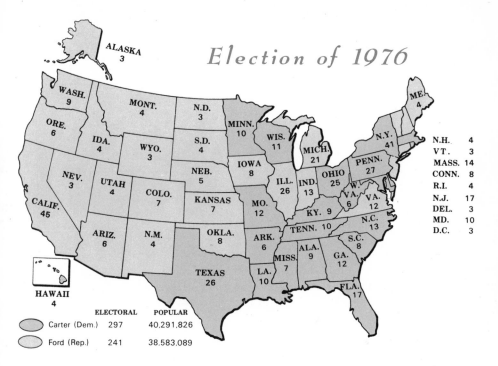

Election of 1976

ALASKA 3

WASH. 9 · MONT. 4 · N.D. 3 · MINN. 10 · ORE. 6 · IDA. 4 · WYO. 3 · S.D. 4 · WIS. 11 · MICH. 21 · N.Y. 41 · ME. 4 · NEV. 3 · UTAH 4 · COLO. 7 · NEB. 5 · IOWA 8 · ILL. 26 · IND. 13 · OHIO 25 · PENN. 27 · W.VA. 6 · CALIF. 45 · ARIZ. 6 · N.M. 4 · KANSAS 7 · MO. 12 · KY. 9 · VA. 12 · N.C. 13 · OKLA. 8 · ARK. 6 · TENN. 10 · S.C. 8 · TEXAS 26 · LA. 10 · MISS. 7 · ALA. 9 · GA. 12 · FLA. 17

HAWAII 4

N.H. 4
VT. 3
MASS. 14
CONN. 8
R.I. 4
N.J. 17
DEL. 3
MD. 10
D.C. 3

	ELECTORAL	POPULAR
Carter (Dem.)	297	40,291,826
Ford (Rep.)	241	38,583,089

and the Democrats maintained control of Congress by wide margins.

Carter's position was not substantially stronger than Ford's had been. He had won by only a narrow margin, 51 percent to 48, suggesting that his victory was more a party than a personal victory, and turnout had been rather low, only 53 percent of the people of voting age. Although he needed to build strength for himself, the Democratic party had overwhelming control of Congress.

Carter's sense of his weaknesses affected his appointments. Although he had campaigned as an "outsider" critical of much of the past, he now turned frequently to people of experience, including experience in the development of American foreign and military policies, such as Cyrus Vance, who became Secretary of State, Harold Brown, who became Secretary of Defense, and James Schlesinger, top man on energy. He also courted businessmen by appointing W. Michael Blumenthal as Secretary of the Treasury and Bert Lance as head of the Office of Management and Budget.

Carter also devoted much of his energy in the early months of his presidency to the building of popular support. He made great efforts to demonstrate that he was a "people's President," not an imperial type. In a variety of ways, he sought, as one commentator observed, to dram-

President Carter and Rosalynn Carter stroll down Pennsylvania Avenue after the inauguration (*Wide World Photo*)

atize "the qualities of morality, frugality, simplicity, candor, and compassion for which the voters have been searching." He hoped to restore confidence in government as well as to establish confidence in himself; he emphasized cultivation of "the people" rather than the interests," and he relied heavily on both television and direct contacts.

As these efforts moved forward, Carter pressed his solutions to the nation's problems. At first, slow economic growth and high unemployment seemed especially pressing—7.3 percent of the work force did not have jobs when he took office and the percentage jumped to 7.5 as a result of a very severe winter. To stimulate the economy, he proposed a $23 to $30 billion program for the next year and a half, including increased spending but with emphasis on tax cuts. Carter hoped that such a package would encourage businessmen to invest. But as unemployment began to decline in the spring, he dropped a major feature of this program—the tax rebate—and shifted his attention to inflation. Rejecting wage and price controls, he made several anti-inflation proposals and promised to balance the budget by the end of his term.

In foreign affairs, the new President emphasized the Middle East, Russia, the arms race, and human rights. He pressed Israel to withdraw to "defensible borders" close to those she had had before the 1967 war and to accept a "homeland" for the Palestinians in exchange for Arab recognition of her right to exist in peace, and he backed up his pronouncements with meetings with many of the Middle Eastern leaders. He pressed the Russians to agree to cuts in the nuclear arsenals and criticized them for violations of human rights. Well-informed about nuclear weapons, he was fearful of them and of both their spread to other nations and the Russian-American arms race. And the campaign for human rights became the centerpiece of his foreign policy. Seeking to overcome negative views of American foreign policy, he criticized many countries, including Russia, for human rights violations, but he relied chiefly on words to promote change.

In addition to efforts to curb the arms race, Carter made several other moves of importance for military policy. He pardoned draft evaders, and he announced that American troops would be withdrawn from South Korea during the next four to five years and that the United States would strengthen South Korean forces and rely upon air and sea power for its own contributions in Asia. He also resisted pressure for construction of the B-1 bomber, regarding it as unnecessary and costly and preferring to develop cruise missiles and improve the B-52.

Late in April 1977, Carter introduced proposals for the energy crisis. They envisioned a smooth transition to an era of scarce and high-priced oil and relied heavily on the taxing power to encourage people to shift from large to small automobiles, to cut back on the miles they drove, to insulate their homes and buildings and to shift from natural gas and oil to coal, nuclear power, and solar energy. Warning of a bleak future, praising conservation, appealing to patriotism and criticizing the "special interests," Carter, others in the Administration, and the Democratic National Committee waged an intensive campaign to build support for this program.

Not everyone applauded Carter's efforts. American Jews grew alarmed about his proposals on Israel's boundaries; some liberals, labor leaders, and blacks charged that he did not have enough interest in the poor and the unemployed; congressmen complained about his hostility to water projects that they favored; champions of military power protested against his plans for South Korea and his decision on the B-1; many people, inside as well as outside the U.S., allies as well as Russians, charged that the human rights campaign was meddling and harmful to international relations; the Russians rejected his proposal for cuts in the nuclear arsenals; and businessmen could not convince themselves that Carter was good for business. Diverse groups, including the automobile, oil, utility and coal industries, and environmentalists, found flaws in the energy program, charging that it would produce a recession, escalate inflation, increase pollution, enlarge the bureaucracy, depend too heavily on taxation, add to the dangers from nuclear power, provide inadequate encouragement for efforts to find and develop new sources of oil and gas and increase coal production, increase the profits of the energy companies, penalize those who must drive to work and continue the nation's dependence on the automobile rather than promote the development of mass transit systems.

In spite of his critics, Carter made progress. By May, unemployment had dropped below 7 percent, and by midsummer, Congress, while contributing to his decision to drop the tax rebate, had passed most of his economic stimulus package, granted him authority to reorganize the federal government, compromised with him on water projects, endorsed his proposal for a Department of Energy and seemed ready to pass most of his other energy proposals. He had learned how to work with Congress and had quite good relations with congressional leaders. Most important from his point of view, he had widespread popular support. More than 60 percent of the people approved of his performance.

It was too early to suggest that the crisis in national leadership had ended. Both Johnson and Nixon had enjoyed high ratings before their popularity collapsed, and Carter faced some difficult problems. In fact, his troubles mounted in the second half of his first year when his closest adviser, Bert Lance, resigned under fire, Congress failed to enact his energy package, many Senators and others opposed his Panama Canal treaty, and his popularity skidded. Yet, the prestige of his office was much greater than it had been only a few years before, and his own prestige was far above Johnson's and Nixon's in their dark days.

Another New Era?

As the American people moved through the mid-seventies, they seemed to be entering into another new era in their history. At least some of the signs suggested that very significant changes were taking place or would soon do so. Yet, the forces of resistance also had strength, and the emergence of a new America was only a possibility, not a certainty.

Race relations were very different from what they had been only a short time before, and the possibility of further change in this area of American life was quite strong. The economic progress that blacks had made in the 1960s was not duplicated in the 1970s, and the economic gap between whites and blacks remained substantial. In mid-decade, the median income for white families was above $14,000, but for blacks it was below $9,000. More than 30 percent of the blacks lived below the poverty line, but only 10 percent of the whites did so; more than 13 percent of the blacks were unemployed, as many as 40 percent of black youth in urban areas, while fewer than 7 percent of the white workers did not have jobs. Obviously, racial discrimination in employment remained a fact of American life. Another, racial segregation, was especially obvious in Northern residential patterns and school systems.

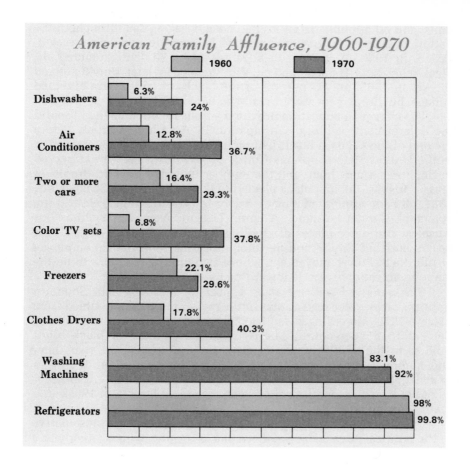

American Family Affluence, 1960-1970

1960 · 1970

Dishwashers	6.3% / 24%
Air Conditioners	12.8% / 36.7%
Two or more cars	16.4% / 29.3%
Color TV sets	6.8% / 37.8%
Freezers	22.1% / 29.6%
Clothes Dryers	17.8% / 40.3%
Washing Machines	83.1% / 92%
Refrigerators	98% / 99.8%

Racism persisted, expressed by some scholars as well as by groups like the Ku Klux Klan. Many blacks needed help and received it from a welfare system that was available to everyone in need. It had many critics, many of whom charged that it weakened the family and the urge for self-improvement. And many blacks were bitterly discontented, even alienated, and expressed their alienation in drug addiction and crime and in the looting that erupted during New York City's electrical blackout in the summer of 1977.

However, Jim Crow—the laws supporting and promoting segregation, discrimination, and disenfranchisement—had been destroyed by the civil rights movement, and the black middle class, the people who had the required temperament, education, and money, had many more opportunities open to them than ever before. Hotels, motels, restaurants, and other public facilities had been desegregated throughout the nation, and considerable progress had been made in school desegregation. In 1960, 99 percent of Southern black students attended all-black schools; in 1969, 50 percent did; three years later, only 8 percent did so. In 1965, only 5 percent of the blacks of college age attended college, but 10 percent were in college ten years later.

The change in education provided a basis for other changes; so did the enlargement of black participation in American politics. Before the end of the 1960s, a black, Thurgood Marshall, had been appointed to the United States Supreme Court. By 1971, thirteen blacks served in Congress, a new high, and the number included Edward Brooke of Massachusetts, the first black elected to the United States Senate since 1881. Johnson appointed a black mayor for Washington, D.C., and the voters of Gary, Cleveland, Atlanta, Detroit, Newark, Wichita, Los Angeles, and other places elected black mayors. The National Urban League and the NAACP modified their programs, reflecting the emphases of the Black Power movement. These two groups continue to be the main organizational efforts toward racial justice.

Blacks moved forward at an especially rapid pace in Southern politics. Black voter registration in the region more than doubled from 1964 to 1969, increasing from 25 to 60 percent in Alabama and from 10 percent to 65 percent in Mississippi. The number of black office holders in the South jumped from 70 in 1965 to 665 five years later and included Mayor Charles Evers of Fayette, Mississippi, a brother of a slain civil rights worker, a sheriff in Lowndes County, Alabama— a county in which no blacks had been registered to vote in 1965—and many legislators.

By 1977, Andrew Young was the most conspicuous representative of the political advance of Southern blacks. Young, whose father was a dentist, was a young clergyman, and one of King's top lieutenants. Young in 1972 had become the first black elected to Congress from Georgia since Reconstruction. In 1976, he allied with Jimmy Carter and helped him move to victory as the two men formed a new black-white coalition in the South that defeated Wallace and then Ford. Young became the nation's new ambassador to the United Nations after Carter moved into the White House and emerged quickly as a prominent, outspoken, and controversial member of the Administration, criticising racism and advocating majority (black) rule in southern Africa.

All barriers to change in race relations had not been swept away. Battles raged over the busing of school children from one neighborhood to another, a method that seemed to be the only way of integrating schools in some areas. It was resisted by people who resented the long time-consuming rides for children and/or preferred that schools mirror the segregation that existed in housing arrangements. Other battles focused on "affirmative action" programs requiring universities, businesses, and other institutions to enroll or employ a certain percentage of blacks, among other minorities. Seeking to open doors previously closed or only narrowly open, the programs were defended as necessary to overcome the results of discrimination in the past but criticized as unfair to a new generation. Also, some black leaders criticized Carter, reminding him that he would not be President if blacks had not voted for him in such large numbers and charging that he was not paying enough attention to the problems of black Americans.

Although change was not the only part of the story of race relations, it was an important part, and the relations between men and women were also changing. A woman's movement that had emerged in the 1960s was largely responsible. It had an ideology, devised by Simone de Beauvoir, Betty Friedan, Kate Millett, Gloria Steinem, and others. They maintained that American women had suffered a great set-back after 1945 with the development of what Friedan called the "feminine mystique" and insisted that women must break out of their "prison" by developing interests outside the home. Assuming that homemakers were unhappy and eager for careers, the ideology called for radical modification of cultural stereotypes, the creation of new community institutions like child-care centers, and a concerted campaign by women to develop lifelong commitments to the professions and business.

The development of this set of ideas was not solely responsible for the emergence of "women's liberation." It was influenced by the civil rights movement, which provided inspiration concerning goals and methods. The great increase in the employment of women since 1940 also influenced the movement. The change affected the thinking of women who worked and of other people who came into contact with them, including their daughters. As a consequence, by the time the ideology began to take shape a substantial number of women were ready and willing to embrace it. Title VII of the Civil Rights Act of 1964—in addition to race, color, creed and national origin—forbids sex as a basis of discrimination. This facilitated job demands.

Although not a solid power bloc, the woman's movement was united by a set of demands. The movement contained reformers like Friedan, who founded the National Organization for Women in 1966, and Steinem, the publisher of Ms., which first appeared on the newsstands in 1972, and the movement also housed Millett and other radicals, many of whom were militantly hostile to men. All members demanded an end to job discrimination. They resented low salaries and wages and limits on the variety of jobs open to women, especially the limited opportunities for high-paying and high-prestige positions. The movement also demanded reform of abortion laws, and educational programs focusing on the history of women and other dimensions of their lives.

Demanding change in women's status and role, the movement affected many aspects of American life. It encouraged women to get

Feminist Protesters (*United Press International*)

an education, and the percentage of college students who were women increased from 38 in 1966 to 47 in 1976. It encouraged women to seek jobs outside the home, and the percentage of women who had them moved from 40 in the late 1960s to 48 in 1976, and the increase in quantity was accompanied by some improvements in the quality of job opportunities for women. Also, the movement was one of the forces responsible for changes in family life: later marriages, fewer children, higher standards of living, tension over responsibilities for the home and children, and the increase in divorces.

Women's liberation also had an impact on politics. It quickly demonstrated an ability to make news and affect the thinking of people outside the women's organizations. A proposed Equal Rights Amendment to the Constitution, which had been bottled up in Congress since the 1920s and declared that "Equality of rights under the law shall not be denied or abridged by any state on account of sex," suddenly moved forward, passed by Congress in 1971-72 and ratified by thirty-four states by 1975. Several states liberalized their abortion laws, and a decision by the United States Supreme Court in 1973 established the right to have an abortion. Women became more important in party politics, playing large and prominent roles in the Democratic National Convention and other events. Carter made a substantial effort to find women for major jobs and appointed two—Juanita Kreps and Patricia Harris—to his cabinet; another woman, Patricia Derrian, contributed significantly to the human rights campaign, and still others, including the President's wife, played other important roles in the administration.

The movement did not, however, promote a revolution. It encountered strong opposition at many points from exponents of traditional ideas. Many men regarded it as threatening to ways of life they valued, put their own careers first, refused to take major responsibilities for housework, insisted that mothers must play the major roles in the raising of children, and resented competition from women in tight job markets. But men were not the only opponents. The movement was largely a white, upper-middle-class activity composed chiefly of women in the professions. Working-class women opposed it because they wanted the protective legislation that the movement in its quest for equality wished to destroy. Many black women regarded feminism as diversionary, and many women of all classes and races believed in and liked the old order.

Two movements developed to resist the new feminism. One was spearheaded by Phyllis Schlafly, a well-known conservative and articulate champion of traditional ideas about woman's place and role. Viewing ERA as a symbol of the undermining of the old values, she battled against it. The other counterforce, the "right-to-life" movement, focused on abortion and had the support of Catholics, Mormons, and other religious groups and of general conservative organizations.

Leaders of the National Women's Movement   *(Wide World Photo)*

The forces of resistance also influenced the politics of the period. The Presidents expressed opposition to some demands of the woman's movement, including child-care centers and abortion. The Supreme Court decided in 1976 that an employer need not make disability payments for absence from work caused by pregnancy, and the Court and the Congress the following year ruled against the use of public funds for abortions, supporting laws that had been passed in fifteen states. By then, the ERA had been defeated in several states, was three states short of the thirty-eight required for ratification and seemed headed for failure by the March 1979 deadline.

The sexual relations between men and women were also changing and controversial. In fact, the signs of change were so numerous that many observers spoke of a "sexual revolution." The term exaggerated the rate and amount of change for the development had been apparent since the 1920s and still had many opponents who put limits on it.

Nevertheless, many Americans were rebelling against the old morality. Modifications in the pornography laws facilitated the development by permitting the publication of works dealing explicitly with sexual activities, and the contraceptive pill, which was widely available and easily used, also facilitated the "sexual revolution" by reducing the risks of sexual intercourse. The forces of change were represented in a somewhat cautious way by the widely read *Playboy* magazine, which had been founded in 1954, and in unrestrained ways by magazines such as *Hustler* that were sold widely by the mid-seventies. Nudity and sexual activity in plays and movies, popular songs dealing with sex in undisguised ways, the growing number of books offering advice on the ways of achieving sexual satisfaction, and the increasing attention to sex on television also testified to change. The increase, in spite of the pill, in the percentage of births that were illegitimate pointed to an increase in premarital and extramarital intercourse. The increase from 664,000 in 1970 to at least 1.3 million in 1977 in the number of unmarried people of the opposite sex who lived together also expressed changes in attitudes.

The emergence of a "Gay Liberation" movement supplied additional evidence of change. The movement was designed to promote tolerance and even a positive public attitude toward homosexuality. A number of communities, states, government agencies, and corporations changed their laws and practices, the media began to give homosexuality more favorable treatment, and several congressmen sponsored a gay rights amendment to the Civil Rights Act.

In the sexual area, however, the forces of change encountered much resistance. Following a Supreme Court decision in 1973 allowing communities to set their own standards of obscenity, actors, publishers and others were arrested and convicted for violations of state and local obscenity laws, and a campaign developed in many parts of the country against pornography, massage parlors, "adult" bookstores and theaters, magazines, and other features of the "revolution." Many people, including President Carter, criticized unmarried couples who were living together, expressing concern that the practice was weakening an important institution—marriage—and regarding it as sinful, and the vast majority of Americans agreed with the critics. Discrimination against homosexuals persisted in many areas, and they suffered from several unfavorable judicial decisions.

In 1977, a former beauty queen, Anita Bryant, emerged as a prominent champion of the old morality. A devout Baptist as well as a PR person, Ms. Bryant was concerned about America's "Decadence, moral decay, and permissiveness" and became known to some as "the Carry Nation of the sexual counter-revolution" as a result of her successful leadership of a "Save Our Children" campaign against a new Miami ordinance banning discrimination against gays in housing, jobs, and public accommodations. Arguing that such laws encouraged the spread of homosexuality and discouraged homosexuals from changing their sexual practices, she expanded her campaign to other parts of the country, including the nation's capital.

In a very different area—the nation's relations with the rest of the world, the forces of change and the forces of resistance were also at work. If the former succeeded, the distinguishing feature of the period since the early 1940s—the global role of the United States—could be destroyed. American thinking about foreign affairs was being affected by the "lessons" of the 1960s just as earlier it had been influenced by the "lessons" of the 1930s. A "Vietnam analogy" competed with a "Munich analogy" and suggested the dangers of involvement rather than the dangers of isolation.

Isolationist attitudes had more strength in the 1970s than they had had for many years. In reaction to the American defeat in Vietnam, many Americans now insisted that the United States must not go to war again unless it was attacked. They questioned all commitments, especially those with "non-free" regimes, and all overseas activity, and they opposed intervention in such trouble spots as Portugal, Angola, Zaire, and Italy where the establishment of Communist power and influence seemed likely. Some people favored an American withdrawal from the Middle East so as to avoid confrontation and conflict with the Arabs and Russia. Critics of America's global role subjected the instruments of involvement—the military, the Central Intelligence Agency, and multinationals—to sharp attack. The CIA, for example, was assaulted for violations of the rights of Americans by intercepting mail and other practices and for interference in the politics of other nations by engaging in assassination and bribery.

Like the isolationists of the 1930s, the critics now attacked both economic groups and the Presidency. The multinational corporations, such as ITT, were often blamed for the large role that the nation was playing as well as criticized for the methods they employed. American foreign policy, it seemed, was not designed to protect freedom and democracy but was designed to protect and promote the foreign investments of these giants, which totaled $119 billion by 1974. The arms producers, like the Lockheed Aircraft Corporation, were criticized. In pursuit of foreign sales, which amounted to nearly $10 billion in 1975, these companies, investigators revealed, bribed and paid kickbacks to foreign officials. And the power of the Presidency, which seemed so important in such adventures as Vietnam, needed to be reduced. Congress needed to play a larger role in foreign affairs so as to keep the nation out of trouble.

The old isolationist argument that involvement abroad would corrupt the United States had emerged once again—but with a twist. Now, the charge was that involvement *had* corrupted the nation. The evidence offered in support of the charge was substantial.

Much of the criticism of America's global activities came from liberals. Earlier, while there had been many liberal isolationists in the 1930s, most liberals had been champions of a large role in world affairs. Then, they had been alarmed by the power and ambitions of Hitler's Germany and of the Soviet Union. Now, many liberals attacked arguments that Russia was growing more powerful, ambitious and dangerous.

The critics did have many opponents. They held on to the beliefs about the importance of the rest of the world to the United States and of American power. Some believed that the American position in the world had deteriorated. Many, such as Senator Henry Jackson, from Washington state, still feared Russian power and ambitions and believed that American resistance—the Containment Policy—continued to be important. They remained convinced that Russia would gain influence—perhaps control—of the areas from which the United States withdrew, and they insisted that, although it had failed in Vietnam, Containment had succeeded in the most important places—in Western Europe and Japan. And concern about the fate of Israel, as well as worry about the Soviet Union, contributed to the defense of a substantial American role in the world.

As the late seventies approached, no one could predict how far the nation would retreat from world affairs. It seemed that the United States would not try to do as much as it had under Kennedy and Johnson. Few if any people had the confidence in American power that had developed by 1965. The Carter administration was dominated by men who had learned the lessons of the 1930s and believed that the United States must be militarily strong and politically active in world affairs, but the administration was also affected by the more recent lessons and thus seemed certain to be more cautious than LBJ and less likely to use military force. Carter also responded to concern about the corruption of America with a crusade for human rights, hoping that thereby the United States would "regain the moral stature we once had." When a new generation comes to power that knows little about the 1930s and gets its insights about foreign affairs from the 1960s, the United States may concentrate only on its "own affairs" and cease to be a global power.

Another profound change seemed to be a possibility. By the mid-seventies, most Americans believed that economic growth might soon end. It had been a major feature of American history since the beginning and had been valued very highly since the 1940s. America would be a very different place if permanent stagnation or decline displaced growth.

Before the end of the 1960s, some Americans had begun to question seriously the possibility of continued economic growth. Most of the questioning had come from the "environmentalists" who emphasized pollution as the major product of economic growth and subjected a central figure of American life—the automobile—to especially heavy attack. In addition to warning about pollution, the environmentalists also warned that the American people, who consumed and wasted products at an unmatched pace, would soon run short of raw materials. The environmentalists disagreed with one another as well as with others about the likelihood of finding ways both to eliminate pollution and continue economic growth, and they promoted many efforts to protect and improve the environment. Often, their proposals were opposed by adherents to the growth philosophy who argued that the proposals would damage or destroy industries and produce unemployment.

In 1972, the fears about the future were expressed dramatically in the Club of Rome's report on *The Limits of Growth*. It predicted that continued growth in production and population would lead to catastrophe in 100 years. The report stimulated widespread debate.

The future of the economy was questioned more frequently following the emergence of the "Energy Crisis" in the fall of 1973. In October, the Arabs banned oil exports to the United States and several other countries, doing so after Egypt and Syria had attacked Israel. The move expressed resentment of aid for Israel and recognized the dependence of the United States and other countries on Middle Eastern oil. Next, the Arabs and others used the Organization of Petroleum Exporting Countries to quadruple oil prices. The moves, which were accomplished without retaliation by the United States and with the collaboration of the multinational oil companies, resulted in shortages of gasoline for several months, higher prices and recession in the United States and even more severe problems in Japan, Western Europe and many poor countries that were even more dependent than the U.S. on oil from the Middle East. In the next three years, OPEC pushed oil prices even higher.

For Americans, the existence of the energy crisis was reconfirmed by the severe winter of 1977-1978. It placed great demands on the natural gas industry, which supplied energy for nearly half of the homes and industries, and the industry did not meet all of the demands. Thus, many parts of the country suffered from gas shortages that forced offices, factories, and schools to close for extended periods and increased unemployment.

The problems affected the major sources of energy but did not produce immediate changes in American practices. Oil and natural gas supplied 75 percent of the nation's energy, but the people did not cut back on their use of them or on the import of oil. Imports, in fact, continued to grow. Some people had to do without from time to time, and minor conservation methods, such as a reduction in the speed limit for automobiles and other users of the highways, were adopted. Americans had long regarded the automobile as a necessity for transportation

Three Presidents Meeting During the Funeral Ceremony for
Senator Hubert H. Humphrey *(Wide World Photo)*

to work, amusement centers, and anything involving their daily lives.

The problems did enlarge the debate over the economic future. Many prophets predicted that stagnation and decline would soon displace growth, and some of them suggested that the change would lead to intense social conflict and force the nation to move in an authoritarian direction. A few observers of the future challenged these prophecies with the suggestion that Americans could find happiness at a much lower standard of living. A more widely endorsed challenge came from those who insisted that the potential supply of oil and natural gas was large enough to supply the nation's needs for many years and the nation needed only to pay the prices required to encourage the petroleum industry to search for and develop the supplies. The grim forecasts were challenged also by those who insisted that science, technology, industry, and government would come to the rescue, promoting conservation, providing more efficient ways of using energy, such as smaller automobiles and mass transit, and developing adequate substitutes for oil, including coal and nuclear and solar power. But pessimists insisted that the automobile and oil companies would block the necessary changes, the capital requirements could not be met, much time would be required to develop nuclear and solar energy, dependence on nuclear power would be very dangerous and dependence on coal would seriously damage the environment. More optimistic types maintained that the nation could enjoy a happy future if it destroyed the power of the oil companies or substituted socialism for capitalism.

Is a new America, one that differs radically from the America of the past, now taking shape? The study of history does not enable us to answer this question confidently for it does not show us the choices that will be made. Yet, the study of history can alert us to the forces that are swirling about us and playing upon us, and it can help us make those choices.

SUGGESTIONS FOR FURTHER READING

Chafe, William H., *The American Woman: Her Changing Social, Economic, and Political Roles, 1920-1970.* New York, Oxford University Press, 1972.

Engler, Robert, *The Brotherhood of Oil: Energy Policy and the Public Interest.* Chicago, University of Chicago Press, 1977.

Grantham, Dewey W., *The United States since 1945: The Ordeal of Power.* New York, McGraw-Hill Book Co., 1976.

Hamby, Alonzo L., *The Imperial Years; The United States since 1939.* New York, Weybright and Talley, 1976.

Hodgson, Godfrey, *America in Our Time.* New York, Doubleday, 1977.

Witcover, Jules, *Marathon: The Pursuit of the Presidency 1972-1976.* New York, The Viking Press, 1977.

Wittner, Lawrence S., *Cold War America: From Hiroshima to Watergate.* New York, Praeger Publishers, 1974.

The
American
Republic

Appendix

Declaration of Independence

When, in the Course of human events, it becomes necessary for one people to dissolve the political bands which have connected them with another, and to assume, among the Powers of the earth, the separate and equal station to which the Laws of Nature and of Nature's God entitle them, a decent respect to the opinions of mankind requires that they should declare the causes which impel them to the separation.

We hold these truths to be self-evident, that all men are created equal, that they are endowed by their Creator with certain unalienable Rights, that among these, are Life, Liberty, and the pursuit of Happiness. That, to secure these rights, Governments are instituted among Men, deriving their just Powers from the consent of the governed. That, whenever any form of Government becomes destructive of these ends, it is the Right of the People to alter or to abolish it, and to institute new Government, laying its foundation on such Principles, and organizing its Powers in such form, as to them shall seem most likely to effect their Safety and Happiness. Prudence, indeed, will dictate that Governments long established should not be changed for light and transient causes; and, accordingly, all experience hath shewn, that mankind are more disposed to suffer, while evils are sufferable, than to right themselves by abolishing the forms to which they are accustomed. But, when a long train of abuses and usurpations, pursuing invariably the same Object, evinces a design to reduce them under absolute Despotism, it is their right, it is their duty, to throw off such Government, and to provide new Guards for their future Security. Such has been the patient sufferance of these Colonies; and such is now the necessity which constrains them to alter their former Systems of Government. The history of the present King of Great Britain is a history of repeated injuries and usurpations, all having in direct object the establishment of an absolute Tyranny over these States. To prove this, let Facts be submitted to a candid world.

He has refused his Assent to Laws the most wholesome and necessary for the public good.

He has forbidden his Governors to pass Laws of immediate and pressing importance, unless suspended in their operation till his Assent should be obtained; and when so suspended, he has utterly neglected to attend to them.

He has refused to pass other Laws for the accommodation of large districts of People, unless those People would relinquish the right of Representation in the legislature; a right inestimable to them and formidable to tyrants only.

He has called together legislative bodies at places unusual, uncomfortable, and distant from the depository of their Public Records, for the sole Purpose of fatiguing them into compliance with his measures.

He has dissolved Representative Houses repeatedly, for opposing, with manly firmness, his invasions on the rights of the People.

He has refused for a long time, after such dissolutions, to cause others to be elected; whereby the Legislative Powers, incapable of Annihilation, have returned to the People at large for their exercise; the State remaining in the mean time exposed to all the dangers of invasion from without, and convulsions within.

He has endeavoured to prevent the Population of these States; for that purpose obstructing the Laws for Naturalization of Foreigners; refusing to pass others to encourage their migrations hither, and raising the conditions of new Appropriations of Lands.

He has obstructed the Administration of Justice, by refusing his Assent to Laws for establishing Judiciary Powers.

He has made Judges dependent on his Will alone, for the tenure of their offices, and the amount and payment of their salaries.

He has erected a multitude of New Officers, and sent hither swarms of Officers to harrass our People, and eat out their substance.

He has kept among us, in times of Peace, Standing Armies, without the Consent of our legislatures.

He has affected to render the Military independent of and superior to the Civil Power.

He has combined with others to subject us to a jurisdiction foreign to our constitution, and unacknowledged by our laws; giving his Assent to their Acts of pretended Legislation:

For quartering large bodies of armed troops among us:

For protecting them, by a mock Trial, from Punishment for any Murders which they should commit on the Inhabitants of these States:

For cutting off our Trade with all parts of the world:

For imposing Taxes on us without our Consent:

For depriving us, in many cases, of the benefits of Trial by Jury:

For transporting us beyond Seas to be tried for pretended offences:

For abolishing the free System of English Laws in a neighbouring province, establishing therein an Arbitrary government, and enlarging its Boundaries, so as to render it at once an example and fit instrument for introducing the same absolute rule into these Colonies:

For taking away our Charters, abolishing our most valuable Laws, and altering fundamentally the Forms of our Governments:

For suspending our own Legislatures, and declaring themselves invested with Power to legislate for us in all cases whatsoever.

He has abdicated Government here, by declaring us out of his protection, and waging War against us.

He has plundered our seas, ravaged our Coasts, burnt our towns, and destroyed the Lives of our People.

He is at this time transporting large Armies of foreign Mercenaries to compleat the works of death, desolation and tyranny, already begun with circumstances of Cruelty and perfidy scarcely paralleled in the most barbarous ages, and totally unworthy the Head of a civilized nation.

He has constrained our fellow Citizens, taken Captive on the high Seas, to bear Arms against their Country, to become the executioners of their friends and Brethren, or to fall themselves by their Hands.

He has excited domestic insurrections amongst us, and has endeavoured to bring on the inhabitants of our frontiers, the merciless Indian Savages, whose known rule of warfare, is an undistinguished destruction of all ages, sexes and conditions.

In every stage of these Oppressions, We have Petitioned for Redress, in the most humble terms: Our repeated Petitions, have been answered only by repeated injury. A Prince, whose character is thus marked by every act which may define a Tyrant, is unfit to be the ruler of a free People.

Nor have We been wanting in attentions to our British brethren. We have warned them from time to time of attempts by their legislature to extend an unwarrantable jurisdiction over us. We have reminded them of the circumstances of our emigration and settlement here. We have appealed to their native justice and magnanimity, and we have conjured them by the ties of our common kindred, to disavow these usurpations, which, would inevitably interrupt our connexions and correspondence. They too have been deaf to the voice of justice and consanguinity. We must, therefore, acquiesce in the necessity, which denounces our Separation, and hold them, as we hold the rest of mankind, Enemies in war, in Peace Friends.

WE, THEREFORE, the Representatives of the UNITED STATES OF AMERICA, in GENERAL CONGRESS assembled, appealing to the Supreme Judge of the World for the rectitude of our intentions, DO, in the Name, and by Authority of the good People of these Colonies, solemnly PUBLISH and DECLARE, That these United Colonies are, and of Right, ought to be FREE AND INDEPENDENT STATES; that they are Absolved from all Allegiance to the British Crown, and that all political connexion between them and the State of Great Britain, is and ought to be totally dissolved; and that, as FREE and INDEPENDENT STATES, they have full Power to levy War, conclude Peace, contract Alliances, establish Commerce, and to do all other Acts and Things which INDEPENDENT STATES may of right do. AND for the support of this Declaration, with a firm reliance on the protection of divine Providence, we mutually pledge to each other our Lives, our Fortunes, and our sacred Honour.

The Constitution of the United States of America

We the people of the United States, in Order to form a more perfect Union, establish Justice, insure domestic Tranquility, provide for the common defence, promote the general Welfare, and secure the Blessings of Liberty to ourselves and our Posterity, do ordain and establish this Constitution for the United States of America.

Article I

Section 1. All legislative Powers herein granted shall be vested in a Congress of the United States, which shall consist of a Senate and House of Representatives.

Section 2. The House of Representatives shall be composed of Members chosen every second Year by the People of the several States, and the Electors in each State shall have the Qualifications requisite for Electors of the most numerous Branch of the State Legislature.

No Person shall be a Representative who shall not have attained to the Age of twenty-five Years, and been seven Years a Citizen of the United States, and who shall not, when elected, be an Inhabitant of that state in which he shall be chosen.

[Representatives and direct Taxes shall be apportioned among the several States which may be included within this Union, according to their respective Numbers, which shall be determined by adding to the whole Number of free Persons, including those bound to Service for a Term of Years, and excluding Indians not taxed, three fifths of all other Persons.][1] The actual Enumeration shall be made within three Years after the first Meeting of the Congress of the United States, and within every subsequent Term of ten Years, in such Manner as they shall by Law direct. The Number of Representatives shall not exceed one for every thirty Thousand, but each State shall have at Least one Representative; and until such enumeration shall be made, the State of New Hampshire shall be entitled to chuse three, Massachusetts eight, Rhode-Island and Providence Plantations one, Connecticut five, New-York six, New Jersey four, Pennsylvania eight, Delaware one, Maryland six, Virginia ten, North Carolina five, South Carolina five, and Georgia three.

When vacancies happen in the Representation from any State, the Executive Authority thereof shall issue Writs of Election to fill such Vacancies.

The House of Representatives shall chuse their Speaker and other Officers; and shall have

the sole Power of Impeachment.

Section 3. The Senate of the United States shall be composed of two Senators from each State, [chosen by the Legislature thereof,][2] for six Years; and each Senator shall have one Vote.

Immediately after they shall be assembled in Consequence of the first Election, they shall be divided as equally as may be into three Classes. The Seats of the Senators of the first Class shall be vacated at the Expiration of the second Year, of the Second Class at the Expiration of the fourth Year, and of the third Class at the Expiration of the sixth Year, so that one-third may be chosen every second year; [and if Vacancies happen by Resignation, or otherwise, during the Recess of the Legislature of any State, the Executive thereof may make temporary Appointments until the next Meeting of the Legislature, which shall then fill such Vacancies].[3]

No Person shall be a Senator who shall not have attained to the Age of thirty Years, and been nine Years a Citizen of the United States, and who shall not, when elected, be an Inhabitant of that State in which he shall be chosen.

The Vice-President of the United States shall be President of the Senate, but shall have no vote, unless they be equally divided.

The Senate shall chuse their other Officers, and also a President pro tempore, in the absence of the Vice-President, or when he shall exercise the Office of the President of the United States.

The Senate shall have the sole

Power to try all Impeachments. When sitting for that purpose, they shall be on Oath or Affirmation. When the President of the United States is tried, the Chief Justice shall preside. And no person shall be convicted without the Concurrence of two thirds of the Members present.

Judgment in Cases of Impeachment shall not extend further than to removal from Office, and disqualification to hold and enjoy any Office of honor, Trust, or Profit under the United States: but the Party convicted shall nevertheless be liable and subject to Indictment, Trial, Judgment, and Punishment, according to Law.

Section 4. The Times, Places and Manner of holding Elections for Senators and Representatives, shall be prescribed in each state by the Legislature thereof; but the Congress may at any time by Law make or alter such Regulations, except as to the Places of Chusing Senators.

The Congress shall assemble at least once in every Year, and such Meeting shall [be on the first Monday in December,]⁴ unless they shall by Law appoint a different Day.

Section 5. Each House shall be the Judge of the Elections, Returns and Qualifications of its own Members, and a Majority of each shall constitute a Quorum to do Business; but a smaller number may adjourn from day to day, and may be authorized to compel the Attendance of absent Members, in such Manner, and under such Penalties, as each House may provide.

Each House may determine the Rules of its Proceedings, punish its Members for disorderly Behavior, and, with the Concurrence of two thirds, expel a Member.

Each House shall keep a Journal of its Proceedings, and from time to time publish the same, excepting such Parts as may in their Judgment require Secrecy; and the Yeas and Nays of the Members of either House on any question shall, at the Desire of one fifth of those Present, be entered on the Journal.

Neither House, during the Session of Congress, shall, without the Consent of the other, adjourn for more than three days, nor to any other Place than that in which the two Houses shall be sitting.

Section 6. The Senators and Representatives shall receive a Compensation for their Services, to be ascertained by Law, and paid out of the Treasury of the United States. They shall in all Cases, except Treason, Felony, and Breach of the Peace, be privileged from Arrest during their Attendance at the Session of their respective Houses, and in going to and returning from the same; and for any Speech or Debate in either House, they shall not be questioned in any other Place.

No Senator or Representative shall, during the Time for which he was elected, be appointed to any civil Office under the Authority of the United States, which shall have been created, or the Emoluments whereof shall have been increased, during such time; and no Person holding any Office under the United States shall be a Member of either House during his continuance in Office.

Section 7. All Bills for raising Revenue shall originate in the House of Representatives; but the Senate may propose or concur with Amendments as on other bills.

Every Bill which shall have passed the House of Representatives and the Senate, shall, before it become a Law, be presented to the President of the United States; If he approve he shall sign it, but if not he shall return it, with his Objections, to that House in which it shall have originated, who shall enter the Objections at large on their Journal, and proceed to reconsider it. If after such Reconsideration two thirds of that House shall agree to pass the bill, it shall be sent, together with the objections, to the other House, by which it shall likewise be reconsidered, and if approved by two thirds of that House, it shall become a Law. But in all such Cases the Votes of both Houses shall be determined by Yeas and Nays, and the Names of the Persons voting for and against the Bill shall be entered on the Journal of each House respectively. If any Bill shall not be returned by the President within ten Days (Sundays excepted) after it shall have been presented to him, the Same shall be a Law, in like Manner as if he had signed it, unless the Congress by their Adjournment prevent its Return, in which Case it shall not be a Law.

Every Order, Resolution, or Vote to which the Concurrence of the Senate and House of Representa-

tives may be necessary (except on a question of Adjournment) shall be presented to the President of the United States; and before the Same shall take Effect, shall be approved by him, or being disapproved by him, shall be repassed by two thirds of the Senate and House of Representatives, according to the Rules and Limitations prescribed in the Case of a Bill.

Section 8. The Congress shall have Power To lay and collect Taxes, Duties, Imposts and Excises, to pay the Debts and provide for the common Defence and general Welfare of the United States; but all Duties, Imposts and Excises shall be uniform throughout the United States;

To borrow money on the credit of the United States;

To regulate Commerce with foreign Nations, and among the several States, and with the Indian Tribes;

To establish an uniform Rule of Naturalization, and uniform Laws on the subject of Bankruptcies throughout the United States;

To coin Money, regulate the Value thereof, and of foreign Coin, and fix the Standard of Weights and Measures;

To provide for the Punishment of counterfeiting the Securities and current Coin of the United States;

To establish Post Offices and post Roads;

To promote the Progress of Science and useful Arts, by securing for limited Times to Authors and Inventors the exclusive Right to their respective Writings and Discoveries;

To constitute Tribunals inferior to the Supreme Court;

To define and punish Piracies and Felonies committed on the high Seas, and offenses against the Law of Nations;

To declare War, grant Letters of Marque and Reprisal, and make Rules concerning Captures on Land and Water;

To raise and support Armies, but no Appropriation of Money to that Use shall be for a longer Term than two Years;

To provide and maintain a Navy;

To make Rules for the Government and Regulation of the land and naval forces;

To provide for calling forth the Militia to execute the Laws of the Union, suppress Insurrections and repel Invasions;

To provide for organizing, arming, and disciplining the Militia, and for governing such Part of them as may be employed in the Service of the United States, reserving to the States respectively, the Appointment of the Officers, and the Authority of training the Militia according to the discipline prescribed by Congress;

To exercise exclusive Legislation in all Cases whatsoever, over such District (not exceeding ten Miles square) as may, by Cession of particular States, and the acceptance of Congress, become the Seat of the Government of the United States, and to exercise like Authority over all Places purchased by the Consent of the Legislature of the State in which the Same shall be, for the Erection of Forts, Magazines, Arsenals, dock-Yards, and other needful Buildings;—And

To make all Laws which shall be necessary and proper for carrying into Execution the foregoing Powers, and all other Powers vested by this Constitution in the Government of the United States, or in any Department or Officer thereof.

Section 9. The Migration or Importation of such Persons as any of the States now existing shall think proper to admit shall not be prohibited by the Congress prior to the Year one thousand eight hundred and eight, but a tax or duty may be imposed on such Importation, not exceeding ten dollars for each Person.

The privilege of the Writ of Habeas Corpus shall not be suspended, unless when in Cases of Rebellion or Invasion the public Safety may require it.

No Bill of Attainder or ex post facto Law shall be passed.

[No capitation, or other direct, Tax shall be laid unless in Proportion to the Census or Enumeration herein before directed to be taken.][5]

No Tax or Duty shall be laid on Articles exported from any State.

No Preference shall be given by any Regulation of Revenue to the Ports of one State over those of another: nor shall Vessels bound to, or from, one State, be obliged to enter, clear, or pay Duties in another.

No Money shall be drawn from the Treasury, but in Consequence of Appropriations made by Law; and a regular Statement and Account of the Receipts and Expenditures of all public Money shall be published from time to time.

No Title of Nobility shall be granted by the United States: And no Person holding any Office of Profit or Trust under them, shall, without the Consent of the Congress, accept of any present, Emolument, Office, or Title, of any kind whatever, from any King, Prince, or foreign State.

Section 10. No State shall enter into any Treaty, Alliance, or Confederation; grant Letters of Marque and Reprisal; coin Money; emit Bills of Credit; make any Thing but gold and silver Coin a Tender in Payment of Debts; pass any Bill of Attainder, ex post facto Law, or Law impairing the Obligation of Contracts, or grant any Title of Nobility.

No State shall, without the Consent of the Congress, lay any Imposts or Duties on Imports or Exports, except what may be absolutely necessary for executing its inspection Laws: and the net Produce of all Duties and Imposts, laid by any State or Imports or Exports, shall be for the use of the Treasury of the United States; and all such Laws shall be subject to the Revision and Control of the Congress.

No State shall, without the Consent of Congress, lay any duty of Tonnage, keep Troops, or Ships of War in time of Peace, enter into any Agreement or Compact with another State, or with a foreign Power, or engage in War, unless actually invaded, or in such imminent Danger as will not admit of delay.

Article II

Section 1. The executive Power shall be vested in a President of the United States of America. He shall hold his Office during the Term of four years, and, together with the Vice-President, chosen for the same Term, be elected, as follows:

Each State shall appoint, in such Manner as the Legislature thereof may direct, a Number of Electors, equal to the whole Number of Senators and Representatives to which the State may be entitled in the Congress: but no Senator or Representative, or Person holding an Office of Trust or Profit under the United States, shall be appointed an Elector.

[The Electors shall meet in their respective States, and vote by Ballot for two persons, of whom one at least shall not be an Inhabitant of the same State with themselves. And they shall make a List of all the Persons voted for, and of the Number of Votes for each; which List they shall sign and certify, and transmit sealed to the Seat of the Government of the United States, directed to the President of the Senate. The President of the Senate shall, in the Presence of the Senate and House of Representatives, open all the Certificates, and the Votes shall then be counted. The Person having the greatest Number of Votes shall be the President, if such Number be a Majority of the whole Number of Electors appointed; and if there be more than one who have such Majority, and have an equal Number of Votes, then the House of Representatives shall immediately chuse by Ballot one of them for President; and if no Person have a Majority, then from the five highest on the List the said House shall in like Manner chuse the President. But in chusing the President, the Votes shall be taken by States, the Representation from each State having one Vote; a quorum for this Purpose shall consist of a Member or Members from two-thirds of the States, and a Majority of all the States shall be necessary to a Choice. In every Case, after the Choice of the President, the Person having the greatest Number of Votes of the Electors shall be the Vice-President. But if there should remain two or more who have equal votes, the Senate shall chuse from them by Ballot the Vice-President.][6]

The Congress may determine the Time of chusing the Electors, and the Day on which they shall give their Votes; which Day shall be the same throughout the United States.

No person except a natural-born Citizen, or a Citizen of the United States, at the time of the Adoption of this Constitution, shall be eligible to the Office of President; neither shall any Person be eligible to the Office who shall not have attained to the Age of thirty-five years, and been fourteen Years a Resident within the United States.

[In Case of the Removal of the President from Office, or of his Death, Resignation, or Inability to discharge the Powers and Duties of the said Office, the same shall devolve on the Vice-President, and the Congress may by Law provide for the Case of Removal, Death, Resignation, or Inability, both of the President and Vice-President, declaring what Officer shall then act as President, and such Officer shall act accordingly, until the disability be removed, or a President shall be elected.][7]

The President shall, at stated Times, receive for his Services a Compensation, which shall neither be increased nor diminished during the Period for which he shall have been elected, and he shall not receive within that Period any other Emolument from the United States, or any of them.

Before he enter on the execution of his Office, he shall take the following Oath or Affirmation:—"I do solemnly swear (or affirm) that I will faithfully execute the Office of President of the United States, and will, to the best of my Ability, preserve, protect, and defend the Constitution of the United States."

Section 2. The President shall be Commander in Chief of the Army and Navy of the United States, and of the Militia of the several States, when called into the actual Service of the United States; he may require the Opinion, in writing, of the principal Officer in each of the executive Departments, upon any subject relating to the Duties of their respective Offices, and he shall have Power to Grant Reprieves and Pardons for Offenses against the United States, except in Cases of Impeachment.

He shall have Power, by and with the Advice and Consent of the Senate, to make Treaties, provided two thirds of the Senators present concur; and he shall nominate, and by and with the Advice and Consent of the Senate, shall appoint Ambassadors, other public Ministers and Consuls, Judges of the supreme Court, and all other Officers of the United States, whose Appointments are not herein otherwise provided for, and which shall be established by Law: but the Congress may by Law vest the Appointment of such inferior Officers, as they think proper, in the President alone, in the Courts of Law, or in the Heads of Departments.

The President shall have Power to fill up all Vacancies that may happen during the Recess of the Senate, by granting Commissions which shall expire at the End of their next Session.

Section 3. He shall from time to time give to the Congress Information of the State of the Union, and recommend to their Consideration such Measures as he shall judge necessary and expedient; he may, on extraordinary occasions, convene both Houses, or either of them, and in Case of Disagreement between them, with respect to the Time of Adjournment, he may adjourn them to such Time as he shall think proper; he shall receive Ambassadors and other public Ministers; he shall take Care that the Laws be faithfully executed, and shall Commission all the Officers of the United States.

Section 4. The President, Vice-President and all civil Officers of the United States, shall be removed from Office on Impeach-

ment for, and Conviction of, Treason, Bribery, or other high Crimes and Misdemeanors.

Article III

Section 1. The judicial Power of the United States, shall be vested in one supreme Court, and in such inferior Courts as the Congress may from time to time ordain and establish. The Judges, both of the supreme and inferior Courts, shall hold their Offices during good Behaviour, and shall, at stated Times, receive for their Services, a Compensation, which shall not be diminished during their Continuance in Office.

Section 2. The judicial Power shall extend to all Cases, in Law and Equity, arising under this Constitution, the Laws of the United States, and treaties made, or which shall be made, under their Authority;—to all Cases affecting ambassadors, other public ministers and consuls;—to all cases of admiralty and maritime Jurisdiction;—to Controversies to which the United States shall be a Party;—to Controversies between two or more States;—[between a State and Citizens of another State;]⁸—between Citizens of different States,—between Citizens of the same State claiming Lands under Grants of different States, and between a State, or the Citizens thereof, and foreign States, Citizens or Subjects.

In all Cases affecting Ambassadors, other public Ministers and Consuls, and those in which a State shall be Party, the supreme Court shall have original Jurisdiction. In all the other Cases before mentioned, the supreme Court shall have appellate Jurisdiction, both as to Law and Fact, with such Exceptions, and under such Regulations as the Congress shall make.

The trial of all Crimes, except in Cases of Impeachment, shall be by Jury; and such Trial shall be held in the State where the said Crimes shall have been committed; but when not committed within any State, the Trial shall be at such Place or Places as the Congress may by Law have directed.

Section 3. Treason against the United States, shall consist only in levying War against them, or in adhering to their Enemies, giving them Aid and Comfort. No Person shall be convicted of Treason unless on the Testimony of two Witnesses to the same overt Act, or on Confession in open Court.

The Congress shall have power to declare the Punishment of Treason, but no Attainder of Treason shall work Corruption of Blood, or Forfeiture except during the Life of the Person attainted.

Article IV

Section 1. Full Faith and Credit shall be given in each State to the public Acts, Records, and judicial Proceedings of every other State. And the Congress may by general Laws prescribe the Manner in which such Acts, Records and Proceedings shall be proved, and the Effect thereof.

Section 2. The Citizens of each State shall be entitled to all Privileges and Immunities of Citizens in the several States.

A Person charged in any State with Treason, Felony, or other Crime, who shall flee from Justice, and be found in another State, shall on demand of the executive Authority of the State from which he fled, be delivered up, to be removed to the State having Jurisdiction of the crime.

[No Person held to Service or Labour in one State, under the Laws thereof, escaping into another, shall, in Consequence of any Law or Regulation therein, be discharged from such Service or Labour, but shall be delivered up on Claim of the Party to whom such Service or Labour may be due.][9]

Section 3. New States may be admitted by the Congress into this Union; but no new State shall be formed or erected within the Jurisdiction of any other State; nor any State be formed by the Junction of two or more States, or parts of States, without the Consent of the Legislatures of the States concerned as well as of the Congress.

The Congress shall have Power to dispose of and make all needful Rules and Regulations respecting the Territory or other Property belonging to the United States; and nothing in this Constitution shall be so construed as to Prejudice any Claims of the United States, or of any particular State.

Section 4. The United States shall guarantee to every State in this Union a Republican Form of Government, and shall protect each of them against Invasion; and on Application of the Legislature, or of the Executive (when the Legislature cannot be convened) against domestic Violence.

Article V

The Congress, whenever two-thirds of both Houses shall deem it necessary, shall propose Amendments to this Constitution, or, on the Application of the Legislatures of two-thirds of the several States, shall call a Convention for proposing Amendments, which, in either Case, shall be valid to all Intents and Purposes, as part of this Constitution, when ratified by the Legislatures of three-fourths of the several States, or by Conventions in three-fourths thereof, as the one or the other Mode of Ratification may be proposed by the Congress; Provided that no Amendment which may be made prior to the Year One thousand eight hundred and eight shall in any Manner affect the first and fourth Clauses in the Ninth Section of the first Article; and that no State, without its Consent, shall be deprived of its equal Suffrage in the Senate.

Article VI

All Debts contracted and Engagements entered into, before the Adoption of this Constitution, shall be as valid against the United States under this Constitution, as under the Confederation.

This Constitution, and the Laws of the United States which shall be made in Pursuance thereof; and all Treaties made, or which shall be made, under the Authority of the United States, shall be the supreme Law of the Land; and the Judges in every State shall be bound thereby, any Thing in the Constitution or Laws of any State to the Contrary notwithstanding.

The Senators and Representatives before mentioned, and the Members of the several State Legislatures, and all executive and judicial Officers, both of the United States and of the several States, shall be bound by Oath or Affirmation to support this Constitution; but no religious Test shall ever be required as a qualification to any Office or public Trust under the United States.

Article VII

The Ratification of the Conventions of nine States shall be sufficient for the Establishment of this Constitution between the States so ratifying the same.

Done in Convention by the Unanimous Consent of the States present the Seventeenth Day of September in the Year of our Lord one thousand seven hundred and Eighty seven, and of the Independence of the United States of America the Twelfth. In Witness whereof We have hereunto subscribed our Names.

Articles in Addition to, and Amendment of, the Constitution of the Untied States of America, Proposed by Congress, and Ratified by the Legislatures of the Several States, Pursuant to the Fifth Article of the Original Constitution.

Amendment I[10]

Congress shall make no law respecting an establishment of religion, or prohibiting the free exercise thereof; or abridging the freedom of speech, or of the press; or the right of the people peaceably to assemble, and to petition the Government for a redress of grievances.

Amendment II

A well regulated Militia, being necessary to the security of a free State, the right of the people to keep and bear Arms shall not be infringed.

Amendment III

No Soldier shall, in time of peace, be quartered in any house, without the consent of the Owner, nor in time of war, but in a manner to be prescribed by law.

Amendment IV

The right of the people to be secure in their persons, houses, papers, and effects, against unreasonable searches and seizures, shall not be violated, and no Warrants shall issue, but upon probable cause, supported by Oath or affirmation, and particularly describing the place to be searched, and the persons or things to be seized.

Amendment V

No person shall be held to answer for a capital or otherwise infamous crime, unless on a presentment or indictment of a Grand Jury, except in cases arising in the land or naval forces, or in the Militia, when in actual service in time of War or public danger; nor shall any person be subject for the same offence to be twice put in jeopardy of life or limb; nor shall be compelled in any criminal case to be a witness against himself, nor be deprived of life, liberty, or property, without due process of law; nor shall private property be taken for public use, without just compensation.

Amendment VI

In all criminal prosecutions, the accused shall enjoy the right to a speedy and public trial, by an impartial jury of the State and district wherein the crime shall have been committed, which district shall have been previously ascertained by law, and to be informed of the nature and cause of the accusation; to be confronted with the witnesses against him; to have compulsory process for obtaining witnesses in his favor, and to have the Assistance of Counsel for his defence.

Amendment VII

In suits at common law, where the value in controversy shall exceed twenty dollars, the right of trial by jury shall be preserved, and no fact tried by a jury, shall be otherwise reexamined in any Court of the United States, than according to the rules of the common law.

Amendment VIII

Excessive bail shall not be required, nor excessive fines imposed, nor cruel and unusual punishments inflicted.

Amendment IX

The enumeration in the Constitution, of certain rights, shall not be construed to deny or disparage others retained by the people.

Amendment X

The powers not delegated to the United States by the Constitution, nor prohibited by it to the States, are reserved to the States respectively, or to the people.

Amendment XI (1798)[11]

The Judicial power of the United States shall not be construed to extend to any suit in law or equity, commenced or prosecuted against one of the United States by Citizens of another State, or by Citizens or Subjects of any Foreign State.

Amendment XII (1804)

The Electors shall meet in their respective States and vote by ballot for President and Vice-President, one of whom, at least, shall not be an inhabitant of the same State with themselves; they shall name in their ballots the person voted for as President, and in distinct ballots the person voted for as Vice-President, and they shall make distinct lists of all persons voted for as President, and of all persons voted for as Vice-President, and of the number of votes for each, which lists they shall sign and certify, and transmit sealed to the seat of the government of the United States, directed to the President of the Senate;— The President of the Senate shall, in the presence of the Senate and House of Representatives, open all the certificates and the votes shall then be counted;—The person having the greatest number of votes for President, shall be the President, if such number be a majority of the whole number of Electors appointed; and if no person have such majority, then from the persons having the highest numbers not exceeding three on the list of those voted for as President, the House of Representatives shall choose immediately, by ballot, the President. But in choosing the President, the votes shall be taken by states, the representation from each state having one vote; a quorum for this purpose shall consist of a member or members from two-thirds of the states, and a majority of all the states shall be necessary to a choice. [And if the House of Representatives shall not choose a President whenever the right of choice shall devolve upon them, before the fourth day of March next following, then the Vice-President shall act as President, as in the case of the death or other constitutional disability of the President.][12]—The person having the greatest number of votes as Vice-President, shall be the Vice-President, if such number be a majority of the whole number of Electors appointed, and if no person have a majority, then from the two highest numbers on the list, the Senate shall choose the Vice-President; a quorum for the purpose shall consist of two-thirds of the whole number of Senators, and a majority of the whole number shall be necessary to a choice. But no person constitutionally ineligible to the office of President shall be eligible to that of Vice-President of the United States.

Amendment XIII (1865)

Section 1. Neither slavery nor involuntary servitude, except as a punishment for crime whereof the party shall have been duly convicted, shall exist within the United States, or any place subject to their jurisdiction.

Section 2. Congress shall have power to enforce this article by appropriate legislation.

Amendment XIV (1868)

Section 1. All persons born or naturalized in the United States, and subject to the jurisdiction thereof, are citizens of the United States and of the State wherein they reside. No State shall make or enforce any law which shall abridge the privileges or immunities of citizens of the United States; nor shall any State deprive any person of life, liberty, or property, without due process of law; nor deny to any person within its jurisdiction the equal protection of the laws.

Section 2. Representatives shall be apportioned among the several States according to their respective numbers, counting the whole number of persons in each State, excluding Indians not taxed. But when the right to vote at any election for the choice of electors for President and Vice-President of the United States, Representatives in Congress, the Executive and Judicial officers of a State, or the members of the Legislature thereof, is denied to any of the male inhabitants of such State, being twenty-one years of age, and citizens of the United States, or in any way abridged, except for participation in rebellion, or other crime, the basis of representation therein shall be reduced in the proportion which the number of such male citizens shall bear to the whole number of male citizens twenty-one years of age in such State.

Section 3. No person shall be a Senator or Representative in Congress, or elector of President and Vice-President, or hold any office, civil or military, under the United States, or under any State, who, having previously taken an oath, as a member of Congress, or as an officer of the United States, or as a member of any State legislature, or as an executive or judicial officer of any State, to support the Constitution of the United States, shall have engaged in insurrection or rebellion against the same, or given aid or comfort to the enemies thereof. But Congress may by a vote of two-thirds of each House, remove such disability.

Section 4. The validity of the public debt of the United States, authorized by law, including debts incurred for payment of pensions and bounties for services in suppressing insurrection or rebellion, shall not be questioned.

But neither the United States nor any State shall assume or pay any debt or obligation incurred in aid of insurrection or rebellion against the United States, or any claim for the loss or emancipation of any slave; but all such debts, obligations, and claims shall be held illegal and void.

Section 5. The Congress shall have the power to enforce, by appropriate legislation, the provisions of this article.

Amendment XV (1870)

Section 1. The right of citizens of the United States to vote shall not be denied or abridged by the United States or by any State on account of race, color, or previous condition of servitude—

Section 2. The Congress shall have power to enforce this article by appropriate legislation.

Amendment XVI (1913)

The Congress shall have power to lay and collect taxes on incomes, from whatever source derived, without apportionment among the several States, and without regard to any census or enumeration.

Amendment XVII (1913)

The Senate of the United States shall be composed of two Senators from each State, elected by the people thereof, for six years; and each Senator shall have one vote. The electors in each State shall have the qualifications requisite for electors of the most numerous branch of the State legislatures.

When vacancies happen in the representation of any State in the Senate, the executive authority of such State shall issue writs of election to fill such vacancies: *Provided,* That the legislature of any State may empower the executive thereof to make temporary appointments until the people fill the vacancies by election as the legislature may direct.

This amendment shall not be so construed as to affect the election or term of any Senator chosen before it becomes valid as part of the Constitution.

Amendment XVIII (1919)[13]

Section 1. After one year from the ratification of this article the manufacture, sale, or transportation of intoxicating liquors within, the importation thereof into, or the exportation thereof from the United States and all territory subject to the jurisdiction thereof for beverage purposes is hereby prohibited.

Section 2. The Congress and the several States shall have concurrent power to enforce this article by appropriate legislation.

Section 3. This article shall be inoperative unless it shall have been ratified as an amendment to the Constitution by the legislatures of the several States, as provided in the Constitution, within seven years from the date of the submission hereof to the States by the Congress.

Amendment XIX (1920)

The right of citizens of the United States to vote shall not be denied or abridged by the United States or by any State on account of sex.

Congress shall have power to enforce this article by appropriate legislation.

Amendment XX (1933)

Section 1. The terms of the President and Vice-President shall end at noon on the 20th day of January, and the terms of Senators and Representatives at noon on the 3d day of January, of the years in which such terms would have ended if this article had not been ratified; and the terms of their successors shall then begin.

Section 2. The Congress shall assemble at least once in every year, and such meeting shall begin at noon on the 3d day of January, unless they shall by law appoint a different day.

Section 3. If, at the time fixed for the beginning of the term of the President, the President elect shall have died, the Vice-President elect shall become President. If a President shall not have been chosen before the time fixed for the beginning of his term, or if the President elect shall have failed to qualify, then the Vice-President elect shall act as President until a President shall have qualified; and the Congress may by law provide for the case wherein neither a President elect nor a Vice-President elect shall have qualified, declaring who shall then act as President, or the manner in which one who is to act shall be selected, and such person shall act accordingly until a President or Vice-President shall have qualified.

Section 4. The Congress may by law provide for the case of the death of any of the persons from whom the House of Representatives may choose a President whenever the right of choice shall have devolved upon them, and for the case of the death of any of the persons from whom the Senate may choose a Vice-President whenever the right of choice shall have devolved upon them.

Section 5. Sections 1 and 2 shall take effect on the 15th day of October following the ratification of this article.

Section 6. This article shall be inoperative unless it shall have been ratified as an amendment to the Constitution by the legislatures of three-fourths of the several States within seven years from the date of its submission.

Amendment XXI (1933)

Section 1. The eighteenth article of amendment to the Constitution of the United States is hereby repealed.

Section 2. The transportation or importation into any State, Territory, or possession of the United States for delivery or use therein of intoxicating liquors, in violation of the laws thereof, is hereby prohibited.

Section 3. This article shall be inoperative unless it shall have been ratified as an amendment to the Constitution by conventions in the several States, as provided in the Constitution, within seven years from the date of the submission hereof to the States by the Congress.

Amendment XXII (1951)

No person shall be elected to the office of the President more than twice, and no person who has held the office of President, or acted as President, for more than two years of a term to which some other person was elected President shall be elected to the office of the President more than once.

But this Article shall not apply to any person holding the office of President when this Article was proposed by the Congress, and shall not prevent any person who may be holding the office of President, or acting as President, during the term within which this Article becomes operative from holding the office of President or acting as President during the remainder of such term.

Amendment XXIII (1961)

Section 1. The District constituting the seat of Government of the United States shall appoint in such manner as the Congress may direct:

A number of electors of President and Vice-President equal to the whole number of Senators and Representatives in Congress to which the District would be entitled if it were a State, but in no event more than the least populous State; they shall be in addition to those appointed by the States, but they shall be considered, for the purposes of the election of President and Vice-President, to be electors appointed by the State; and they shall meet in the District and perform such duties as provide

by the twelfth article of amendment.

Section 2. The Congress shall have power to enforce this article by appropriate legislation.

Amendment XXIV (1964)

Section 1. The right of citizens of the United States to vote in any primary or other election for President or Vice-President, for electors for President or Vice-President, or for Senator or Representative in Congress, shall not be denied or abridged by the United States or any State by reason of failure to pay any poll tax or other tax.

Section 2. The Congress shall have power to enforce this article by appropriate legislation.

Amendment XXV (1967)

Section 1. In case of the removal of the President from office or of his death or resignation, the Vice-President shall become President.

Section 2. Whenever there is a vacancy in the office of the Vice-President, the President shall nominate a Vice-President who shall take office upon confirmation by a majority vote of both Houses of Congress.

Section 3. Whenever the President transmits to the President pro tempore of the Senate and the Speaker of the House of Representatives his written declaration that he is unable to discharge the powers and duties of his office, and until he transmits to them a written declaration to the contrary, such powers and duties shall be discharged by the Vice-President as Acting President.

Section 4. Whether the Vice-President and a majority of either the principal officers of the executive department or of such other body as Congress may by law provide, transmit to the President pro tempore of the Senate and the Speaker of the House of Representatives their written declaration that the President is unable to discharge the powers and duties of his office, the Vice-President shall immediately assume the powers and duties of the office as Acting President.

Thereafter, when the President transmits to the President pro tempore of the Senate and the Speaker of the House of Representatives his written declaration that no inability exists, he shall resume the powers and duties of his office unless the Vice-President and a majority of either the principal officers of the executive department or of such other body as Congress may by law provide, transmit within four days to the President pro tempore of the Senate and the Speaker of the House of Representatives their written declaration that the President is unable to discharge the powers and duties of his office. Thereupon Congress shall decide the issue, assembling within forty-eight hours for that purpose if not in session. If the Congress, within twenty-one days after receipt of the latter written declaration, or, if Congress is not in session, within twenty-one days after Congress is required to assemble, determines by two-thirds vote of

both Houses that the President is unable to discharge the powers and duties of his office, the Vice-President shall continue to discharge the same as Acting President; otherwise, the President shall resume the powers and duties of his office.

Amendment XXVI (1971)

Section 1. The right of citizens of the United States, who are eighteen years of age or older, to vote shall not be denied or abridged by the United States or by any State on account of age.

Section 2. The Congress shall have power to enforce this article by appropriate legislation.

[1] Modified by the Fourteenth and Sixteenth amendments.

[2] Superseded by the Seventeenth Amendment.

[3] Modified by the Seventeenth Amendment.

[4] Superseded by the Twentieth Amendment.

[5] Modified by the Sixteenth Amendment.

[6] Superseded by the Twelfth Amendment.

[7] Modified by the Twenty-fifth Amendment.

[8] Modified by the Eleventh Amendment.

[9] Superseded by the Thirteenth Amendment.

[10] The first ten amendments were passed by Congress September 25, 1789. They were ratified by three-fourths of the states December 15, 1791.

[11] Date of ratification.

[12] Superseded by the Twentieth Amendment.

[13] Repealed by the Twenty-first Amendment.

Admission of States

(See p. 117 for order in which the original thirteen entered the Union.)

Order of Admission	State	Date of Admission
14	Vermont	March 4, 1791
15	Kentucky	June 1, 1792
16	Tennessee	June 1, 1796
17	Ohio	March 1, 1803
18	Louisiana	April 30, 1812
19	Indiana	December 11, 1816
20	Mississippi	December 10, 1817
21	Illinois	December 3, 1818
22	Alabama	December 14, 1819
23	Maine	March 15, 1820
24	Missouri	August 10, 1821
25	Arkansas	June 15, 1836
26	Michigan	January 26, 1837
27	Florida	March 3, 1845
28	Texas	December 29, 1845
29	Iowa	December 28, 1846
30	Wisconsin	May 29, 1848
31	California	September 9, 1850

32	Minnesota	May 11, 1858
33	Oregon	February 14, 1859
34	Kansas	January 29, 1861
35	West Virginia	June 20, 1863
36	Nevada	October 31, 1864
37	Nebraska	March 1, 1867
38	Colorado	August 1, 1876
39	North Dakota	November 2, 1889
40	South Dakota	November 2, 1889
41	Montana	November 8, 1889
42	Washington	November 11, 1889
43	Idaho	July 3, 1890
44	Wyoming	July 10, 1890
45	Utah	January 4, 1896
46	Oklahoma	November 16, 1907
47	New Mexico	January 6, 1912
48	Arizona	February 14, 1912
49	Alaska	January 3, 1959
50	Hawaii	August 21, 1959

Presidents & Vice-Presidents

Term	President	Vice-President
1789-1793	George Washington	John Adams
1793-1797	George Washington	John Adams
1797-1801	John Adams	Thomas Jefferson
1801-1805	Thomas Jefferson	Aaron Burr
1805-1809	Thomas Jefferson	George Clinton
1809-1813	James Madison	George Clinton (d. 1812)
1813-1817	James Madison	Elbridge Gerry (d. 1814)
1817-1821	James Monroe	Daniel D. Tompkins
1821-1825	James Monroe	Daniel D. Tompkins
1825-1829	John Quincy Adams	John C. Calhoun
1829-1833	Andrew Jackson	John C. Calhoun (resigned 1832)
1833-1837	Andrew Jackson	Martin Van Buren
1837-1841	Martin Van Buren	Richard M. Johnson
1841-1845	William H. Harrison (d. 1841)	John Tyler
	John Tyler	
1845-1849	James K. Polk	George M. Dallas
1849-1853	Zachary Taylor (d. 1850)	Milliard Fillmore
	Milliard Fillmore	
1853-1857	Franklin Pierce	William R. D. King (d. 1853)
1857-1861	James Buchanan	John C. Breckinridge
1861-1865	Abraham Lincoln	Hannibal Hamlin

1865-1869	Abraham Lincoln (d. 1865)	Andrew Johnson
	Andrew Johnson	
1869-1873	Ulysses S. Grant	Schuyler Colfax
1873-1877	Ulysses S. Grant	Henry Wilson (d. 1875)
1877-1881	Rutherford B. Hayes	William A. Wheeler
1881-1885	James A. Garfield (d. 1881)	Chester A. Arthur
	Chester A. Arthur	
1885-1889	Grover Cleveland	Thomas A. Hendricks (d. 1885)
1889-1893	Benjamin Harrison	Levi P. Morton
1893-1897	Grover Cleveland	Adlai E. Stevenson
1897-1901	William McKinley	Garret A. Hobart (d. 1899)
1901-1905	William McKinley (d. 1901)	Theodore Roosevelt
	Theodore Roosevelt	
1905-1909	Theodore Roosevelt	Charles W. Fairbanks
1909-1913	William H. Taft	James S. Sherman (d. 1912)
1913-1917	Woodrow Wilson	Thomas R. Marshall
1917-1921	Woodrow Wilson	Thomas R. Marshall
1921-1925	Warren G. Harding (d. 1923)	Calvin Coolidge
	Calvin Coolidge	
1925-1929	Calvin Coolidge	Charles G. Dawes
1929-1933	Herbert C. Hoover	Charles Curtis
1933-1937	Franklin D. Roosevelt	John N. Garner
1937-1941	Franklin D. Roosevelt	John N. Garner
1941-1945	Franklin D. Roosevelt	Henry A. Wallace
1945-1949	Franklin D. Roosevelt (d. 1945)	Harry S Truman
	Harry S Truman	
1949-1953	Harry S Truman	Alben W. Barkley
1953-1957	Dwight D. Eisenhower	Richard M. Nixon
1957-1961	Dwight D. Eisenhower	Richard M. Nixon
1961-1965	John F. Kennedy (d. 1963)	Lyndon B. Johnson
	Lyndon B. Johnson	
1965-1969	Lyndon B. Johnson	Hubert H. Humphrey
1969-1973	Richard M. Nixon	Spiro T. Agnew
1973-1977	Richard M. Nixon (resigned 1974)	Spiro T. Agnew (resigned 1973)
	Gerald R. Ford	Gerald R. Ford (appointed 1973)
1977-	James E. Carter, Jr.	Walter Mondale

Presidential Elections*

Election	Candidates	Parties	Popular Vote	Electoral Vote
1789	GEORGE WASHINGTON	No party designations		69
	John Adams			34
	Minor Candidates			35
1792	GEORGE WASHINGTON	No party designations		132
	John Adams			77
	George Clinton			50
	Minor Candidates			5
1796	JOHN ADAMS	Federalist		71
	Thomas Jefferson	Democratic-Republican		68
	Thomas Pinckney	Federalist		59
	Aaron Burr	Democratic-Republican		30
	Minor Candidates			48
1800	THOMAS JEFFERSON	Democratic-Republican		73
	Aaron Burr	Democratic-Republican		73
	John Adams	Federalist		65
	Charles C. Pinckney	Federalist		64
	John Jay	Federalist		1

*Candidates receiving less than 1% of the popular vote are omitted. Before the 12th Amendment (1804) the Electoral College voted for two presidential candidates, and the runner-up became Vice President. Basic figures are taken from *Historical Statistics of the United States, 1789-1945*, pp. 288-290.

Election	Candidates	Parties	Popular Vote	Electoral Vote
1804	THOMAS JEFFERSON	Democratic-Republican		162
	Charles C. Pinckney	Federalist		14
1808	JAMES MADISON	Democratic-Republican		122
	Charles C. Pinckney	Federalist		47
	George Clinton	Democratic-Republican		6
1812	JAMES MADISON	Democratic-Republican		128
	DeWitt Clinton	Federalist		89
1816	JAMES MONROE	Democratic-Republican		183
	Rufus King	Federalist		34
1820	JAMES MONROE	Democratic-Republican		231
	John Q. Adams	Independent Republican		1
1824	JOHN Q. ADAMS (Min.)*	Democratic-Republican	108,740	84
	Andrew Jackson	Democratic-Republican	153,544	99
	William H. Crawford	Democratic-Republican	46,618	41
	Henry Clay	Democratic-Republican	47,136	37
1828	ANDREW JACKSON	Democratic	647,286	178
	John Q. Adams	National Republican	508,064	83
1832	ANDREW JACKSON	Democratic	687,502	219
	Henry Clay	National Republican	530,189	49
	William Wirt	Anti-Masonic	33,108	7
	John Floyd	National Republican		11
1836	MARTIN VAN BUREN	Democratic	762,678	170
	William H. Harrison	Whig		73
	Hugh L. White	Whig	736,656	26
	Daniel Webster	Whig		14
	W. P. Mangum	Whig		11
1840	WILLIAM H. HARRISON	Whig	1,275,016	234
	Martin Van Buren	Democratic	1,129,102	60
1844	JAMES K. POLK (Min.)*	Democratic	1,337,243	170
	Henry Clay	Whig	1,299,062	105
	James G. Birney	Liberty	62,300	
1848	ZACHARY TAYLOR (Min.)*	Whig	1,360,099	163
	Lewis Cass	Democratic	1,220,544	127
	Martin Van Buren	Free Soil	291,263	
1852	FRANKLIN PIERCE	Democratic	1,601,274	254
	Winfield Scott	Whig	1,386,580	42
	John P. Hale	Free Soil	155,825	
1856	JAMES BUCHANAN (Min.)*	Democratic	1,838,169	174
	John C. Frémont	Republican	1,341,264	114
	Millard Fillmore	American	874,534	8
1860	ABRAHAM LINCOLN (Min.)*	Republican	1,866,452	180
	Stephen A. Douglas	Democratic	1,375,157	12
	John C. Breckinridge	Democratic	847,953	72
	John Bell	Constitutional Union	590,631	39
1864	ABRAHAM LINCOLN	Union	2,213,665	212
	George B. McClellan	Democratic	1,802,237	21
1868	ULYSSES S. GRANT	Republican	3,012,833	214
	Horatio Seymour	Democratic	2,703,249	80
1872	ULYSSES S. GRANT	Republican	3,597,132	286
	Horace Greeley	Democratic and Liberal Republican	2,834,125	66

*"Min." indicates minority President—one receiving less than 50% of all popular votes.

Election	Candidates	Parties	Popular Vote	Electoral Vote
1876	RUTHERFORD B. HAYES (Min.)*	Republican	4,036,298	185
	Samuel J. Tilden	Democratic	4,300,590	184
1880	JAMES A. GARFIELD (Min.)*	Republican	4,454,416	214
	Winfield S. Hancock	Democratic	4,444,952	155
	James B. Weaver	Greenback-Labor	308,578	
1884	GROVER CLEVELAND (Min.)*	Democratic	4,874,986	219
	James G. Blaine	Republican	4,851,981	182
	Benjamin F. Butler	Greenback-Labor	175,370	
	John P. St. John	Prohibition	150,369	
1888	BENJAMIN HARRISON (Min.)*	Republican	5,439,853	233
	Grover Cleveland	Democratic	5,540,309	168
	Clinton B. Fisk	Prohibition	249,506	
	Anson J. Streeter	Union Labor	146,935	
1892	GROVER CLEVELAND (Min.)*	Democratic	5,556,918	277
	Benjamin Harrison	Republican	5,176,108	145
	James B. Weaver	People's	1,041,028	22
	John Bidwell	Prohibition	264,133	
1896	WILLIAM McKINLEY	Republican	7,104,779	271
	William J. Bryan	Democratic	6,502,925	176
1900	WILLIAM McKINLEY	Republican	7,292,530	292
	William J. Bryan	Democratic; Populist	6,358,133	155
	John C. Woolley	Prohibition	208,914	
1904	THEODORE ROOSEVELT	Republican	7,628,834	336
	Alton B. Parker	Democratic	5,084,401	140
	Eugene V. Debs	Socialist	402,460	
	Silas C. Swallow	Prohibition	258,536	
1908	WILLIAM H. TAFT	Republican	7,678,908	321
	William J. Bryan	Democratic	6,409,104	162
	Eugene V. Debs	Socialist	420,793	
	Eugene W. Chafin	Prohibition	253,840	
1912	WOODROW WILSON (Min.)*	Democratic	6,286,820	435
	Theodore Roosevelt	Progressive	4,126,020	88
	William H. Taft	Republican	3,483,922	8
	Eugene V. Debs	Socialist	900,672	
	Eugene W. Chafin	Prohibition	206,275	
1916	WOODROW WILSON (Min.)*	Democratic	9,129,606	277
	Charles E. Hughes	Republican	8,538,221	254
	A. L. Benson	Socialist	585,113	
	J. F. Hanly	Prohibition	220,506	
1920	WARREN G. HARDING	Republican	16,152,200	404
	James M. Cox	Democratic	9,147,353	127
	Eugene V. Debs	Socialist	919,799	
	P. P. Christensen	Farmer-Labor	265,411	
1924	CALVIN COOLIDGE	Republican	15,725,016	382
	John W. Davis	Democratic	8,386,503	136
	Robert M. LaFollette	Progressive	4,822,856	13
1928	HERBERT C. HOOVER	Republican	21,391,381	444
	Alfred E. Smith	Democratic	15,016,443	87
1932	FRANKLIN D. ROOSEVELT	Democratic	22,821,857	472
	Herbert C. Hoover	Republican	15,761,841	59
	Norman Thomas	Socialist	881,951	

*"Min." indicates minority President—one receiving less than 50% of all popular votes.

Election	Candidates	Parties	Popular Vote	Electoral Vote
1936	FRANKLIN D. ROOSEVELT	Democratic	27,751,597	523
	Alfred M. Landon	Republican	16,679,583	8
	William Lemke	Union, etc.	882,479	
1940	FRANKLIN D. ROOSEVELT	Democratic	27,244,160	449
	Wendell L. Wilkie	Republican	22,305,198	82
1944	FRANKLIN D. ROOSEVELT	Democratic	25,602,504	432
	Thomas F. Dewey	Republican	22,006,285	99
1948	HARRY S TRUMAN (Min.)*	Democratic	24,105,695	303
	Thomas E. Dewey	Republican	21,969,170	189
	J. Strom Thurmond	States' Rights Democratic	1,169,021	39
	Henry A. Wallace	Progressive	1,156,103	
1952	DWIGHT D. EISENHOWER	Republican	33,778,963	442
	Adlai E. Stevenson	Democratic	27,314,992	89
1956	DWIGHT D. EISENHOWER	Republican	35,590,472	457
	Adlai E. Stevenson	Democratic	26,022,752	73
1960	JOHN F. KENNEDY (Min.)*	Democratic	34,221,531	303
	Richard M. Nixon	Republican	34,107,474	219
1964	LYNDON B. JOHNSON	Democratic	43,126,233	486
	Barry M. Goldwater	Republican	27,174,989	52
1968	RICHARD M. NIXON (Min.)*	Republican	31,783,783	301
	Hubert H. Humphrey	Democratic	31,271,839	191
	George C. Wallace	American Independent	9,899,557	46
1972	RICHARD M. NIXON	Republican	47,168,963	520
	George S. McGovern	Democratic	29,169,615	17
1976	JAMES E. CARTER, JR.	Democratic	40,827,292	297
	Gerald R. Ford	Republican	39,146,157	240

*"Min." indicates minority President—one receiving less than 50% of all popular votes.

Justices of the Supreme Court

Name (Chief Justices in Italics)	Service (Terms)	(Years)
John Jay (N.Y.)	1789-1795	6
John Rutledge (S.C.)	1789-1791	2
William Cushing (Mass.)	1789-1810	21
James Wilson (Pa.)	1789-1798	9
John Blair (Va.)	1789-1796	7
James Iredell (N.C.)	1790-1799	9
Thomas Johnson (Md.)	1792-1793	½
William Paterson (N.J.)	1793-1806	13
John Rutledge (S.C.)*	1795-1795	
Samuel Chase (Md.)	1796-1811	15
Oliver Ellsworth (Conn.)	1796-1800	4
Bushrod Washington (Va.)	1798-1829	31
Alfred Moore (N.C.)	1800-1804	4
John Marshall (Va.)	1801-1835	34
William Johnson (S.C.)	1804-1834	30
Brock Livingston (N.Y.)	1806-1823	17
Thomas Todd (Ky.)	1807-1826	19
Joseph Story (Mass.)	1811-1845	34
Gabriel Duval (Md.)	1811-1835	24
Smith Thompson (N.Y.)	1823-1843	20

Name (Chief Justices in Italics)	Service (Terms)	(Years)
Robert Trimble (Ky.)	1826-1828	2
John McLean (Ohio)	1829-1861	32
Henry Baldwin (Pa.)	1830-1844	14
James M. Wayne (Ga.)	1835-1867	32
Roger B. Taney (Md.)	1836-1864	28
Philip P. Barbour (Va.)	1836-1841	5
John Catron (Tenn.)	1837-1865	28
John McKinley (Ala.)	1837-1852	15
Peter V. Daniel (Va.)	1841-1860	19
Samuel Nelson (N.Y.)	1845-1872	27
Levi Woodbury (N.H.)	1845-1851	6
Robert C. Grier (Pa.)	1846-1870	24
Benjamin R. Curtis (Mass.)	1851-1857	6
John A. Campbell (Ala.)	1853-1861	8
Nathan Clifford (Maine)	1858-1881	23
Noah H. Swayne (Ohio)	1862-1861	19
Samuel F. Miller (Iowa)	1862-1890	28
David Davis (Ill.)	1862-1877	15
Stephen J. Field (Calif.)	1863-1897	34
Salmon P. Chase (Ohio)	1864-1873	9
William Strong (Pa.)	1870-1880	10
Joseph P. Bradley (N.J.)	1870-1892	22
Ward Hunt (N.Y.)	1872-1882	10
Morrison R. Waite (Ohio)	1874-1888	14
John M. Harlan (Ky.)	1877-1911	34
William B. Woods (Ga.)	1880-1887	7
Stanley Matthews (Ohio)	1881-1889	8
Horace Gray (Mass.)	1881-1902	21
Samuel Blatchford (N.Y.)	1882-1893	11
Lucius Q. Lamar (Miss.)	1888-1893	5
Melville W. Fuller (Ill.)	1888-1910	22
David J. Brewer (Kans.)	1889-1910	21
Henry B. Brown (Mich.)	1890-1906	16
George Shiras, Jr. (Pa.)	1892-1903	11
Howell E. Jackson (Tenn.)	1893-1895	2
Edward D. White (La.)	1894-1910	16
Rufus W. Peckham (N.Y.)	1895-1909	14
Joseph McKenna (Calif.)	1898-1925	27
Oliver W. Holmes (Mass.)	1902-1932	30
William R. Day (Ohio)	1903-1922	19
William H. Moody (Mass.)	1906-1910	4
Horace H. Lurton (Tenn.)	1910-1914	4
Edward D. White (La.)	1910-1921	11
Charles E. Hughes (N.Y.)	1910-1916	6
Willis Van Devanter (Wyo.)	1911-1937	26
Joseph R. Lamar (Ga.)	1911-1916	5
Mahlon Pitney (N.J.)	1912-1922	10
James C. McReynolds (Tenn.)	1914-1941	27
Louis D. Brandeis (Mass.)	1916-1939	23
John H. Clarke (Ohio)	1916-1922	6
William H. Taft (Conn.)	1921-1930	9
George Sutherland (Utah)	1922-1938	16

Name (Chief Justices in Italics)	Service (Terms)	Service (Years)
Pierce Butler (Minn.)	1923-1939	16
Edward T. Sanford (Tenn.)	1923-1930	7
Harlan F. Stone (N.Y.)	1925-1941	16
Charles E. Hughes (N.Y.)	1930-1941	11
Owen J. Roberts (Pa.)	1930-1945	15
Benjamin N. Cardozo (N.Y.)	1932-1938	6
Hugo L. Black (Ala.)	1937-1971	34
Stanley F. Reed (Ky.)	1938-1957	19
Felix Frankfurter (Mass.)	1939-1962	23
William O. Douglas (Conn.)	1939-1975	36
Frank Murphy (Mich.)	1940-1949	9
Harlan F. Stone (N.Y.)	1941-1946	5
James F. Byrnes (S.C.)	1941-1942	1
Robert H. Jackson (N.Y.)	1941-1954	13
Wiley B. Rutledge (Iowa)	1943-1949	6
Harold H. Burton (Ohio)	1945-1958	13
Fred M. Vinson (Ky.)	1946-1953	7
Tom C. Clark (Tex.)	1949-1967	18
Sherman Minton (Ind.)	1949-1956	7
Earl Warren (Calif.)	1953-1969	16
John M. Harlan (N.Y.)	1955-1971	16
William J. Brennan (N.J.)	1956-	
Charles E. Whittaker (Mo.)	1957-1962	5
Potter Stewart (Ohio)	1958-	
Byron R. White (Colo.)	1962-	
Arthur J. Goldberg (Ill.)	1962-1965	3
Abe Fortas (Tenn.)	1965-1969	4
Thurgood Marshall (Md.)	1967-	
Warren E. Burger (Minn.)	1969-	
Harry A. Blackmun (Minn.)	1970-	
Lewis F. Powell, Jr. (Va.)	1971-	
William H. Rehnquist (Ariz.)	1971-	
John Paul Stevens (Ill.)	1975-	

Index